THE SOCIALIST REGISTER 1991

SOCIALIST REGISTER 1991

COMMUNIST REGIMES: THE AFTERMATH

Edited by
RALPH MILIBAND
LEO PANITCH

THE MERLIN PRESS
LONDON

First published in 1991
by The Merlin Press Ltd
10 Malden Road
London NW5 3HR

Second impression October 1991

British Library Cataloguing in Publication Data

The Socialist Register. — 1991
  1. Socialism — Serials
  I. Miliband, Ralph   II. Panitch, Leo
355'.005

ISBN 0-85036-419-1
ISBN 0-85036-420-0 Pbk

Typesetting by
Heather Hems, Tower House, Gillingham, Dorset

Printed and bound in Great Britain by
Biddles Ltd, Guildford and King's Lynn

TABLE OF CONTENTS

PREFACE

This twenty-seventh volume of the *Socialist Register* is primarily devoted to the daunting questions posed for socialists by the transformations which the USSR and the former Communist regimes of Eastern Europe are going through. The editors of and contributors to the *Socialist Register* over the past quarter century have fostered no illusions regarding the dictatorial nature of these regimes, and have presented over the years many analyses of their limits and contradictions. The emergence of "glasnost" in the USSR since 1985 followed by the dramatic democratic revolutions in Eastern Europe in 1989-90 were events of great historic importance, and they appeared to offer some promise for positive developments in international relations as well as for democratic socialist prospects. Today, we must ask what already remains of such promise as we witness the prospects for democratic socialism marginalized by capitalist and chauvinist forces and sentiments in Eastern Europe and the USSR, not to mention the growing economic and military ruthlessness of an unchecked global capitalism lustily proclaiming its "new world order". The Left must reassess the whole Communist experience, and draw appropriate lessons, in light of the collapse of authoritarian communism; it must do so, however, also mindful of the costs and consequences of an authoritarian capitalism rushing in to pick up the pieces.

The essays in this volume attempt to understand the aftermath of Communist regimes in terms of its global as well as local political, economic and ideological implications, including the implications it has for the meaning and prospects of democratic socialism. While they also analyze the long-term, internal and external, causes of the crisis of the authoritarian communism, their primary focus is on providing detailed accounts of current developments, above all in relation to investigating the contradictory nature of the simultaneous processes of "democratization" and "marketization", and the complex old and new social forces, ideas and struggles involved. Regardless of whether our contributors see the Communist regimes as having represented the distortion and ultimate failure of a particular kind of socialism, or as never having amounted to any kind of socialism at all due to their divorce between socialism and democracy, the conclusions they draw regarding what is happening in the aftermath of Communist regimes still point to democratic socialism as the only humane alternative. The most daunting questions this volume raises, therefore, are those concerned with how to go about making viable the vision and prospect of democratic socialism at the end of the twentieth century.

We are extremely pleased to count among our contributors a number who are closely associated with the struggle for democratic socialism in some of the very countries which are the focus of this volume. Alexander Buzgalin and Andrei Kalganov of Moscow were the founders of the Marxist Platform in the Communist Party two years ago; in the past year Buzgalin has been elected as a member of the Central Committee of the CPSU, and Kalganov has been elected as a member of the Central Committee of the Russian Communist Party. Tadeusz Kowalik, an historian of socialist economic thought in the Academy of Sciences in Warsaw, was an adviser to Solidarity in its founding years; he is associated today with the self-management wing of Solidarity, in opposition to the policies of the current Polish government. Peter Bihari, a lecturer at the Budapest University of Economics in Budapest, became editor two years ago of the theoretical journal of the Hungarian Socialist Party, and has contributed to the development of a new circle of young socialist economists in Hungary. For his part, Carlos Vilas, a frequent contributor to the *Socialist Register* in recent years, worked in Nicaragua between 1980 and the beginning of 1990 as a consultant to various government agencies and international organizations. He is now a Fellow at the Interdisciplinary Centre for Research in the Humanities, UNAM, Mexico.

Among our other contributors, John Saville was one of the founders of the *Socialist Register* in 1964 and for twenty-five years one of its co-editors. Sam Gindin is Research Director and Assistant to the President of the Canadian Autoworkers Union. David Mandel teaches political science at the Université du Québec a Montréal; and Justin Schwartz is in the Department of Philosophy at Ohio State University in Columbus. Patrick Flaherty, since completing his Ph.D. in Government at Harvard University, has been an independent scholar living in Woburn, Mass. Both Robert Cox and Ernest Mandel teach political economy, the former in the Department of Political Science at York University in Toronto, and the latter at the Free University in Brussels. Daniel Singer is an independent writer living in Paris who is European Editor of *The Nation*. Susan Woodward is currently a Visiting Fellow at The Brookings Institution in Washington, D.C.; and Michael Lebowitz teaches in the Department of Economics at Simon Fraser University in Vancouver.

We are very grateful to all our contributors, although we must, as always, point out that neither they nor the editors necessarily agree with everything that appears in the volume. Special thanks are due to Mike Gonzales, Hugh Jenkins and Eszter Pásztor for their translations of the articles by Vilas, Buzgalin and Kolganov, and Bihari respectively. We also appreciate the advice and support we have had from Susan Lowes of Monthly Review Press. Finally, as had been the case with every volume of the *Socialist Register*, Martin Eve of Merlin Press deserves much of the credit for his great help with all aspects of production. We are most grateful for his consistent encouragement and support.

March 1991

L.P.
R.M.

THE COMMUNIST EXPERIENCE:
A PERSONAL APPRAISAL

John Saville

In the preface to the English edition of 1888 of the *Communist Manifesto* Frederick Engels explained why the Manifesto of 1848 could not have been called a *socialist* Manifesto. He continued:

> By Socialists, in 1847, were understood, on the one hand the adherents of the various Utopian systems: Owenites in England, Fourierists in France, both of them already reduced to the position of mere sects, and gradually dying out; on the other hand, the most multifarious social quacks, who by all manner of tinkering professed to redress, without any danger to capital and profit, all sorts of social grievances, in both cases men outside the working class movement, and looking rather to the 'educated' classes for support. Whatever portion of the working class had become convinced of the insufficiency of mere political revolutions, and had proclaimed the necessity of a total change, called itself Communist. It was a crude, rough-hewn, purely instinctive sort of communism; still it touched the cardinal point and was powerful enough amongst the working class to produce the Utopian communism of Cabet in France, and of Weitling in Germany. Thus, in 1847, socialism was a middle class movement, communism a working class movement. Socialism was, on the Continent at least, 'respectable'; communism was the very opposite. And as our notion, from the very beginning, was that 'the emancipation of the working class must be the act of the working class itself', there could be no doubt as to which of the two names we must take. Moreover, we have, ever since, been far from repudiating it.[1]

The time has now come for such a denial and repudiation. The period of Communism, centred upon the history of the Soviet Union since 1917, and of the countries of Eastern Europe since the late 1940s, which gave inspiration and hope to millions of people all over the world, has now ended in discredit and dishonour. There are still parts of the world — South Africa is an obvious example — where the name Communist Party still carries respect; but in Europe especially the name and the organisation are synonymous with economic incompetence and material ineptitude of a massive kind, together with the bitter political regimes of Stalinism. The disappearance of any credible alternative to capitalism in any part of the world today requires the most serious examination and analysis of the historical factors involved in the momentous events of 1989/1990. For someone like the present writer, who spent twenty-two years in the British

Communist Party until 1956, the enquiry is not into the nature and character of Stalinism and the extensive deformations occurring in countries which called themselves socialist, because that exploration began seriously in the year of Khrushchev's speech, and has continued since. It is rather the survey of the period as a whole and of a sombre assessment of the future of socialism. 'Goodbye to All That' is the triumphalist cry of the enemies of socialism, but the hostility of the propertied classes everywhere has always been unrelenting. What we have to appreciate, however, is that cynicism towards the socialist project extends to very large numbers of ordinary people in the advanced industrial world, and that there is here a very serious discussion and debate to be revived and renewed. Such a debate cannot ignore the central problems of the contemporary world where a majority of the world's population remain in economic bondage, poverty and material degradation to whose conditions the industrialised sectors have always and continuously contributed.

It is necessary to begin, not with 1917, but with the three decades or so preceding the outbreak of the first great war of the twentieth century. It was in these earlier decades that there emerged the modern labour movements of Europe, and, to a more limited extent, of the United States and other countries of mostly white settlement. Continued technological change in the closing decades of the nineteenth century was producing the conditions for the assembly line: it was the age of steel and electricity superseding the first main stage of industrialisation based upon coal and iron. The advanced world was on the threshold of Fordism; and it was in these years that the ideas of socialism, anarchism, and especially in some parts of Europe, of marxism, gradually took hold of the minds of quite large sections of working people. Internationalism, and solidarity with the struggles of other nations has a long history: in modern times notably with the revolutionary France of the 1790s; but there was now developiing a new sort of awareness of the interrelatedness of national struggles. The Paris Commune was a landmark in this appreciation that 'All Men are Brethren';[2] and Victor Serge, nearly four decades later, provided in his Memoirs an illustration of the growing internationalism throughout Europe. The occasion was the execution of the famous Spanish educationalist, Francisco Ferrer, in early October 1909. Ferrer was first an anarchist and then, in the later part of his life, a radical free-thinker concerned with education of a new kind; anti-militarist, anti-clerical, rationalistic and humanitarian. His Modern School became internationally known. Following a general uprising in Barcelona, with which Ferrer had no connection, he was framed, tried, and found guilty, and quickly brought before a firing squad. All Europe knew it was a judicial murder; and Serge described the reaction:

I had written, even before his arrest, the first article in the great Press campaign conducted on his behalf. His transparent innocence, his educational activity, his courage as an independent thinker, and even his man-in-the-street appearance endeared him infinitely to the whole of Europe that was, at the time, liberal by sentiment and in intense ferment. A true international consciousnes was growing from year to year, step by step with the progress of capitalist civilisation. Frontiers were crossed without formalities, some trade unions subsidised travel for their members; commercial and intellectual exchanges seemed to be unifying the world. Already in 1905 the anti-Semitic pogroms in Russia had roused a universal wave of condemnation. From one end of the Continent to the other (except in Russia and Turkey) the judicial murder of Ferrer had, within twenty-four hours, moved whole populations to incensed protest. [3]

The spread of this internationalist sentiment was sharply reversed with the beginning of the first world war; but over the war years the horrendous carnage on both Western and Eastern fronts violently assaulted the consciousness of both combatants and civilians; and when the Bolsheviks took power in October 1917 it seemed to the socialists of Europe and in other continents that a beacon of light was now shining through the gloom of death and destruction. For many who were living at the time of the Russian revolution it was the electrifying moment of their whole lives. The people had taken power; the appeal of the new Soviet government was to the oppressed masses of the world; and in the colonial countries of European imperialism, the message of liberation and independence was never again to go unheard. Lenin and the Bolsheviks understood their own revolution as the precursor of the world revolution which would overthrow capitalism and put a new kind of society in its place. The national Communist Parties which established themselves immediately after the ending of the war and came together under the banner of the Communist International, shared the belief they were part of a world movement that through their disciplined leadership of the working people would achieve their revolutionary aims and objectives. For more than three decades after 1917 there was much that could support these ideas and ideals. The war which began in 1914 brought about the collapse of liberal democracies in one European country after another; and for the next forty years world capitalism moved through successive crises. Economic collapse on a world scale was followed by the conquest of power by Nazism in Germany; and the black night descended. The civil war in Spain and the outbreak of the second world war: for the propertied classes the world was staggering from one catastrophe to another. Fear — a bitter savage fear of communism, and of the potential power of ordinary working people — dominated the politics of international relations.

By the 1930s, together with the introduction of the Five Year Plans, these developments enhanced the role and place of the Soviet Union in world affairs, and strengthened the loyalty and devotion to the cause of workers' power on the part of increasing numbers of militant workers and a growing minority of intellectuals. We have become increasingly aware, in the most recent decades, of the bitter paradox of the history of the 1930s. On the one hand the ideal of the first workers' state won wider support than ever before in the minds of many sections of the international labour movement. The initiatives the Soviet Union took to build a unity against fascism; their support for Republican Spain; the vigorous part which national communist parties played against their own propertied classes who were appeasing the fascist powers and encouraging them to turn eastwards against Soviet Russia: all contributed to the growing support being enjoyed by the Communist parties in Europe and in many countries of the world. On the other hand it was in the same decade that Stalinist repression inside the Soviet Union became an integral part of the social order. The brutal realities of the tyranny inside the boundaries of the Soviet state which became known to any significant numbers of militants in the rest of the world was remarkably limited; and the different level of awareness in different countries was striking. In Britain, for example, the Trotskyist movement was numerically very small, and intellectually feeble, and appreciation of the nature and character of Stalinism was confined to very few within the broad labour movement. No doubt if war had not come in September 1939 the debates over the Soviet trials of 1936-8 would have led to a clearer understanding of the oppressive and bloody regime that Stalin presided over. But while the Nazi-Soviet Pact encouraged some anti-Soviet sentiment, the German attack upon Russia in June 1941, the sacrifices of the Soviet people in their Homeric struggles against German and other armies, the recognition that the overwhelming strength of the German forces were concentrated on the Eastern Front, and that if Russia had been defeated there would have been no victory over fascism: all induced a torrent of sympathy and support for the Soviet Union. It swept through the non-fascist world and was irrepressible in its warmth and responsiveness. Why and how this sympathy, apparently so deeply felt, so quickly evaporated after 1945 is a matter for complex historical analysis, for which the brief summary below offers only a few elementary pointers.

We must begin with the situation in 1945 when the crucial victories of the Red Army in the defeat of fascism together with the heroic record of the Communist parties in Europe, and within the national liberation struggles of South-East Asia, lifted the menace of bolshevism for the propertied classes of the whole world to new levels of awareness. The counter-revolution had already been widely discussed within the British Foreign Office and the American State

Department — and in other parts of their respective State organisations; and countervailing measures were already planned or in process of initiation. Within a month of the invasion of Normandy, in the summer of 1944 and nearly a year before the war with Germany was concluded, the planning staff of the British Chiefs of Staff were setting down on paper the possibility that Germany might have to be re-armed to counter the Russian menace;[4] and in the United States the list of required military and air force bases round the world were being seriously considered from 1943 on. When the Labour Government in Britain came to power in July 1945 there was no change in foreign policy, and it can be seriously argued that Ernest Bevin was more single-minded in his anti-Sovietism than a Conservative government would have been: not least because the opposition to Eden and Churchill carrying through the policies that Bevin achieved would have been much stronger and much more vociferous. Whitehall was more single minded in the early months of peace than was Washington in its anti-Soviet policies, but the forces for counter-revolution in the United States were always strong, and grew stronger month by month. George Kennan's Long Telegram was written as early as February 1946 — five months after the end of the war with Japan — and it provided the anti-Soviet groups in Washington with their theoretical guide-lines. Both countries, with the United States dominating, co-ordinated the strategy and tactics of the Cold War. The leadership of the British TUC and that of the American Federation of Labor played a not unimportant part in this global strategy;[5] and the Vatican, always reactionary, undertook a much more extended role than is usually appreciated. Above all, the capitalist west won the propaganda battle for the minds of their peoples, greatly aided by a Soviet Foreign policy that at times was stunningly incompetent and on a day to day basis exhibited attitudes of harsh stupidity and cruelty. The Soviet Union was not expansionist beyond its requirements of a cordon sanitaire on its western borders; and the widely believed idea that Russia was waiting only for the opportunity to march across Europe, or into the Middle East, is no longer accepted even by orthodox historians.[6] It was the great lie upon which the Cold War was nourished; but the ways in which the Soviet Union pursued its foreign affairs bears a considerable responsibility for its continued nourishment. The Soviet Union, it needs to be emphasised, was not, however, the major architect of the Cold War; that dishonour belongs firmly to the United States and the United Kingdom. Anti-Soviet policies began on the first day of the 1917 Revolution, and what has happened after 1945 has been their intensification and expansion.

If we take 1950 as roughly the year when the immediate post-war reconstruction had been achieved — in both the West and the East —

the decades which followed provided western capitalism with two developments of quite crucial importance in the struggle against the Soviet Union and its allies. The first was an economic boom of global proportions the like of which had never previously been experienced; and in the course of the boom the technology of Fordism began to move into the automation of the computer age. Within the Soviet Union itself the rapid development of Cold War practices by the western powers encouraged the intensification of an already pervasive Stalinism, and the fortress mentality which ensued effectively eliminated any forces for political change. The imposition of Stalinist regimes in Eastern Europe was followed by the fabrication of treason trials on the Russian model, and within the Soviet Union the doctors' plot would no doubt have offered the spectacle of the pre-war trials had it not been for the death of Stalin himself.

The consequences of the increased repression inside Russia, and the stories reaching the West of the cruelties within the Soviet zones of occupation, inevitably stimulated a growing recognition of the nature of Stalinism as it had developed through the 1930s and after. There was unquestionably exaggeration in many of the accounts that were published in the popular press, but the realities of the labour camps began to imprint themselves upon popular consciousness, and the ideals, and ideas, of socialism began slowly to wither; much aided by the rising standards of living that have been such a notable feature of the lives of most working people from the 1950s on. The mass Communist parties of Italy and France, with their outstanding record during the period of resistance, suffered less than other left-wing parties, but a steady seepage of support and membership has been a common feature in all the countries of advanced capitalism. Social-democratic parties — the word is used in the classical sense — have become steadily more reformist, and steadily less challenging to the capitalist system. The history of decline of the communist party in Britain in the decade or so after 1945 was slower than it might otherwise have been, partly because the American-British alliance was pursuing a counter-revolutionary policy on a global scale, but in Britain especially because the disintegration of the Empire was being met with bloody repression in Kenya, Malaya, Cyprus; and no socialist or communist could offer anything but opposition. It was when Khrushchev in 1956 officially pronounced upon the tyrannies and mass persecutions and executions of the Stalin era, all the doubts and misgivings now came together and produced a world wide crisis in the Communist movements that was accentuated by the invasion of Hungary in the autumn of the same year. Some of the smaller communist parties, the British among them, started to fall apart; and only the momentum of their past slowed down their inevitable decline.

There might have been some possibilities of renewal, both within the Soviet Union and inside the national Communist parties; but if Britain is any example, the forces of the old established bureaucracy, and the intellectual tyranny of old ideas, effectively submerged the possibilities of renewal. It is now clear that for a complex of reasons the Soviet Union found impossible to restructure the economy to take account of a rapidly changing technology, to develop a consumer goods market,[7] and to introduce a general flexibility in economic organisation at all levels. The results we have seen in the tumultuous events of 1989-1990.

*   *   *

It is time to clothe this brief historical account with personal experience, my own in particular. What has happened in the year to 1990 has been an historical moment of great significance, not only for Europe and the relations with the United States, but on a world scale. Without question, there has taken place a major defeat of the socialist idea and ideal. It matters not that a majority of socialists in the world had long been aware of the internal problems of the USSR: its lack of elementary democratic procedures and the absence of civil rights, even though the excesses of the Stalin era seemed to have gone in Russia itself. Violations of human decency were common enough in the countries of Eastern Europe. The evil deeds of the bourgeois democracies were many but this was no argument to set against the common knowledge of what was happening in the countries of professed socialism, as the dwindling membership and influence of the communist parties in most countries were only too obvious a reflection. The shouts of triumph from bourgeois commentators are only to be expected, including the idiotic prophecy of Francis Fukuyama that 1989 was the end of history and the future belonged to the liberal free market; but what is much more of concern is the intellectual and political collapse of those on the Left, especially noticeable among people who remained within their own communist parties, that the whole Communist experience was a disaster, and that we either have to begin again or recognise that what is so widely and euphemistically called the market economy has proved its economic superiority. In many important matters we have indeed to begin again, and the process in historical terms will be long and bitter. To suggest, however, that the Communist experience has been a folly is seriously to misunderstand — indeed fundamentally to misunderstand — what it meant in global political terms, in the national politics of individual countries and within the individuals themselves who played their minor parts in the historical experience. We have all begun to understand, much more clearly than ever before, what the radicals of the early nineteenth felt when they remembered the wonderful hopes they had all experienced with the Revolution in France, and witnessed its descent into Bonapartism thereafter. William Hazlitt is once again required reading.

Analytical accounts of the Communist experience in Britain are rare, as are serious memoirs of communist party militants. We are therefore much in debt to Raphael Samuel for his three articles in *New Left Review* (Nos 154, 156, and 165, 1985-87) although there is a great deal to disagree with in his accounts. He has, however, put up a number of important landmarks for serious discussion and debate, and we must all be grateful for this massive outpouring of argument and historical fact.

My own comments mainly relate to the concluding section in his first part in which he discusses the background to his membership of the Communist Party. 'Family Communism' he titles it, and his opening words: 'I was brought up as a true believer' provides the introduction to a remarkable story of his childhood and teenage days within a Jewish milieu in which twelve members of his family, including some by marriage, were Communist Party activists. For his mother's generation, he tells us, 'Communism, though not intended as such, was a way of being English, a bridge by which the children of the ghetto entered the national culture'. For Raphael himself:

> Like many Communists of my time, I combined a powerful sense of apartness with a craving for recognition, alternating gestures of defiance with a desire to be ordinary and accepted as one of the crowd. If one wanted to be charitable, one might say that it was the unresolvable duality on which British Communists find themselves impaled today.[8]

I do not in any way deny the validity of Raphael Samuel's own personal history as he has set it down in these fascinating pages but the historian in him might have made the crucial point that it was a very unusual history, typical of many Jewish comrades but not in any way relevant to most of the working class militants who joined the Communist Party in its first thirty years or so, and not relevant either to most of the non-Jewish intellectuals who also became members. Anyone familiar with the intellectual and social history of the American Communist Party, especially in the New York area, will recognise many similarities with Raphael's own experience; and the American documentation is more prolific and more illuminating than anything we have so far produced on this side of the Atlantic. The point needs to be made at the outset that this is a very old country; there is a native radicalism among ordinary people which goes back a very long way, and the Communist Party which was founded in 1920 grew out of these traditions: a source, no doubt, of both its strengths and its weaknesses.

There is a further point to be made in this context. One of the problems of Raphael's approach is that it offers strong support for the widely used argument that the Communist Party was a substitute for the Church; that Party members showed many of the characteristics of religious believers; and it follows, although Raphael does not make specifically this particular point, that when disillusionment sets in and resignation from the Party was accepted, it was 'The God that Failed'. Let it be acknowledged that there were many inside the Communist Party whose commitment was total to the point of religious conviction. To work in any organisation of the Left requires a spiritual dedication, in some degree or other; without it there can be no sustained involvement against the powers of darkness, in whatever period of history or however defined. The history of radicalism in the past three centuries has been expressed in different language at different times, and in the twentieth century the language has often, not always, been expressed in secular terms. Faith, in some degree or other, a set of beliefs, a moral conviction, however inadequately articulated, there must always be; but for most people in this century dedication in the cause of human emancipation has stopped short of an intense religiosity which Doris Lessing so beautifully portrayed in her short story 'The Day That Stalin Died'.[9] There are two points to be made in this context. The first is that political dedication in Britain of the kind experienced in the Communist Party has not in any way been unique to that Party. It has been represented within many individuals during the history of radicalism in these islands. Tommy Ramsay, born around 1810 in Durham county, spent his whole life preaching the necessity of organisation to the pitmen of his county. He was in the great strike of the Pitman's Union of Tyne and Wear in 1832, and in every major conflict thereafter. On many occasions he was victimised, and made homeless, and by the last years of his life was being refused employment from one end of the county to another. Like so many Durham miners he was a chapel-goer. Less than a year before he died, on June 15, 1872, he was a speaker at the first annual gala of Durham miners and their families; and looking over the great crowd of about 30,000, Tommy Ramsay spoke with feeling and great emotion at the unity of the workers for which he had striven so long: 'Lord, now let thy servant depart in peace, for mine eyes have seen Thy salvation'. Just about a hundred years later Jack Nicholson died. He had been secretary of the Hull Trades Council for over thirty years; always on the Left but never a Communist Party member; and he worked seven days and nights a week. The day after his death his widow collected all his papers, pamphlets, books — and Jack was a magpie who saved everything and kept a mass of material in the shed at the bottom of his garden — and burned the lot. A funeral pyre to commemorate the bitter years of neglect that Jack's devotion to the working class cause had conferred upon her.

Those who have been totally committed to the Union, or the Co-operative Society, or the Labour Party, or the Communist Party have, however, always been in a minority, and often a small minority. This is my second point: that in every political/social organisation, however revolutionary its principles or however strict its formal discipline, it has been unusual, except in times of crisis, for all their members to offer a commitment that was total. The minority of the totally committed have been surrounded by far larger numbers whose general agreement can be accepted, but whose practical contribution will never match that of the fervent minority of activists. It could not be otherwise. There are a myriad of reasons in most lives for not being a totally committed political activist. Bourgeois society constantly inculcates individualism and self-interest. On another plane, there are families to be worked for and cared for. There are many other things in life than politics, broadly defined, and a life of political activism can for some be intellectually and emotionally constricting. For most people to move into a position of opposition brings with it difficulties, problems, stress and strain; and for working people often hardship and oppression of varying kinds.

And so to my personal history. I refer to brief biographical details, not because the history of one individual is of any particular significance, unless the person concerned is of national importance which the present writer emphatically is not, but because the variety of experience in the Communist movement in its most expansive period requires emphasis. Ordinary people, those who were in the majority of communist recruits in the years between the wars and during the second war itself, came from a wide sample of the population. Unlike Raphael Samuel, for example, I myself had no need to develop a sense of belonging: I did belong, and it never occurred to me to have any doubts about my position. It was not at all that I belonged to the privileged groups of society, except in the important sense that I was never subject to material insecurity. Most of my life as a child and a teenager was lived in a comfortable petty-bourgeois family milieu. I had the advantage — which became more obvious to me later in life — that I spent my first four years in a working class home in a small industrial town in Lincolnshire where I was offered all the love and emotional security that young children need, even though my own mother was away working in London. From the age of six my mother and I moved into a lower middle class environment, into a house in which my mother acted as housekeeper, and in a few years married the man she worked for (her first husband, my father, had been killed during the first world war). My mother was an active Anglican, and my step sister and I went to church twice a day on Sundays, and I sang in the choir. Later, when I had become a communicant, I became a server, an assistant to the priest. I was never committed in a religious sense and by the time I was fourteen I had ceased consciously to be a Christian; but it made no difference to my life-style. There was no point in creating a family upheaval, and the church provided an extremely lively social life for its teenagers. So I continued to go to Church, enjoying the singing and in later life being grateful for the knowledge I acquired of the Old and New Testaments, but much more at the time the round of tennis, dancing, family parties that group life round the Church brought with it. Until the age of sixteen when I took the equivalent of today's 'O' levels, I was uninterested in academic work, much to the dismay of my mother, but I was increasingly competent at most sports and I was exploring the mysteries of life with the help of girls at the local convent school. I was willingly, and pleasantly, seduced when I was sixteen by the elder sister of my current girl friend, and in my sixth form years I was occasionally offered a return of her favours. The last two years at what was a very good grammar school were very different from those that had gone before. For reasons which I cannot explain but must have been connected with the excellent teaching in the sixth forms, I turned over from being idle at my books and began working extremely hard. I continued a range of sports and ended my last year at school as Captain of the school, and captain of association football, swimming and athletics. In all three I represented my county of Essex. I entered the London School of Economics in the autumn of 1934, with a junior scholarship, to which was automatically added a County Major scholarship; and I joined the Communist Party within two months.

I became a member of the Communist Party without any sense of exultation although it would be wrong to deny in any way the intellectual excitement that a discovery of marxism created. Moreover it is not difficult to understand why intelligent young men and women joined the Communist Party from the mid-1930s on. For one thing the stupidities of the 'social-fascist' period were mostly over, but much more important was the world capitalist crisis, the ravages of which were still blindingly obvious, both in Britain and in the world as a whole. Fascism had come to power in Germany in the early months of 1933, a description which it is too easy to understand in an academic way without appreciating the passionate hostility that developed against its bestialities among my contemporaries. At the same time the feebleness of the Labour Party leadership following its ignominious defeat in 1931 developed a scepticism towards social-democracy which in my case has never abated. There was a general failure of the Labour

Party to offer a sustained opposition to the National Government; a refusal to provide any support for the national Hunger Marches which Wal Hannington and his comrades so successfully organised; its advice to the labour movement not to oppose Mosley and his fascists on the streets; the endorsement which was given to the infamous policy of Non-Intervention in the first eighteen months of the Spanish civil war: who could support these broken-backed politicians by joining their Party? Quite a lot of Communists did, of course, infusing a vigour in local and regional Labour groups which would not otherwise have been there. [10]

For young intellectuals with any generosity of spirit there were additional factors beyond the poverty of so many of their own people, and the brutalities of fascism. Bourgeois society was under increasing criticism for its callousness, greed and cultural emptiness. *Left Review*, especially in its first years, was as lively a journal as one could wish for; [11] and within my own intellectual environment of LSE the sterility of the orthodox economics of Lionel Robbins and von Hayek was taken as given. Against the leading economists there was Harold Laski whose influence on the present writer was far-reaching. Laski drove one into the library, while Communist Party activity often involved the streets. It has, however, often been remarked that communist students were expected to be 'good' students, and this has not seldom been misinterpreted. I speak here for myself but to be a good student meant that if you were going to play any part in the undermining of bourgeois society, it was necessary to be able to engage the philosophers and cultural apologists of bourgeois society on their own ground. Long before I read Gramsci this was my understanding of what was involved in being a 'good' student. There was never a suggestion that it was the necessary road to an affluent career in the future; there was indeed something of an unemployment problem for graduates. Intellectual competence to the highest level of one's ability was assumed to be a desirable good, and in one's Final year at LSE, every member of the Communist Party was excused all political activity, and it was expected that you would get the best degree that you were capable of.

What the LSE years provided was a continuous confirmation of the marxist analysis of contemporary capitalism. It was, it needs to be emphasised, not a dogmatic marxism that went unquestioned. In the matter of Russia matters were different, and that question is discussed briefly below. The marxism that we taught ourselves was based first upon the writings of Marx and Engels, and the literature of classical marxism that was gradually being made available. For me, the publication of the *Selected Correspondence* in 1934 was of major significance. No one could read the letters of Marx and Engels without becoming aware of how conscious they were of the complexities of their contemporary world and of historical explanation in general. There was also a growing volume of work upon British history. Apart from the Marx-Engels Correspondence, superbly edited by Dona Torr, John Strachey's *The Coming Struggle for Power* which had its fourth edition in 1934 (first appearing in 1932) was an exciting intellectual experience and there was Hessen's study of 'The Social Roots of Newton's Principia' which made such an impact upon the radically minded young scientists of the 1930s.[12] I got a great deal from Theodore Rothstein's *From Chartism to Labourism*, which I have always thought an under-rated text[13] and in 1937 Allen Hutt produced *The Post-War History of the British Working Class*, and in the following year A. L. Morton's *A People's History of England* provided the Left with an alternative version of their island's history. I started collecting socialist and communist literature from my early days as a student — not least through the annual *Daily Worker* bazaars in London — and I began reading the left wing literature of the early labour movement with *Labour Monthly*, which carried a good deal of historical material, probably the most important. I also went beyond Britain. Laski in his lectures encouraged his listeners to read the French writers of the Enlightenment, and I did; and he also talked a great deal about the contemporary United States with whose radical literture I gradually became familiar. I cannot recall why I became fascinated with the history of modern China, but my reading began with Louis Fischer's *The Soviets and World Affairs* (1930), and went on from there. When the Left Book Club began in the summer of 1936 the range of world politics available widened considerably. In all this we were fortunate to have access to the LSE library, one of the few academic institutions with an international labour and socialist collection.

It is necessary to emphasise the intensity of intellectual debate and discussion during my formative years at LSE. For one thing nearly half the total student body were post-graduate students and they seemed to use the junior common room more than their own but more important, we all ate together in the same refectory. Among communist students — and the nominal total at one time was around a hundred members — 'Bolshevik self-criticism' was a phrase commonly on our lips — mainly as a joke, it must be said — but we did assume that it was incumbent upon us to evaluate critically the national and international situation. All our party meetings opened with a political discussion and although Palme Dutt's 'Notes of the Month' in *Labour Monthly* were always taken to be the most important signposts to be followed, I do not recall that they were accepted without question. In general, of course, the major issues of the years from 1934 to the beginning of war were in broad terms agreed upon by all or most of the Left in Britain. The exception was the internal situation in Soviet Russia, with the political trials of the Old Bolsheviks in the years 1936 to 1938 as the centrepiece of argument and discussion. One of my contemporaries was Alec Nove with whom I argued for many hours about the trials. He was right and I was wrong, although it is always necessary to appreciate why so many others were wrong with me. It was not the case in the United States where there was a Trotskyist movement of some intellectual liveliness; but there was surprisingly little critical comment from within the United Kingdom. It was not wholly absent and some of the best minds of the labour movement were either sceptical or in firm opposition. The *New Stateman* articulated the doubts; the *Manchester Guardian* kept its columns open to all points of view; H. N. Brailsford, the greatest socialist journalist of the inter-war years, consistently regretted and sharply criticised the trials; and Emrys Hughes, editor of the Scottish *Forward* attacked the procedures of the trials and maintained a principled policy of opposition while keeping his columns open to different views. What must be appreciated however are two things, and these are put forward not in an apologetic sense but as historical explanation: the first was that the weight of evidence available to British readers on the Left was overwhelmingly in support of the trials; and the second was the international situation through 1937 and 1938. Bukharin was shot three days after the Nazis marched into Austria in March 1938; Munich provided the major betrayal in the autumn of the same year; and the Spanish Republic collapsed in the early months of 1939. [14]

These were years when we learned that the British ruling classes were wholly unscrupulous and that they would go to any lengths to protect what they regarded as their fundamental interests; that the hostility to the Soviet Union, and to their serious challengers on the Left, was all-pervasive; that the leadership of the Labour Party and the TUC could never be expected to offer any significant opposition to the ruling groups, and that only pressure from below could be expected to achieve some degree of change. Certainly I never believed that socialism for Britain was on the agenda, and my view has not altered for the past half century. In personal terms what I learned from my communist years at LSE was intellectual discipline and a strong commitment to party work. This was not true of the majority of my student comrades since most left the Communist Party either during the war or within a few years of the end of the war; but few resigned with feelings of bitterness that expressed themselves in the kind of denunciation that has not been uncommon with the American Communist Party or in certain of the Communist parties of

Europe. I would guess that my practical commitment was always stronger than the majority of my friends, and that my six years in the army during world war two were important in strengthening my political position. Before however expanding that statement, let me just say that student political life in the Communist Party was exciting, very lively intellectually, and fun. Leonard Woolf titled his memoirs of the years between the wars *Downhill All the Way* and on any rational assessment this was a wholly reasonable description of an exceedingly unpleasant and grim period of world history. But we were young in the 'thirties, and youth has a resilience and a buoyancy that shines through the darkening vistas of the future. It was not that we were pharisaical in our denunciations of the evils of fascism, or the hypocrisy of our own politicians; but we still had hope and there was a life before us. So alongside our serious study, and our whole-hearted support for Republican Spain and our deeply felt emotions when the Spanish cause began to be overwhelmed, we also led a happy social life: we danced, we had lots of parties at which memory suggests we seemed to be singing much of the time, we fell in love, and we went to Paris for five pounds a week: a skilled worker's wage. We were young, and learning about life was still exciting.

I graduated in the summer of 1937 with what is known as a good degree; and I was unemployed for the next nine months, in the end having to take a job in business. In my period of unemployment I worked on a voluntary basis for Dorothy Woodman's Union of Democratic Control and in particular for the China Campaign Committee. I also became London organiser for the student communist party, and in the year before war broke out I began to work with the London organisation of the National Unemployed Workers Movement, and thereby made the acquaintance of one of the great militants of Communist history, Wal Hannington. The London organiser was Don Renton, who had fought in Spain.

My own political education broadened considerably during the six years of war. I was called up in the spring of 1940 and refused to take an officer's training course that was soon offered me. It was all a matter of accent. The political advice the Communist Party offered was that all comrades who were offered commissions should take them, and this seemed to me quite the wrong approach. I had a number of arguments with senior party officials at King Street — which was the national headquarters of the Party in Covent Garden — and went away unconvinced, and unchanged in my attitude. My argument was that it would be wrong to enter a class-based structure that it would be impossible to change, and moreover that if there was any 'trouble' — I had no idea in 1940 what 'trouble' meant — it would be more sensible to be in the NAAFI canteen with ordinary

soldiers than in the officer's mess. The irony of my army career was
that I was soon promoted to be gun sergeant in charge of a heavy anti-
aircraft detachment: we were on 3.7 inch guns which fired a shell
weighing about half a hundredweight. This promotion I did not object
to, since all the fifteen in my gun detachment had joined up the same
time as myself, and by this time we were all friends. Most were labour-
ing working men from the East End of London, and with one other I
was the only middle-class member of the group. I talked politics a lot
of the time, and my wife sent me each week a bundle of literature
which I sold on a regular basis. The trouble came after about
18 months. We had spent the year of the blitz — August 1940 to May
1941 on the docks in Liverpool, and had been firing almost every
night. It was very hard work, and occasionally dangerous, and there
developed strong bonds of comradeship between all of us. By this time
I was known throughout the Battery (a Battery is made up of eight
guns) as a Red, or so I was informed by the Quarter-master Sergeant
one day who asked me where I got all the literature that I sold each
week; and it was therefore with some surprise that I learned I was to
be promoted to sergeant-major to take over a new Battery that was
about to be formed. My own unit was scheduled to go abroad: to
North Africa as it turned out. I refused the promotion, was brought
before the colonel of the regiment, and after half an hour was still
saying no. When I returned to my own Battery I was told by the Major
— with whom I had good relations — that the Colonel was giving me
the option of accepting promotion or a posting to Iceland, where the
tour of duty was two years. I accepted promotion.

I spent a year in the Shetlands and then transferred into a course
for Gunnery Instructors. It was a three months course and if you
passed you became one of the élite groups in the Royal Artillery. I was
still with the rank of sergeant major, and after becoming highly
specialised in German gunnery equipment, and therefore expecting a
posting to the second front in Europe, I was shipped to India where I
remained for the last two years of my army career.

My Indian years were to be crucial in the way my political thinking
developed and in the commitment to my socialist ideals. It was not
just the poverty, although the early months of contact with the levels
of material degradation that the masses endured were numbing and
never ceased to shock. As a contemporary liberal commentator said:
'It burns like acid into the brain.' Even more was association with
members of the Indian Communist Party. I had known in England
that I was going to India, and went carrying letters to the Party leaders
in Bombay, where the Party headquarters were. Mohan
Kumaramangalam[15] was president of the Cambridge Union just
before the war — a close friend of Victor Kiernan — and he was now

the youngest member of the Central Committee. Through him, of course, I met all the leading members of the Party including its General Secretary P. C. Joshi, and wherever I went in India I made contact with the local Party. So did many other British communists, I should add. What impressed me, and it has always remained with me, was the self-sacrifice and dedication of the full-time Party workers. I had contact, to a much more limited extent, with the rank and file. I gave talks to peasant groups and on two occasions to industrial workers but real contact was much more difficult, not least because of the language problem. I became reasonably fluent in Urdu — I had to because for much of my time I was attached to Indian regiments — but it was Army Urdu full of English gunnery expressions.

To listen to these Party activists, some of whom had been terrorists in their youth, and to their stories of underground work and their life in prison, was both exhilarating and sobering, much more the latter than the former. British Imperialism became a reality of a kind that is not always accessible from books although one must never underestimate the importance of anti-imperialist writing. I had one extraordinary piece of luck at the end of the war with Japan, in that friends were able to obtain educational leave of absence for me to attend the Bombay School of Economics. My own headquarters knew nothing of this; it took them two and a half months to find me; and during that period I worked every day at the Party headquarters while living with a liberal Quaker family in a middle class area of the city.

British Communists throughout the armed forces very often engaged in political activity. There was no directive of any kind from the British Party, but it was the obvious thing to do. At one RAF camp outside Karachi they put up a communist candidate at a mock general election in the summer of 1945; and there was earlier, of course, the famous Cairo Parliament in which Communists and left Labourites worked together. In my own case I had succeeded in forming discussion groups and in selling literature during most of my time in Britain. Shetland was an exception, but in India there were Communist groups in a number of places I visited; and since in my role as gunnery instructor I travelled around a good deal, I had rather more opportunity than most of making contacts. The last months in India were in political terms the most lively. I had returned to Karachi following my sabbatical at the Bombay School of Economics, and while there was absolutely nothing for anyone to do except wait for demobilisation, I was banished to take charge of an empty site nearer the town; a move which suited me very well. We had a party group of about twenty-five, of which I was chairman. Most were RAF and it was the biggest station in the region which carried through a ten day strike as protest against the slow rate of demobilisation. The CP group had not initiated the protest but it was a Party decision on the evening of the first day to move in and provide leadership; and this was done. It was obviously quite a radically minded camp of over 5,000 RAF (I had earlier spoken for an hour at a meeting of over 600 against British military intervention in Greece, and we had won overwhelming support). This is not the place to tell the story of the strike, which received widespread publicity all over India and also in Britain, with questions in Parliament, except to mention the courage and steadfastness of the small group of Communists who directed the strike; and especially Arthur Attwood, an electrician from the London area who was later arrested, kept in solidary confinement and who was only released after a three month campaign in the United Kingdom. An examplar of the working class communist militant. [16]

The Indian experience toughened me in a number of ways. It made me appreciate more sharply than ever before the class nature of British society, with the hierarchical character of the army only the most extreme example of a social structure immanent throughout British life. The army everywhere was class-bound, and for every officer in combat role there were probably ten in the long line behind, enjoying the best food and the best conditions that were available. Life on troopships probably illustrated the different treatment of the common soldiery and the officer classes more strikingly than in any other situation; but in India, partly no doubt because of imperialist rule for so long, the class distinctions were more blatant than in Europe, or so it seemed to me. Railway travel illustrated differences of approach to the worth of the various levels of army life. India is a very large country; and there was a constant movement of troops across the continent. Journeys could take two or three days, sometimes longer, and travel conditions were often uncomfortable and disagreeable. The Indian railways did not have through coaches; each coach in the first and second class was self contained. Officers travelled first; warrant officers like myself second; and the rest third class, where the seats were wooden and where there might or might not be reserved compartments for British troops. Subsistence pay was on the usual graduated scale. I reckoned to spend around ten rupees on food and drink on a day's journey. The scale for privates was four rupees a day, moving up to ten to twelve rupees for warrant officers, with junior officers beginning just above that level. First and second class coaches had uncrowded sleeping accommodation, ice boxes renewed at every main stop, and generally bearable conditions. Travel for the ordinary soldier was always unpleasant; in the hot season exceedingly unpleasant.

India also exhibited the racism of the British in obnoxious ways. Again there was the long tradition of white superiority into which the conscript Army fitted very easily. It was my common experience that young soldiers were horrified at their first contact with the poverty of the Indian peoples, and were willing to concede that as the responsible power the Empire should go; but within three months the 'wogs' were being blamed for their filthy conditions of living, for their destitution and poverty, and for the often cringing attitudes that were the inevitable accompaniment. Clive Branson's *British Soldier in India* is one of the great pieces of anti-imperialist writing, and offers a more authentic account of army life and army attitudes than any other I have read (Branson's biography is in volume 2, *Dictionary of Labour Biography*, 1974). He was a troop sergeant in an armoured corps and was constantly confronted with the racism of ordinary British soldiers. In my own case in this respect I had a different, and easier, experience than Branson. Much of the time I was attached to Indian regiments, which had British officers who were always careful in their attitudes towards their own men; and for another I never became part of any British unit but was always an outsider. Travelling around, of course, meant a certain amount of confrontation with unpleasant attitudes towards the people of India and I never lost any opportunity to use my rank of sergeant-major to put down racist opinions; but such occasions were relatively rare.

I returned to England at the end of March 1946 with my Communist convictions strengthened. I had seen imperialism at its revolting worst, and I had followed closely the reactionary foreign policy of the British government which became more pronounced as the war came to an end. The military intervention in Greece in December 1944 was the outstanding public demonstration that the old order had changed not at all and that the Labour leaders in the War Cabinet, Attlee and Bevin in particular, were wholeheartedly with Churchill in his counter-revolutionary actions. Since I was in India at the end of the war I was more aware than most of the central part which the British army played in re-establishing the French in what was becoming known as Vietnam — the bulk of 'British' troops were of course Indians and Gurkhas — and the parallel action in Indonesia on behalf of the Dutch against the national movement. [17]

I remained in the Communist Party for another ten years. It was the decade of the Cold War, of civil conflict of the bloodiest kind in Korea, and of a series of rearguard actions by Britain as the imperialist basis of the metropolitan country was steadily eroded. Indian independence was achieved in 1947 because the British had not the resources to hold India in subjection; but where military action was practicable, as in Malaya, Kenya, Cyprus, British troops were used against those who seemed to believe that the right to exercise sovereignty over your own country was inalienable. These military exercises were accompanied with varying degrees of atrocities; the full details only gradually became known, and in the case of Mau Mau in Kenya it has taken forty years before the full extent of the brutalities perpetrated by the British have become known. No socialist could support the foreign policy of the Attlee-Bevin regime between 1945 and 1951 and of the Conservative governments thereafter. The military and political subordination of Britain to the United States was already becoming defined, but again the full details of the subservience involved — not least in the establishment of over 150 American military installations in the United Kingdom — has only slowly been revealed. The continued support for the Soviet Union, as noted above, was based above all upon the heroic struggles of the Russian people against German fascism; but it was less easy to remain a Communist from about 1947 than in the previous decade. Some of the reasons have already been briefly touched upon, but the McCarthy years in the USA were devastating to the Left in general and not only to the communists, while in Britain the Cold War was more repressive than is usually suggested.

The British Communist Party lost remarkably few of its intellectuals before 1956. It was, after all, our own country Britain, which was carrying through its infamous policies in colonial countries, and which had already destroyed the chances of democracy in Greece while avoiding any action against Franco Spain; and whatever else was happening in the world, our main responsibility was for British actions round the world. For radicals of all kinds, there are always these difficult choices to be made; and for communists after 1945 the problems were acute and became increasingly so. I can only offer my own history. Hindsight can often be misleading and inaccurate, and it is always tempting to re-write one's own life in rational terms. Certainly this is a serious problem for communists although it is apparently not such a problem for liberals and social-democrats when confronted with the history of the barbarism of their own bourgeois democracies. Those who in the last resort come down on the side of contemporary capitalism have no choice but to engage in hypocrisy, sanctimoniousness and double talk. We have lived in the bloodiest century in recorded history and the present (January 1991) war in the Middle East is the latest infamy in the savage and violent chronicle of the twentieth century. Marxism, in my Anglo-Saxon version, is a morality that does not accept ethical justification for unpleasant deeds that have to be done. I myself was aware of labour camps in the Soviet Union though not of their extent nor of the brutality practised within them; I thought the Lysenko controversy both unfortunate and unnecessary, as with the cultural pronouncements of Zhdanov; and I finished reading James Klugman's

From Trotsky to Tito sceptical and unconvinced. I was a personal friend of Klugman, and I have to record that I did not tell him of the many doubts I had of his book. The pre-war Moscow trials were being much written about, but it was not, in my recollection, an issue of any importance in the labour movement circles in which I moved, and it never became a matter of serious discussion. I should add that before the war and after I personally never met a Trotskyist, or was confronted by one at any meeting I addressed; and the same was true, with only a very few exceptions, of members of the ILP. The one controversy that related to internal developments of the Soviet Union, as against matters of foreign policy, was anti-semitism; and here I took an uncompromising stand against any suggestion that it existed in Russia. There were two reasons: the first was that we had all become extremely wary of the bourgeois press, and with very good reason in many cases; and the second was personal to myself. I had a large circle of Jewish friends, some of them first generation emigrés from Russia. They spoke Russian and had Russian contacts. Hyman Levy, professor of mathematics at Imperial College, was among my Jewish comrades, but there were many others who are still living. Why should I believe the bourgeois press and not my political comrades?

There is another reason, of great importance in my own life, and in the lives of many others, why the Communist Party provided an organisation one was proud to belong to. There were some members I positively disliked, and mistrusted; there were others I tolerated; but most were comrades in the meaning of the term: friendly, dedicated and self-sacrificing. Not all were wholly committed, but that can never be expected; but the British Communist Party had a solid base in the working class and a quite large group of intellectuals who were not dilettante but serious in their political and intellectual work. I was fortunate to be of the generation that established the Communist historians' group[18] and for ten years we exchanged ideas and developed our marxism into what we hoped were creative channels. It was not chance that when the secret speech of Khrushchev was made known in the West, that it was members of the historian's group who were the most active among the Party intellectuals in demanding a full and uninhibited debate and discussion.

I do not propose to discuss in any detail the traumatic events of 1956 when at least 8,000 members left the Communist Party. There was already a serious discussion, and many misgivings, when Edward Thompson and I published the first number of the *Reasoner* in the summer of 1956; and the third issue over the weekend when Soviet troops invaded Hungary. At that point we both resigned having come to the conclusion a couple of months earlier that it was improbable we would ever be able to shift the top leadership into an honest discussion of the revelations in the secret speech, and their implications for the history of the Soviet Union. The bitterness against us was intense, much more acerbic than some recent colloquia have suggested. It needs to be emphasised that the idea of resigning from the Communist Party was not in our minds when we began the *Reasoner* and it was only in the following months that we recognised, with great reluctance, the fundamental conservatism, not only of the leadership but of many of the rank and file. It was all too understandable, as was the steady decline of the Communist Party in the next twenty years. The momentum of the past kept the party going through the nineteen sixties, but as their prominent trade union leaders either resigned or retired because of age, the failure to recruit the young, the refusal to analyse seriously the phenomena of Stalinism in its many aspects: all contributed to the disintegration of the organisational basis of the Party in the 1980s. [19]

*　　　　　*　　　　　*

For the first time in the history of the modern labour movement in Britain, from the 1880s to the present day, there is no effective political grouping to the left of the mainstream labour and trade union organisations. The Trotskyist and later more generally *gauchiste* groupings have remained marginal, and above all they have failed to recruit a substantial working class base. There have been two war situations in the 1980s. The first was the wholly unnecessary Falklands War, and the second was the Middle East war which began in January 1991. In both situations the official Labour and trade union leadership accepted the lead of the Tories: that, after all, was not unexpected. While there has been an active minority of Labour MPs, and organisations such as CND and ad hoc anti-war committees, it is the absence of an effective political organisation capable of co-ordinating the whole range of political opposition that is disturbing. There are more marxists in Britain today than there have ever been; there are more socialist books on the shelves than at any previous period; and there are serious journals of the Left. The gap, however, between socialist theory and socialist practice continues to widen, and while we are not yet in the American situation, where an annual meeting of 3,000 socialist scholars can meet in New York, with almost no impact on practical politics, we do seem to be moving, albeit slowly, in the same direction.

The Communist experience in Britain, although it was never more than a minority experience, does offer some important lessons for socialist work and activity in the present and in the future. It represented, it must be emphasised again, an historic moment in the development of the labour movement in Britain which is not likely to be repeated in the same terms in the future. More than two decades before 1918 recognition of the urgent necessity of an independent socialist educational movement had led to the efforts of the Socialist Labour Party in Scotland, and the Plebs League and the National Council of Labour Colleges in South Wales and elsewhere. This is a permanent requirement for any socialist movement: an independent educational movement, separate from the mainstream of colleges and universities. It may be admitted that the facilities in the British system for adults to re-enter education are growing, but they touch only a fraction of the total working population, and their curricula are usually orthodox or near orthodox. More importantly, many trade unions today have much improved facilities for their members, often with radically-minded tutors. There still remains, however, a quite crucial area of political information and analysis which only a socialist educational movement could supply. Today there is no shortage of materials for study: we know far more about the workings of bourgeois society than at any previous period in the history of capitalism. We cannot predict the future; that was always a myth, but we can explain what is happening today, and what might happen tomorrow, in greater detail and with more accuracy than ever before. What is lacking are the organisational facilities for providing regular discussion and instruction: instruction based upon debate and argument, with no one bringing down the Tablets from on high.

The second, and perhaps the crucial component of any viable movement in the future, is the world of trade unionism. For more than a decade after its foundation the British Communist Party was uncertain in its attitudes towards the existing trade union movement. The major problem was whether Party members should work within the existing reformist unions or establish independent revolutionary organisations. Attitudes became more sectarian during the Third Period, when the Comintern imposed the Class Against Class line upon the theory and practice of the world communist movement. With the rise of fascism in Germany in 1933 the approach towards the reformist trade unions changed. In most countries the majority of working people who were organised, were in reformist trade unions, and no revolutionary socialist could ignore the fact.

What has never happened in Britain, except to a minor extent and on a localised scale, was the emergence of a labour/socialist culture that pervaded ordinary peoples' ways of life. Scotland and South Wales have developed a mixture of nationalist and labour ideas that provided an ethos absent in most of England. It is reasonable to argue that such a culture, albeit in a not very pronounced way, was beginning to develop during the inter-war years and the war years, but it declined rapidly after 1950. Here the unions must be seen as the starting point. It will be necessary first to have recruited as large a proportion of the working population as can be achieved, and this means increasingly women and ethnic minorities. Whatever the personal motivation for joining a union, organisation on a basic economistic level is the first and necessary step. With intelligent leadership a tradition can be built within a union which achieves three things: the first, the organisation of most workers to the point of the closed shop; the second, the intimate involvement of the union and its members, at all levels, in the technology, managerial working styles, as well as working conditions, within the particular industry; and third, the political education of their membership towards an understanding of their place in the world at large. Political education must be interpreted broadly, not just in terms of classes and tutors. It should be social as well as straight educational, involving families and groups. In the 21st century the Union has to organise a wide range of social, sporting and intellectual activities outside and beyond what has come to be regarded as the normal range of union responsibilities; working towards the creation of a labour/socialist culture on an international plane; one that is not self-contained, as was the life inside the German Social-Democratic Party before World War One, but open and influential within the wider community. The role and place of the union in the coming decades is crucial; it must be European at least in its international contacts; and what must not happen is the American experience. All this will require an imagination, a fertility of ideas, a richness of social invention that has so far eluded the whole of the Left in Britain; and while the bitter years of the Thatcher era have begun to produce the beginnings of new concepts and new ideas, it will be a long haul.

The final requirement for a socialist renewal is unquestionably the most difficult. Communist parties, in their most successful years were highly disciplined, united in their purposes, and provided with a vigorous and dynamic leadership. The tougher the situation the more these qualities were needed, and it was at the extreme end of the human condition — the Resistance and above all the concentration camp — that there was exhibited in a remarkable way the resilience, the courage, and the indomitable spirit of ordinary men and women. Unlike most of the world, we in Britain live in a bourgeois democracy; a society which is a good deal less democratic than its apologists suggest, but one in which certain liberties are available, if not guaranteed, and in which the possibility of reformist change is realisable. A highly disciplined political party is no longer practical politics except for very small groups whose nature and character encourages a dogmatism that ensures a high turnover of membership. The essence of capitalist democracy has not however changed; the world of global capitalism has not changed. Since 1945 there have been at least 150 wars, large and small, mostly in Third World countries, fought with armaments supplied by the advanced industrial nations, some of whom, Britain included, accept the sale of arms to the rest of the world as an essential item in their balance of payments. The problem therefore remains: how to develop movements for change, for societies that offer adequate material living standards with democratic liberties for all. We know how at least two-thirds of the world will exist in the 21st century. They will continue as they are now: half-starved when they are not suffering from periods of complete starvation. We can expect tribal wars, national wars, and continued exploitation by the advanced industrial countries. The 20th century has been horrendous: the torture and the killings of many millions; it may be overtaken by the century which follows. In the industrial world there will be remarkable shifts in the centres of power, and whether this will lead to a repetition of the uneasy peace of the second half of the twentieth century, or to wars between major powers, it is impossible at this time to predict. What we do know is that assuming peace and sustained economic growth, bourgeois societies will continue to develop their appetites for greed; corruption will deepen; and violence within communities will increase. We can look at New York and Calcutta today and see the future.

In the long run, that is, within two or three centuries, all may be different; but it will only be different if we begin to develop methods of opposition to the degeneracy already afflicting America and Europe; methods that draw upon the humanist spirit which over the centuries has been very slowly maturing. In political terms we have to find ways of working that draw upon the revolutionary ideas and practices of the past century without the flawed organisational structures within which the Communist experience has crumbled and disintegrated. This, so it seems to me, is our major task: to search for new forms of organisation in which socialist intellectuals will join forces with a core of working class militants to create movements without illusions; firm in their understanding that the struggle will be long and hard; and founded upon a comradeship that will sustain and support the self-discipline and self-sacrifice without which the principles, and the aims, of the Good Old Cause will never be achieved.

NOTES

1. Karl Marx, *Selected Works*, Vol. I (1942), pp. 201-2.

2. This was the motto of the German Workers' Education Society which was founded in London in 1840; and it was taken over by the Fraternal Democrats which G. J. Harney established in 1847. For the latter, A. R. Schoyen, *The Chartist Challenge* (1958), Ch. 6 and all subsequent writing on Chartism will have some relevant material.

3. Quoted, *Dictionary of Labour Biography* (eds. J. M. Bellamy and J. Saville), Vol. VII, p. 239.

4. A British Chiefs of Staff document dated 20 July 1944 discussed future problems and included the words: "however unpalatable the fact might be, there might well come a time when we should have to rely on her [ie. German] assistance against a hostile Russia". This appeared six weeks after the Allied landing in Normandy, with another nine months of the war in Europe in the future: COS (44) 24 8th Meeting (0) (14), Public Record Office, Kew, London.

5. There is a full and excellent account of the involvement of the British TUC and the American Federation of Labor with their respective Foreign Offices in the development of Cold War strategies in Peter Weiler, *British Labour and the Cold War* (Stanford, 1988).

6. And also by politicians who played a part in the early days of the Cold War. Denis Healey, *The Time of My Life* (1989) describes his role as International Secretary of the British Labour Party from January 1946: 'Like most Western observers at the time, I believed that Stalin's behaviour showed that he was bent on the military conquest of Western Europe. I now think we were all mistaken. . .' (p. 101). What Mr Healey does not go on to say is that as a result of this mistaken judgement forty years of Cold War followed.

7. It is widely accepted by economists that part of the problems of the capitalist world in Europe during the years between the wars was the failure to develop their home markets, and that a considerable part of the boom of the post war era was the great upsurge of consumer demand that economic policies encouraged.

8. *New Left Review*, No 154 (November/December 1985), p. 53.

9. *New Reasoner*, No 2 (Autumn 1957), pp. 30-39.

10. In the last years of the 1930s, before the outbreak of war, quite a sizeable number of members of the Communist Party worked inside the Labour Party. In most cases their membership of the Communist Party was not known; but there was no doubt that a good deal of active political life was thereby injected into what was so often a lethargic electoral organisation. London was a particularly important centre. There is a brief discussion in Noreen Branson, *History of the Communist Party of Great Britain, 1927-1941* (1985), p. 157. I had personal experience of these matters since for a short time in 1937-8 I was secretary of my local Communist branch in my home town of Romford, Essex.

11. The volumes of *Left Review* were reprinted by Cass in 1970 and were the occasion of a sparkling commentary by Edward Thompson, *Times Literary Supplement*, 19 February 1971.

12. The most useful account of the radicalisation of the scientists of the 1930s is G. Werskey, *The Visible College. A Collective Biography of British Scientists and Socialists in the 1930s* (1978).

13. Reprinted in 1983, with an introduction by John Saville.

14. For a somewhat fuller discussion of the background to the trials in Britain, although a good deal more documentation is needed, see John Saville, 'May Day 1937', in *Essays in Labour History, 1917-1938* (eds. A. Briggs and J. Saville, 1977), esp. pp. 259-270.

15. For a brief biography, see *Dictionary of Labour Biography*, Vol. 5, pp. 132-4.

16. The full story of Arthur Attwood and the strike at the RAF base at Drigh Rd, Karachi, has not, unfortunately, yet been published. D. N. Pritt, *Autobiography, Part Two. Brasshats and Bureaucrats (1966)*, p. 237 ff, gives a long account of his own crucial involvement in the case. See also R. Kisch, *The Days of the Good Soldiers. Communists in the Armed Forces WWII* (1985), Ch. 10 has some additional material.

18. For a very good journalistic account, written before the official papers became accessible, see George Rosie, *The British in Vietnam. How the Twenty Five Year War Began* (1970); and for a more academic account, P. Denis, *Troubled Days of Peace. Mountbatten and South-East Asia Command, 1945-46* (Manchester, 1987).

19. For which see the essay by Eric Hobsbawm, 'The Historians' Group of the Communist Party', in *Rebels and their Causes in Honour of A. L. Morton* (ed. M. Cornforth, 1978), pp. 21-47.

20. For a brief account of the *Reasoner* period, see John Saville, 'The Twentieth Congress and the British Communist Party', The Socialist Register (1976), pp. 1-23.

PERESTROIKA AND THE PROLETARIAT

Leo Panitch and Sam Gindin

Like most western leftists of our generation, we became socialists despite the Soviet example of authoritarian Communism. We had little patience with an earlier generation given to be more apologetic for many of the events that amounted to a tragic and terrible aberration of socialist ideals. But while we celebrated the turn to political freedom in the USSR since Gorbachev, and the revolutions in Eastern Europe in 1989, we were at the same time disturbed that the trajectory of change appeared towards capitalism. Was a transition to democratic socialism at all on the agenda, if not in Eastern Europe, then at least in the USSR? The answer mattered in terms of the scope for socialist politics in the West. Having been hamstrung in our politics (among many other reasons) by the negative example afforded by authoritarian Communism in the East ("See what socialist revolution leads to!"), were we now to be hamstrung again by the collapse of authoritarian Communism ("Even they have opted for capitalism!")?

With these questions uppermost in mind, we undertook a visit to the Soviet Union in June 1990. In addition to the perspective afforded by meeting some of the intellectuals, journalists, academicians, political leaders and activists who compose Moscow's political class, we especially wanted to see what impact the process of political and economic change was having on workers, and what role they were playing in the process, as this might be revealed in terms of the activities of the party, the trade unions, the informal workers committees and the relation between managers and workers in the enterprises. To this end the Institute of the USA and Canada, our hosts in Moscow, cooperated with the international department of the Automobile and Farm Machinery Industries Workers Union in arranging visits to Yaroslavl (about 400 km. east of Moscow) where a major strike had taken place at a large diesel engine plant in 1987, and to Togliatti (1,000 km. south of Moscow) where the Lada is produced in the largest automobile plant in the world. Although some accounts of the dramatic developments among Soviet miners have been offered by western visitors, there have been very few accounts of

visits with workers in other industries. Although we ran the risk that
we might be treated to a traditionally misleading tour of union-run
polyclinics and pioneer camps, the days we spent in Togliatti and
Yaroslavl with a remarkable new generation of local union leaders
were extremely revealing. As socialists in the West observe the
transformation of the USSR, hope blends with trepidation and often
turns to dismay as events unfold. What makes what we saw of
continuing relevance is especially this: among the many different
struggles that are transforming the Soviet Union today, not the least
important is the class struggle. And it inspired us to see, whatever else
we saw that pointed in very different directions, that the capacity for
struggle on the part of workers still renews itself, as so often in the
past, by opening itself to and reaching for a democratic socialist vision
and purpose.[1]

I. *The Culture of Glasnost*
Five years after Gorbachev's coming to power, the most visible and
important change remains *glasnost* itself. A remarkable discursive
"openness" stands in sharp contrast to the strong sense of
constraint a visitor could palpably feel disfiguring even private
conversation in the earlier era. The confusing (and often just plain
confused) profusion of new movements, parties and workers' groups
reflects a high degree of politicization amidst this absence of
discursive constraint. Indeed, one sociologist told us that surveys have
revealed that Soviet society was increasingly polarizing into two
camps, defined in terms of their positive or negative orientations to
the politicization itself. On one side are the "activists"; on the other
are the "active non-activists", whose insistence on their right to be left
alone to tend their own garden has to be no less militantly asserted in
the face of the overall trend to politicization.

Outside the offices of *Moscow News* a hundred people crowd the
sidewalk debating politics, amidst a profusion of hawkers of crudely
printed newspapers ("Read all about it: How much Raisa Gorbachev
costs the people!"). Some of these papers are religious, some are
pornographic, yet all of them are politicized if only by virtue of the
novelty of their relatively unhindered distribution. But what is
especially important to register is that the street culture of *glasnost* is
as commercial as it is political. The profusion of craft and artist stalls
on the Arbat or at Ismaelovsky Park gives Moscow some of the
vibrancy that was so notably absent in the past. Yet this directly
blends with some of the most unsavoury aspects of the kind of market
freedom we know in the West. There are, near the Arbat, many
beggars pathetically attempting to scrounge a few kopeks by turning
pity for their physical handicap or the visible impoverishment of their

children into some sort of exchange value. Rather more pleasantly interspersed among the stalls are many buskers, such as a jazzband playing with gusto Dixieland renditions of Glen Miller's greatest hits. (The quality of their music is actually much higher than the no less derivative rock music videos that occupy all the air space on daytime television.) Reflecting a far more traditional aspect of Russian culture, a much larger crowd gathers amidst the stalls to hear a poet declaim his verses in the richest of Russian tones. His poems are all political and all splenetically anti-regime. One anti-Gorbachev poem in particular, in which he does a quite brilliant satirical take off of the man himself, produces rapture from the crowd. The crowd includes a clutch of young men in militia uniform who, far from taking notes or making arrests, display in their laughter and applause as much appreciation of the poet's sentiments as every one else.

Thus does the politics of *glasnost* blend with the commercialism of *glasnost*. Indeed, among the crafts on the stalls themselves the hottest new commodity, produced by hundreds of political-artistic entre-preneurs in an array of styles ranging from the most crudely painted to some of high artistic quality, is the "Gorby" doll. Like the traditional Matrushka, it opens up to reveal a succession of dolls inside. Inside Gorbachev one invariably finds first Brezhnev (usually bedecked in his military medals), then Khrushchev (the one we bought is carrying a shoe), then Stalin (ours has a pipe in one hand and, held behind his back, a bloody dagger in the other), then finally, inside Stalin, there is always a tiny Lenin, looking sage or stunned, benevolent or evil, according to the whim, ideological orientation or sense of consumer demand of the dollmaker. Jonathan Steele (*The Guardian*'s correspondent) has bought one of these that goes further: inside Lenin is Czar Nicholas, and inside Nicholas, Peter the Great. He tells us that he has seen others which have a tiny proletarian inside Lenin, and inside him — a traditional Russian muzhik!

As already may be gleaned, Gorbachev is little revered (to put it mildly) in this culture of *glasnost*. Muscovites especially (one heard this less in Togliatti or Yaroslavl) are disdainful of the adulation they sense he is accorded abroad. The things for which we would give him credit, for inaugurating *glasnost* itself or for a foreign policy explicitly designed to undo the knots in which the world has been tied by Cold War attitudes and structures, don't seem to impress people at home. Instead there is the lament (more often the complaint) that after five years he has "done nothing". What is meant by this is, first of all, that he has accomplished nothing to improve the domestic economic situation, above all the economy of consumer shortages; and, second, that the system of privileges for the bureaucratic-administrative elite, the old Communist "nomenklatura", still remains in place. Yeltsin's popularity rests largely on his insistent speaking to this latter theme.

The main test appears to be how quickly life is finally becoming "normal". This is a word much used to describe what people want ("a normal society", "a normal economy", "a normal life") and by this is mainly meant how they perceive most people to live in the United States. There is a strong sense of inferiority to all things American. People especially feel humiliated by their experience as consumers — "We feel this every time we go to the store", Len Karpinsky of *Moscow News* told us. The failure to catch up to America through a statist mode of parallel development has led to a widespread determination to catch up through emulating the American way.

But the American way is a composite of many things. And one sometimes feels that what they may be heading for could well look like the Chicago gangsterland in the 1920s that Brecht so brilliantly used as a backdrop to satirize the roots of fascism in his play "Arturo Ui". The culture of *glasnost* has opened new space for corruption, even as it has led to the exposure (and some prosecution) of some of the more sordid corrupt practices of high officials. As a means of coping with consumer shortages, petty appropriation was always commonplace and remains so: only the minimal surreptitiousness with which this is now done is reflective of *glasnost*. But the half-way house that cooperatives occupy between the market and statist modes of distribution has created new forms of corruption. We were assured by two knowledgeable economists, both very pro-market, that the shortages in the state shops had much more to do with corruption than anything else. According to one example: 500 pounds of meat arrives at a state-run shop and three hundred pounds of it will immediately be sold illicitly at a premium by the manager to a "cooperator", leaving only 200 pounds (or less depending on what informal system exists for the employees to appropriate their take for themselves or friends and relatives) for general distribution in the state shop at the low official price.

There was much talk in Moscow of the mafia as a power in the land, thriving in this half-way house. This seemed to confirm the boasts of one proud self-proclaimed gangster sitting at the hotel restaurant table beside us on our first night in Moscow, who ventured to inform us that the most important thing we needed to understand about his country was that nobody obeyed the law — that the system only worked in so far as everyone broke the law. We wondered, that first night of our trip, when one prostitute telephoned directly to our hotel room at 1.30 am., and yet another at 5.00 am., ("You Canada? Very nice! I come to your room?"), whether this was the pimp who ran the scam of paying the front desk of the trade union hotel to inform him of the telephone numbers of the rooms occupied by the foreigners who registered each day. When we related this the next day to our union host, he said he had complained of this before, but been threatened with his union having difficulty placing guests in the hotel.

We told the story again later, at the office of the new Socialist Party. It is a tiny room in the Rossiya Hotel looking directly over the Kremlin. The office is run by Yufi Ostromov. He is extremely thin and pale, looking every inch like a throwback to a young Menshevik in 1910. But this image is an incongruous one as we watch him constantly answering the telephone, computer on his lap, fax machine at his elbow, with the television across the room emanating its never-ending rock videos. ("Why are you watching this stuff?" "There is nothing else on.") The party's founder, the Marxist intellectual and Moscow City Soviet deputy, Boris Kagarlitsky, arrives as we are relating the incident with the prostitutes at the hotel and he finds the scam rather humourous. In a country with a terrible service sector, he quips, we had been offered the best of what that sector had to offer. He is much more interested in our trip to Togliatti and Yaroslavl, and bade us to report on whomever we might find there that the new party might be likely to recruit for its campaign for democratic socialism. *Glasnost* has many faces.

II. *Unions and Workers: A New Beginning?*
In 1987, when industrial democracy and self-management (along with cost-accounting) were the watchwords of perestroika, the Supreme Soviet passed a Law on State Enterprises which established that all the employees of each enterprise were to be constituted as a labour collective, empowered to elect managerial personnel as well as a representative council which would participate in managerial decisions and monitor their implementation and administration. An excellent example of how laws alone do not transform power relations occurred in December 1987 at the Yaroslavl Autodiesel Associated Works, where 40,000 workers are employed, and where a seven day strike took place over management's proposed work schedule for 1988.

At issue had been the "Communist Subbotniks", the "voluntary" Saturday work which Lenin in *A Great Beginning* (1919) had described as follows:

> Communist subbotniks are of such enormous historical significance precisely because they demonstrate the conscious and voluntary initiative of the workers in developing the productivity of labour, in adopting a new labour discipline, in creating socialist conditions of economy and life. . . [S]tarving workers, surrounded by malicious counter-revolutionary agitation. . . are organising "communist subbotniks", working overtime *without any pay*, and achieving *an enormous increase in productivity of labour* in spite of the fact they are weary, tormented and exhausted by malnutrition. Is this not supreme heroism? Is this not the beginning of a change of momentous significance?. . . Communism is the higher productivity of

labour — compared with that existing under capitalism — of voluntary, class conscious and united workers employing advanced techniques. Communist subbotniks are extraordinarily valuable as the *actual* beginning of *communism.* . . [2]

It perhaps says more about the actual demarche of Soviet Communism than anything else that these "Communist subbotniks", institutionalised as they were by management and unions over the ensuing decades throughout industry, have come to be called "Black Saturdays" by the workers themselves. Victor Reuther (who worked in the early 1930s in Gorky before going on to help found the United Auto Workers in the United States) told us that workers had a song in the 1930s, "We are just cogs in the big machine", and that they loved it and sang it enthusiastically on their way to work. Be that as it may, the image such a song conjures up, in the decade of Stalinism's greatest advances in terms of industrial productivity at the greatest human cost, is certainly very different from that of the free voluntarist working class subject of history which Lenin saw in embryo in the Communist subbotniks. Gorbachev's own "new beginning" sought to break definitively with Stalinism not only for its inhumanity but because the "big machine" could not continue to meet the definition of the Communist project as minimally set out by Lenin in terms of the "higher productivity of labour. . . employing advanced techniques". But far from unleashing the missing agent of "the conscious and voluntary initiative of the workers", which inspired Lenin's definition of Communism, the opening provided by Gorbachev rather was taken up by workers as an opportunity finally to rid themselves of the hated "Black Saturdays".

The issue came to a head in Yaroslavl late in 1987 when the management of the diesel engine plant put forward the work schedule for 1988. In the face of evident worker resentment with the Subbotniks (management had always found them useful at the end of each month when they were scrambling to meet planned production quotas — this was known as "storming the plan") their number had been reduced from 21 in 1986 to 19 in 1987. For 1988, management proposed to reduce the number of Black Saturdays to 15 and to compensate for them by reducing the basic weekly shift by 10 minutes off the eight hour day. It seems the workers were hardly surprised when the trade union committee endorsed management's plan, but when the new collective council did so, this so manifestly frustrated the expectations raised by the newly established "participatory" structure (in a classic example of cooptation, the director general of the plant had managed to get himself elected as chairman of the council) that this was the spark that started the strike. The strike, replete with mass meetings at the plant gates and marches to the director's office, was led by an informal group of rank and file workers. Notably, with the trade union committee effectively side-lined as a cipher of management, the 1987 Law also layed the basis for the resolution of the dispute. The Law had provided that in extra-ordinary circumstances workers might call for a general assembly of the entire labour collective, and during one of the confrontations between the strikers and the general director it was agreed that the issue would be put to 700 delegates directly elected by workers from the various sections of the plant. It was at this meeting that a com-promise was arranged — with the director guaranteeing that there would only be eight Black Saturdays in the 1989 work schedule. This strike received considerable attention in the Soviet press. An opinion poll by *Izvestia* found that 69% of the worker respondents approved of the stand the Yaroslavl workers against Black Saturdays. [3]

One of our main interests in visiting Yaroslavl and Togliatti in 1990 was to try to see what had happened with the new structures of industrial democracy that had only just been established in the auto-mobile industry when the 1987 strike took place. Little did we know, when we arranged the visit, that on the day after we arrived in the Soviet Union, a new Law on Enterprises would be passed which would renege considerably on the powers given to the labour collectives in the 1987 Law. Managerial personnel (except for brigade leaders) were no longer to be elected by the collective, and ultimate authority in the enterprises was to pass to a new enterprise council based on parity representation between managers and workers. If the 1987 Law was inspired by radical Yugoslav self-management notions, the 1990 Law was clearly based on the more tepid example of West German co-determination. Perestroika had taken a clear turn, one which put less stress on the "voluntary, class conscious and united" participation of workers. The questions that immediately arose for us concerned why this shift had taken place and what the response of workers to it would be.

The Trade Union Central

The official trade unions in the USSR have always been directly enmeshed in the ruling apparatus. Their leadership was a secondary, but by no means entirely powerless, element in the bureaucracy. They were conveyor belts downward to the workers of party, ministerial and managerial decisions; recruiting stations for those who showed the inclination and aptitude to rise in the hierarchy; organizers of worker passivity amidst ersatz displays of mass support. Their control of resources in the form of the considerable "social wage" (health clinics, housing, pensions, vacation camps, cultural centres) at the enterprise level — yielded them whatever social base they could genuinely claim (especially since wages were set centrally by the ministries) and furnished the backbone of their power vis-à-vis workers — leaving aside, of course, the coercive apparatus they could call on to suppress dissent.

Today, the central trade union apparatus, the AUCCTU, is widely regarded as an "empty shell", a phrase we first heard from Kagarlitsky, but was repeated by the local union leadership in Togliatti, who added that it was "harmless, and perceived as irrelevant". They told us that throughout the auto industry, and in many others, the central union apparatus had lost considerable power to the locals. The national leadership knows that it must evolve a new role: "We are first year students in how to act as trade unionists," Alexander Kashirin, President of the Central Committee of the Autoworkers Union, told us. They are caught, as it were, in a pincer movement between their declining power in the party and vis-à-vis the Government, on the one hand, and the local unions' assertion of their independence on the other. But what new role does the central apparatus see itself as playing? At the moment, their orientation is mainly reactive and defensive. Kashirin told us that the AUCCTU accepted the market economy "in principle". He used a chillingly familiar phrase that we were to hear time and again: "There is no alternative." He confirmed western press reports that the leadership of the AUCCTU played an important role in the decision to hold a referendum on the price reform, their thinking being that it will only obtain popular approval if a package of compensatory laws designed to maintain living standards and "keep social stability" is introduced beforehand. "There is already much unemployment in Central Asia," he says, "and the market economy will put many people out of jobs everywhere." One of the laws that the unions hope will be passed by the Supreme Soviet would offer a guarantee of full employment, and provide for unemployment compensation and retraining. (But does not the latter suggest that they accept that the former guarantee will only be formal?)

Kashirin claimed that in the previous year, the AUCCTU had "done everything to prevent limiting the rights of working people in the enterprises". But the examples he gave all pertained to resisting price increases. No mention was made about working conditions, or health and safety, or technological change. Most significantly, the AUCCTU leadership clearly put up no opposition whatever to the new Law on Enterprises despite the fact that it considerably retracted the democratic powers that workers had formally been accorded in the 1987 Law. In terms very similar to what we were to hear later from the Deputy Director of the Autodiesel enterprise in Yaroslavl, Kashirin tells us that the collective councils in the enterprise "are no longer needed". There was much conflict between the Councils and the local unions. On the other hand, they tried to "take over" management of the enterprise and encouraged workers to ignore managerial commands. He personally would like even the new parity council of the enterprise to be dominated by "specialists" in finance, technology, etc. Although this is not yet the official position of the AUCTU, measures to ensure this are "being discussed".

It is very clear that the official unions, at least at the national level, still define their role in terms of an alliance with managers. Kashirin tells us that the unions are not "eliminating the possibility of strike action", and are looking into the question of establishing strike funds. "For seventy years we were never able to even think of strikes. Now we are just learning the necessary skills involved. There are others who are ahead of us in this and are challenging us. But we see strikes as a measure of last resort. Each strike hurts another part of the working class. For this reason, we accepted last year the law on strikes." This law goes well beyond Canadian labour legislation in restricting the right to strike.

Who are these others that are "ahead" of the official unions and challenging them in this respect? Although there are three other local organizations that have formed at the national level (SOTSPROF, the United Front of Working People, and the Russian Federation of Independent Labour Organizations, which held a founding conference in May 1990), it is by no means clear that any of these new centrals have significant organizational strength, nor that the latter two have very much independence from the old union leadership. Notably the local leaders and activists we met in two major industrial centres knew little or nothing about them. It would appear that in so far as there are any effective challenges to the old union practices, they primarily exist at the local level, except for the League of Miners. At this level there are many informal workers' committees working outside of the official unions. But we were told by one of the closest observers of the "informals" that in virtually all strong industrial areas the local unions (and often the local Communist party organization) have already been taken over by a new brand of activists and leaders; or at least bureaucrats have ceded much influence to them since they have to defend local interests to hold onto their positions.

Togliatti

The three days we spent in Togliatti as guests of the Trade Union Committee of the Volga Automobile Associated Works (VAZ) provided us with an excellent opportunity to observe this new local unionism first hand. If the newly elected trade union leaders we met with there, almost all between the ages of 35 and 42, are "first year students in trade unionism", they are among the quickest students we have ever met. Certainly in their economic and political intelligence and sophistication, as well as in their confidence as organizers and their openness to searching for new approaches and ideas, they outshone most trade union leaders in the West. Perhaps this is only a reflection of the kind of abilities that come to the fore in the working class when a society is in the process of transition. Perhaps it also says that, amidst all the repression of authoritarian Communism, some qualities of leadership of the kind that Gramsci best defined in the communist tradition were nevertheless seeded, even if not organizationally nurtured anywhere to the extent that they should have been. In any case, we formed the strong impression — only after pressing them very hard with questions that trade unionists in the West would certainly have considered impertinent — that the local leadership in Togliatti are very committed to becoming effective democratic representatives of their members' interests.

Togliatti is a 27 year old city on the Volga about 1,000 kilometres southeast of Moscow which is totally dominated by the VAZ empire of highly integrated assembly, parts, foundry and machine plants. By virtue of its concentration of all aspects of car production, it has always been highly independent of the central planning apparatus. The assembly plant's three parallel assembly lines stretch out for some three kilometres. It is organized like car assembly plants in North America were twenty years ago (i.e. when it was built with the help of Fiat) and the machinery, including the robots, while not necessarily of that vintage, are based on models that date back that far. VAZ produces 750,000 vehicles each year, about 40% of these are exported, and about half of the exports go to the West. It is in good part due to its direct access to hard currency that there is no consumer crisis in Togliatti. The enterprise shops are full. Only fruit was in short supply while we were there, and one of the union vice-presidents was about to travel to Georgia to secure supply.

The massive assembly plant, where we spent a half day and where we were free to talk to workers as we wished, is dirtier and noisier than plants in North America. Apart from this, the most striking difference is that at least half of the assembly line workers are women. In North America, the most gender integrated assembly plant has, at most, twenty percent women workers. Remarkably, many of the women are wearing sandals, while no one in a western plant would be permitted to go without protective footwear. A group of women on the line tell us that they put much more effort into their work than the men do. When we turn to the men who hear this and ask if this is true, they laugh and say: "Of course!" At breaks one generally sees men and women sitting separately, but not always, and it is obvious that some romantic attachments are formed at work. Indeed, one unforgettable scene on the line was of a young man and woman, having completed putting electrical wiring into the car frame that just passed their station, running around to each other for a passionate kiss before the next car made its way to them along the line. It appeared to us, although we can say nothing from what we saw about the incidence of absenteeism, that the workers are working harder than they do in North American assembly plants. No generalizations should be drawn from this, but it is nevertheless worth noting in light of the conventional wisdom that job security makes the Soviet worker lazy.

At a tiny shop stewards office near the cafeteria, a 55 year old male steward was meeting with three thirtyish women who were discussing their maternity benefits. He was the head of a group of thirteen elected stewards representing a section of 900 assembly line workers, and ten of the thirteen were women. Only the chief steward's position was full-time; he had been elected for a two year term and was not a party member. As we discussed the degree of activism and democracy in the union, he told us that his section was having a meeting the following Saturday to discuss the impending price increases and what the union should do about them; 300 delegates had been elected — one for every three workers — and on the basis of precedent (such meetings were held about once a month) he expected that about 280 would attend. He mentioned all this casually, as if there was nothing remarkable about such a form of delegate democracy. Could it be that, long buried beneath the Stalinist structures and practices, the 1917 revolution had left some legacy of direct and delegate democracy which was now coming back to life?

In Togliatti, all union positions, from the Chair, vice-chair and seven vice-presidents to the chief stewards in every shop (in the auto industry every 700 workers are allotted a full-time representative) have been elected in contested elections over the last two or three years. The system of open elections appears to have been sparked by the example of the elections for managerial personnel and workers councils inaugurated under the auspices of the 1987 Law on Enterprises, but it is not clear that this was the cause, rather than the moment of opportunity, for this change from the top-down system of appointments, nominations and ersatz elections in the past. In fact, the Communist Party Secretary at VAZ told us that the idea for the 1987 Law was born at a factory Communist party committee meeting in Togliatti in 1985. This emerged out of a "strong feeling that the old system limited participation and productivity in so far as sole responsibility fell on management and the trade union bureaucracy and most workers had no way to participate in decisions on the process of production". But the main change in labour-management relations in Togliatti pertains mostly to the behaviour of the union. In contrast with what happened in Yaroslavl, the union leaders dated their experience with "fighting management" back to a similar attempt to knock twelve minutes off each working day in exchange for "Black Saturday" work. It was the union that resisted this in Togliatti and managed to get the management to retreat on this completely without a strike.

It is clear that the new local party and union leadership are close allies. As with Gorbachev at the national level (although they are a generation younger), they did not stage a coup against the old leadership but rather developed within the local union and party organizations and waited for the retirement of the old guard. Most of them are skilled engineers and technicians (the traditional recruiting ground for industrial and political leadership) and many were Komsommol leaders 15 or 20 years ago. Thus as with Gorbachev, with whom they clearly share a common trajectory and perspective (these kinds of local leaders were clearly in 1985 his real political base), their rise is not a product of the new system of elections. Rather, they repeatedly insisted that the key thing about their being freely elected was that it gave them legitimacy among the workers, so that they could go to the workers with this or that initiative and say: "You elected me — now you have to support me."

The strongest material grounds for their support continues to rest on the considerable facilities run by the union in Togliatti: the massive cultural centre with its cinema, concert halls and library; the preventative health care and herb medicine clinic where 15,000 workers a year spend two weeks; the network of pioneer camps for the kids (staffed by auto workers — mainly women — who leave the plant for the summer months to run the camps). Moreover, these facilities are run in the spirit of *glasnost*. The staff at the pioneer camp told us that they have been completely liberated from the previous "narrow-minded" party control over their curriculum. A particular blessing was that they no longer had to waste the children's time and energy practising the songs that the party used to want them to perform for visiting dignitaries. Among the two million volumes loaned from the library in the past year, Nabokov — long associated in the Soviet Union with "decadent" literature and support for the Whites in the civil war — was the most popular of the authors. The cultural centre regularly sponsors rock concerts, although we were told that there is a serious problem in Togliatti with teenage gang violence — which was attributed to young people having too few cultural outlets in the city.

Of course, the union leadership enjoy perks that go with holding office, not least the excellent meals we enjoyed with them and some opportunity for foreign travel. How many workers get access to the union-owned yacht on which we spent a pleasant few hours, or to the union mini-vans with their drivers which were at the beck and call of our hosts? One of these vans was equipped with a television, which was clearly a status symbol (and indeed not much more, since it only worked when the van was standing still). But these perks are probably not any greater, relative to their members, than most union leaders have in the West. When we told one of the vice-presidents that we were going to ask workers on the assembly line whether they saw these new leaders as apparachiks, he said if they did they would be partly right, as they were the "new apparat" now. When we put this question to about a dozen men and women taking a break from the line, this immediately sparked an argument among them pro and con, but there was a general consensus that the leaders were more responsive for being elected. Another smaller group clearly didn't want to discuss the question, or any other, but rather preferred to be left alone to get on with their lunch. But this would have been the typical attitude we would have confronted had we bothered a group of workers with our questions during their break in a North American plant.

Below the top leadership level, there are some thirty elected committees representing different groups of workers in the vast VAZ enterprise, within which there is also a large network of elected shop stewards. We were told that 50% of those who hold union positions are women, which would reflect the gender composition of the workforce itself. But when we met a group of thirty who were the chairs and/or vice-chairs of these committees, only four were women. The chairman of the Trade Union Committee had asked us to open the proceedings by talking about unions and autoworkers in Canada. Hoping to steer the subsequent discussion towards these issues, we put particular emphasis on unemployment, restrictions on the right to strike, and problematic aspects in the relation between leaders and rank and file workers (the latter included a brief primer on Roberto Michel's "iron law of oligarchy" in working class organizations). A heavy-set man in his sixties opened the discussion with a question on how extensive the sports facilities were for workers in our car plants (clearly making a point thereby on how comparatively blessed their own workers were). He followed with a claim that the turn to markets in the USSR would not necessarily lead to unemployment due to the retraining schemes being planned. (While he was speaking the Chair of the Trade Union Committee whispered to us: "Not a problem in theory — but in practice?") The same man then followed with a statement which offered a defence of democratic centralism. He had not gotten very far in this before he was forcefully interrupted by the vice-chair of the union committee in the foundry, a vivacious woman in her early thirties (most of the foundry's 9,000 workers are men), who insisted that we needed to know who was speaking. "That is the deputy director of the enterprise," she loudly proclaimed to much laughter and assent all around, and went on to insist that the thesis on oligarchy very much applied to the practice of democratic centralism. At this point we asked what difference the union elections had made and a 57 year old manual worker responded forcefully that over 27 years of working he had never held a union position because he wasn't a member of the party, but now he had been elected. The Chair of the Trade Union Committee in a parts plant then turned the discussion to the market, arguing that it would force the unions to take up the issues of protecting workers from the rise in prices, and looking at the Deputy Director, said they would be taking this up with the enterprise management. Notably, a number of questions were then put to us on how strike funds worked in Canadian unions.

There was, in fact, an interesting work action that very day in Togliatti. For all we were told about how the union had become more independent and far more active over the past two years, it is never-theless significant that there is an informal workers' club in Togliatti which operates outside of the union. (Perhaps this was why the Chair of the Trade Union Committee refused to take any credit for the union's activism, ascribing it rather to the fact that "people were really active now, especially workers.") The workers' club had recently distributed leaflets putting forth a set of demands on improving the "work environment", and had challenged the union leadership to take these up with management. On the Friday before we had arrived the union had taken these demands to management and apparently gotten them resolved, inclusive of a promise to install equipment to control the level of emmissions in the plant. But on the Monday morning, management had announced — without telling the union — that they might at the same time reduce wages by taking away the compensation given for working in poor conditions. On the following day, the union organized a "collective headache", with large groups of workers leaving their station to go to the medical staff. The union leaders were convinced that management had intended to sabotage the union, to teach them a lesson about not cooperating with the workers' club. But they were equally convinced that this was a strategic blunder by management, since the union was strong enough to win on this issue. Indeed the amount of time the union leadership spent with us on the very day this work action was going on provided some measure of their degree of confidence about the strength of their organization on the shop floor.

In general, the union leadership saw the workers' club as playing "a very useful role". One described them as a "barometer", another as a "catalyst". Since so much of the leadership's time and energy is involved with the extensive network of clinics, shops, vacation camps, and cultural centres run by the union, they see the workers' clubs as "crucial for raising discontents" and helping the union "pinpoint what the priorities ought to be". The leaders in the clubs are people who have left and rejected the party. One of the union vice-presidents described them as "extremist" in the sense that they put forward "impractical" demands, but the vice-chair of the union saw them in different terms: "They are active workers, not passive like most. In some ways they are personalities like the union leaders themselves, and are engaged in a power struggle for leadership of the workers. Ideologically they range from greens to social democrats, but they are, in a positive way, searching."

An important area of disagreement between the workers' club and the union leadership is over whether skilled engineering and technical staff ought to be members of the union. In fact this was the main topic at a meeting between the chairman of the trade union committee in the foundry and leaders of the workers' club the day of the "collective headache" work action. In so far as managerial personnel, who are drawn from this stratum, are still union members, and in so far as there has been traditionally a high degree of career interchange between union leadership and managerial positions, this clearly is an important element in the "power struggle" currently taking place. The chair of the union in the foundry, speaking with us immediately after this meeting, expressed both puzzlement and dismay at the position being taken by the workers' club on this. He is a 35 year old engineer, highly committed to working with the workers' club and to making the union more independent of management. He insisted that engineers and technicians were not a class apart despite their education but "still workers like the rest". He pressed us closely on whether unions in the West reflect such divisions and how marxist theory should comprehend them. There was much interest in the Lucas Aerospace example of technicians sharing their skills with manual workers to the end of developing alternate production schemes to prevent layoffs or plant closures.

It is clear that this new union leadership is itself searching precisely how to define their role in an independent manner from management. There was in Togliatti, as everywhere else in the world auto industry, interest in Japanese styles of management. The union leaders we talked to about this were not overtly hostile to this, but were aware of the passivity of Japanese unions. One of them recounted to us his amazement when he discovered on a visit to Japan that collective agreements prohibited the posting of union bulletins on the shop floor. "We would never allow this here." We were questioned closely on how strike funds worked in Canada and the extent to which they effectively sustained workers and their families during strikes. At the same time, they were concerned lest strike action would have the effect of making an enterprise uncompetitive, thereby leading to a loss of jobs. As we used the instance of the Canadian autoworkers' successful strike against General Motors to emphasize the importance of unions having the capacity to make independent judgements regarding the financial position of corporations, they expressed their concern about their dependence on management for information and the need, at the local union level, for the economic expertise that would enable an independent assessment of that information.

It is notable in this respect that, although Togliatti appears to have provided the prototype for the 1987 Law on State Enterprises, the Head of the workers council at VAZ (a manual worker in his late fifties) told us that the existence of the Council "had made little difference". The Communist Party Secretary took the position that in so far as the structures established in the 1987 Law had not worked it was because the idea behind it had been distorted in other enterprises. Part of this was due to the fact that managers had coopted the labour collective councils, but part of it was due to the fact that the higher the level of the managerial position, the more difficult it was for workers to decide whom to vote for. The new Law "took into account the mistakes which had been made and which we felt in our practice here. It ought to be the manager who made the final decisions. The limit of the workers council's power is the power of the manager. Theoretically the workers council had been the collective master of the enterprise, but practically it had not been." He saw the new Law as "neither here or there". Although the local union leaders did not appear very exercised about the new law, it was by no means clear that they entirely shared these views. Indeed, they told us that not only the union committee but the Communist Party Secretary had sent a document with their deputy to the Supreme Soviet opposing the new Law. But neither was it clear that they had done much to consult with the rank and file on this. Shortly after the new Law was passed (just a few days after we left Togliatti), the workers on the main assembly line issued a strong condemnation of the failure to have submitted it to the labour collectives for discussion.

How then do they see the future? It was easier for them to formulate their views on the mistakes of the past. We were told by the vice-chairman of the trade union committee: "In so far as workers are backward and underdeveloped, this is because there has in fact been no real political education since 1924. The workers were made fools of by the Party." They are also unanimously of the view that the command economy had failed. They are proud of the autonomy that VAZ has had from the central plan and do not appear terribly troubled that Togliatti is "an island of economic stability" while other cities are experiencing severe shortages. Yet at the same time many of them asserted repeatedly that communist values must never be given up. In the CP Secretary's view the problem with the Soviet Union was that it had tried "to set those values up apart from life — now it was necessary to let life take its course". The central material condition he was referring to was that "the free market is dynamic around the world" — and life taking its course meant that a stage of integration with international capitalism was necessary before the material conditions for communist values could be established. (He admitted this sounded naive about the benefits of the "free market", but this was because "we have had no experience with markets".) In Togliatti this would entail the establishment of joint ventures with western capital which they believed would still remain under the control of VAZ.

The union leadership, while certainly not opposing joint ventures, expressed considerable concern that the integration with Western capitalism would lead to a "Latin Americanization" of the Soviet economy. They were cognizant of and concerned by the rush to embrace capitalism in Eastern Europe (while at the same time highly supportive of the democratic revolutions there, including independence from the USSR; indeed, one of them spoke movingly about the trauma of having been one of the young soldiers sent to Czechoslovakia in 1968). But they doubted that the conditions for the reestablishment of capitalism existed in the USSR, and were certain that the workers would not accept a radical market reform short of it being forced upon them by a return to authoritarian government. At the same time, they were worried that price increases and the inevitable pressure to compensate for this by wage increases would lead both the "centre" and local enterprise managers to cut back on the resources needed to maintain the collective services the unions run for workers. They claimed that signs of this were already visible. Yet, such a turn away from collective consumption might be sustained by the widespread egoism they detected among workers. As the deputy chair of the trade union committee put it: "Egoism is everywhere. People respect what is 'mine', but have no respect for what is 'ours'. People's apartments are neat and well maintained, but the hallways are a shambles." Our own glimpse of the city, where the grass was uncut and streets pot-holed, confirmed this. We began to dub this "private poverty and public squalor".

Notably, a large group of independent candidates, allied with the

Komsommol in Togliatti, had been elected to the municipal soviet on an ecology platform. The union leaders had stayed away from the municipal soviet elections and "let the ecologists win". But the reason they gave for this was rather cynical. Without an effective tax base the municipal soviet had no capacity to accomplish anything (the local government even had to come to the union for 60,000 roubles to stage a celebration for the 25th anniversary of the founding of the city). The union leaders were sure the ecologists would lose the election next time since they would not command the resources which alone would enable them to carry out their promises. As for the Komsommol, they (like the workers' club) were given some credit for "searching", but there was also some feeling among the union leaders that the Komsommol had lost its ideological bearing, had become too single issue oriented, too "commercial", too "populist". The Komsommol leader did indeed express to us support for private property and the market, but his overall political orientation was quite similar to those who are trying to build networks among local social movements in the West. He was especially proud that the Komsommol itself had started a taxi service for the elderly and "drop in" creches near cinemas. The ecology movement in Togliatti had worked through the Komsommol to get the union to sponsor a symposium on the environment. The union leaders agreed that while workers had been "backward" on this until recently it was the main issue in Togliatti now. Yet, on this issue, as on most others, it still appeared that the direction and pace of change in Togliatti hinged very largely on the position that would be taken by the Communist local union leadership.

The union leaders thought it likely that a real crisis would come in the fall or winter if the government moved ahead with its proposed market reforms. Yet it seemed to us that a great deal would ride on what this level of leaders did in this crisis. Indeed, we could sense that they were coming to recognize this themselves. They did not rule out the possibility that they might leave the Communist Party, but we could never get clear the criteria on which they would make this decision. Certainly they were not visibly aligned with any faction in the party and they were suspicious of Yeltsin, who they thought capable of authoritarian populism.

Yaroslavl

Yaroslavl, an ancient capital of Russia with a much more diversified economy and social structure (including a large intelligentsia associated with the many institutes of higher education and culture) provided a sharp contrast to the new single-industry city of Togliatti. The architectural splendour of Yaroslavl, with its many frescoed churches and monasteries built by the powerful merchants and nobles of the 17th century, puts to shame the modern city further south on the Volga built by Italian and Soviet industrialists and planners so many centuries later. (While in Togliatti no church at all was in sight, the restoration of churches — including one of them completely surrounded by a chemical plant — is a major industry in Yaroslavl all by itself.) A local Popular Front of informal movements had formed in the city in 1988 and within it was a broad informal workers' group which had its roots in the 1987 strike at Autodiesel. The popular front had been holding mass meetings in a local stadium of some 1,000 people every Saturday over the past year. Among 178 municipal soviet deputies, some 20% were elected on a Popular Front ticket, and they worked closely with the many Communist party deputies who were aligned with the Democratic Platform in the party.

The Autodiesel enterprise, the largest in the city, had produced its 650 horsepower engines for truck and tractor plants in Byelorussia. This meant they had little autonomy from the central planning apparatus, and very little direct access to hard currency, such as VAZ enjoys in Togliatti. In a meeting with the deputy director, we were told that until 1990 only those enterprises integrated enough to produce a final product had secured much autonomy. Having finally secured more independence from the plan, they are looking to export engines directly themselves. This will mean cutting back delivery to the plants in Byelorussia, but there were no advantages to Auto-diesel any longer in enjoying the monopoly position they had with these plants, which were likely to be forced to close down. Displaying very much a "sauve qui peut" attitude, the manager was coldly un-concerned about their fate. Autodiesel is now being allowed to keep 50% of its profit, but since their profitability level is only 4%, their main problem is where they will secure new capital. They have some slim hopes of obtaining this from one of several banks that have been created recently (including an AutoBank formed by 200 enterprises in the industry) or from a partner they may be able to sell the engines to in the West.

Although the state probably will remain the main source of credit, it is clear that the pressure is very great to solve the problem of obtain-ing the new capital by increasing the extraction of surplus from the workers. The manager tells us that the main reforms that are now needed are those that would give enterprises flexibility in wage and employment levels, which still are dictated by Gosplan. "Bonuses are important now, but workers feel they are underpaid in terms of the centrally set basic rates, and they therefore demand bonuses regardless of productivity. Work discipline and motivation is very low now. Only if workers feel their income is dependent on the enterprise rather than the centre will they work better." When we suggest that workers in the plant in Togliatti seemed to be working harder than in North American plants, he explains this in terms of the plant there having been built according to western standards, where "technology controls the workplace".

He considers the victory that the workers won on "Black Saturdays" to have been a disaster. Not only did it have the effect of a significant loss in the volume of production, it established the working collective council as a real power in the enterprise, something that he insists did not happen elsewhere despite the provisions of the 1987 Law. "Nothing good came of that Law. The workers' level of culture meant that not very conscious or educated workers were elected to the councils. The democracy came before the culture. The Law is being changed now because many directors of enterprises refused to remain directors if they lost their decision making power. Instead of taking quick professional decisions, there were long involved discussions that dragged out. These inevitably ended with redistribution questions coming first, since these are the problems closer to the people, while the main questions of production and modernization were ignored."

It is very clear that what this manager means when he says workers will work better if their income is dependent on the enterprise rather than the centre is that managers will have more control over workers. There are the makings of very serious class struggle in relation to this strategy, for as we immediately saw when we left his office to meet the union representatives, their support of enterprise autonomy has primarily to do with a conception of workers control. Again asked to begin the meeting with an opening statement of our own, we did so by putting directly the question of how much the situation had changed since the strike and then conveying to them what the deputy director had just told us and asking for their reaction to it. There were 24 people there, most of them elected leaders in various sections of the plant, and one of them also the vice-president of the informal workers' club. Sixteen of them were women — and the women were older (in their forties or fifties) and not nearly as western looking in their dress as those we had met in Togliatti. Overall, they looked, put simply, poorer. But they were also more eloquent and direct. We kept almost verbatim notes of this meeting.

Woman I: "Before the change, almost all decisions were made by the administration. Now there must be consultation with the trade union committee and the workers have a much greater say. The trade union has more say in questions of social infrastructure, but also on wages and bonuses. Elections themselves have acquired a much more representative character, including elections of delegates for conferences."

Woman II: "I am a representative of a work collective. There were direct elections with six candidates per position. When there are so many candidates, this indicates that people are not sure who to choose."

Man I: "The reason the informal organization arose was because the union has to put so much energy into providing collective services. This is necessary in non-market economy."

Man II: "The transition to the market worries people in terms of prices as well as shortages. This increases the role of the union."

Man III: "I am the representative of the informal workers group which emerged here two years ago. We felt that the traditional administrative power structure in the factory would talk much about change, but not do much in fact. Lots of talk but no action. Not much was tried by the traditional union structure, so workers elected their own representatives to defend their rights and their wages and conditions. Up to now the trade unions are still too much engaged in social functions. For so many years people have been kept in a passive position, they may have become passive themselves and refused to believe the trade unions would be participating in the changes. And the opposition in the union to change is still strong, especially to democracy. Very few workers are satisfied with the pace of change in the trade unions. [At this point there were many shouts of disagreement.] Well, maybe not so many people are participating in the workers' clubs, but those that are are the real activists. There is an idea for the workers of the Russian Federation to have a new union created. There is already a new confederation of labour in Siberia. We sent a delegate to a conference held in May."

Man IV: "I don't agree with everything he said, especially what he said about passive workers. The election of Yeltsin is a serious sign of victory by democratic forces. Since these workers' clubs are organized and uniting, this is also proof of a movement. At this level, the trade union represents workers well. This was seen in the reduction of subbotniks even before the strike."

Man III (the informal group representative again): "About what the deputy director said. If discipline is low, it is because workers were so alienated from the means of production that they developed poor working habits. The main question now is how the independence of the enterprises will change this. The workers' clubs are fighting for collective ownership of the means of production along with the independence of enterprises. But this is being undermined. For example, the proposed price rise is a purely bureaucratic administrative decision by the centre."

Woman III: "We have to recognise that the managers do need independence on technical decisions."

Woman IV: "Control by the Ministries is still there, and this limits managers' power as well as the workers' collectives' power. So the enterprises must become free of the Ministries first of all, and then the workers' collective councils will really become strong."

We had stayed out of the discussion to this point, but as there seemed general assent to this last comment, we interjected to ask whether the new law on enterprises passed earlier in the week did not already negate what they expected in terms of the power of the workers' collectives once the enterprises became autonomous. They appeared confused and said that they had heard that a new law was being considered but did not really know what was in it. When we said that we had been told in Togliatti and by their national union president that the law had already been passed last Monday and that it removed the power of the collective to elect managers and had established a new parity council to oversee decision making in the enterprise, there was uproar in the room. The main reaction was that this was proof of how the system at the centre, despite the new parliamentary institutions, remained undemocratic, the same bureaucratic system that delivered decisions from on high without popular involvement. The Chair of the trade union committee spoke up at this point (for the only time during the meeting) and tried to cool things out by saying: "We are not yet owners of the means of production. When we are we will have more rights." A middle-aged woman, who had to this point been silent, followed this with a long and eloquent speech on the meaning of socialism. It ended with this bald statement: "When the state owns the means of production, then they appoint managers. But if socialism really means that workers own the means of production, then they should elect managers." Another woman disagreed: "Not everyone feels all managers should be elected. People who were not competent enough were elected." The informal representative inter-jected forcefully: "A good manager should have nothing to be afraid of." There seemed overwhelming assent to this, and when he went on to say that he was in favour of municipal soviets plus workers in each enterprise having joint control of the enterprises, they all agreed.

They were anxious to turn the discussion towards the situation in Canada. Significantly, the first question was whether managers were members of the unions as in the USSR. This was followed by a series of questions on the right to strike in Canada. And, then, surprisingly, given the clearly syndicalist approach he had taken throughout the meeting, the informal workers' club vice-president, raised a naive question, the kind we were later to hear put by Moscow liberal intellectuals, who are keen to deny the contemporary relevance of drawing any conceptual distinction between capitalism and socialism: "We hear that there is socialization of the means of production going on in the United States." When we asked him what he could possibly mean, it turned out that he had heard about profit sharing schemes by corporations. It seemed to us that such naivete might presage the workers' clubs demands for industrial democracy being sooner or later bought off with the issuance of shares to individual workers which would leave them with no effective democratic control over their enterprises. This led us to offer a sketch of the reality of such schemes in the West, which ended with an expression of the need to democratize our system in order to displace our ruling class of capitalists, just as they needed to democratize their system to displace ruling "nomenklatura" class.

Our translator at this point thought it necessary to preface her translation by telling them that we were speaking as western marxists, but when she had finished translating what we had said about our respective ruling classes, there was a burst of spontaneous and enthusiastic applause throughout the room. The trade union chairman thought this an appropriate moment to end the meeting.

The union chairman, elected two years ago, is a Communist party member in his early forties, and seemingly very committed to the democratic changes taking place and to making the union an effective representative of its workers. One measure of this commitment was that he had recently been offered a senior management position and had responded to this in uncharacteristic fashion for a union official. He had gone to the union council, told them of the offer and said he wanted to put the matter in their hands, since they had elected him and he was responsible to them rather than to management. They told him they wanted him to reject the offer, and he did so.

When we pressed him on the degree of independence the union now had from the party, he stressed that a key to this was the fact that the industrial committees of the regional party apparatus had been abolished, and since they had been the locus of party control over both unions and enterprises, this was an important factor in understanding the transition that both local unions and enterprises were going through. But he was anxious to get on to another matter that he considered far more important. He demanded to know what "social justice" meant in our view. We clearly had not agreed with the deputy director's call for flexibility on wages and employment, but was it socially just that some workers do nothing at work, or don't even show up for work and yet get paid the same as those who work hard? He proceeded to make a strong defence of income differentials in the workplace, and, if necessary, the right of managers to fire unproductive workers. We responded that it was hardly socially just to tie income to a measure of productivity since this was not only a factor of individual worker effort, but the way the labour process was organized in each plant and the nature of the technology. Workers who are in two different plants and are working just as hard would, on the measure he was proposing, be paid wildly different amounts. Moreover, what would be socially accomplished by firing someone who didn't work hard? Since he was in favour of full employment, he would just be passing the problem which that worker's lack of effort represented to another enterprise. In the end, we appeared to come to an agreement that the essential problem was not an individual one to be solved by introducing the discipline of the labour market, but was related to alienation from the polity and from a labour process workers did not control.

As we went on to discuss the role that unions could play in relation to this, we noted that we were surprised that union leaders in Togliatti and Yaroslavl seemed not to know each other or even anything about each other, let alone actually discuss these matters together. He complimented us for having in such a short space of time "grasped the essential point" about the working class in the Soviet Union. There were virtually no linkages across the unions, even in the auto industry, at the base. Democratic centralism, which fostered this division as a matter of organizational principle, has produced its negation in terms of local hostility to the centre, but it had left that hostility embedded in a series of unconnected localisms. Yet the very passage of the new law on enterprises, with virtually no allowance for input from the rank and file representatives, may exactly have been the shock needed to overcome this problem. While the political class in Moscow debated the 500 day crash privatization plan, two very broadly based meetings took place later in 1990, the first in Togliatti at the end of August and the second in Moscow in December, bringing together hundreds of delegates from local labour collective councils and workers' committees to protest the new law on enterprises and to found a new all-union labour organization. As David Mandel recounts in his detailed account in this volume,[4] these meetings were little covered in either the Soviet or the Western press, but that is hardly a measure of their significance.

III. *The Perspective from Moscow*
One advantage of visiting Moscow after visiting the provinces was that it encouraged some healthy scepticism about the ready generalizations which the political class of intellectuals, journalists and politicians that predominate in the capital are wont to paint for the visitor. Nevertheless, it was also refreshing and instructive to meet with this political class amidst the discursive openness of *glasnost*. For what this political class in Moscow thinks and intends (and it now openly thinks and intends many different and even contradictory things) still remains the focal point for everything else that is going on in the Soviet Union.

It is true that Moscow may be losing control over the vast geographic space, with its great diversity of peoples, gradually assembled under the old czarist empire. Indeed, it is arguable that only the Bolshevik revolution, with its unique blend of inter-nationalism and coercion prevailing through the civil war, preserved most of that immense space as a distinct territorial-political entity at the end of World War One. It is in this light that not only the Baltics', but also Poland's, undoing of Stalin's reclamation of those bits of the old empire that were lost after 1917, needs to be understood. And an even larger drama of detachment from the territorial reach of the old empire is now being played out in many areas that were retained under a new regime after 1917. But while projects to break with or secure or extend autonomy from the centre are seemingly ubiquitous in the Soviet Union today, all eyes still turn to Moscow in order to discern the ways in which the projects of the political class there will complement or frustrate, promote or prevent, the decentring process that so markedly motivates politics everywhere else.

Moreover, Moscow remains the communications hub of the Soviet Union: it is a political class's business, after all, to collect, control and dispense information. And while the information received in Moscow is by no means complete (indeed what the political class does not know about a society in transition probably exceeds what it does know), such "facts" as become generally "known" in the Soviet Union still primarily make their way through Moscow. Indeed, it is arguable that the rest of the country now relies *more* on Moscow for credible information than in the days when everything was filtered through, or concealed behind, the Party line. Despite all the centrifugal localisms that are asserting themselves so insistently, Moscow remains the summit that affords the broadest perspective.

Of course we are using the term political class here rather loosely. We mean it not in the sense of the tightly organized personnel that staffed the upper reaches of the party-state apparatus under the rigid rules of democratic centralism and Stalinist statecraft. The political class in this sense is dying, although it is by no means yet dead, in the Soviet Union. Rather we use the term as one might use it in a liberal democracy, to refer to those who make their living by and off politics — making, opposing, advising, commenting and reporting on state policy at the centre. This includes in Moscow today a broad array of people whose common passion for politics and quite uniform socio-economic profile (male, salaried, university educated) is not inconsistent with a diversity of goals for the future and interpretations of the reality today.

There was a broad consensus among virtually everyone in the political class we talked to in Moscow that the whole country was in the throes of a severe economic crisis. Its immediate symptoms were a massive hidden inflation in the context of consumer shortages existing alongside a vast pool of savings (estimates vary on the size of this, from 300 to 600 billion roubles) which at present could neither be spent on the limited goods available or tapped for investment purposes. The structural roots of this crisis were generally located in the following factors: the "extensive" nature of Soviet economic development wherein something akin to what has come to be called "Fordism" in the West (that is, a virtuous circle of mass production and mass consumption) never developed; the hyper-centralization of production which inhibited modernization and technological innovation; the rigidities of the bureaucratically administered system of distribution, made worse by the effects of underinvestment in infrastructure; the historic defeat of the agricultural classes in the 1930s forced collectivization, and the consequent low agricultural productivity due to superexploitation in the form of extremely poor wages and conditions; the increase in real wages in industry and services since the 1960s, which neither domestic production nor imports (especially after the fall in oil prices ended hopes of a hard currency windfall) were capable of soaking up and recycling.

The effects of all these long-standing problems appear to have been rendered more severe by the disruption to the old political-administrative system introduced by Gorbachev's revolution from above, and at the same time rendered more visible with *glasnost*. It was generally agreed no structure in the political-administrative system was functioning smoothly. Even the security system, which had been the most efficient, no longer works well and is incapable of coping with what is generally recognized as a crime wave. Yet no one we met thought it possible to go back to the old system as it had evolved under Brezhnev, even if there were those who blame the incompleteness or, on the other hand, the rapidity, of the changes since 1985 as the cause of the current crisis and its many discontents.

To borrow a phrase from someone who is heard of much less these days than at the outset of perestroika, what is to be done? Notably, everyone we talked with in Moscow took the view that the package of market reforms which the Ryzhkov Government had announced, and especially the price increases on basic necessities scheduled to come into effect on July 1st, was unacceptable to the population. And, indeed, as we watched on our last day in Moscow the Supreme Soviet decide to postpone the introduction of this package, an aura of foregone conclusion pervaded the rather desultory debate. Yet there can be no doubt that the overwhelming orientation among the political class, inside and outside the Communist Party, is towards finding both short-term and long-term solutions to the economic crisis through the more or less gradual turn to "markets". But although this word sets the terms of all debate and discussion these days (far more than "democracy"), it conceals as much as it reveals — not least because it does not capture the political changes that are seen as inseparably connected to solving the economic problems. It is necessary, therefore, to take a much closer look at the various orientations and tendencies within the political class.

Let us begin with the Central Committee of the Communist Party. The Gorbachev leadership group, having taken the driver's seat in 1985 of the old locomotive at the head of the stalled Soviet train, suffered many slings and arrows in the run up to the July 1990 party congress, but it clearly secured there its hold over the controls. The railway metaphor, however strained, is an apt one, and not only because the frustrations of perestroika so far call to mind the freight trains that are reputedly loaded with goods but stuck at sidings all over the country. It is also a good one because this leadership still understands what it is doing in terms of the "locomotive of history" following along the tracks set by the development of the forces of production. It wants to find a way to get back on the track set by capitalism's development of these forces of production, having accepted that the Bolshevik attempt to construct a parallel track was not only unorthodox in terms of the classics of historical materialism (it obviously does not bother them much to be unorthodox) but futile. Their view is that it is necessary to integrate with a stage of dynamic world capitalism: this alone will lay the basis for the eventual emergence of socialism on solid foundations. The people who lead the Bolshevik party, in so far as one wants to understand them in terms relevant to the political history of Marxism in the Soviet Union, are Mensheviks.

These were precisely the terms in which their philosophy and strategy was presented to us by Andrei Grachev, the deputy head of the international committee of the Central Committee. Responsible for theoretical issues, close to Yakovlev and influential with Gorbachev (with whom he had just returned from the United States, having handled the media side of the visit), this very handsome, expensively dressed (Gucci?) 52-year-old (Paul Newman could play him in *Reds II*), talked with us for two hours on subjects that ranged from Gramsci's conception of the party to Togliatti today. The goal of the Gorbachev leadership, he told us, is "normalcy", by which was meant a stage of parliamentary democracy and market relations. "But this is *only* a stage. For this is not where we should have landed in the end. But we should have made use of the universal aspects of parliamentary democracy and markets, which we ignored before. The goal is to arrive to the point that socialism grows out of normal capitalist society." When we taxed him with the likely costs in human misery of a transition to such a stage, he responded: "We are not too afraid of going too far towards capitalism, as there is great resistance to it here. There is a strong spiritual basis in this society which does not accept the excesses of capitalism. This is the traditional collectivism which goes back before 1917." In light of this, the cultural success of the revolution which led to broad education eventually produced a political consciousness that demanded a democratic version of socialism. That was why he believed "we have a good chance of reaching a Scandinavian, more cooperative version" of the stage they needed to go through. He did not dissent when we said this sounded classically Menshevik.

Unlike so many other enthusiasts for the market and multi-party elections we met in Moscow, Grachev displayed a sophisticated appreciation of the limits and contradictions of democratic capitalism. Nor was he apologetic about the limits of the Gorbachev reforms. For instance, when we told him about the anger we had witnessed among workers in Yaroslavl that they had only heard about the passage of the new law on enterprises by the Supreme Soviet from us, he saw this as an instance of the negative aspect of parliamentarism, its elitism, and the separation, apart from the act of voting for representatives, between decision making and the people. "Many of the new structures which were a year ago seen as incredible developments for this society are now questioned because they see the negative aspect of bourgeois parliamentarism, while not yet having any evidence of the positive benefits." He insisted, however, that the impression we had from Togliatti and Yaroslavl that the municipal soviet elections amounted to little, in so far as the local soviets had no tax base, was wrong in that the intention had been made clear all along (and this was now in the process of being passed through the Supreme Soviet) for the local soviets to get directly the taxes from citizens and enterprises and then only pass a portion of these along to the centre.

When we expressed surprise that this was not known even by the Communist trade union leaders we had met in Togliatti, he explained this in terms of the unfortunate existence of "a filter between the party at the top in the centre and the lower levels". Asked what this meant, he turned the discussion to the Party. Even in the Polituro Gorbachev had only a minority behind him since 1985. He constantly had to strike compromises there, and in the Central Committee, which "did not reflect reality". As a result, "the power at the top no longer represents the balance of opinion in the country as a whole. It is like a vacuum chamber underneath the sea, resistant to the great pressure upon it from outside." When in response to the emergence of the Democratic Platform inside the party, the Central Committee had issued a statement on the impermissibility of factions amidst a strong defence of democratic centralism, the text had in fact been drafted by the Politburo without even consultations with the Central Committee. All this reflected "old fashioned" compromises at the top forced on Gorbachev in terms of his minority position. On the other hand, especially in the run up to the July Congress, he told us it was fascinating to observe how the old apparatchiks, who had gotten where they were by never stirring from their desks, keeping their noses down, pushing paper and following orders "were discovering how to be creative politicians", making speeches, organizing opinion to the end of holding on to the old system.

Coming out of the Congress, the Party would have to confront four fundamental but absolutely necessary changes: "First, to convince people that it means what it says; that is, that it will not remain a party-state and that it is sincere in looking for a role separated from the state, as an organization and movement. Second, to redefine its relation to other movements and parties. Having accepted the principle of a multi-party system, it must renounce its monopoly of power and respect fair play with other forces. And it must do so because it believes in socialism and social justice and because it believes it can get support politically from people, rather than just rule administratively. Third, self-renewal: the internal remaking of the party. It must stop being vertical and monolithic from the top. It must become a lively party which would be open for internal debate and with horizontal connections across the base. Finally, we have to look at the role of parties in general, which is declining everywhere in the face of the social movements. We need to allow for movements here. And it is possible that the Party may not be able to survive their attacks.".

The importance of the July Congress in this respect was emphasized when we met with Yuri Krasin and Alexander Galkin, Rector and Deputy-Rector of the Central Committee's Institute of Social Sciences. "This is the Party's last chance not to lag behind the popular desire for change," Krasin (who is also a delegate to the Moscow City Soviet) told us. "A rapid polarization in the party is taking place and polarization in Russia always leads to extreme conflict." The only way to avoid it was for the Congress to consolidate around a "centrist" stand. But the question being asked was whether there was such a centre with a stand to consolidate around. "Gorbachev's stand is eclectic of left and right, rather than an independent stand." They were enthusiastic, however, about the programme of the Moscow party which had just been published that day in *Pravda*. It proposed constitutional changes in the direction of federalism along with market reforms. This was the basis of the kind of centrist position needed even if its weak point was that it was "imprecise and not concrete".

In general, Krasin and Galkin supported a shift in the party towards the positions of the Democratic Platform. The Central Committee's response to the Democratic Platform in February had been entirely negative. This reflected the fact that the conservatives were in a majority. The strength of the conservatives lay in the fact that they had a considerable social base given their control over the dispensation of resources. Yet a shift had taken place in the run up to the Congress, in so far as the conservatives seem to have decided to retreat. They were mainly concerned with how to protect their pensions and privileges at the lower level, accepting that it was inevitable that certain things were going to change at the top. It was significant, therefore, that the latest version of the party's platform did not use the term democratic centralism any more. In Krasin and Galkin's own view (no doubt shared by the Gorbachev leadership) it was "quite clear that we should drop democratic centralism, but not change to such an extent as to make impossible a distinct party position. We need to change the activities of the party from extreme centralism, which undermines all activity and produces passivity." The undermining of the regional Oblast party committees was very important in this respect but had yielded its own problems. "Now that the party was removed from control of the Oblasts, we have found that there is no coordination among the regions. But that is not the proper role of the party. The party should elaborate policy and achieve political support — not just electoral — but the party has failed to learn how to do this yet. Even the party cadres are not anything but managers, former engineers and agronomists who are no good as party cadres. They block the kind of changes needed towards allowing the party to survive."

Yet they insisted at the same time that "a lot of democratic elements" had been elected as delegates to the Congress and were therefore optimistic about its outcome in terms of the party coming to support a centrist position around Gorbachev. And it was imperative that this happen at the Congress. "There is a threat of populism. When Yeltsin says his own path to the market does not mean raising prices, he does not reveal how, yet the population believes him. Yeltsin has said he will appeal to the people over the heads of the Central Committee. This is dangerous. The majority in the party are sick and tired of confrontation and could support a centre position such as that offered by the Communist Party in the Moscow City Soviet. If this happens the party may survive. If not, then there will be a split and a favourable position for populism, for popular support for someone who will promise to put everything in order. This will be a right-wing populism no matter what the slogans."

There was no question in their minds that the solution to the country's immediate economic problems depended on the political changes in the party. "The Government recognized the need for an immediate transition to a market economy, but at the moment it is impossible to do it because the Government's credit is so low here, as in contrast with Poland." But the real problem, in their view, was that the transition to the market is impossible with such a great disparity between the mass of money in circulation and the small number of commodities available. "Even if we raise prices threefold there will be nothing on our shelves." Their analysis of the inflationary problem was that the economic reforms to date had destroyed the barrier between money in circulation and credits between enterprises. The cooperatives can now convert credits, which were previously just bookkeeping devices, into money. The solution Krasin and Galkin were pressing on the Central Committee involved freezing access to money in order to set the market in motion. What they had in mind was similar in their view to what Western European governments had done right after World War II. Enterprises would be given credits which would allow them to pay wages, but a portion of wages as well as money currently in circulation would be turned into bonds which would pay a certain rate of interest. In this way the state would obtain an important lever over the economy which would allow it to control inflation. As certain goods became available, the government would make it possible to buy them with bonds. They believed this would avoid the problem of the seizing up of production as had occurred in Brazil. "If we don't do this there will not be an immediate adoption of market mechanisms. And we will eventually end up with a solution like Poland or a return to the old administrative system."

It was clear that the reformers in the Communist Party were looking for a market solution less drastic than Poland's not only because of their antipathy to "the excesses of capitalism", but because the party lacked the legitimacy to survive such a drastic imposition of hardship on the population. We got the strong sense while we were in Moscow that a very sizeable section of the political class were strongly in favour of a rapprochement between Yeltsin and Gorbachev, and were actively pushing for it, as the sole immediate means of laying the political grounds for a market reform. While we were in Moscow, Yeltsin, in an interview in *Moscow News*, had promised a market reform which would not cut real incomes. It is significant that even Krasin and Galkin, who clearly saw this as sheer demagogy, conceded that "the population believes him", and most people we spoke with shared their view on the political danger entailed in a continuing open split between Gorbachev and Yeltsin. As we were told by Len Karpinsky, the highly respected columnist for *Moscow News*: "Yeltsin has great credibility. The main issue is to stop the quarrel between Gorbachev and Yeltsin, and Gorbachev has to take the first step."

Karpinsky's estimation of Yeltsin was in fact very favourable: "Gorbachev's refusal to congratulate Yeltsin on his recent election was perceived as an underestimation of this event. Yeltsin is still a symbol of democratic developments in this society. When he was elected people in small towns were congratulating themselves. He is a mass psychological phenomenon. It is with his name people identify the chance of changing something. His election was seen as only justice given his popular support which was flouted in his earlier expulsion by the leadership from his position at the head of the Moscow Party. Now, this is the first time that one of the leaders of the Democratic Front has come to occupy a leading position in the structures of power in the country. He has behaved courageously in many situations. Many other leaders did this in words not in deeds. This doesn't mean I have illusions about his personality. He has many weaknesses, but he is flexible and can change. We are not guaranteed from Bonapartist tendencies from Gorbachev. Yeltsin can provide a balance against this. Gorbachev has lost much credibility. Maybe in reality it is not so, but for the mentality of the people Yeltsin is the figure who gives hope of perestroika continuing."

Such views can not be taken lightly, coming from someone like Karpinsky. Until 1972, when he was expelled for writing a critical history of the party, he had been a senior party educator. A year ago he had been invited to rejoin the party and did so because "it was a different party than the one that expelled me and I wanted to take part in the changes they promised. And if I had not joined, I would have not been allowed to join the *Moscow News* editorial board. It was decided at very high levels. I was not the kind of person who could have been hidden in the crowd, since I had held senior positions before I had been expelled." This perhaps suggested that the party was not quite as different from the one that had expelled him? "The Communist Party still controls personnel and management positions. It still does not influence through its representatives but through administration. There is still no way to move through the career structure except through the party. The party should allow itself to go into opposition to rethink its whole philosophy. Those who hold to the ideas of communism and socialism will stay in the party and many are good and honest people."

Yet how honest was *Moscow News* itself in the entirely uncritical approach it had taken on the virtues of the market? It had been the scourge of the double-speak of the old apparatus and set the standard for independent comment and good investigative journalism. Increasingly it was proving itself craven in following a market line. In the interview with Yeltsin, he had not even been asked to clarify how he could conceivably introduce the market without raising prices and affecting real incomes. Over the past year *Moscow News* had published an article which made the absurd claim that there was no capital accumulation in Sweden. Another article had lavished praise on a group of cooperators who had built a pig farm on the outskirts of Moscow and proven their entrepreneurship by producing pork at a third the cost of the state farms. Senior citizens who lived next to the farm had complained to the authorities because of the smell and when it was closed down *Moscow News* presented this only in terms of this being proof that the old bureaucracy was still in power. Karpinsky granted that the authorities were right to close the farm. "That was the socialist thing to do. But you have to understand the feeling of humiliation people feel under the existing system. This explains our strong desire to move to economic freedom. There are those who say we need a stong hand to introduce the market. We believe we can avoid this through enterprise ownership or mixed ownership and a variety of social guarantees. The problem with *Moscow News* in this respect is that there are few people who are capable of profound theoretical thinking about these issues."

But we encountered remarkable naivete about markets and capitalism even among very capable economists, who are by no means admirers of Milton Friedman. Even though their mode of analysis is that of neo-classical economics, they are naively of the view that capitalism no longer exists in the West. It is not just a matter of paying little attention to the contradictions that Keynesianism ran into, but actually of believing that institutions like West German Co-determination meant that managers and workers really were equal partners who fully shared in making investment decisions, or that the great number of cooperative enterprises in Italy meant that the cooperatives controlled the Italian economy. Such naivete is a product of wishful thinking, a hope that a transition to market relations will be something less brutal and more democratic than it is likely to be.

From what we saw of the cooperators movement (private enterprises in all but name), they are rather more hard hearted and less naive. Certainly Andrei Fadin, the political editor of *Commersant*, the newspaper of the movement (which is a joint venture with a group in Chicago, and which bills itself as "Russia's Business Weekly") knows what the capitalist road he advocates means in terms of hardship for millions of people and the uneven development it will spawn. (This is not to say that the newspaper itself is so honest, by any means. Indeed it paints capitalism in glorious colours.) The morning we spent with Fadin over the kitchen table in the tiny and shabby apartment out of which the newspaper is produced provided a very sharp counterpoint, in substance as well as in surroundings, to our meetings with the advisors to the party's Central Committee or with the liberal economists we met. Fadin has had a fascinating personal history. He had been one of the Marxist dissidents in Moscow imprisoned, along with Roy Medvedev and Boris Kagarlitsky, in the late 1970s. We were put on to him by an extremely knowledgeable American Marxist sovietologist who had described him as the most perceptive analyst of the informal movements. Fadin had moved through the informals to being a militant in the Social Democratic party and to a political position of an explicit endorsement of capitalism. Yet his account of the economic and political crisis today and of the effects of a transition to capitalism was informed by a surer materialist analysis than the softer analyses of those who hoped for an easy transition to a Swedish type of capitalism.

Fadin was easily as candid about the state of the informal as Grachev and Krasin had been about the state of the Communist Party. "The informal movement is over," he told us, since all of the informals had already formalized structures as parties and legal associations. "There was only a short epoch between illegal existence and de facto legalisation. Moreover, having had a common enemy in the old structure of power was what united the informals. In August 1987 there took place the first meeting of all the informals. Now there is no common enemy. There are many enemies and many goals. They cannot be a movement together. Separately, they are too little and unknown to have an influence. They have not lost the character of a movement altogether and maybe they will eventually organise links with a strike movement through the Socialist party or the Social Democrats, but not yet. It is interesting also that the newspapers tied to emerging parties like the Constitutional Democrats (CADETS) or *Republica*, the paper of the Estonian Social Democrats, or the paper of SAJUDIS in Lithuania, or the Democratic Union paper are all under pressure to conform to the party line. In contrast, the official Communist Party press is more independent than ever — for instance the Komsommol Moscow paper, which everybody reads. All the new parties will remain marginal, on the political periphery until the Communist Party splits up."

Fadin was convinced, as well, that until this occurred no market reforms would succeed. He predicted a strike wave starting in the summer, of which the price increases would only be a spark. The bureaucrats and local functionaries in the provinces would support the strike wave against the centre to hold on to their local base. "The strikers from the one side and the functionaries from the other can prevent market reform. Local soviets can distribute some goods in reserve for emergency situations and will do so during the strikes. They can also get orders on credit from Kolkhozes. This will compensate for the absence of strike pay.".

These strikes would prevent the Government's attempt to limit the market reform only to a consumer market. "There is no possibility of establishing a consumer market without a capital market and a labour market. This can begin with dynamic zones. There may not be universal opposition from workers since significant sections of workers have an interest in such a reform, especially those in resources and in privileged machine industries as well as in commerce and transport branches that are undeveloped now because of artificial limitations by the central power. They will support a shift from capital goods production to consumer goods. This support will sharpen the effects of market reform for the better and limit the need for authoritarianism to impose the market. By the same token only strikes in raw materials, transportation, a few consumption goods and a few service sectors (especially medical and teaching services) can be successful. The rest can hold out on strike as long as they want. The system does not need them."

Fadin then proceeded to sketch the situation region by region. Armenia, Azerbaijan, the Baltics would all spawn a full market economy. Central Asia only had a black market now, but "this can be legalized since it works. The only thing that doesn't exist there is a labour market due to the old feudal system of tied labour." As for the Ukraine, Fadin's view was that it would split. "The eastern Russified zone with heavy machine industries will be in a bad situation in a market economy and no strikes will help them. The western Ukraine that has no heavy industrial base can be successful with a market economy because they have an orientation to consumer goods. This overlaps with the political orientation. The western Ukraine is nationalist and anti-Russian. The eastern Ukraine is Russified. The coal industry will support the market. It is already in an alliance with the cooperators — an alliance between an emerging bourgeoisie and the workers."

The only thing that could save the USSR as presently constituted would be a military coup d'etat. And if the conservatives succeeded in blocking market reform for two to three years there would be a bloody civil war. The outcome would be incalculable since armaments are spread around the republics and paramilitary organizations have emerged in Moldavia and Azerbaijan. Moreover, the control by the officers over the troops is weak, since "40% of military personnel is of Asiatic origin and this percentage is rising; they are in the lowest levels of the hierarchy, most of them are raw recruits. This is a ready base of a nationalized split in the army, which we already see in the Lithuanians deserting and the Armenians insisting on not serving outside their region." Short of a coup or civil war, nothing could stop most of the republics taking their own direction. And mediation between the republics could only be through markets since the central power was lost. "This is why Yeltsin says market mediation between republics on the basis of world prices. Russia will sell raw materials to the other regions and they will try to sell consumption goods to Russia. If Russia buys consumption goods from the West instead that will be the end of the empire, with vast movements of Russian refugees from the regions. In a few years there will be a series of countries in a loose federation. The Baltics will be included in the EEC."

Capitalist modernization through the market depended on the large pool of savings being mobilized through the sale of shares in state enterprises. This would lay the basis of a capital market, which would be quite concentrated since the most recent data (five years ago) showed only 4% of the population held 40% of the savings. Another route was to legalize foreign currency ownership and the legalisation of foreign enterprises, not just joint ventures. Fadin had no illusions about the kind of development this would lead to. The outcome for Russia was either a South Korean or Brazilian path to modernization, and he preferred the former, since the Brazilian route would leave a hundred million people destitute. "Moscow, Leningrad, the far east and the northern region, and unfortunately even most of the western region will be the 'vegetative sector of the economy', as the Brazilians say. The role of government will be to soften the effects of this uneven development."

Although it seems bizarre to western leftists, such advocates of the market are designated as being "the left" among the political class. Yet the question remains whether there are not those who, while also opposed to those who seek to preserve the undemocratic party-state structures, nevertheless are searching for a socialist route out of the crisis. There are, but they are thin on the ground among the political class. Vadim Rogovin, a sociologist who engaged himself in an important debate against those who advocate a more unequal income distribution as the best means of producing incentives, and who is just finishing a major study of the Left Opposition in the 1920s, told us that the tendency among the political class at the outset of perestroika to look back to NEP as a model for reform was already a thing of the past. "They have now been able to read Bukharin and have discovered that he really was a communist, so he is no longer their hero." Rogovin told us that he had always believed that when the system finally really opened up about its history people would recognize that Trotsky was right. But instead Trotsky has come to be treated as in the same category as Stalin in recent years and Lenin no longer is seen as much different either. At best they are seen as irrelevant, according to Rogovin, who had a recent, already type-set, article on Trotsky pulled from *Ogonyok*, the popular intellectual weekly, while we were in Moscow. "Increasingly among the intellectuals here the heroes are the Whites, Solzhenytsin and Nabokov. If you can show you had an ancestor who was a merchant or a kulak, it is now a badge of honour."

The only organized political expressions that articulate a socialist vision (untainted, at least, by a preliminary stage of integration with capitalism) seem to be the small Marxist Platform in the Communist Party led by Alexander Buzgalin, and the newly-formed Socialist

Party led by Boris Kagarlitsky. From our discussions with both of them, it is clear that there is not much that separates them ideologically except their estimation of the potential space for socialist mobilization inside the Communist Party. Indeed, Kagarlitsky's only criticism of Buzgalin was that he had not left the Communist Party (which he had only joined two years before) for the Socialist party. Buzgalin's group (which does get some attention paid to it — we saw him interviewed on the popular nightly programme *'Vreyma'*) perhaps tends more towards worker self-management as the road forward, while Kagarlitsky's party places greater stress on local soviets as the building blocks of a democratic socialist alternative.

The perspective of the Socialist Party, as articulated for us by Kagarlitsky on the basis of the party's programme for its founding conference in June, begins from the following premises. Neither capitalism nor social democracy will take hold in the Soviet Union, since there is neither an indigenous bourgeoisie or a "protestant ethic" culture to sustain them. The industrial working class remains the key social base for a political project. In looking for alternatives, the unit of analysis must not be the enterprise, but the system; the question of who owns the enterprises misses the point. From these premises, the Socialist Party proceeds to the argument that a "soft" market reform of the kind advanced so far by the Government will fail and that this will be followed by more radical market reforms (a "shock treatment" like Poland) which will fail again. This will usher in a major political crisis, with the possibility of a "market stalinist" outcome. But this will not be accepted easily. The alternative to it, in as highly politicized a climate as exists in the country, will be not by the unions, but by new political parties like the Socialist Party, which will put forward democratic socialism as preferable to market authoritarianism. They will advocate municipalization of the means of production under the local soviets economic and political control. On top of this there will be higher levels of representation through which the coordination of democratic planning and investment will occur, supplemented by a commodity market as a stage to a higher form of socialism.

Although the analysis remains sketchy in the extreme regarding how such a regime would cope with an immediate economic crisis and how the higher levels of representation above the local soviet level would bear the burden of the complex decision-making that would fall to them, we saw from our visits to Togliatti and Yaroslavl that the slogan of "real power to the soviets" might indeed garner significant support from workers. But it seemed to us that the Socialist party's scenario underestimates the degree to which it was the unions and workers' clubs to which the industrial workers would turn in the face of "shock treatment". What is certainly clear is that the Socialist Party is a tiny, ill-organized force not dissimilar to the political groupuscules on the far left that we have known so well in the West. It had only some 300 members, and from what we could see when we attended a branch meeting in Moscow with Kagarlitsky they are mainly students and young intellectual workers. Such was the degree of disorganization in both Moscow and Leningrad, where their support was primarily concentrated, that the founding conference was almost cancelled just two weeks before it was due to begin.

Under these conditions, Buzgalin's Marxist Platform inside the Communist Party may well have more to say for it. Buzgalin himself was elected to the Central Committee at the July Congress. Our experience with the young Communist trade union cadre suggested to us that there was indeed a strong base for creative leadership within the party. Yet, if any scenario, among those that were painted for us in Moscow, rang most true it was unfortunately the one put forward by Fadin, although we were not convinced that there would be nearly as much support as he presumed from workers for what he candidly admitted would be a terrible transition to a dependent capitalism, not least because even a "South Korean route" would involve the restriction on free trade unionism that would be very difficult to suppress now that it had sunk roots among workers. Moreover, we were not convinced that the section of the Communist political class represented by people like Grachev were to be easily written off as Fadin, on what we would call the right, properly speaking, or Kagarlitsky, on the left, were wont to do.

We had put three objections to Grachev, from the perspective of the Western left, concerning his Menshevik strategy. First, as regards his confidence that their capitalist stage would be relatively benign, did he take account the fact that even the Swedish model was in danger of collapsing under the weight of the new mobility and globalization of financial capital? Second, what were socialists in the Third World to make of a strategy, emanating from the Soviet Union, that seemed to condemn them to living with the status of dependent capitalisms? And finally, was he not at all bothered that the Western left, having had to endure the charge earlier that socialist ideals lead to the gulag, were now to be subjected to the charge that even Soviet Communists had come to accept the virtues of the capitalist market? Grachev responded by saying that "all this could be answered if the left in the West and the Third World can make sense of perestroika. We really believe that democracy is not synonymous with bourgeois democracy; that the market is not synonymous with capitalist markets; that socialism is not a system of shock absorbers but a whole car. We know we won't, because we can't, go too far to become a capitalist country. Socialism is a living creature which can live without coercion and distortion, which has power in people's consciousness and willingness to work for it and arrange social life so that the freedom of one does not become a barrier on the freedom of others. It is just that the next stage in the advance of socialism now falls on the Western left before it falls on the Soviets."

As we left the Soviet Union to attend a meeting in Quebec City concerned with regrouping the Canadian left on the basis of general socialist principles that were very close to those Grachev articulated here, we recognized that in his very last comment Grachev was probably right. It is interesting to speculate about whether Soviet Communists are passing the buck or passing the torch. But either way, the more important question, for the left in the West, is: are we up to it?

NOTES

1. It may help set the context of this visit if the reader is reminded that we arrived when Boris Yeltsin had just been elected President of the Supreme Soviet of the Russian Federation; the USSR Supreme Soviet was debating ex-Prime Minister Ryzhkov's package of price increases, scheduled for July 1st; the Moscow City Soviet had imposed resident restrictions on access to the shops in reaction to the run on goods induced by the anticipation of these price increases; and the Communist Party was readying itself for its July Congress. It perhaps needs to be stressed that neither of us are experts on the Soviet Union, nor do either of us speak Russian. One of us had been there ten years ago, the other twenty years ago. In so far as we were able to prepare ourselves, we are especially indebted to Bernie Frolic, David Mandel, Patrick Flaherty, Monty Johnston, Robin Blackburn, Kerri McCuaig and George Hewison. Once in the Soviet Union, we had to rely on the considerable language skills, organizing ability, boundless patience and energy of our hosts and translators, Lucy Nemova of the Institute and Gennaddy Korsikov of the autoworkers union. For additional guidance and translation we were aided by Helena Mouzhevljova, who teaches at the Moscow Arts Institute and serves as a translator on contract for the union at the princely sum of five roubles a day. Out of this particular joint venture, no one, and least of all Helena, was going to make a profit.
2. Lenin, *Selected Works*, Vol. III (Moscow: Progress, 1971), pp. 233, 236.
3. See David Mandel, " 'Revolutionary Reform' in Soviet Factories", *The Socialist Register 1989*, (London: Merlin Press, 1989); and Fred Weir, *The Soviet Revolution: Shaking the World Again*, (Toronto: Progress, 1990).
4. See, in this volume, David Mandel, "The Struggle for Power in the Soviet Economy".

A FUTURE FOR SOCIALISM IN THE USSR?

Justin Schwartz

The fate of socialism is linked to the crisis in the USSR, the first nation to profess socialism as an ideal. But as the Soviet Union prepares to drop "socialist" from its name,[1] it is opportune to inquire whether there is a future for socialism in the USSR. Whether we think so, however, depends in part on whether we think it had a past. "Actually existing socialism" — we need a new term, perhaps "formerly existing socialism" — is not socialism as historically understood, for example, by Marx, involving a democratically controlled economy and a state subordinate to society. The Soviet system is not socialist in this sense but is essentially Stalinist, both in its historical origin and its character, involving a command economy and a dictatorial state.[2]

The Stalinist system forfeited its moral authority by repressiveness and lost its economic legitimacy by unsuccessfully competing with the West on the consumerist grounds that favour capitalism instead of the democratic ones that favour socialism. Having delivered neither prosperity nor democracy, it is in disintegration. Socialism in the USSR would thus require not reclaiming a lost revolutionary achievement, for, despite the early aspirations of the Bolsheviks, the USSR was never socialist, but a systematic transformation of society, not a restructuring (perestroika) but a revolutionary reconstruction.

In a crisis situation prediction is speculative, but the short-term prospects for a socialist reconstruction of Soviet society, in the classical sense of the term, are slim. Such a project finds support in some sectors of an increasingly organized and mobilized working class, at least in the Slavic republics, but Soviet workers are sharply divided along ethnic and national lines. Moreover, socialism is not on the agenda of the main groups struggling for mastery in the Soviet elite. Gorbachev's programme of perestroika appears to have run its course as he turns to force to maintain the Union against nationalist separatism. The increasingly dominant liberal intelligentsia, rallying around Boris Yeltsin in the Russian Republic, are explicitly pro-capitalist. But the split in interests between the working class and the new middle classes as well as growing centrifugal nationalism

67

threatens a liberal capitalist reconstitution of Soviet society as much as a socialist one. To many Soviets, political deadlock, civil war, and authoritarian nationalism seem more probable for the present than either a socialist or a liberal outcome. Any happier resolution of the crisis will have to overcome these tendencies.

Stalinism versus Socialism

Given the current doubts in the USSR and elsewhere about whether "socialism" has any definite meaning, it is worthwhile to explain why that sense fails to apply to the USSR. Both analytical clarity and the prospects of the left require a sharp distinction between Stalinism and classical or Marxist socialism. This distinction has a long tradition on the non-Stalinist left and is widely echoed in the USSR today. Most of the leading Gorbachev supporters interviewed by Stephen Cohen and Katrina vanden Heuvel in 1989 agreed that the Soviet system was not socialist.[3] No society fully lives up to its ideals, but the USSR was at best an authoritarian welfare state. If we say it was "backward" or "deformed" socialism, we will need a new term for what Marx meant.[4] While noncapitalist because it abolished private property in the means of production, Stalinism is closer to what Marx dismisses as "crude communism", a "levelling down to a preconceived minimum", an "abstract negation of the whole world of culture and civilization".[5]

The essential features of the Soviet system were constructed by the Stalinist bureaucracy in the 1930s.[6] They involved: (1) a single party dictatorship, in which all public life was dominated by a Party bureaucracy and (2) a command economy, in which decisions about production and investment were made by bureaucratic fiat. Rather than being the expression or result of workers' self-rule, the establishment of the system was due, as Soviet economists Nikolai Shmelev and Vladimir Popov argue, to the dominance of the Soviet bureaucracy, a stratum whose interests "directly opposed [the] interests" of the workers and peasants, as shown by the tremendous resistance broken only by forced collectivization and the Great Terror of the 1930s. "The command-administrative system", Shmelev and Popov argue, "was the logical way for the bureaucracy to develop, given the absence of effective control from below".[7] In an isolated and relatively backward country, lacking strong democratic traditions, and where a militant but extremely small working class had been decimated by civil war, the bureaucracy was able to impose Stalinism as a noncapitalist crash modernization programme.

Contrast this to Marx's socialism, not out of deference to the Master's Voice but to undermine the Soviets' claim to Marx's legacy and because the ideal of socialism has, to this day, no more powerful proponent. With respect to politics, Marx gave the party no special role (much less a monopoly one) in a socialist society. [8] He was deeply suspicious of state power. He opposed

> set[ting] the state 'free'. . . as in Russia. Freedom consists in converting the state from an organ superimposed upon society into one completely subordinate to it, and even today forms of the state are more or less free to the extent that they restrict the 'freedom of the state'. [9]

Rather than creating an omnipotent dictatorship, the workers' state, in Marx's account of the Paris Commune, would "amputate" the "merely repressive organs of the old governmental power" [the army and the police], returning its "legitimate functions" to the responsible agents of society, democratically elected and modestly compensated. "Nothing could be more foreign to the spirit of the Commune to supersede universal suffrage by hierarchic investiture," [10] i.e., by the principle of *nomenklatura* or bureaucratic rule which underpins Stalinist politics.

With respect to economics, Marx does suggest wresting "by degrees, all capital from the bourgeoisie. . . centraliz[ing] all instruments of production in the hands of the State. . ." But given his view of the revolutionary state as *"the proletariat organized as ruling class"*, [11] the proposal is best read as urging extensive workers' control rather than Stalinist nationalization. Abolition of markets, moreover, is not mentioned in the list of suggested measures in the *Manifesto*; market relations among worker-controlled enterprises are consistent with Marx's account of "the first phase of communist society" (usually identified with socialism). [12] Even in the "higher phase", where commodity production is supposedly abolished, Marx advocates not economic administration by bureaucratic diktat but

> that socialized man, the associated producers, govern the human metabolism with nature in a rational way, bringing it under their collective control instead of being dominated by it as a blind power, accomplishing it with the least expenditure of energy and in conditions most worthy and appropriate for their human nature. [13]

Rather than having a bureaucratic state seize the surplus and hand out wages and welfare benefits, finally, Marx insists on workers' control of the social product (capital) as well as of production. The workers *themselves* deduct from this investment funds, "general costs of administration", and funds "for the common satisfaction of needs. . . and for those unable to work", and finally individual means of subsistence. [14]

The picture is of "an association of free men, working with the means of production held in common, and expanding their. . . labour power in full self-awareness". [15] It is a picture and not a model (which is badly needed [16]), but the picture imposes constraints on any model which might be called socialist. These include three main features:

(1) a democratic, decentralized state in which the working class is politically dominant, and (2) workers' control of production, and (3) democratic control of investment. It is difficult to imagine anything further from the Stalinist system.

Whether classical socialism, so understood, is possible or likely is an open question. Neoliberal triumphalism to the contrary, history has pronounced judgment on Stalinism, but socialism has not failed because it has not been tried. Some may worry (or hope) that this defence consigns socialism to the museum of utopian ideals, condemned by Marx's own insistence that "Communism is not. . . an *ideal* to which reality [will] have to adjust itself [but] the *real* movement which abolishes the present state of affairs."[17]

Now my topic is the future of socialism *in the USSR*, not the future of socialism in general. But were I to address the larger topic, I would discuss working class movements, which time after time, in periods of upheaval throughout the world, reproduce, often without theoretical rationale, the democratic structures of workers' control which, despite his animadversions against "ideals", are Marx's ideal: from the Paris Commune of 1871, through the Russian soviets of 1905 and 1917, the workers' committees of the general strikes in Seattle in 1918 and San Francisco in 1934, the British general strike of 1926, the communes of Republican Spain in 1936-39, to the workers' councils of Hungary 1956, Czechoslovakia 1968, the Solidarnosc of 1979-81, and the Soviet miners'committees of 1989. A revolutionary class, Marx writes:

> finds the content and material for its own revolutionary activity directly in its own situation: foes to be laid low, measures dictated by the needs of the struggles to be taken; the consequences of its own deeds drive it on. It makes no theoretical inquiries into its own task.[18]

On the historical record, such spontaneous strivings are clearly *insufficient* for socialism. While traditional vanguardism on the Leninist model is bankrupt, some sort of conscious organization and leadership would be required; what sort, no one knows today. Nonetheless the historical record offers some support for Marx's claim that the working class has the potential to be such a revolutionary class with the aspirations to and interests in collective self-rule he attributed to it, even if it could not attain these ends alone, without the active support (and without actively supporting) the aspirations of other oppressed groups.

A Future for "Socialism"?

Even in the Soviet Union, the term "socialism" has been tainted by its appropriation by Stalinism. The language of Marxism suffers today, in Eastern Europe and to an increasing extent in the USSR, under an even stronger anathema than it does in the capitalist democracies. This lethal legacy in time may fade, particularly if the emergent capitalism in the East is of the predatory third world variety and living standards in the West continue to decline. The collapse of Stalinism may allow a renewal of socialism, finally free from Stalin's shadow. A renewed socialist movement might not call itself Marxist, but that is for the best. "Whatever may be the scientific value of a doctrine," Victor Serge remarked, "from the moment it becomes governmental, interests of State will cease to allow it the possibility of impartial inquiry [and] lead it. . . to exempt itself from criticism."[19] Marxism's strength is as a critical theory of society; a socialist movement will be better served if it stays that way.

But socialists must face the possibility that the term "socialism" is not just tainted, but, like "Communism", irremediably poisoned. That does not mean the end of the socialist project if Marxist theory correctly identifies major sources of capitalist instability and class-based tendencies towards collective self-rule. The project depends not on the appeal of a theory but on the reality and power of the tendencies the theory identifies. But if the terms and theory are unusable for political reasons (rather than because they are empty or false), socialists would be in the position of the English peasant revolutionaries of 1381, of whom William Morris wrote:

> . . . I pondered. . . how men fight and lose the battle, and the thing they fought for comes about in spite of their defeat, and when it comes it turns out not to be what they meant, and other men have to fight for what they meant under another name. . .[20]

It is too soon to tell whether this is the fate of "socialism" as a term or Marxism as a theory; if it is, socialists will have to rediscover all the insights of the tradition under "another name". This would be extremely difficult. Just now we have no other name. "Democracy", a current favourite candidate among post-Marxists and ex-socialist radicals,[21] is at present too vague and theoretically underdeveloped. Today those who aspire to the kind of collective self-rule which is the traditional goal of socialists face the choice of explaining either why what they want *isn't* socialism or why *Stalinism* wasn't socialism. In both cases they must explain *what* they want. On the principle of not kicking away the ladder while we are climbing it, I take the latter choice. Socialism requires a reformation, doubtless. But after all, Luther still called himself a Christian.

The Character of Perestroika

At the beginning of 1991 it appears that Gorbachev's programme of perestroika has failed. The programme has been abandoned in all but name by all the main elements in Soviet society, including Gorbachev himself. An analysis of the prospects for socialism in the Soviet Union, if any, therefore calls for an examination of the course of that programme as history. We may consider the situation from above and from below. First, the perspective from the Soviet elite. Here the struggle has developed in three distinct phases: (1) the battle for perestroika, (2) the disillusionment of the intelligentsia, and (3) the rise of the neoliberal "radicals".

The first phase was the articulation of perestroika. It lasted from Gorbachev's appointment as CPSU General Secretary in 1985 to the special 19th Party Conference in 1988. [22] In this period Gorbachev and the reformers went to battle with the conservatives in the bureaucracy, i.e. defenders of the Stalinist system as it matured under Brezhnev, over his developing reform programme. Gorbachev was the leader of the "Thaw" generation of Soviet leaders who came to maturity under Khrushchev, hating the crimes and brutality of Stalinism but hoping for a progressive revitalization of a modified Soviet system. Seeking, and initially finding, support among the Soviet intelligentsia, these leaders saw perestroika as a renewal of a Soviet system cleansed of the excesses and irrationalities of Stalinism, a return to "Leninist roots", particularly the "market socialist" Lenin of the New Economic Policy. (Lenin himself considered the NEP a sort of state capitalism. [23]) In 1989 Gorbachev adviser Alexander Yakolev told Cohen and vanden Heuvel that the alternative to perestroika is "the death of socialism". [24] Most of their other interviewees agreed.

There is little doubt that Gorbachev and (in this phase) the reformers sincerely saw themselves as defenders of something they called socialism. But so did Stalin and his epigones. We cannot take such professions at face value. If Stalinism was not socialist, how socialist was perestroika? Consider each of the main components of the programme: glasnost and "democratization", new thinking in foreign policy, and economic reform.

The glasnost component of the reform programme, while in part a step towards liberal democracy, also pointed towards socialism in allowing the relatively unfettered self-organization of popular movements and organizations and vastly increased freedom of speech and the press. These are necessary though not sufficient conditions of socialism from below. If socialism is workers' self-rule, there is no socialism without freedom of assembly and the press. Gorbachev's liberalizing steps in this direction led to an explosion of at least 30,000 "unofficial" civic organizations, [25] although they did not go far enough, and reluctantly abandoned the "leading role of the Party" in March 1990 only under the pressure of the collapse of East European

Communism.

The socialist character of Gorbachev's foreign policy, however, is doubtful. Gorbachev's goals of disarmament and nonintervention are commendable from a socialist perspective. Traditionally socialists oppose militarism and support self-determination. Stalinism broke sharply with these policies in all but name. But the Soviet abandonment of erratic and cynical support for national liberation in the third world, notably in Nicaragua and South Africa, indicates that the "new political thinking" is a continuation in a different key of the Stalinist doctrine of "socialism in one country", i.e. pursuit of perceived Soviet national interest, not socialist internationalist interests.[26] The point is reinforced by Soviet acquiescence to US pressure for withdrawal of Vietnam from Cambodia in the face of a possible Khmer Rouge return, and more recently, Soviet accommodation to the US military action against Iraq.

There should be no misplaced nostalgia for the era of Soviet intervention in Afghanistan, support for murderous regimes like Mengitsu's Ethiopia, and extensive participation in the international arms trade. But unprincipled and unsocialist as the old Soviet policy was, its effect was to create a space where poor nations might attempt to organize their affairs at some distance from the domination of multinational capitalism, a space which has now largely vanished. The "new thinking" cannot be regarded as socialist.

Most importantly, the economic component of perestroika was more liberal than socialist.[27] These proposed reforms sought to break the bureaucratic logjams blocking economic growth and to motivate an apathetic workforce by the undemocratic imposition of market mechanisms from above. The main reforms advocated by economic advisers Abel Aganbegyan, Tatyana Zaslavskaya, and later, Leonard Albakin, included extensive privatization, unemployment as a means of labour discipline (that is, to make workers work harder), wider income differentials to overcome "a psychology of levelling", i.e. solidaristic egalitarianism, and reduction in social programmes.[28] Market mechanisms are not necessarily unsocialist,[29] but the key aspects of Gorbachev's reforms involved an attack on working class benefits with only a promise that increased growth would trickle down.

This was called "social justice",[30] but whatever relation it has to justice, it is not socialist.[31] A minimal requirement for a socialist programme is that it promote working class interests and working class self-organization. Desultory introduction of workplace elections for managers gave workers no real say over the direction and tempo of the changes and none at all over the disposition of the social product, which remained in the hands of bureaucratic managers. In Marxist terms, the reforms would have meant increased exploitation of the working class.

The 1988 Party Conference was the high point of the first phase, when Gorbachev appeared to have won Party agreement to his programme. It is now clear that this was illusory at least in the crucial economic sphere. Gorbachev had a free hand in foreign policy and glasnost, once announced, was irreversible. But the economic changes were not systematically implemented. In part this was because the bureaucracy was able to block implementation of economic reforms by inaction and countermanding of changes, however many Brezhnevites Gorbachev removed from the Politburo.

The main obstacles seem to be at the lower levels of the bureaucracy; the two best known high-level "conservatives", former Party ideology chief and agriculture secretary Yegor Ligachev and former Prime Minister Nikolai Ryzkhov, were not advocates of the old system but of a more gradual change to a "regulated market economy", i.e., of an earlier version of perestroika, the programme, essentially, of the 27th Party Congress from 1986. Of the two, Ligachev is the more conservative, an advocate of something like Andropov's reform programme of moderate perestroika and little glasnost. And neither were more able than Gorbachev to implement the reforms they saw fit. Perestroika thus never really happened.

As the pseudonymous cold warrior "Z" summed it up, "the half-reforms introduced so far have unsettled the old economic structures without putting new ones in their place". [32] At the 28th Party Congress the head of the State Planning Commission, Yuri Maslykov, agreed: "At present centralized state planning, which was the lynchpin of the command system, has been [largely] destroyed. . . [and] has lost its determining role in the functioning. . . of the economy." [33] The result was a steady deterioration of already poor economic performance in a context of rising unrest partly occasioned by glasnost. According to (inflated) official statistics, growth in the gross national product, after rising from about 3.2% in 1986 to 5.6% in 1988 dropped *below zero* by 1990; CIA figures are even more bleak, indicating a drop from 4% growth in 1986 to -2.3% in 1990, while the Washington consulting firm Planecon estimates an increase in inflation from about 4% in 1986 to 10% in 1990. [34] Perhaps 15% of the Soviet population, around 48 million people, lives below the absurdly low official poverty line of 75 roubles a month. [35]

That perestroika failed does not mean that the Soviet system was unreformable. As the *Economist* observes, "paradoxically. . . the Soviet Union has not yet proved that economic reform cannot work", because it has not been tried. [36] While some reform programme might have worked, Gorbachev's was doomed to frustration because it embodied contradictory goals. The basic problem is that reform in either a capitalist or a socialist direction would require dismantling the domination of the Party apparat over Soviet society, but Gorbachev wanted to retain a cleaned-up version of bureaucratic rule. In the end he could not have it both ways.

In a capitalist trajectory, Gorbachev might have retreated from the Party to the state, pursuing a more radical version of Andropov's programme of imposing market reforms by force. Here he might have adopted the role of a Soviet Pinochet, advocated (as I discuss below) by some of the radical intelligentsia. This would have required strict limits on democratization, particularly in rights of popular organization and independent unions, while permitting the intelligentsia the freedom to discredit Stalinism. But his commitment to glasnost prevented this; and he counted on popular support to overcome bureaucratic resistance.

In a socialist trajectory, Gorbachev might have redeemed the promise of the October Revolution, handing over the farms and factories to the workers' and peasants' soviets while dismantling the apparatus of Party-state control. But he apparently believes that the CPSU really is the repository of the socialist project. His late and reluctant abandonment of "the leading role of the Party" (in March 1990) shows that he suffers under the limits of his background as an apparatchik. He is a reforming, even a visionary bureaucrat, but a bureaucrat nonetheless and not, despite his self-image, a socialist. Doubtless this is not just a psychological limitation but an expression of the stratum he represents. The upshot was deadlock, immobility, and failure.

The Disaffection of the Intelligentsia

The failure of economic perestroika led to the second phase: increasing disaffection with socialist goals and ideals among the intelligentsia. The extent of disaffection is indicated by Yuri Bandara's *Moscow News* article mocking the hopes (shared by that journal) of the 1986 27th Party Congress on the eve of the 28th Congress in 1990. "Four years later", *Moscow News* asked the Soviet reader, "how much of your former self remains?"[37] (It is not impossible that this is a conscious echo of Reagan's 1980 election slogan, "Are you better off today than you were four years ago?")

A younger generation of managers and intellectuals became increasingly vocal in their admiration for capitalism as a model of a working economy and "normal, civilized society", as the popular catch-phrase goes. Writers like Alexander Tsypko, until recently with the ideological department of the CPSU Central Committee, asked openly, "Is it worth risking the fate of the country. . . of perestroika, for a couple of words ['communism' and 'socialism'] which have long since become absurd?" At a December 1989 conference on socialism he criticized Marx for "wanting to subject the logic of the economy to morality", as nice a statement of the basic impulse behind socialism as there is.[38]

Tsypko may be extreme in his overtly Thatcherite advocacy of "the older, time-tested values" of "neoconservatism, neoliberalism, bypassing social democracy" but he is not alone in rejecting socialism, even if others prefer Western European social democracy. (Among the Soviet intelligentsia, however, as among those of Poland and Hungary, Thatcherism and Reaganism are probably more popular than these ideologies are in their home countries.) The chief Soviet philosophical journal, *Voprosy Filosofii*, has begun a serialized translation of the Austrian economist Friedrich A. von Hayek's 1944 *The Road to Serfdom*, a text which defends the idea that any government intervention in the economy leads to Nazism or Stalinism.[39] The economist Nikolai Shmelev became famous for "Shmelev's law", which states that "Everything which is economically efficient is moral."[40]

Together with liberal journals like *Ogonyok*, the weekly *Moscow News*, formerly the flagship of perestroika, became a leading voice in the disillusionment with socialism and the romance with 19th century liberalism, regularly publishing articles which would do justice to Milton Friedman. The emigre Valery Chalidze, who lives in Vermont, but evidently not in the United States, writes on the issue of "socio-economic rights", to, e.g., a job, a place to live, or medical care:

> In free enterprise societies, the individual is free to take care of himself. . .
> Unfortunately many people would impose the socio-economic rights doctrine on the
> free enterprise society, thus violating other fundamental civil rights. . .;
> compell[ing]. . . those who provide for themselves, to deny themselves certain things
> in order to provide for the poor. . . To a certain extent this exists, but it is public
> philanthropy. One should not regard this philanthropy as a socio-economic right.[41]

The disaffected initially found political representation in the Congress of People's Deputies in Andrei Sakharov's Inter-Regional Group, comprised largely of reforming bureaucrats like Yeltsin, liberals and radicals. A social democrat rather than a neoliberal, Sakharov had given up on socialism in any sence in the mid-1970s.

It's clear that the Soviet intelligentsia and the younger managerial elite have come to identify socialism with the historical aberration of an anti-society that was inefficient at everything but repression. Conversely they identify democracy with liberal capitalism. The image of capitalism they have is rosy, to be sure. Russians "have not gone through a phase of rationalizing" and "freed themselves. . . from a mythological perception of reality", journalist

Heksei Kiva writes, and so "give preference to rather unrealistic but grandiose plans over undertakings which are modest but actually feasible".[42] She is speaking of the October Revolution, but the point applies to the magical picture of capitalism favoured by many Soviet intellectuals. The Yugoslav philosopher Mihalio Markovic suggests that they have accepted the simplified picture of 19th century laissez faire capitalism presented in (old) Soviet propaganda and merely reversed the value signs: they had said it was bad, now they say it is good.[43]

But it's not at all clear why this should be. After all, they did not accept the propagandistic picture of the Soviet system as democratic. Why would they accept that it was socialist? A different conception of socialism, together with a sharp critique of authoritarian bureaucracy could be found in the writings of Marx, which were widely available to Soviet citizens. (One might wonder why Marx's writings were not suppressed as "anti-state propaganda", which indeed they are.)

This question has not been posed either by those who celebrate the phenomenon or those who mourn it. By contrast, the "apostasy" of ex-leftist anti-Communist *Western* intellectuals has received considerable attention.[44] Yet such an attitudinal shift surely calls for explanation. If we reject that proposed by the intelligentsia themselves, that they have simply recognized the truth of the Western anti-communists' critique of socialism, six factors seem relevant in the intelligentsia's disillusionment.

1. The success of the bureaucracy in appropriating an appallingly distorted version of the vocabulary of Marxism (official Marxism-Leninism) as a justification for the system. The failure of the system then worked, by *modus tollens*, to discredit Marxism and its socialist goals. The successful appropriation may be attributed partly to a stultifying system of indoctrination at every level of education, in which people were forced to regurgitate obviously dishonest material from textbooks of catatonic dullness and to confine their intellectual work to the limits set by official ideology.[45] (The masochistic might try to read some official Marxism-Leninism just to see why the intelligentsia might find it useless.)

Creative, original texts of Marxist theory were not used in this education, and the best Marxist work from the West was banned because of its critical attitude towards the USSR. Nor was creative Marxism permitted within the USSR. It is significant that from the 1920s until recently Soviet Marxism made no contribution whatsoever to the flourishing of Marxist theory in the 20th century. Boris Kagarlitsky is one of the few significant Soviet Marxist theorists since Trotsky. The writings of Marx were indeed available, but the citizenry was inoculated against their effect. Thus when Gorbachev spokesman

Gedenny Gerasimov told editors of the conservative *National Review* in 1990 that resistance to perestroika was due to the fact that "Some people read too much Marx", he was in error: Marx is little read in the USSR.

2. The adoption of consumerist values in the place of democratic ones, as mentioned before, which highlights Western capitalism's strength. By consumerism I mean measuring the quality of life merely in terms of material wealth and security, by the quantity of goods one has. Material well-being *is* important, but socialism emphasizes the democratic value of collective self-determination *as well*. (Liberal capitalism confines this value to politics and delegates it to professionals.) Rather than offering Marx's "free association of producers" with the spiritual and (perhaps) material benefits of self-organization in economic as well as political matters, the Soviet system's ideologues offered increased material wealth in exchange for autonomy, a similar tradeoff to that presented to the majority in advanced capitalist societies, although with far less autonomy and a lower although more secure level of material well-being.

Clearly the Stalinists were operating at an ideological disadvantage, and the extensive censorship which prevailed under the old system about conditions in the West suggests that they knew it. The offer nonetheless worked to some extent as long as the low standard of living rose through the early-mid 1970s. But with the onset of economic stagnation in the late 1970s, when growth rates fell from 8.9% (inflated official figures) in 1966-70 to 4% in 1981-83, [46] to below zero today, the USSR began to lose the ideological cold war. The failure of Khrushchev's promise to "bury" the West under an avalanche of toothbrushes, razors, nylon stockings, and tinned foodstuffs was traced correctly to bureaucratic centralization, the "command-administrative system". The intelligentsia identified the command economy as the differentia of a system which is neither democratic nor capitalist, hence, by elimination, socialist. (This is a false dichotomy.)

3. Another source of disillusionment was the repeated failures of attempts to reform the economic system from Khrushchev to Kosygin to Gorbachev himself. [47] This raises doubts about the viability of a system that they identified as socialist, and thus of the socialist ideal itself. Tsypko himself says that communism died ideologically under *Brezhnev* — not under Stalin. [48] Sociologically this is inaccurate, as demonstrated by the intelligentsia's enthusiasm for perestroika in the first phase of the struggle. But the retrospective revision of the ideological shift supports the idea that it was the system's resistance to change that helped to subvert the appeal of socialist ideals.

Despite all the cynicism about official Marxism-Leninism and the bureaucratic dictatorship, however, commitments that were broadly socialist retained their hold on both reformers and some dissidents until quite recently. Even the young Solzhenitsyn (of *Caner Ward* and *The First Circle*) and the Sakharov of *Progress, Coexistence, and Intellectual Freedom* framed their critiques in what were in some sense socialist terms, as Roy and Zhores Medvedev always have. The non-dissident intelligentsia, like Yegor Yakolev, editor of *Moscow News*, or Fydor Burlatsky, ideologist of Khrushchev's Thaw, are very recent converts to liberalism.[49] Even Tsypko, while insisting on the continuity between Marx's socialism and Stalin, argued in late 1988 that Marxism and "our socialist practice" could be freed from Stalinist "deformations", which he attributed in part to a "Rousseauist and not the Marxist view of man".[50] What explains the *timing* of the current, drastic abandonment of aspirations on the part of the intelligentsia to restore (as the perestroichiki saw it) or to create "socialism with a human face"?

4. The "ideology of perestroika", in particular Gorbachev's abandonment of class analysis for what he calls "universal human values", had the unintended effect of paving the way for the adoption of self-describedly bourgeois values. Class analysis was not helped by the official representation of Soviet state policy as identical to the interests of the working class. Interviewing Yuri Prokofyev, a Moscow city Party official, Yegor Yakolev remarked, "I can't see how to link. . . a teaching of class struggle with the priority of human values." "It is not correct to give preference to any class or stratum of society," replied Prokofyev, "Human values come first."[51] Gorbachev's intent was doubtless to affirm humanism and human rights in the face of official lawlessness carried out in the name of "class values" — in reality, the values of the bureaucracy — but the shift provided an Archimedian point for the ideological abandonment of working class interests.[52]

5. More deeply, there is the social position of the intelligentsia as a new middle class whose interests are distinct from those of the working class.[53] Whatever its defects, the system created a large, educated middle class. In 1987, 21 million Soviets had a higher education, up from 1 million in 1939.[54] These people are not bourgeois, but they might hope to become bourgeois, and they certainly wish to enjoy the material and other benefits and opportunities which their counterparts do in the West. It is not surprising if, losing hope that the system will enable them to do this, they adopt an ideology that they expect will further their interests, as well as happily coinciding, as they see it, with "universal human values".

I do not mean to suggest that this is a cynical choice: people cannot choose their beliefs and values in such a calculated way. But people who are not fanatics will revise their ideas if their aspirations are not met, and the new middle class aspires to a way of life available to people like them in Western capitalist countries. Little if anything in the Soviet system works to promote a solidaristic identification of the intelligentsia with the working class that would lead to a belief that only socialist democracy can offer a decent life for *all* citizens, workers and intellectuals alike. Official propaganda which decreed such solidarity has the opposite effect, if anything.

6. Most immediately, the collapse of Communism in Eastern Europe, and Eastern Europeans' rejection of a third way, i.e., socialism rather than Communism or capitalism, spurred the disaffection considerably, leaving Soviet intelligentsia feeling that they were saddled with an unworkable, outmoded system. (In Eastern Europe, Communism suffered under the additional ideological burden of being an unpopular imposition by a hated foreign power; this may contribute to the pro-capitalist turn in that region. [55]) Gorbachev's foreign policy of reversing the Brezhnev doctrine, and maintaining nonintervention in the affairs of former Soviet satellites, a policy which was a major factor in the Eastern European revolutions, thus undermined his own hopes for what he took to be socialist renewal there and at home.

Radical Accession and the End of Perestroika

These factors contributed to the third phase, the accession to power of the Soviet "left". In a politically astute move, the disaffected intelligentsia have appropriated the designation "left", excluding socialism in the classical sense from a political spectrum where the "right" defends some version of the existing command-administrative system. The "left", who are pro-market right-wingers in Western terms, are more accurately called the "radicals". [56]

In the March 1990 municipal elections, radical coalitions swept city council elections in Moscow and Leningrad, free marketeers Gavril Popov and Antoly Sobchack respectively taking the mayoralities of these cities. A new Leningrad council member spoke publicly of proceeding "from communism, through socialism, to Reaganism". [57] As statues of Lenin were taken down in cities across the USSR, [58] there was talk of restoring Leningrad's prerevolutionary name of Petrograd. In Moscow, Popov pointedly hired a private cooperative to repave city roads. [59] More importantly, the immensely popular Boris Yeltsin, then recently elected president of the Russian Republic, led an exodus from the Party at the 28th Party Congress, taking Popov, Sobchack and other leading members of the radical Democratic Platform faction with him. (Yeltsin seems not to be principled radical but a populist politician; his autobiography is remarkably devoid of political thought. [60])

The significance of the radicals' accession to political power is brought out by Yeltsin's endorsement of Stanislav Shatalin's 500-day plan to take the Soviet economy on the Polish route to free market capitalism. Speaking to a Plenary session of the CPSU Central Committee in February 1990, Shatalin, a long-time Party member, said that "The concept of a 'democratic humane socialism'[the catch phrase of the Party programme for the 28th Congress] is an absurdity." [61] Writing that "humanity has not developed anything more efficient than a market economy [which requires] private property and profit", Shatalin proposed to sell off 80% of state-owned industry, privatize land, decontrol prices, and drastically reduce foreign aid and social welfare benefits. The plan was un-workable, requiring the sale of 46,000 industrial enterprises and 76,000 commercial ones, worth almost three trillion roubles (two trillion after depreciation), in less than two years. [62] The timetable was fantasy. Margaret Thatcher, with far more support than the Soviet regime, was able to privatize only 5% of Britain's much smaller nationalized sector in ten years. And the money — 1,400 roubles per capita — wasn't there if the assets were not given away at fire-sale prices.

Moreover, as Gorbachev correctly complained, such a plan would risk even greater social upheaval, leaving perhaps 30-35 million jobless, according to V. Shcherbakov, Chair of the State Labour Committee. [63] "Those who declare we can have a new economy in 1991 or 1992 are simply adventurists. . . with suicidal inclinations", Shatalin himself said in April 1990 — shortly before proposing the plan — warning that without creating a market infrastructure and a social protection mechanism, hasty privatization would lead to a disaster "more terrible than the great crisis of the late 1920s and early 1930s". [64] Given the scale of the catastrophe of forced collectivization, these are very strong words.

The evidence of the Polish drive towards capitalism bears him out. [65] The appalling pain consequent on Poland's IMF programme lost Tadeuz Mazowiecki's Solidarnosc government the election in November 1990, and Lech Walesa may find the Solidarnosc name a wasting asset if, as promised, he accelerates that programme. The Soviet regime, though, has no legitimacy to forfeit. The import of the Shatalin plan appears to have been ideological rather than practical, indicating the antisocialist commitments of the now ascendent group in the Soviet elite and not offering a serious programme for change.

Economic reform is at a standstill. The Shatalin plan was approved by the Russian Republican parliament, but by the early November date when it was supposed to go into effect, Shatalin himself declared the plan "a failure", saying that it "cannot now be put into effect".[66] After suffering in one year legislative defeat of three successive proposals for economic reorganization, drafted under the then Prime Minister Ryzhkov, Gorbachev waffled, first indicating approval of the Shatalin Plan and then withdrawing it. (A rare democratic proposal to subject its provision for the privatization of land to a referendum was an attempt to defeat this key and unpopular measure.) In October 1990, Gorbachev won approval in the Union parliament for a broadly similar plan, which Shatalin and Yeltsin vigorously attacked as inflationary and overly centralized, but there is no more reason to think that it will be implemented than were either its predecessors or rivals.

Given the absence of any serious idea of a way forward in economics, Gorbachev's real response to the impasse was a governmental reshuffle in November (incidentally abolishing Ryzhkov's position of Prime Minister), replacing the Union Council of Ministers as the chief executive agency with a Federation Council, comprised of the presidents of the several Republics and headed by himself. He also requested and won approval for extensive presidential powers for enforcement of his decrees over Republican recalcitrance like that manifested in Russia's support of the Shatalin plan, but in a situation of declining central authority these theoretically sweeping powers are more formal than real.

The View from Below
But the struggle in the elite is only half the story. From below, we may consider the perspective from the Soviet working class. This is a group of considerable social weight. The Soviet system has created a large, educated working class as well as a large middle class. Manual workers are 62.7% of the Soviet population, up from 37% in 1940; 86% of these workers have more than primary education, as opposed to less than 10% in 1939.[67] As *Moscow News* acknowledges with some frustration, "What do the workers want? First, they want socialism. Second, they want the dismantling of the command system." (*Moscow News* denies these goals are compatible.)[68] Three kinds of evidence support these claims.

First, insofar as surveys are indicative, there is widespread scepticism about unregulated markets in capital and labour. An all-Union poll in late 1989 found that three quarters of the respondents favoured private ownership of small business; only one quarter supported it and 57% strongly opposed it for large industry. Half of the respondents thought private wage labour was permissible, but three fifths of these thought it should be strongly regulated. The analyst concludes that a Western-style market economy (capitalism) has "only 25-30% support. The majority, while not opposed to private property, want to keep it on a strictly limited scale." [69]

In January 1990 an all-Union poll on attitudes towards key terms found a 61% "pro" (17% "con") response to the term "socialism" as opposed to a 34% "pro" (38% "con") response to "capitalism"; "competition" got a 74% "pro" (10% "con") response. [70] This result is consistent with the first. Pro-socialist attitudes, though, may be declining. According to Tatyana Zaslavskaya, a Fall 1990 poll indicated only 10-20% support for "the socialist choice", and that mainly from the older generation. [71] In the latter two polls it is unclear, however, what respondents intended by the terms (whether, for example, they thought that "the socialist choice" meant the existing regime, or whether their image of capitalism is as romantic as that of some intellectuals), so answers to specific questions about property rights and wage labour are probably more revealing. Despite the volatility of attitudes, I suspect these replies are not much changed among the Soviet workers.

Why should this be the case? The success of indoctrination is relevant here: Soviet workers have been taught to associate the idea of socialism with the notion of a good society. In particular the idea that the working class is the hope of the future offers a dignity to labour that may to some degree offset the miserable condition of Soviet workers. But interests matter too, which is why the Soviet workers, unlike the intelligentsia, do not allow the failure of the system to destroy their socialist commitments. While their material situation is far worse than that of much of the intelligentsia, they are unlikely to find attractive free market solutions designed to coerce them to work harder and deprive them of social benefits and jobs. An easy pace of work, guaranteed jobs, and a low but strong social safety net are among the few benefits of the Soviet system. By themselves those benefits might promote conservatism (and to some extent do), but in general, as *Moscow News* admits, Soviet workers appear to share the general disgust and disillusionment with Stalinism and the "command-administrative system". They are, however, not unreasonably concerned that reforms preserve what they have or offer them something as good, and here socialist democracy is more attractive than free market capitalism.

A more dynamic sign of worker support for socialism (as opposed to the existing system) is the miners' strike of summer 1989 and the rise of independent trade union activism. 300,000-500,000 miners walked out in July 1989 in the first large-scale labour action of perestroika. [72] In addition to economic demands about wages and working conditions, they demanded industrial democracy, workers' self-management, a ban on private cooperatives (which are regarded as predatory), repeal of the USSR constitution's Article Six (stating the "leading role" of the CPSU), and direct elections for the Congress of People's Deputies and the Supreme Soviet chairmanship — one of Gorbachev's jobs. [73] In the Fall of 1989, Kuzbas miners established a Union of Workers which publishes its own paper (*Nasha Gazeta*). Miners in the Donetsk basin, Vorkuta, and other strike centres set up ongoing political organizations to defend workers' interests.

Worker activism continued into 1990. In May, a Congress of Workers' Organizations, with representatives of 58 organizations from 46 cities decided to form an independent workers' movement for united action. "The workers' movement is not only broadening but becoming highly politicized," *Sovetskaya Rossiia* reported. [74] In June, the miners' strike committees voted to form an independent miners' union, and a 24-hour warning strike was held on the anniversary of the 1989 strike, to demand the resignation of the Union government and the removal of Party control from the state and the economy. [75] The independent trade union Sotsprof, the Confederation of Socialist Trade Unions, claims a membership of 250,000 workers Union-wide. [76] Oleg Veronin, a leader of Sotsprof, says, "Among workers the idea that socialism is dead is not popular. It is popular among the middle class and intellectuals." [77] (Veronin means by "socialism" roughly classical socialism.)

In terms of political organization, the independent trade union movement has strong links to a new Socialist Party, formed June 1990 and led by the young political theorist Boris Kagarlitsky. Sergei Tomkin, an SP leader, says that the party aims to become a mass labour party "serving the interests of the working class". Socialism, he thinks, is not a system but "a set of political principles — democracy, collective organization of production, workers' self-management, and the right of nations to self determination." [78] The SP claimed 1,000 members at its formation (this may be an exaggeration).

Some observers have compared the SP to analogous tiny and marginal groups in the West which share its classical socialist politics; but while this is correct in terms of size and influence on the larger polity, it is misleading. First, *all* the new political formations in the USSR are tiny and marginal. Second, while socialist groups in most Western societies are marginalized because liberal capitalism enjoys hegemonic legitimacy, no social force, particularly not the CPSU, has such legitimacy in the USSR. In this context, the group (and more importantly the socialist tendency it represents) has more weight than its Western counterparts. This is reflected in the judgment of two journals hostile to its perspective. It was given a four out of ten rating in terms of political importance by *The Economist* in May 1990, equal to that given the neoStalinist Communist Party of Russia; *Moscow News* listed it as one of the three formations to watch as the CPSU disintegrates or splits. [79]

The conventional wisdom (here and among the perestroichiki) that the workers are largely a "conservative" force who support the Stalinist system is false. But there are strong conservative elements among the workers. This means that the working class is far from united. Setting aside the tiny, fascistic Pamyat group, Veronin worries about the appeal of groups like the United Front of Workers, founded October 1989, whose leader, Veniamin Yarin, *The Economist* describes as a populist in the Peronist mould. The UFW may have more than 5,000 members, mostly unskilled workers fearful for their jobs. This provides abasis for alliance with moderate and conservative elements in the apparat. The neoStalinist heroine Nina Andreyeva, author of a notorious anti-perestroika letter published before the 19th Party Conference, [80] attended a meeting founding a Russian-wide UFW.

Unlike other workers' organizations, the UFW does not criticize bureaucratic privilege. [81] Its positions are indicated by the placards at a small demonstration in Moscow during the 28th Congress, which included demands to "Reject the conversion to a market economy", "Condemn groundless attacks on the Armed Forces and the KGB", and "Retain CPSU organizations at enterprises". Its support, however, may be indicated by the size of the demonstration: at a time when rallies can bring tens or hundreds of thousands into the streets, the action drew around 200 people. [82] Whether this specific group has any prospects, it represents a potentially strong current in the working class. The UFW has links to the conservative (as distinct from the more radical and democratic) elements in the Marxist Platform of the CPSU, headed by Yegor Ligachev. *The Economist*, however, gives both a seven out of ten weight in political importance.

The Spectre of Pinochet
The conflict between the workers and the intelligentsia bodes ill for either a democratic socialist or a liberal capitalist resolution to the Soviet crisis. Perestroika, the reform programme for modernizing the old system, appears to have failed for lack of trying. But the possibility of a deadlock, in which the workers use their newly-won political organization and democratic rights to block the radical plans for a transition to capitalism, and the intelligentsia use their newly-won offices to block worker demands for self-management and industrial democracy, raises new threats. The situation is reminiscent

of Marx's account of "Bonapartism", in which, he says, a deadlock in the class struggle creates a space for a military or other dictatorship, with the state asserting its own corporate interests over that of the major contending social groups. [83]

Writing about the changes in Eastern Europe and the USSR, the economist Gavril Popov, radical mayor of Moscow and a self-styled "democrat", says that "the forms of democracy being established [here] are exceptionally contradictory and in a very short time will lead to serious internal conflict". More honest than many radicals, Popov admits that "We could not have overthrown the powerful totalitarian system without the active participation of millions of ordinary people." But while "the masses long for fairness and economic equality", they will not get these from Popov. "Now we must create a society with. . . private property. . . denationalization, privatization, and inequality. . . This will be a society of economic inequality." Since "if we cannot denationalize and privatize property we will be attacked by waves of workers fighting for their interests. . ." he says, "we must seek new mechanisms and institutions of political power that will depend less on populism". [84]

These mechanisms are specified more boldly by some radicals, like Igor Klymakin and Andranak Migranyan, who talk of "an authoritarian transition to democracy", invoking Jeane Kirkpatrick's authoritarian-totalitarian distinction. "While the highly complex process of forming. . . a civil society is in process," Migranyan writes, "it is important that a firm authoritarian regime be maintained in the political sphere." [85] (In the context, "civil society" means "the capitalist market". [86]) More baldly, he says, "At the moment [February 1990] I'm for a dictatorship." Klymakin explains:

> Democratization doesn't necessarily encourage reform. For instance, a leader decides to introduce a market economy. Will his idea get support from the people? Of course not! 80% will oppose him. [87]

Today one can read in the pages of *Moscow News* uncritical praise for the Pinochet regime. Yuri Korolov, a former adviser to the Allende government of Chile, writes in "Pinochet and Us" that "overdue reforms in Chile were carried out by an authoritarian regime". [88]

No wonder Boris Kagarlitsky worries abut "market Stalinism", the undemocratic, forcible imposition of market relations on unwilling Soviet workers. [89] The deadlock threatens newly-won democracy as well as a resolution of the economic crisis. Polls suggest that a significant minority of Soviets might support repression under some circumstances: 25% of respondents to an all-Union poll in December 1989 agreed that "our people are in constant need of a strong hand". [90] That hand might emerge if the deadlock continues.

Gorbachev, the Nobel Peace Prize laureate, was disinclined to use force to promote economic reform, but has resorted to it reluctantly (although often unwisely) in dealing with nationalist separatism. Although secession would be economically irrational for small republics, failing a new Union treaty centrifugal nationalism threatens to take the Soviet empire the way of the Austro-Hungarian or Ottoman empires.

Under popular pressure, every republic has declared some sort of autonomy. The Russian Republic itself, under Yeltsin, asserts that Republican law takes precedence over central policy and has torpedoed central government policy with regard to Russian resources and banking. In many nonRussian Republics, separatist and ethnic strife flickers at the edge of civil war, the worst case being the Azerbaijani-Armenian conflict over the Armenian Nagorno-Karabakh district in Azerbaijan, raging since early 1988. After months of anti-Armenian pogroms and armed defiance of requests for a peaceful resolution of difficulties, Gorbachev sent in troops.[91]

Less understandably, Gorbachev imposed an armed blockade against Lithuania during the first half of 1990 when argument failed to persuade that republic to revoke its declaration of independence. In mid-January 1991, Gorbachev sent the tanks into Lithuania and Latvia, and a dozen or more demonstrators were killed in scenes reminiscent of Hungary 1956 or Prague 1968. Gorbachev responded to severe press criticism of the crackdown by unsuccessfully seeking a parliamentary suspension of the new law on press freedom, a cornerstone of glasnost.

Even before things turned ugly in the Baltics, Gorbachev's turn to the "forces of order" — the Army and the KGB — at the end of 1990, caused concern among his inner circle. Worry about the danger of "dictatorship" prompted the spectacular resignation of Foreign Minister Eduard Shevardnadze in December 1990, although whether this worry was then directed at Gorbachev is still unclear. It is also unclear whether the "forces of order" ultimately have the resources to enforce either an unwilling Union or an unpopular economic programme. The Soviet Union, in desperate need of foreign aid, might not be able to risk the Western reaction to such a move without international distraction. The crackdown in the Baltics could not have occurred without the war in the Gulf.[92]

The preference of some radicals for an "authoritarian" imposition of a market system, though, could meet with a better Western response than an attempt to maintain the Union by force. The *Economist* editorialized approvingly that Gorbachev might yet become a Soviet Pinochet.[93] It is not impossible that he, or some radical successor, might take advantage of a forcible maintenance of the Union to impose market-oriented reforms at bayonet-point.

The militarized suppression of Baltic independence is widely regarded as Gorbachev's throwing in his hand with the "forces of order", the Army, the KGB, and the remaining conservatives. If this is correct, it is unlikely that a turn to the "right" can succeed. Gorbachev has accomplished the destruction of the old system if not the creation of a new one. He will be unable to pronounce that "Order reigns in Vilnius, Riga, Moscow". There is in a deep sense no order to maintain. In such conditions of instability, the prospects are more like Timisoara than Tienanmen Square. Either Brezhnevite repression or a more radical "Andropovite" programme of enforced marketization will find active, angry resistance from both workers and separatists.

And beyond Gorbachev and the radicals are the archaic, primitive nationalist forces of Pamyat in Russia and the pogromchiki in Armenia, Azerbaijan, and elsewhere, which threaten a dozen or more "strong hands" if the Union fragments. The rising strength of right-wing authoritarian nationalism in Eastern Europe suggests that this threat is not idle. Still, no outcome is determined and the only out-come almost certainly foreclosed appears to be a restoration or reform of the old system. The "strong hand" cannot maintain what has been destroyed. Perestroika has run its course. The "authoritarian road" to some sort of capitalism is open. Is there a future for socialism in the USSR? Perhaps the only response is that attributed to Zhou Enlai when asked if he thought the French Revolution had succeeded. He replied, "It's too soon to tell." [94]

NOTES

1. A new proposed name is the Union of Sovereign Soviet Republics, allowing the country to retain the initials "USSR". Gorbachev suggested this in this new draft Union treaty in December 1990; the name change was voted down, but it can only be a matter of time.

2. There is no good term for Soviet-style systems. This reflects our poor under-standing of their dynamics. "Actually existing socialism" suffers under the double disadvantage that the noun never applied and the adjectives are rapidly ceasing to apply. "State capitalism", or "social-imperialism" rely on dubious theories that capitalism had been restored in the USSR. The "command-administrative system", the term favoured in the USSR, is accurate but awkward; the "bureaucratic system", the nearest natural English translation, properly places bureaucracy in the centre but perhaps fails to differentiate the system from bureaucratized modern capitalism. The "statist system" ignores the role of the Party shadow-state. The "Stalinist system", my choice, risks the mis-understanding that the terror of high Stalinism characterized a system which was in most of its career merely repressive. With the caveat that it did not, I somewhat reluctantly use this expression.

3. Stephen Cohen and Katrina vanden Heuvel, *Voices of Glasnost* (New York: Norton, 1989), p. 69.

4. As expressed, for example in Isaac Deutscher's epigram, "Socialism in a backward country is backward socialism", cited in Carl Marzani, "On Interring Communism and Exalting Capitalism", *Monthly Review*, January 1990 (Special Supplement), p. 24.

5. Karl Marx, *Economic and Philosophic Manuscripts*, Karl Mark and Frederick Engels, *Collected Works* [MECW] (New York: International Publishers, 1975-), vol. 3, pp. 294-95.

6. Elements of the Stalinist system were put in place earlier, notably the single-Party dictatorship, established by the Bolsheviks in 1919 during the Civil War. Moreover the economic policy of "War Communism" (1918-21) bears certain affinities to the Stalinist command-administrative system. Despite Bolshevik high-handedness and repressiveness, which excited the concern, e.g., of Rosa Luxemburg as well as less sympathetic observers, it is widely recognized that the Stalinist system was qualitatively different from various emergency measures, conceived as temporary and not called socialist, that the Bolsheviks (often unwisely and unjustly) took during a period of revolution, civil war, and their aftermath.
    I don't want to enter into a fruitless dispute about whether "the germ of all Stalinism was in Bolshevism at its beginning". As the antiStalinist revolutionary Victor Serge wrote on this question, "I have no objection [to this]. Only, Bolshevism also contained many other germs. . . To judge the living man by the death germs which the autopsy reveals in his corpse — and which he may have carried in him since his birth — is this very sensible?" (*Memoirs of a Revolutionary*, trans. Peter Sedgwick [Oxford: Oxford University Press, 1963], pp. xv-xvi).

7. Nikolai Shmelev and Vladimir Popov, *The Turning Point* (New York: Doubleday, 1989), pp. 69, 74-75. Their analysis of the roots and defects of the Stalinist system is among the clearest and best available; it is curiously reminiscent of Trotsky's in *The Revolution Betrayed*.

8. In the *Communist Manifesto*, Marx and Engels says, "The Communists *do not form a separate party* opposed to other working class parties. . . [they are], practically the most advanced and resolute section of the working class parties of every nation" (MECW, vol. 6, p. 496, emphasis added).

9. Marx, *Critique of the Gotha Programme*, MECW, vol. 24, p. 94.

10. Marx, *The Civil War in France*, MECW, vol. 22, pp. 332-33.

11. Marx and Engels, *Manifesto*, MECW, vol. 6, pp. 332-33. Note also the relative gradualism of the "by degrees"; Marx does not appear to have supposed that the "expropriators would be expropriated" in a stroke.

12. Marx, *Critique of the Gotha Programme*, MECW, vol. 24, p. 87.

13. Marx, *Capital*, vol. III, trans. David Fernbach (New York: Vintage Books, 1981), p. 959.

14. Marx, *Critique of the Gotha Programme*, MECW, vol. 24, pp. 84-85.

15. Marx, *Capital*, vol. I, trans. Ben Fowkes (New York: Penguin Books, 1976), p. 171.

16. For some attempts at articulating models, see the works cited in note 29 below.

17. Marx and Engels, *The German Ideology*, MECW, vol. 5, p. 49.

18. Marx, *The Class Struggles in France*, MECW, vol. 10, p. 56.

19. Serge, *Memoirs*, p. 375.

20. William Morris, *A Dream of John Ball*, in *Three Works by William Morris*, ed. A. L. Morton (New York: International Publishers, 1968), p. 53.

21. See for example, Samuel Bowles and Herbert Gintis, *Democracy and Capitalism* (New York: Basic Books, 1987) and (from a "postmodern" perspective) Ernest Laclau and Chantal Mouffe, *Hegemony and Socialist Strategy*, trans. Winston Moore and Paul Cammack (New York: Verso, 1985); Milton

Fisk, in a forthcoming paper, "A New Face for Socialism in the 1990s", offers some effective criticisms of this move.

22. A special Party Conference was called midway between the regular Party Congresses in 1986 and 1990 because of the widespread sense that a major policy reorientation could not wait.

23. "The alternative [to War Communism] (and this is the only sensible and the last *possible* policy) is not to. . . put the lock on the development of capitalism, but to channel it into *state capitalism*", wrote Lenin in *The Tax in Kind: The Significance of the New Policy and Its Conditions* (1921), in *Selected Works*, vol. 3 (Moscow: Progress Publishers, 1975), p. 539.

24. Cohen and vanden Heuvel, *Voices of Glasnost*, p. 69.

25. David Lane, *Soviet Society Under Perestroika* (Boston: Unwin & Hyman, 1990), p. 96. This figure is from a *Pravda* report in November 1987; it is almost certainly larger today.

26. See Justin Schwartz, "Common Interests or Class Politics? The Ideology of Gorbachev's New Foreign Policy", *Against the Current* 24, January-February 1990, pp. 32-35 and Michael Fischer and James Petras, "From Malta to Panama: The Third World's Uncertain Future", *Against the Current* 27, July-August 1990, pp. 42-45. My previous analysis was more sympathetic than what I say here.

27. David Mandel, "Economic Reform and Democracy in the Soviet Union", in *Socialist Register 1988: Problems of Socialist Renewal, East and West*, ed. Ralph Miliband, Leo Panitch, and John Saville (London: Merlin Press, 1988), pp. 132-53; "Perestroika and the Working Class", *Against the Current* 20, May-June 1989, pp. 22-31 and "Why Soviet Workers Resist", *Against the Current* 28, September-October 1990, pp. 24-28.

28. A good survey is Anders Aslund, *Gorbachev's Struggle for Economic Reform* (Ithaca: Cornell University Press, 1989). Aslund (a Swede!) critizes Gorbachev for not being liberal enough.

29. See my "Socialism, Markets, Democracy", unpublished manuscript. A fuller presentation of the sort of market socialist model I favour is David Schweikart, *Capitalism or Workers' Control?* (New York: Praeger, 1980).

30. Cohen and vanden Heuvel, *Voices of Glasnost*, pp. 126-28. See also James Scanlan, "Known Direction, Unknown Goals: Social Justice vs. Equality in Soviet 'New Thinking'," paper presented at Harrogate Conference on the USSR, May 1990.

31. Justice is a value decried by Marx. See *Critique of the Gotha Programme*. This has produced a great deal of discussion recently in the West. See, e.g., Alan Buchanan, *Marx and Justice* (Totowa, NJ: Rowen and Allenheld, 1982); Norman Geras, "The Controversy About Marx and Justice", *New Left Review* 150 (1985), pp. 211-67, and Richard Peffer's magisterial, *Marxism, Morality, and Social Justice* (Princeton: Princeton University Press, 1989). This is not the place to argue the point, but I think Marx was wrong to denigrate the importance of justice and that perestroika cannot be considered a restoration of justice for the working class and other subordinate groups in Soviet society.

32. "Z", "To the Stalin Mausoleum", *Daedelus*, Winter 1990, p. 331. After about 25 pages of anticommunist theology in the grand style, "Z" changes key and gives as crisp and accurate an account of the weaknesses of perestroika as one might wish to have; given subsequent events his analysis has proved more prescient than the optimistic assessments shared until recently by many liberals and socialists (myself included).

33. *Pravda*, July 5, 1990, reprinted in *The Current Digest of the Soviet Press* [CDSP] XLII. 29, August 22, 1990.

34. *New York Times*, September 16, 1990.

35. Lane, *Soviet Society Under Perestroika*, p. 148.
36. *The Economist*, October 20, 1990.
37. Yuri Bandura, "Discoveries Made in Retrospect", *Moscow News*, July 8, 1990.
38. Alexander Tsypko, "The Fate of the Socialist Idea", *Moscow News*, July 1, 1990; "Was Marx a Socialist?" in *The Phenomenon of Socialism* (Moscow: Global Research Institute, 1990), pp. 44, 46. Tsypko, who knows his Marx, here recalls Marx's censure of the amorality of "political economy" in the *Economic and Philosophic Manuscripts*: "Do I obey economic laws if I extract money by offering my body for sale. . . or if I sell my friend to the Moroccans?. . . Then the political economist replies to me: You do not transgress my laws, but see what Cousin Ethics and Cousin Religion have to say about it. My *political economic* ethics have nothing to reproach you with". (MECW, vol. 3, p. 310).
39. *Voprosy Filosofii* 1990 (10).
40. Cohen and vanden Heuvel, *Voices of Glasnost*, pp. 151-52. Shmelev's own position, as expounded in Shmelev and Popov, *The Turning Point*, is actually closer to the sort of market socialism advocated by Schweikart or Alec Nove. But that is not the way the "law" is taken, nor is his market socialism (if he still holds it) the basis of his popularity among the intelligentsia.
41. Valery Chalidze, "Socioeconomic Rights, East and West", *Moscow News*, January 29, 1990. In "On the Reason of the People's Wealth" (April 15, 1990) he attributes this to entrepreneurial brilliance and nothing else — particularly not to the efforts of workers.
42. Heksei Kiva, "October in the Mirror of Utopias and Anti-Utopias", *Izvestia*, November 5, 1990, reprinted in CDSP XLII. 44, December 5, 1990.
43. Mihalio Markovic, "The Meaning of the Changes in Eastern Europe and the USSR", *Against the Current*, forthcoming.
44. Not least from the anti-Communists themselves; the classic of the genre is *The God That Failed*, ed. Richard Crossman (New York: Bantam, 1950); for an account from the left, see Isaac Deutscher's review of this volume, "The Ex-Communist's Conscience", in *Russia in Transition*, rev. ed. (New York: Grove Press, 1960), pp. 223-36. The best book-length study (also from the left) is Alan Wald, *The New York Intellectuals* (Chapel Hill: University of North Carolina Press, 1987).
45. See Stephen White, "The Effectiveness of Political Propaganda in the USSR", in *The Soviet Polity in the Modern Era*, ed. Erik Hoffman and Robin Laird (New York: Aldine, 1984), pp. 663-90. James Scanlan, *Marxism in the USSR* (Ithaca: Cornell University Press, 1985), gives a sense of the oppressiveness of official Marxism-Leninism.
46. Lane, *Soviet Society Under Perestroika*, p. 9.
47. For a history, see Ed Hewett, *Reforming the Soviet Economy* (Washington D.C.: Brookings Institution, 1988).
48. *Moscow News*, July 1, 1990.
49. Unless they were being disingenuous, these individuals and others interviewed by Cohen and vanden Heuvel retained socialist ideals, as they understood them in perestroikan terms, as late as early 1989.
50. Alexander Tsypko, "On Zones Closed to Thought" and "The Roots of Stalinism", *Nauka i zhizn*, 11 and 12 (November and December, 1988), reprinted in CDSP XLI. 10, April 5, 1989 and XLI. 11, April 12, 1989. He holds, implausibly, that "Stalin never overstepped the bounds of Marxism. . . in his speeches and writings" (if not his actions); a fairly startling claim, in view of Stalin's main theoretical theses, e.g., the possibility of socialism in one country and of a revolution from above, which contradict Marx's conviction that socialism can only be international and the product of working class self-activity from below.

51.   *Moscow News*, February 25, 1990.
52.   Milton Fisk, "Marxism in the USSR Today", forthcoming in *Studies in Soviet Thought*, explores this "new humanism" and its effects from a Marxist point of view. Fisk is the most articulate writer today defending a sophisticated account of class-based values. See his *Ethics and Society* (New York: Humanities Press, 1980) and *The State and Justice* (Cambridge: Cambridge University Press, 1989).
53.   This is explored in two studies of the Gorbachev period from the perspective of modernization theory: Moshe Lewin's *The Gorbachev Phenomenon* (Berkeley: University of California Press, 1988) and Geoffrey Hosking, *The Awakening of the Soviet Union* (Cambridge, MA: Harvard University Press, 1990).
54.   David Lane, *Soviet Society Under Perestroika*, p. 139.
55.   Especially in Hungary, Poland, and increasingly in Czechoslovakia. Eastern Germany is a special case because of the desire for reunification. Romania and Bulgaria are less far advanced on this road.
56.   If one wants to preserve the etymological sense of "radical" as "going to the root" this term is also unhappy. Unfortunately "neoconservative" or "neoliberal" are terms which have specific connotations in Western politics that would be extremely misleading in a Soviet context. Boris Kagarlitsky calls them "liberals", and while this may be correct in the 19th century economic sense of "liberal", it overstates their commitment to democracy and liberal rights. So "radical", in the sense of "extremist", will have to do.
57.   Quoted in Manning Marable, "Rethinking American Marxism", *Monthly Review*, January 1991, 40.
58.   Yuri Solmonov, "Lenin's Monuments: A Tug-of-War", *Moscow News*, September 9, 1990.
59.   "Co-Op Wizard Rings Moscow", *Moscow News*, October 14, 1990.
60.   Boris Yeltsin, *Against the Grain* (New York: Summit, 1990). Even *The Economist* says that "Presumably Yeltsin [acted] in the name of some ideas or policies, but he barely mentions them" in the book (March 24, 1990). A practical politician utterly lacking in theory, Yeltsin appears to have a genuine populist revulsion against privilege — the source of his popular appeal — but also a good eye for the main chance.
61.   *Pravda*, February 8, 1980.
62.   *The Economist*, September 15, 1990.
63.   *Izvestia*, August 7, 1990, reprinted in CDSP XLII. 32, September 12, 1990. Shcherbakov, it should be noted, was speaking as a proponent of the Union government's more moderate version of a plan for marketization, which he claimed would leave 8 million unemployed but provide an adequate safety net.
64.   *Izvestia*, April 12, 1990, reprinted in CDSP XLII. 17, May 30, 1990. See also Patrick Flaherty, "Behind 'Shatalinomics'," *The Guardian* (U.S.), October 10, 1990.
65.   See Jon Weiner, "Capitalist Shock Therapy", *The Nation*, June 25, 1990.
66.   Stanislav Shatalin, et. al., "Why the 500 Days Program is Unfeasible Today", *Komsomolskaya Pravda*, November 4, 1990, reprinted in CDSP XLII. 45, December 12, 1990.
67.   Lane, *Soviet Society Under Perestroika*, pp. 135-36.
68.   *Moscow News*, September 30, 1990.
69.   Cited in David Mandel, "Worker Consciousness and the Socialist Alternative: The Ideological Struggle for the Soviet Working Class", unpublished manuscript.
70.   *Moscow News*, January 21, 1990.
71.   *Komsomolskaya Pravda*, October 30, 1990, reprinted in CDSP XLII. 44, December 5, 1990.
72.   The best account of the strike is Theodore Friedgut and Lewis Sieglebaum,

"Perestroika From Below: The Soviet Miner's Strike and Its Aftermath", *New Left Review* 181 (May-June 1990), pp. 1-32.

73. *Manchester Guardian Weekly*, June 30, 1990.

74. *Sovetskaya Rossiia*, May 17, 1990, reprinted in CDSP XLII. 23, July 11, 1990.

75. *Izvestia*, June 11, 15, 1990, reprinted in CDSP XLII. 24, July 18, 1990; July 11, 1990, reprinted in CDSP XLII. 28, August 15, 1990.

76. "Workers Begin to Organize", *Moscow News*, September 16, 1990.

77. *Socialist Worker* (U.S.), April 1990.

78. "The USSR's New Opposition", *Socialist Worker* (U.S.), September 1990.

79. "Guide to Soviet Democracy", *The Economist*, May 26, 1990; "Public Movements in the USSR", *Moscow News*, February 25, 1990.

80. Nina Andreyeva, "I Cannot Forego Principles", *Sovetskaya Rossiia*, March 13, 1988, reprinted in Lane, *Soviet Society Under Perestroika*, pp. 108-17.

81. See Mandel, "Worker Consciousness", for discussion.

82. *Izvestia*, July 4, 1990, reprinted in CDSP XLII. 25, August 8, 1990.

83. Marx, *The Eighteenth Brumaire of Louis Bonaparte*, MECW, vol. II, pp. 99-197, especially pp. 141-43; 184-97.

84. Gavril Popov, "Dangers of Democracy", *New York Review of Books*, August 16, 1990.

85. Andranak Migranyan, "The Long Road to the European Home", *Novy Mir*, July, 1989, reprinted in CDSP, XLI. 42, 1989. Migranyan does not seem to have reflected that Kirkpatrick's theory was that "totalitarian" regimes are supposedly frozen and incapable of change, an idea seriously compromised by both perestroika itself, despite its deadlock, and by the Eastern European revolutions of 1989.

86. Migranyan's use of "civil society", incidentally, corresponds more closely to Marx's sense of the term than to the sense of the term used today in Eastern Europe. Following Hegel, Marx used the expression *"buergerliche Gesellschaft"* [bourgeois society], usually translated "civil society"; implicitly contraposing *Gesellschaft*, a merely instrumental association for the advancement of individual ends, to *Gemeinschaft*, which has a connotation of community and mutuality. Something like this latter, more Gramscian, sense indicating popular organization independent of the state, is what Vaclav Havel and other Eastern European advocates of "civil society" favour. Like many Soviet intellectuals today, Migranyan prefers the former.

87. *Literary Gazette International*, February and March, 1990. Unlike Migranyan, Klymakin denies that he advocates authoritarianism; he simply regards it as probable.

88. *Moscow News*, April 1, 1990.

89. Boris Kagarlitsky, "The Importance of Being Marxist", *New Left Review* 178 (November-December 1989), p. 33. Kagarlitsky declines to call market Stalinism a form of capitalism.

90. *Moscow News*, March 25, 1990.

91. For an overview and background to this crisis, see Ronald Suny, "The Revenge of the Past: Socialism and Ethnic Conflict in Transcaucasia", *New Left Review* 184 (November-December 1990), pp. 5-34.

92. Here Shevardnadze must bear some responsibility for enabling the conditions under which the Baltic crackdown could occur. He was an architect of the Soviet rapprochement with the West and as responsible as anyone for the policy of Soviet accommodation to the US buildup for war against Iraq.

93. *The Economist*, December 22, 1990. Rumours of a military coup abound. See Andrei Nuikin, "Military Coup in the USSR?" (*Moscow News*, September 30, 1990). I regard this worry as unfounded. The military, always strictly subordinate to civilian authority, has never been an effective player in Soviet

high politics. Nor is there a Russian tradition of military rule. But one might imagine a situation in which radical civilian authorities, frustrated with democratic deadlock, order in the troops.

94.   Thanks for constructive suggestions are due to Ron Aronson, Matthew Evangelista, David Finkel, Milton Fisk, Phil Gasper, Andrew Oldenquist, Leo Panitch, Mihalio Markovic, Kurt Mosser, Bernard Rosen, Bruce Rosenstock and Yana Yakhina.

THE STRUGGLE FOR POWER IN THE SOVIET ECONOMY[1]

David Mandel

"It is now our turn to reject that which has not withstood the test of history. They often try to frighten us that the market is exploitation, the restoration of capitalism, the rule of the shadow economy. In reality, we are talking about the transition to a civilized, cultured market, open to all honest and industrious people."

(From the appeal of the Russian Parliament to the population to support the "500-Day Plan for the Transition to the Market".)[2]

"I recently read in your paper [. . .] 'Employees of the state sector are prepared to become hired workers only on condition that their wages rise significantly.' [. . .] I don't know of any workers in the state sector who would be prepared to become hired slaves. And what can a 'significant' increase, say a doubling, of wages give them if prices rise 5-10 times and if mass unemployment sets in? Criminals, who have amassed capital, are becoming a class of owners and rulers of the destiny of the state."

(From the letter of a worker of Kharkov region.)[3]

This article treats developments in the Soviet labour movement as they relate to the issue of power in the economy. The first section presents certain elements of the current economic situation that have brought the issue of power to the fore. There follows an examination of the forms, spontaneous and organized, through which workers have responded to it. A final section evaluates the significance of the self-management current in the labour movement from a socialist perspective.

Of Markets and Mafias

In early December 1990, a journalist at the liberal daily *Komsomol'skaya pravda* purchased a pig from a farmer and brought it to the kolkhoz (private) market to sell. The market price of meat had doubled over the last half year to 30-35 roubles a kilo[4] (with a 33-66% rise only over the past month alone), and he wanted to understand why. He made the rounds of sixteen of Moscow's 33 markets but everywhere was refused access to the counters where he would have been able to offer his meat for sale to the public. Finally, at the Riga market, Moscow's largest, after paying a "crazy" bribe to the butcher and inspector, he was given a counter among the egg dealers. He posted a sign: "Cheapest Meat at the Market" and started to sell at five times below the going price. The reaction was swift. A man purchased a very large piece of meat only to run back a few minutes later shouting that the meat was infected. When this false accusation failed to deter the other clients, our journalist was denied access to the scales, under the pretext that his meat was dirty. He then began to sell the meat unweighed, upon which four large men attempted to drag him away. "The markets of the capital," he concluded, "where, in principle, free economic laws should hold sway, are today completely monopolized. [. . .] The mafia structure of a single market rakes in several tens of thousands of roubles a day. The whole path is thickly paved with bribes."[5]

73% of the respondents in a survey conducted in sixteen regions of the Soviet Union in the summer of 1990 stated that their ability to influence political life had not increased over the past two years.[6] In another survey in Moscow in the fall of 1990, 60% claimed that "power in the localities belongs not to the soviets but to the chiefs of the mafia".[7] In the sixth year of the prestroika, people are waking up to the realization that despite the increased freedom of speech, the competitive elections, and the removal of the party apparatus from the levers of political power, they themselves remain almost as powerless as ever. People, who only a year ago were fervent supporters of the schemes of the radical marketeers, now typically express fear that the elimination of state control over the economy means that "it will all fall into the hands of the mafia". The term "mafia" reflects the popular perception of a growing fusion of the bureaucracy, especially the economic administrators, with the "affairistes" of the private sector.[8] These are the people who hold power in the economy, and so also in society.

Any Soviet citizen can readily offer a list of examples drawn from personal experience to support this view. The "mafia" has lately also become a major theme of the press, liberal as well as conservative (there is no mass socialist press). As a social phenomenon, its contours are illusive and fluctuating — its shadowy character is in the nature of the beast. But the term most often refers to two principal kinds of related activity: the creation and maintenance of shortages by monopoly structures,[9] and the illicit transfer of state resources and funds into private hands. Both involve the collusion of administrators of the state sector with the "shadow" [tenevaya] economy, itself often indistinguishable from the legitimate private sector. The "mafia" was not, of course, born under Gorbachev, as the trials at the start of the perestroika surrounding Rashidov's reign in Kazakhstan amply showed. But with the further weakening of central control and the legalization of the private sector, the "Rashidovshchina" has become much more generalized. The following are some additional examples of "mafia" activity; these could easily be multiplied.

In September 1990, a deputy of the Moscow Soviet travelled to Astrakhan' to find out why tomatoes and watermelons were arriving from this southern region in such small quantities. The local Astrakhan' authorities showed him a pile of telegrams sent by administrators of Moscow's produce wholesale-retail network instructing them to stop shipment because of an oversupply in Moscow, which, of course, did not exist. "Prices are now mostly 'by agreement'," explained the deputy. "The less goods, the higher their price can soar. Who profits from this reduced supply of vegetables? Those who sell them. I consider that mafia links along the lines warehouse-shop-speculator are real!"[10] As for dry goods, the director of a Moscow department store chain estimates that only 18% of the goods in high demand that are produced and imported actually reach the ordinary consumer.[11] Enormous lines stretch around state shops, while at the private markets — and sometimes only a few yards from the door of the state shop itself — one can purchase the same goods without any wait for several times the state price.

The Soviet Union has imported hundreds of millions of dollars worth of medicine over the past two years. Yet even simple aspirin has become a rare find in the pharmacies. According to the director of a Moscow pharmaceutical trading firm, most of the imported drugs are not those that are in most demand, and no one consulted her about this.[12] But someone surely made a bundle in pay-offs from the exporters. Anyone with enough money can obtain needed drugs by bribing the pharmacy or warehouse manager, or at the black market or at Moscow's little-known, but now quite legal, foreign currency drug store. According to one report, the volume of illegal trade in medicine is already approaching that of the state pharmacies.[13]

Besides economic gain, shortages also play a useful political role for those interested in maintaining popular quiescence. People are so preoccupied with the material struggle for survival that they have little time or energy for sustained political activity. (This is, of course, not to claim that the shortages are the result of a political conspiracy, though in some cases even this hypothesis should not be dismissed. In any case, one can argue with confidence that, were it not for the political role played by the shortages, efforts to deal with them would be more intense and successful.) And when political tensions rise dangerously, "defitsit" (scarce goods — literally "shortage") is suddenly "thrown out" onto the market. According to a resident of the industrial town of Sverdlovsk, soon after a mass political demonstration, the authorities "began to 'throw out' Austrian boots,

Rumanian blouses and deodorant from somewhere or other. Naturally, lines sprang up, then lists, guardians of the lists and guardians of the night lines. The people are busy, they have become active". The committee elected at the demonstration soon found itself isolated from the rest of the population.[14]

As shortages grow more serious, the practice of selling "defitsit" directly in the enterprises has expanded. This is a common and quite effective tool in the hands of the administration for reinforcing the workers' dependence. A worker who speaks up against management might miss out. At the same time, there are never enough goods to go around, and the squabbling over who is to receive what can seriously undermine solidarity within the collective. This practice also has a deeply corrupting influence on workers, since the goods that are sold are often not scarce basic consumer goods but items such as cars, electronic equipment, video cassettes and French perfumes, which the workers then resell at a large profit. Management is, of course, perfectly aware of this.

Shortages also serve as a political football for conservatives and liberals who want to discredit each other. With the potato crop rotting in the fields, party officials accused the "democrats", elected to the soviets in the spring of 1990, of doing nothing to mobilize their constituents for the harvest. (This used to be the role of the party apparatus until it was stripped of its administrative functions in the economy.) The liberal press, in its turn, blamed the conservatives for sowing panic in order to discredit the "democrats". The "democrats" pointed their finger at the central economic apparatus for failing to take measures in time, when the problem was foreseeable even a year ago. Indeed, the first reaction of Gavriil Popov, Moscow's liberal mayor, was to refuse to mobilize his constituents, suggesting instead that the incompetent ministerial apparatus be sent to the fields.

Leonid Sukhov, a taxi driver from Kharkov and member of the USSR Parliament, expressed a widespread view when he suggested that "someone" is consciously creating a desperate situation with the aim of preparing the workers psychologically to accept any reform, including the market.[15] The "democrats" argue that they lack real power to change the situation. And while there is much truth to this claim, they have done little to mobilize the population in order to change the correlation of forces. There is a general reluctance on the part of liberals, stemming from their ideological orientation as well as from more concrete political considerations, to apply "administrative" methods — the only ones that could be effective against monopoly — to rein in the "mafia". For, as the Russian-born American economist Vasily Leontieff has argued, today's mafia is tomorrow's class of "civilized" capitalists.

Direct robbery of the consumer is only one source of "mafia" profits. Parallel to this, and sometimes overlapping, is theft from the state. This also takes many forms. Workers tell of the "pocket" co-operatives[16] and joint ventures set up by enterprise management for the illicit sale abroad or to the private sector of raw materials and semi-manufactured goods. For example, the director of the state research and manufacturing association Gidrolizprom authorized the creation of the co-operative Khimtekhnika and transferred to it — free of charge — the association's large store of defective titanium hydrolysis apparatuses. Khimtekhnika, which began with no assets of its own, traded these for from six to nine million roubles worth of computers and video players, of which Gidrolizprom saw none. After several narrow escapes from the economic police and tax inspectors, Khimtekhnika's directors transferred these assets to a joint Soviet-Swiss venture, Intercomplex, created specially for that purpose. (Joint ventures enjoy a two-year tax holiday.) Since then, the Gidrolizprom association has been disbanded. Its former institutes and factory, now independent, face large debts and bleak futures. Not so the former director of Gidrolizprom, who now stands at the helm of Intercomplex.[17]

Subcontracting work to co-operatives is a common way of turning non-cash credits into cash. In the Soviet economy, monetary exchanges between state enterprises take the form of bookkeeping transactions between the State Bank accounts of the different enterprises. In such exchanges (po beznalichnomu raschetu), no cash changes hands. On the other hand, in transactions between state enterprises and co-operatives, which are non-state enterprises, cash is paid out of these accounts, allowing state managers to receive kickbacks or salaries as members or employees of the co-operative. There are also fortunes to be made in foreign dealings. Most of Moscow's "joint venture" construction companies are too busy importing and selling computers to put up any buildings. And why should they, when their profits can reach 4,000%?[18] As a minister in the Latvian government put it, "cooperatives and joint enterprises are often oriented not toward the production of consumer goods but toward their re-distribution. From the state's pockets into their own. That is, if we are to call things by their name, they are involved in speculation on a very large scale."[19] Under Brezhnev, a "gift" of jeans or whiskey helped to seal foreign export deals to the Soviet Union. Under the perestroika, when foreign dealings have been decentralized, large cash sums of foreign currency have become de rigueur.[20]

Mention must also be made of the party apparatus, many of whose former and current members are using their connections and illegally accumulated wealth to go into business. In Leningrad, for example, the once mighty regional party apparatus has been reduced to 37 people. But they keep busy renting out offices to co-operatives, private banks and foreign companies in the Smolnyi Institute, an historic landmark and prime piece of real estate that rightfully belongs to the people. They have also turned one of the committe's hotels into a joint venture.[21]

But it is not only members and former members of the bureaucratic clans who are involved in these activities. A scandal broke out in the Moscow Soviet when a deputies' club by the name of "Stolitsa" (capital) tried to oust the local temperance society from its premises on Chekhov St. It was discovered that this club's goals are "production and commercial activities". Further inquiry revealed that its founders work in the Soviets' Commission on Economic Policy and Entrepreneurship. *Komsomol'skaya pravda* remarked: "The example of 'Stolitsa', unfortunately, is not unique but is even typical of the existing structure of soviets: different commissions of local soviets often create various commercial organizations and pay part of their profits, not to the local budget, but directly to their founders. And the founders, of course, repay the kindness."[22]

In December 1990, 35 members of the Oktyabr'skii District Soviet in Moscow publicly accused its chairman, Ilya Zaslavskii, a liberal luminary, of "organizing monopoly structures, as similar to classic 'shadow' formations as two peas in a pod [. . .] Judge for yourselves: the chairman of the District Soviet, the chairman of its executive committee, and almost all his deputies, having become heads of the district's political structures, are at the same time directors of co-operatives, commercial banks and firms. [There follows a long list of these enterprises.] Exceptionally favourable conditions are created for the activity of all these firms, and tens of thousands of roubles are being pumped at an intensive rate into their financial accounts from the basic budgetary funds of the district executive committee, that is, they are openly robbing you and me of funds intended for the socio-economic development of the district." The deputies went on to accuse the executive, busy with realizing Zaslavskii's conception of "the market economy and financial independence of the district", of sabotaging the district's vegetable harvest campaign. The housing programme, they argued, was also failing: while the executive was selling state apartments primarily to occupants who openly stated their intention of leaving the country and reselling the apartments for foreign currency or renting them out to foreign companies, 60,000 people in the district still lived in communal apartments.[23]

These developments, the "transition to the market" as the uncontrolled sway of monopoly formations and the illicit transfer of public wealth to private hands, popularly termed the "mafia-ization" of the economy, do not come as a surprise to Soviet Marxists, who are the only ones even to attempt a serious analysis of the underlying causes of the "command" system's failure.[24] They have always insisted that the basic issue in economic reform is power, that is a social issue, and that the market-versus-plan debate is about mechanisms of regulation that in and of themselves do not determine the nature of a social system. The failure of the "command" system cannot be explained by simply citing the allegedly "utopian nature of a planned economy", though the Marxists themselves call for a revision of the old socialist model of "one big factory", including a significant expansion the role of market relations in the Soviet economy. But this task, however important, cannot be resolved successfully in the interests of the great majority without directly confronting the issue of power.

For the Marxists, the underlying social cause of the crisis of the old system is the absence of control over the economy's administrators, who after the revolution usurped the power of the economy's official owner, the people, without becoming full owners themselves. Under Stalin, at the origins of the "command economy", some control from above did exist. A manager who failed to carry out assigned tasks knew that he or she would be sanctioned, often in a drastic manner. Khrushchev eliminated the terror but did not replace it with democratic control from below. He merely played with democracy. But even his timid reforms provoked the opposition of the bureaucracy that was able to find allies in the majority of the political leadership. Brezhnev thus came to power as the candidate of the bureaucracy. What Soviets today call "the period of stagnation" was probably the purest expression of the rule of a bureaucracy increasingly free of outside political control. During this period, administrators (especially at the top and middle levels) did not need particularly to fear punishment for failure to carry out official duties. Real sanctions were reserved for those who violated the informal rules, the *esprit de corps*, of the bureaucratic caste mired in corruption.

From this point of view, Gorbachev, though himself a reformer, has favoured the process that he inherited from the Brezhnev régime: today the centre has become almost as powerless as the people themselves against the economic bureaucracy, which is free to exploit its monopoly positions in perfectly predictable ways: restricting the volume of goods put on the market, cutting quality, and raising prices. This is the inevitable consequence of an attempted "revolution from above" which has entrusted economic reform to the bureaucracy itself. Its aim is to preserve the power and privilege of at least a part of the bureaucracy by transforming the mode of domination and exploitation. This, of course, requires bringing new elements into the ruling class and sacrificing some of the old.

The developments in the Soviet economy described above are forcing the liberals to come to terms with the unpleasant reality. Their standard argument that the deepening economic crisis and the "debauch of the mafia" are due to the absence of "real" reform has lost much of its force, since ordinary citizens have already experienced enough of the market to form a quite clear picture of what a "real" transition to the market holds in store for them. In the words of the USSR Minister of Finance: "One can argue whether we are prepared or not for the transition to the market, if competition has been established among producers or if that still remains a very distant goal, but the reality is such that the market is already imperiously intruding into our lives. Over 60% of prices are not under the control of the state. That means that they are rising, and very significantly. [. . .] Monopolism in industry, agriculture and transport has very strong positions." [25] (This is quite an admission, in view of the fact that there has been no official price reform. In the spring of 1990, Gorbachev solemnly promised that there would be no price reform without first consulting the population, itself overwhelmingly opposed to price rises.)

Liberal sociologist Leonid Radzikhovskii argues that the Soviet economy is dominated by a "lumpen-bourgeois ethic: the desire to increase one's own property at the expense of state property, which is 'no one's' property". This has yielded "a unique, historically unprecedented monster — a completely mafiaized economy". All this he attributes, of course, to the socialist revolution itself. But he is not far from the Marxists' analysis when he describes the perestroika as the "privatization of the bureaucratic-mafia structure: the ministry becomes a monopolist concern and the city trade administration — an association of private shops". Nevertheless, he warns that it would be silly to believe that anything else is possible, since the "mafia-nomenklatura" is where the power is. And so, however distasteful, one must hold the course since "only in conditions of open private property will it be possible to begin, drop by drop, to crush monopoly and the mafia, [. . .] millimetre by millimetre to restore the common human ethic[26] and to get rid of the lumpen bourgeoisie". [27] In essence, Radzikhovskii is proposing to hold one's nose and support the revolution from above. He does not even mention the possibility of a popular revolution as an alternative. For wresting power from the "mafia-nomenklatura" by the people itself might jeopardize his goal of a capitalist restoration.

Leningrad's social democrats, advocates of a "mixed" (but predominantly capitalist) economy, have also recently come to the realization that "privatization will mean the transfer of property into the hands of the directors; and the introduction of a market economy — their freedom from any limitations whatsoever". The following are only the most striking of the developments along these lines in their city: "The 26 largest enterprises, having formed the 'Association of Industrial Enterprises', have now founded the bank 'Rossiya', in which they are investing millions of roubles. They have also created the firm 'Nevskaya perspektiva', through which they will buy up [. . .] the consumer goods and food industry of the city along with the trade network — all this, naturally, to help the citizens and Leningrad Soviet. At the conclusion of these operations, the city will still be run by the same old administrative structure, only its elements will enjoy new opportunities, which hitherto were considered criminal." [28]

While this in itself is worrying to the social democrats, who want a "normal" Western-style economy for the Soviet Union, they clearly fear even more that "political instability" and "social unrest" will result. "People in the factories will not wait for long when they discover that society is being ruled by the same actors, leading the same kind of life, along with all their relatives and friends and with a part of the most amenable democrats, the only difference being that they will have exchanged their black Volgas for black Mercedes." The Leningrad social democrats are fervent partisans of what they call the "parliamentary path". "There are two alternatives: try to use the extreme instability of the situation to destroy the remaining conservative structures and on the wave of the mass actions hope to become political leaders 'expressing the interests of the people'; or try to prevent the social explosion by any methods available, preserving the parliamentary path of development of events. The Bolsheviks of 1917 were the most consistent partisans of the first option. [. . .] We know the consequences of trying to make a social revolution." Consequently, the social democrats see the bureaucrats' move from Volgas into Mercedes as virtually inevitable. All they can think to propose is to invite Western capitalists in the hope that they will introduce a "civilizing" element into Soviet business. Another proposal is for the Leningrad Soviet itself to go into business, as a counterweight to the "mafia". But, they sadly note, in that case there would be no guarantee against the Soviet itself becoming "mafia-ized". [29]

The Struggle For Power in the Factories
The growing prominence of the question of power in the economy, as well as the accelerated decline in the general economic situation, have had a direct impact on the labour movement. Labour conflicts in the

first years of the perestroika centred around issues of wages and work conditions, with demands addressed to the enterprise management and sometimes to the ministry.[30] Although wages and conditions still remain central issues, a new type of conflict has emerged over the past year. Rather than putting forth economic demands and pressuring management to meet them, workers are themselves seeking an active role in management of their enterprises. These conflicts, which are more offensive in nature and pose directly the issue of power in the enterprise, have been especially prominent in the crucial machine-construction industry, which unlike coalmining, has not seen any co-ordinated, inter-enterprise strike movement.

At the start of 1990, Moscow's AZLK auto factory, which makes the "Moskvich", seemed even to its handful of activists an unlikely place for an "uprising". Like many of Moscow's factories with large semi-skilled and unskilled labour forces, about two-thirds of the workers here are "limitchiki", workers from the provinces with temporary Moscow residence permits that can be revoked upon dismissal from the factory. They are, therefore, especially vulnerable and generally quiescent. But even the settled Muscovites felt the pressure and corrupting influence of the internal distribution system, which expanded as shortages in the state shops worsened.

True, the year before, something unheard of had occurred at the factory's trade-union conference: someone complained about the purchase of useless machinery in Western Europe. Some speakers blamed this on management's decision to send the director's son (travel to the West is a coveted privilege) rather than workers and engineers who had first-hand knowledge of the specifications. AZLK's workers also remembered how the previous year the director had ignored the decision of the work-collective (self-management) council and adopted a 120,000-car plan target. He went so far as to dismiss his popular assistant director, who had insisted that the plant's capacity was only 80,000. In fact, only 74,000 cars were made in 1989, but the workers received their bonuses anyway, since the director is well-connected and was able to persuade the ministry to "correct" the plan. The adoption of the original plan had allowed him to obtain additional funds, some of which went to buy the machinery that was lying about uninstalled. 1989 also saw the workers reject management's proposed schedule of fifteen "black" (working) Saturdays, when the director, in a nod to the current fashion (since then abandoned, as we shall see), foolishly decided to consult the workers.

But otherwise, the workers looked on in their usual gloomy silence at management's inability rationally to organize production and provide normal work conditions as well as at its deepening corruption. (The huge sums involved in the "shadow" economy and the great demand for the attractive new "Moskvich" have opened up new vistas in this area.) Then came an article in *Komsoml'skaya pravda*, written on information provided by factory activists, describing the poor management at the enterprise. If in 1985, 17,500 workers produced 175,000 cars, in 1989, 16,900 workers made less than half as many. This was followed by a television report that the factory was being fined one and a half million convertible roubles for non-fulfilment of a contract to build a sports car for a West-German firm. The final piece of tinder was provided by the news that the retail price of the "Moskvich" would be raised 50% to 13,500 roubles, even though no substantial improvements had been made. The factory would be allowed to keep 1,000 extra roubles for its needs.

In January 1990, the work-collective council of the assembly shop, led by a group of activist workers (who are also party members), called a shop meeting to discuss the situation. To the surprise of the initiators, workers streamed in from all over the factory and filled up the 800-seat hall and adjacent corridors to overflowing. The following demands were put forward: dismissal of the director and election of a new one; reinstatement of the dismissed assistant director; new elections to the enterprise work-collective council, since the present one was subservient to the administration; no price rise (speakers explained that it might permit the factory to raise wages, but if all enterprises made unjustified price rises, wage gains would soon be wiped out); equalization of the rights of the "limitchiki" with those of permanent residednts; a regular work process, without idle time, "storming", and violation of internal supply schedules; real cost-accounting; and wages paid according to labour (large wage differentials exist from shop to shop for the same kind of work). Some speakers demanded that supervisory and technical personnel be cut and the savings be used to raise the salaries of the remainder in accordance with results.

In a letter to *Pravda*, Sergei Novopol'skii, chairman of the assembly shop's work-collective council and head of the brigade of mechanic-assemblers, explained the underlying impulse behind the explosion: "The main thing is that we are convinced that the perestroika does not need silent workers of the kind the present management would like to see but workers who think, who understand, and who know how to work in a way that is useful for the country." [31] But the director, on his part, attributed it all to "intrigues of the apparatus", which he accused of abusing the new democracy and glasnost. He agreed to hold a referendum on his administration, which he won. [32] The main results of the meeting were new elections to the work-collective council and a halving of the proposed price rise.

The workers were obviously not prepared for sustained activism. In part, this can be attributed to the influence of the economic crisis and the internal distribution system. However, the latter's arbitrary and corrupting nature, while effective in the short run, is particularly degrading to the workers and eventually adds fuel to the explosions, when they finally occur. And most Soviet observers expect these to occur soon. More importantly perhaps, the auto workers' demands were addressed to the enterprise management, but many of their problems could be resolved only at higher, essentially political, levels. Any new movement will have to link up with workers in other enterprises if it is to be effective and take on stable, organized forms.

Only a few weeks after the AZLK meeting, a similar gathering took place several thousand kilometres away at the Sibelektrotyazhmash plant in Novosibirsk which makes large electric generators. Here too workers had never shown much concern for the economic fate of the enterprise. Their complaints were traditionally about the cafeteria's food, bad ventilation and heating, the periodic absence of hot water. In short, it was a typical machine-construction enterprise, except perhaps for the shiny new Toyotas parked in front of the administration building, though these too were becoming a familiar scene in the fifth year of the perestroika. The initiative for the meeting here too came from a group of activists. A few days before, the head of a brigade of turners, himself a member of the factory's party committee, sounded out the shops and met with an enthusiastic response from the workers. The main issue at the meeting was poor management. The director had been elected a year ago but had not carried out his programme: no new forms of work organization had been introduced. Output was half of what it had been twenty years ago, but the work force was the same size. The assembly brigade stood idle for weeks, while workers in the adjacent shop put in ten hour shifts for the same wage. Copper wire worth thousands of roubles was cut up because there were no reels. Technical and production discipline had declined catastrophically. While the director blamed all this on the middle levels of management that he accused of sabotaging his initiatives, the workers complained that they rarely saw him at the factory and never on the shop floor. While the collective was seething and with the conference already in preparation, he took off to Moscow to attend a branch conference of directors. The chief engineer's assertion that things were not so bad since profits had risen 400% over 1976-88 made no impression on the workers.

But the most insistent accusation against management concerned the co-operatives. These had been created to help the enterprise fulfil the state's directive to increase its production of consumer goods. "Where are these goods?" asked the workers. "We don't see any more [on the market] than before. Whom are we fooling?" "The managers are coddling the co-operatives, and the co-operatives are robbing the enterprise blind. Transformer copper is going to the co-operatives, but who signs it out? We produce no copper waste." "The superintendent of the first department received 1500 rubles from one of the fifteen co-operatives organized at the factory to produce consumer goods. [. . .] In essence, this is payment for his having ruined the shop — let's tell things as they really are. The shop is now working to meet the needs of the co-operative, not the factory. Forty welders left the shop for the co-operative, forcing other shops to send their people to help it out. One of the assistants to the chief engineer received 2700 rubles for the construction of a trestle bridge in his spare time. Where does he get it, if he doesn't have a fixed workday!? The party organizer has also dirtied his hands in the co-operatives. He has passed all his work to his assistant and himself is nowhere to be seen. People are sick of all this. It angers us to the bottom of our souls. What is going on around us!? We have to change our life, we cannot go on living like this." [33]

The meeting elected a workers' committee (representing only the blue-collar workers) to take power in the factory and decided to hold new elections to the work-collective committee (which represents all employees: workers, office employees, engineering and technical personnel as well as management), which had been doing little more than distributing "defitsit". The factory's newspaper was removed from the control of the administration, the party and trade-union committees and made responsible to the workers' conference. Managerial, engineering and technical personnel were to be cut in half, and a new director elected. (The workers' committee later decided to give him six more months, after which he would report back to the workers, who would take a final decision.) Characterizing as one-sided the enterprise's relations with the ministry, regional and union governments (it paid them 70% of its income, leaving little for the collective's social development), the meeting decided to negotiate a reduction in its payments. The workers' committee was instructed to study, with the aid of economists, the question of gradually leaving the ministry. (The workers were aware that they might be worse off without the ministry playing its redistributive role within the branch.)

The co-operatives, accused of "pillaging the enterprise's resources and fostering the moral decay of the collective", were ordered off the enterprises's territory, and administrative personnel as well as employees in the financial and accounting departments forbidden to work in them. Full reports on their activities and finances were ordered from the co-operative chairpersons. The meeting also turned its attention to the nefarious effect on the collective of the internal distribution system and decided that henceforth, the sale of scarce consumer goods, food, cars etc., would take place only after this had been approved by a workers' conference. Finally, on the issue of the Toyotas, a report was demanded of the superintendent of the transport department on the cost of maintaining the enterprise's fleet of cars and vans and on his budget in 1989.

The election of a workers' committee is characteristic of many of these conflicts. As one observer put it, "in the majority of cases the work-collective committees [elected by the entire collective] fail to show any independence vis-à-vis management. The work-collective committees were basically created on order from above. [Until the government issued a special instruction, they were often headed by the director.] The workers' committees [representing only the blue-collar workers], on the other hand, are not obligated to anyone at their birth, i.e. they are not the result of initiative from above but of the realization that we are all responsible for changing things and that if we do not, who will?"[34] The formation of workers' committees reflects in part the deepening hostility between workers and "white blouses" in the enterprises — the reduction of administrative and technical personnel is a very popular demand.[35] But it also is a response to the fact, that technical, like administrative personnel, have no right of appeal against dismissals and are therefore more dependent on the director. One of the workers' leaders explained: "The shop engineers are our brothers; they work in the same dirt and face the same difficulties. [. . .] We aren't against them. They should be with us. Our level of knowledge does not allow us to really spread our wings, especially when it comes to economic questions. But for the time being, we have decided to create a workers' committee with representatives only from the working class [. . .] we have a good lever [. . .] — the strike. Management has to consider that possibility and take the proletariat into account. [. . .] But we do include the engineering and technical personnel in the work-collective committee."[36] Another interesting aspect of these conflicts is the initiating role often played by worker party activists. This occurs against the general background of the party's unpopularity among workers, who are leaving it in significant numbers.

At a Vilnius trucking enterprise, whose existence was threatened in the spring of 1990 by Moscow's oil embargo and the republican government's proposed economic reforms, the workers dissolved the work-collective committee and elected a workers' committee, assuming full control of the enterprise. The committee was instructed to take "all measures to organize the enterprise's complete, normal functioning, which has been undermined of late". Among other things, it independently concluded a contract with the Ministry of

Transport of Byelorussia (just across the border from Lithuania), which agreed to supply the enterprise with fuel and parts. "I would never have believed it," commented a member of the administration. "I always thought that the main thing for them was their 19 rubles a day, and to hell with the rest."[37] At a Voronezh machine-construction factory, the director was misappropriating the factory's equipment and materials for his personal benefit. A small, poorly organized enterprise that was in bad economic shape, it nevertheless maintained seven well-paid assistant directors. Spurred on by the party committee, a bare majority of the work-collective committee called a workers' conference. It elected a workers' committee, which it mandated to investigate and restore order in the factory. The director was replaced through competitive elections, and affairs began quickly to improve.[38] At a Novosibirsk machine-construction factory, the workers shut down a co-operative that management had entrusted with the enterprise's supply and transport services. This occurred after a group of workers forced open the assistant manager's safe and found a contract showing him to be an employee of the co-operative which had been selling the factory's raw materials on the side at two and three times the state price.[39] At the VAZ auto factory, the workers first learnt from an interview by the assistant general director in the enterprise newspaper that, as one worker put it, "our clever managers had already prepared a packet of documents for the conversion of VAZ into a concern". In response, the work-collective committee declared VAZ and all its production the property of the work collective.[40]

Conflicts over power in the enterprises, that is over workers' self-management, are destined to grow as the economic and political disintegration of the country continues and factory and ministerial administrations, behind the backs of the workers, who typically suspect the worst, transform enterprises into joint-stock companies, enter them into "concerns", transfer departments to co-operatives, establish joint ventures and commercial banks with enterprise resource and funds.

The Limits of Trade-Unionism

Until recently, however, one could not speak of a self-management movement in the Soviet Union. There were only isolated conflicts over power and committee activity in the enterprises. The organized labour movement, which began with the miners' strike of July 1989, has been characterized by a basically, though by no means exclusively, trade-unionist orientation. After the 1989 strike, the miners transformed their strike committees into workers' committees, which united on a regional basis. Their main function was to monitor fulfilment of the accord with the government Resolution 608 that ended the strike. The miners have also held two national congresses, in June and October

1990. These resulted in the founding of an independent trade union. Unlike the official union, which embraces all the employees of the Ministry of the Coal Industry, the new union limits its membership to non-managerial personnel employed directly by the coal mines or the coal-enrichment factories. The Fifth Conference of Workers' Committees of the Kuzbass, which (along the much smaller Pechora basin), has been the most militant and politicized region, in September 1990 also set as its central goal the formation of a "normal" trade-union movement. [41]

For a movement that arose out of nothing after almost 60 years of very effective repression, these are impressive organizational gains. Nevertheless, this movement is today in crisis. It has not really succeeded in spreading outside of the mines and mining regions. The unions of workers' committees that have arisen in other regions consist mainly of small groups of activists, who emerge out of their isolation only when serious conflict arises in their enterprise. None of the organizations from outside the coalmining areas that attended the Congress of Independent Workers' Organizations and Movements in May 1990 in Novokuznetsk (which founded the Confederation of Labour) has anything resembling a mass base. [42] In the mining areas themselves, rank-and-file activism has declined, and the ties between the unions of workers' committees and the rank-and-file have weakened. [43] Many delegates to the Second Congress of Coalminers in Donetsk at the end of October 1990 were not at all certain that the congress's decision to found a new trade union would meet with an active or enthusiastic response back home in the mines. [44]

This is essentially a crisis of political orientation against the background of the deepening economic crisis. The attempt through strictly trade-unionist activity to protect living standards and labour conditions in a collapsing economy has reached its limits. The miners themselves have recognized that the government lacked the means to carry out certain parts of Resolution 608 and that many of those economic gains that were realized were soon lost to inflation. Moreover, in existing Soviet conditions, a trade-unionist orientation often leads to solidarity between workers and their own administration, often at the expense of the rest of the population that ends up with a bill it can ill afford to pay. For example, the one-day mail carriers' strike on June 15, 1990 was organized by the Ministry of Communications itself. [45] And the second Congress of Miners was financed by the Ministry of the Coal Industry, which had its representatives on the organizing committee. This surely must raise questions about the interests being pursued by the various bureaucratic clans in supporting these movements. [46]

The miners' movement did, of course, put forth important political demands relating to the democratization of the state. But the basic question remained unanswered: what to do with this democracy if and when it was won? The most politicized elements (often those most strongly under liberal influence) have tended to advocate a trade-unionist orientation for the labour movement and, to the extent that they put forth a positive economic programme, a market reform borrowed from the liberals. But this is running up against the same reality that the liberals are now being forced to confront.

Representatives of the Kuzbass Union of Workers' Committees, which under the presidency of Vyacheslav Golikov has had the strongest pro-liberal orientation, participated in the work of the Shatalin-Yavlinskii commission that drew up the 500-Day Plan. This is a programme for the wholesale privatization of the economy and the establishment of a market system in which state regulation plays a subordinate role. [47] The Kuzbass union has been a strong supporter of Boris Yel'tsin and the Russian Parliament, with whom it concluded a social peace accord in exchange for the parliament's support in creating a "zone of joint entrepreneurship" (free-trade zone) in the Kuzbass. But Golikov, in his report to the union's fifth conference at the end of September 1990, was forced to recognize the "deformations" (of the type described here in the first section) that were already occurring in the Kuzbass with the expansion of the private sector and market relations in the region. He appealed "not to leave these processes to themselves without the participation of the toilers. While defending market relations in the economy, we do not intend to allow it to be bought up by existing structures and their functionaries". Yet he offered no practical proposals for preventing this. Similarly, the conference's "Appeal to the Toilers of the Kuzbass" observed that "The programme of transition to market relations and, in the Kuzbass, also the creation of a zone of joint entrepreneurship are on the whole seen positively by the toilers of the region. But at the same time, the shift of the enterprise to cost-accounting and self-financing is already causing job cuts and the closure of unprofitable factories. The transition to market relations will intensify this process by many times." But rather than question the wisdom of this reform, the document merely calls for the creation of "genuine trade unions" to defend the workers. [48]

The liberal orientation of the Kuzbass leaders is to a large extent premissed upon their understanding that the region is well-situated to benefit from the market. The cost of extracting coal in the Kuzbass is relatively low, since the industry here is comparatively new and the coal close to the surface, often allowing open-pit mining. Export contracts have already been signed with Japan. (Some economists, however, argue that Kuzbass optimism will be short-lived. The region is 6,000 kilometres from a port, and the exports are being subsidized by cheap Soviet freight rates. If these rates were raised to the same world levels at which the coal is being sold, there would be no foreign contracts. How long will the railroad agree to subsidize the foreign-currency earnings of the Kuzbass coal industry?) The future, however, does not look so rosy to the Donbass miners. Their mines are old, deep — many are virtually mined-out — and their production costs are high. The transition to the market here threatens the region with mass unemployment and the extinction of entire towns and villages.

It is not surprising, then, that outside the Kuzbass and the Pechora basin (which has export contracts with Sweden through Arctic ports), the miners' movement has been rather less enthusiastic about the market. As the inevitable consequences of a transition to the market, as envisaged by the liberal reformers, become clearer, their lack of enthusiasm is turning into alarm. After the publication of the 500-Day Plan, which calls for an end to subsidies and the eventual freeing of prices, dozens of mining associations and enterprises sent angry telegrams to the government.[49] A delegation of miners from the Yakutugol' Association came to Moscow to protest against the intended dismantling of the industry's central administration and the ending of subsidies. "Natural and geological conditions vary from mine to mine," they explained. "Therefore, they cannot all be equally profitable. In our association the average cost of coal is from one to eighteen rubles, but in Donbass it is 40 to 120 rubles. Without the centralized redistribution of funds, without subsidies, Donbass will not survive. [. . .] Without centralized management, all sorts of misfortunes and shocks await the branch."[50]

Taking note of these concerns, the organizing committee of the Second Congress of Miners decided against endorsing the plan. One of its members, a miner from Karaganda, explained: "There are disputes in the collectives and in the organizing committee [about the transition to the market]. The interesting thing is that we ourselves participated in the creation of one of the programmes — that of Shatalin. [. . .] But we wavered. Why? First of all because the hardest blow will be struck against the extractive industries, and we wanted to first see a separate programme of transition to the market for our branch. Of course, a part of the people understand that it will be necesary to accept certain sacrifices, but there are also many who say: why do I need that market if my interests are violated, if I lose benefits and job seniority? [. . .] We are also worried by the fact that the realization of the Shatalin programme calls for a strong presidential power. Yet just yesterday, we proclaimed the democratization of society and self-management."[51] The organizing committee demanded the maintenance, at least for the transitional period, of the industry's central administration and subsidies. [52] Even the Council of Representatives of the Confederation of Labour, which was subject to strong liberal influence at its founding, also balked at endorsing the 500-Day Plan at its September 1990 meeting in Donetsk. [53]

The differences in orientation among the mining regions manifested themselves from the very start of the Second Congress of Miners at the end of October 1990 in the debate over the agenda. There were three main items: a report on how the decisions of the first congress had been carried out, the transition to the market in the coal industry, including a report by the Minister, and the establishment of an independent trade union. Delegates from the Donbass insisted on allotting an unlimited amount of time to the second question. They felt their region was at stake and that trade unions would be of no use if the mines were closed. Delegates from the Kuzbass, on the other hand, insisted on unlimited time for the third point, since, they argued, whatever system the workers lived under, they would need strong trade unions to defend them. [54]

Though the vast majority of delegates were in favour of a new independent trade union (a significant minority wanted to democratize the old one), a split over these differences in orientation was narrowly averted only at the very end of the congress, when the new trade union was established. But the delegates remained extremely dissatisfied with the report on the transition to the market, even though the Minister had assured them there would be no layoffs in 1991. ("If even one miner is dismissed," he declared, "you won't have to ask me, I will resign myself.") The discussion made it amply clear that although many miners fear the market, they certainly do not want to retain the old system. But the Minister offered no new vision, only the need to ask the government for additional subsidies. The delegates responded with the decision to create their own commission of experts to develop a plan for the industry.

This decision was implicit recognition of the limits of the strictly trade-unionist approach that some of the Kuzbass delegates, like Golikov, were advocating. These delegates argued that the congress's basic task was to create a trade union whose principal function would be to obtain the highest price for the labour power the workers were selling to the "employers" (rabotodateli). But most of the delegates obviously felt that the new union could not leave the tasks of managing and restructuring their industry outside of its purview.

The Emergence of a Self-Management Movement

Although self-management has not played a prominent role in the miners' movement, even those leaders closest to the liberals would no doubt say that they support the idea. One often has the impression that their alliance with the liberals is in no small part based upon a misconception (fed by liberal rhetoric about "people's enterprises" and "returning property to the people") that the market proposed by the "democrats" is a necessary condition for real self-management. In fact, the history of market reform in Yugoslavia, which has had the richest experience in this area, shows that self-management poses severe limits to the free circulation of capital and labour, and as such is incompatible with the efficient functioning of the kind of "full-blooded market" that Gorbachev has said he wants to introduce in the Soviet Union. In Yugoslavia, as well as in the rest of Eastern Europe and the Soviet Union, the "radicalization" of the market reform is being accompanied by a retreat from the self-management idea and the restoration of full private property rights, including the right of owners to manage and sell their enterprises.

But although the self-management orientation has until recently been a minor note in the organized labour movement in the Soviet Union, it was never completely absent. At the May 1990 Congress of Independent Workers' Organizations and Movements, where the influence of certain liberal Moscow intellectuals was strongly felt, a minority "Block of 33" delegates (mostly from outside the mining areas and in particular from the industrial centres of the Urals), argued for an independent labour movement within the broader democratic movement (a position firmly opposed by the liberals[55]) and proposed the following platform as a response to what they described as an offensive against labour's social and political rights: "In no circumstances to deprive the workers of the right to manage their enterprises and to realize the principles of self-management; not to allow the economic reform to be carried out at the expense of workers' interests, through the reduction of their real wages and the spread of unemployment; to oppose the democratization of property relations through the sale of state enterprises to private individuals.[56]

The conflicts over power in the enterprise and the deepening suspicion among workers that destatization will in practice mean the transformation of their enterprises into the property of the bureaucrats and "affairistes" of the "shadow economy" formed the background for the emergence of an organized self-management current in the labour movement in the late summer of 1990. But the immediate impulse was provided by the passage in the USSR Supreme Soviet of a new "Law on Enterprises in the USSR" at its Spring 1990 session. This law, adopted with suspiciously little publicity, supersedes the 1987 "Law on State Enterprises" that had granted broad self-management rights to the work collectives, including the right to elect managerial personnel and to participate in and monitor the administration of the enterprise through their elected work-collective councils.[57] The new law was explained at the time by the need to facilitate the process of democratization and the shift to the market. But the activists who managed to learn of it described it as "depriving the work-collective councils of any real functions in management and in practice reducing them to nothing".[58] Under the new law, which said nothing about self-management, enterprises are to be managed according to their charters, which are to be established by the owners.

A week after the law's adoption, the workers of the main assembly line of the VAZ factory declared: "[We] are deeply angered by the fact that the Supreme Soviet of the USSR, on June 4 1990, passed a 'Law on Enterprises in the USSR', in secret from the people, without first even publishing a draft in the press and submitting it to the collectives for discussion. In essence, a gross provocation has been committed against the toilers of the country. A law affecting the interests of every work collective has been adopted without any consideration for the opinion of the toilers themselves."[59]

In fact, the offensive against self-management, which had never become much of a reality anyway, had begun months earlier with the government's instruction to end the practice of electing managerial personnel. "The absurdity of these elections does not require discussion," wrote the management-oriented journal *EKO*. "This has already been recognized by N. I. Ryzhkov. M. S. Gorbachev, who first proposed them, has not expressed any opinion, but his silence speaks loudly."[60] The liberal ideologues have also participated in this offensive, though often hiding behind self-management rhetoric. Thus, Gorbachev's personal adviser, economist Nikolai Petrakov, has described the creation of councils of stockholders (who are not limited to the enterprise's employees), which will appoint the directors and make key decisions on investments, dividends and profits, as "a sort of step toward self-management free of higher-standing links."[61]

The convocation of the First All-Union Conference of Work-Collective Councils and Workers' Committees in Togliatti on August 31-September 4 1990 was a direct response to the passage of the new law. Attended by about a hundred delegates from enterprises employing some two million employees, it was almost completely ignored by the national media. *Rabochaya tribuna* (Workers' Tribune, published by the Central Committee of the CPSU) was the only central paper to give it any coverage, and this was really incidental to its main interest in responding to the challenge of Nikolai Travkin, leader of the Democratic Party,[62] who said he would eat his hat if the paper published the conference's resolution critical of the government. The crew of the national news programme "Vremya" also came, but its purpose was to film Venyamin Yarin, an "honorary" worker-member of Gorbachev's Presidential Council. Yarin told the conference that the President had entrusted him with the mission of organizing the representatives of the work-control councils around himself and the Presidential Council.[63] Apparently, the conference's failure to respond to this offer explains why no news about it appeared on Soviet television screens.

While the conference approved of the new law's intention of increasing the economic autonomy of enterprises, it otherwise assessed it as anti-democratic, directed against self-management, favouring the arbitrary power of the administration and the ministries and holding back the processes of demonopolization and destatisation. Some did argue that the work-collective councils had been subservient to management and, in any case, they were outmoded now that the government had adopted a policy of privatization[64] that allows for more "progressive" forms of enterprise management. The new law states that enterprises are to be administered according to their charter established by their owner or owners. Since, it was argued, the work collectives are about to become the owners, why make a fuss? If they judged the council to be useful, they could decide to retain it.

But that was the rub: the majority of delegates were not at all certain that the work collectives would inherit the destatized factories. Certainly this was as far from clear in the "500-Day Plan" as it was in the USSR government's "Basic Orientations for the Stabilization of the Economy and the Transition to a Market Economy". Both allow for all forms of property and neither makes specific provision for self-management, let alone for ownership or control by the work collectives. Indeed, if one goes beyond the rhetoric and deliberate fuzziness of sections relating to property and management, their entire thrust is against self-management and for the introduction of full private property rights.[65]

Accordingly, the conference demanded that the work-collective councils themselves be the ones to choose the appropriate form of property for their enterprises. Specifically, they should have two options: they could either become collective owners, without any payment for the enterprise, or they could decide that the enterprise remain state property that would be managed by the councils. In discussing the first option, some argued for payment, since the enterprises were built, not by the collectives, but by the entire society. Others said that property that was obtained for free would not be valued by the collective. But the majority rejected these arguments, not least because the workers simply lack the means to purchase their enterprises. As for management of the enterprises, all were agreed that under both options the administration should be hired employees of the collective and work under its supervision. The meeting declared "impermissible the transformation of ministries into concerns playing the role of leasors or into joint stock companies". It called on the Supreme Soviet to suspend the law until it could be revised to take into account the decisions of the conference and it asked republican parliaments to ignore those provisions that contradicted the self-management provisions of the 1987 law. A new draft law should be submitted to a national discussion. The conference elected an organizing committee to co-ordinate the activities of the work-collective councils and workers' committee throughout the country and to act as their spokesperson. It was instructed to participate in revising the law and to convoke a full congress of self-management committees in December that would establish a permanent organization. [66]

This was the first organized expression of how at least a significant part of the workers see "destatization". It made clear the underlying differences between the motives of the workers' support for market reform and those of the liberals. As noted earlier, rhetoric aside, a "full-blooded market", the liberals' ultimate goal, requires the establishment of full private property rights. The workers, on their part, support market reform and the enterprise autonomy that it would provide as conditions for a more efficient economy and real self-management by the collectives. Although the conference was silent on this, it was implicit in its position that enterprises that become the property of the collectives (there is no question for those that remain state property) could not be divided or sold.

Despite the organizing committee's meagre resources and the difficulty in finding a large enough hall, 700 delegates and 300 observers, mainly workers and engineers, self-management activists from large enterprises that together employ about seven million workers, attended the Founding Congress of Work-Collective Councils and Workers' Committee in Moscow on December 8-10, 1990. Many of the delegates had to pay their own way, and some had even to brave threats from management. [67] But the main purposes of the gathering, to create a permanent organization of self-management committees, to reaffirm the Togliatti conference's position on the "Law on Enterprises in the USSR" and on destatization, and to develop a plan of action were achieved.

The congress founded the Union of Work-Collective Councils and Workers' Committees and elected a council of representatives from the major regions, with three co-chairmen. [68] A heated debate took place over the issue of a warning strike at the start of January to support the congress's programmatic demands. Although a strike was not ruled out, it was decided first to try other means, in particular to act through the republican parliaments. The chairman of the USSR

Supreme Soviet, A. Luk'yanov, tried to reassure the delegates that the Soviet parliament agreed that the self-management councils should have the right to decide all the matters that affect the vital interests of the workers. He invited them to work with the parliament in revising the Laws on the Enterprise and on Property, which, he admitted, had already been overtaken by events. But not all delegates were reassured. Sergei Novopol'skii of the AZLK factory explained that "It does not depend on promises and declarations and not even on the intentions of the other side, but on our decisiveness. If they do not carry out our demands, we will declare a strike." [69]

A dominant theme of the discussions was the danger of a quiet appropriation of state property by bureaucratic clans who are adapting the market to their interests. Much evidence, along the lines cited earlier in this article, was brought to support that fear. The Union's programme of immediate measures took note of the "critical situation in the country linked to the attempt by the administrative-command system to consolidate its power through the appropriation of the property belonging in common to the people and to leave the toilers in the situation of hired labourers deprived of rights". It called on the councils to convene their collectives to hear reports from the administration on its activity "including [that relating to] joint enterprises, small enterprises, co-operatives, as well as its participation in associations and concerns [. . .] and to stop any attempts to transform enterprises behind the back of the collective into concerns, joint stock companies, etc."

The Union's basic goals are the achievement of "legal guarantees and the realization in practice of the voluntary and free choice by the work collectives of forms of property and management", as well as the "drawing of work collectives into the process of managing their enterprises, as one of the main ways of fighting against the totalitarian system in the aim of overcoming the alienation of the toilers from power and from property and the liquidation of the cruel exploitation of the people by the barrack-bureaucratic state". Finally, the "Union unites the labour collectives in the aim of mobilizing their civic activity as a factor for the general improvement of the situation in the country, as a factor of constant positive pressure from below on legislative and executive organs, and, finally, as a factor that will block anti-popular actions and facilitate the precise and swift execution of plans and decisions in the interests of the toilers." [70]

The Self-Management Movement and the Socialist Alternative
From a socialist point of view, the programme of the new Union is not unambiguous, and it is worth looking first at some of the potential dangers it presents. As already noted, although the inalienable and

indivisible nature of the collective's property flows logically from the programme, this is never made explicit. More importantly, there is no overall economic conception. The Union clearly supports market reform (although this too is not really spelled out), but is this reform to lead to a system defined by market relations, i.e. one in which the market dominates and dictates its logic to society, or to one where market relations are a mechanism of economic regulation and co-ordination subordinated to the collective, conscious will of the society? It could be argued that the movement's emphasis on enter-prise autonomy and on ownership by the collective can serve as a basis for an eventual restoration of capitalism as well as for the construction of a socialist economy based upon self-management, depending on whether the accent is on the market or on the collective power of the workers. If it is on the former, there seems little more reason to welcome monopolism based upon workers' self-management than bureaucratic monopolism; both involve the pursuit of particular, corporatist interests at the expense of the collectivity.

With Gorbachev moving to the "right" (in particular his attempt to shore up the Union and the disintegrating economy through extra-ordinary presidential powers based upon a greater reliance on the army and KGB and his appointment of conservatives to certain top posts) and the realization among liberals that "destatization" is not proceeding as they would like (that is, in a way that would give ample influence and reward to the intellectual élite and to a private sector not dependent on bureaucratic whims), some liberals are already toying with the idea of an alliance with the self-management movement, hoping to dominate it. Gavriil Popov has publicly warned of two possible variants of privatization: "the transfer as property to the bureaucracy (along with the trade mafia) of that which they have, so to speak, already been 'managing' so successfully; or democratic privatization, with transfer of the enterprises to the toilers".[71] (A supporter of the 500-Day Plan, Popov no more really wants to see the second option realized than do the bureaucrats he is attacking.) Igor Klyamkin, one of the most insightful liberal ideologues, has now also come around to seeing in Gorbachev the leader of the "revolution from above". Yel'stin, on the other hand, represents for him "new [unnamed] forces"; Yel'tsin wants a "different [unspecified] kind of market". Klyamkin laments the fact that nationalism cannot serve as a basis for "democracy" (i.e. for the liberal intelligentsia and its restorationist project) in Russia, as it does in the other republics. He suggests, however, that such a basis might be constructed from the struggles provoked by destatization, and he calls for "a broad bloc of employees and entrepreneurs".[72]

The hopes pinned on this tactic of harnessing the popular

movement to the liberal programme in the Russian Republic by play-ing up the opposition of a supposedly democratic republican parlia-ment led by Yel'tsin to the undemocratic central government and parliament led by Gorbachev have some basis. The tactic has a major trump in Yel'tsin's personal popularity as an outspoken opponent of the Establishment (though there are some signs that his star too might be waning). Thus, the workers of the VAZ assembly-line, whose resolution was cited above, appealed to Yel'tsin and the Russian parliament to defend their self-management rights against the central government. The programme of the December Congress called on the collectives to work through their republican parliaments and to push for the transfer of their enterprises from Union to republican jurisdiction.

Nevertheless, the liberals' attempt to win the self-management movement to their cause has slight chance of success: their market reform is no more compatible with a revolution from below and genuine self-management than that of the reformist wing of the bureaucracy. And these two groups need each other to realize their programmes, which are really not that different.[73] It was only a little over a year ago that Klyamkin himself wrote that the transition to the market could not be achieved democratically, since the workers are too attached to the idea of social justice.[74] Now, after suddenly "discovering" that Gorbachev, in contrast to Yel'tsin, has embraced the "revolution from above", he nevertheless still concludes (not at all disapprovingly) that a Gorbachev-Yel'tsin alliance is inevitable, though for good measure he adds that it will be a stormy union of convenience. As Sergei Stankevich, deputy mayor of Moscow and one of the leaders of the liberal "Interregional Group" in the USSR Parlia-ment put it in the closing days of 1990: "The situation in the country is critical and by ordinary parliamentary methods, using only our newly-born and still ineffective democracy, it will be impossible to resolve our problems. Therefore, we need a more authoritarian leadership of the reform process."[75] The liberals' so far feeble reaction to Gorbachev's shift to the "right" indicates that Stankevich's views are widely shared by his colleagues, or that, in any case, they can find no acceptable alternative to Gorbachev.

Of course, few would deny the need to restore some semblance of order in the economy. The Presidential decree reactivating and stgrengthening "workers' control" of trade (to be aided by the KGB!) should be seen as a populist gesture on Gorbachev's part.[76] But this measure is not really intended to change the relations of power in the economy. The unmistakable thrust of Gorbachev's latest shift (cer-tainly not his last — the "revolution from above" has only one possible programme: the market) is toward bureaucratic recentralization, which in practice necessarily means strengthening the power of the economic managers vis-à-vis the workers. The All-Union Meeting of Managers of State Enterprises that took place at almost the same time as the self-management congress adopted a strong law-and-order resolution. In contrast to the workers' congress, this gathering, held in the Kremlin's Palace of Congresses, was addressed by Gorbachev himself and received broad press coverage.[77]

As the liberal-apparatus alliance becomes more explicit, so the liberals' success in winning popular support by posing as the only real democrats and the most fearless enemies of the bureaucracy declines. On the other hand, socialists, who so far have remained relatively isolated from their potential social base, are the only ones who embrace the revolution from below and put forth a consistent democratic programme. The self-management movement thus opens up new possibilities for breaking their isolation. Summing up political developments in 1990, Pavel Voshchanov, political observer for *Komsomol'skaya pravda*, lamented "a mass shift to the right in consciousness [. . .] The discrediting of the democratic idea is one of the political outcomes of this last year." By "democratic idea", Voshchanov, of course, means "liberalism". His use of the term "right" is more ambiguous, since it can refer to conservative "defenders of socialism" as well as to genuine socialists (these two groups are indistinguishable to liberals, who are in complete agreement with the conservatives that socialism has already been constructed in the Soviet Union). But there is no evidence of a shift in mass consciousness toward the conservatives, either of the Stalinist or of the Pamyat' (Great-Russian chauvinist) type. On the contrary, the emergence of an organized self-management current demonstrates the continued strength of democratic sentiment among the workers.

The creation of the Union of Work-Collective Committees is itself a sign of the weakening of liberal ideological influence in an important sector of the labour movement. The recognition of the need for co-ordinating their activities indicates that self-management activists are beginning to understand the limits of a corporatist approach to their struggle for enterprise autonomy. Such an approach, which has received strong encouragement from liberals, was to a large degree a spontaneous reaction on the workers' part to their experience with bureaucratic centralism. But this seems to be changing under the impact of what they have already experienced of the market and the threat posed by the growing economic dislocation. "Certain elements very much would like to split up the workers as potential owners," explained a delegate to the Congress from the Elabuga auto factory. "When they are isolated from each other, it will be easier to manipulate them in the service of alien interests. This is one of the reasons we called the congress."[78] Much was said at the congress of the need for a strong central authority capable of restoring respect for laws and harmony among the republics, uniting regions and establishing stable economic relations in a unified economic space. But the congress rejected Gorbachev's authoritarian solution. According to V. Kataev, a delegate from Cheboksar:

> Such an authority cannot be established from above with the aid of a club and decrees. It will be established by the work collectives themselves if they become the complete masters of the socialist property. In that case, as the resolution of the Congress states, the work-collective as owners are prepared to bear full responsibility for the results of the economic activity of their enterprises and for order in the country.[79]

V. Adrianov, co-chairman of the Union and a mechanic on the VAZ assembly line, expressed the outlook of the self-management movement in the following terms:

> The work-collective councils in the enterprises were born of the perestroika. But from the very start, they were separated from each other. Today the time has come to unite. Why? We are standing on the threshold of the market. We are not indifferent when it comes to who will get that part of the national property that will undergo destatization. The aim of our union: through common efforts, to win the possibility for every collective to itself choose the form of property, to itself become, if it so desires, the owner of its enterprise without payment. Only the workers, having become the master, the owners of the property, are capable of stopping the advancing chaos in the economy.
>
> The programmes of transition to the market that have been adopted contain within them the danger of violation of the workers' interests. Exploiting the confusion, the administrative-command apparatus is attempting not only to hold onto the reigns of management, but to become in fact the owners of the means of production, creating concerns, associations, joint-stock companies. As for us, we are left the role of hired labour, the draught force of the economy. We cannot and simply do not have the right to allow that.[80]

If the workers are really going to prevent this, they will have to take up the fight for a socialist path of development. For it alone holds out the prospect of genuine democratization of economic and political relations. While the liberals form alliances with the apparatus in order to push through by authoritarian means a reform that would leave economic power in the hands of a small élite, the socialists emerge as the only real democrats. In a joint declaration at the end of September 1990, a coalition of left parties and groups in Moscow condemned the official reform programmes as:

> One more social experiment that would maintain power and property in a new form in the hands of the party-state bureaucracy and the "affairistes" of the shadow economy. The bosses of the [Brezhnev] period of stagnation want to change the form of their domination. [. . .] And once again, the burden of these transformations will fall entirely upon the shoulders of ordinary people [. . .] Yesterday's "irreconcilable" fighters against the privileges of the partocracy are prepared today

to defend the power of the same nomenklatura, with the only difference that now transactions will occur in cash [pod nalichnyi raschet]. [. . .] The slogans of justice, humanism, and charity, under which the democratic movement of the Perestroika period developed, have been replaced by calls for a cruel economy, a firm hand, and the auctioning off of the nation's wealth. [. . .] It is necessary to overcome the false alternative between totalitarianism and a monopoly-dominated capitalist market and to take our own path, determined by the creative activity of the people where they live and work and by the unity of their actions as a people. In this work, our sympathies lie with social, production and territorial self-management, though this too cannot be imposed from above.

Among the immediate measures proposed in the declaration are: the right of work collectives to determine independently, without purchase, the forms of property, management and self-management in their enterprises; the right of local soviets to manage land and natural resources, monitored by public organizations; the right of republics and other territorial formations to independently determine their status as well as the powers they voluntarily delegate to superordinate organizations; the abolition of presidential power; democratic opposition to the creation of authoritarian national states that refuse national and civil rights to their own minorities; the consistent introduction of full human rights, in particular the abolition of the death penalty, of anti-strike legislation, of all forms of forced labour, of the internal passport regime, and of the political police; the right of the local population through their soviets and through referenda to veto the construction of enterprises on their territory.[81]

Such is the state of glasnost' that none of the mass newspapers would agree to print this declaration. But despite the obstacles posed by the liberal quasi-monopoly of the mass media (tempered only by the minority conservative media), the profoundly democratic nature of the labour movement, and more particularly, the appearance of an organized self-management current within it, give new grounds for optimism about the eventual development of an active, mass base for socialism in the Soviet Union.

NOTES

1. I would like to thank Allen Fenichel, Andrea Levy, Dave Melnychuk and Leo Panitch for their helpful comments on an earlier draft of this arfticle.
2. *Sovetskaya Rossiya*, October 10, 1990.
3. *Rabochaya tribuna*, September 4, 1990.
4. The average industrial wage is about 260 roubles a month.
5. *Komsomol'skaya pravda*, December 12, 1990.
6. *Trud*, July 11, 1990.
7. *Sovetskaya Rossiya*, September 30, 1990.
8. A related term, less frequently used, is "bandokratiya" (from the word "banda" — gang), which one economist has defined as "organized crime that has grown

up on the basis of bureaucratism and merged with it economically, socially and even politically". A. Buzgalin, "Est' li u nas ekspluatatsiyaz", *Sovetskie profsoyuzy*, no. 17-18, 1990, p. 26.

9. Many factors, of course, contribute to the shortages, but among these, monopoly behaviour occupies a special place. For an analysis of the role of monopoly in the Soviet economy, see V. Bogachev, "Monopoliya v sovetskoi ekonomike", *Ekonomicheskie nauki*, no. 6, 1990, pp. 11-22.

10. *Kuranty* (Moscow), October 4, 1990.

11. *Rabochaya tribuna*, October 9, 1990.

12. *Vechernyaya Moskva*, September 27, 1990.

13. "Apteka gde est' vse", *Nedelya*, no. 41, October 8, 1990, p. 5.

14. G. German, "Ochered' ", *Rabochii vestnik* (Perm'), no. 5, May 1990, p. 3.

15. Central Soviet television, September 21, 1990. At the same session, Sukhov also called on the leadership to be honest enough to admit that the better life they are proposing is one that will take place under capitalism. In that case, he suggested, the Communist Party's name should be changed to the Capitalist Party.

16. Soviet co-operatives are often ordinary private enterprises that employ hired labour. Asked in September 1990 what would happen if the state legalized private property, Artem Tarasov, vice-president of the Union of Co-operators, answered: "Nothing. We would simply get rid of the camouflage and call things by their names. [. . .] My co-operative would become a company with private capital." *Rabochaya tribuna*, September 4, 1990.

17. T. Bogacheva, "Rasgosudarastvelenie — ne razgrablenie", *Pravitel'stvennyi vestnik*, no. 50, December 1990, p. 6.

18. Such is the finding of a Moscow research institute. Personal communication by M. Malyutin, director of the sociological service of the Moscow Soviet.

19. I. Litvinova, "Zaslon spekulyatsii", *Nedelya*, no. 42, October 15, 1990, p. 4.

20. Private communications from German and Italian businessmen.

21. From Leningrad television, November 5, 1990. Smolnyi, once a school for girls of the nobility, was seized by the Bolsheviks and other revolutionary organizations in 1917.

22. *Komsomol'skaya pravda*, October 3, 1990.

23. *Rabochaya tribuna*, December 9, 1990.

24. Non-Russian readers will find Soviet analyses that share this basic framework in D. Mandel (ed.), *La perestroika: économie et société*, Québec: Presses de l'Université du Québec, 1990 (articles by V. Bogachev, V. Dementev, Yu Sukhotin) as well as in the review *Alternatives* (Montreal and Moscow) no. 1, forthcoming Spring 1991 (articles by V. Buzgalin, B. Kagarlitskii, A. Kolganov, Yu Sukhotin, G. Rakitskaya, B. Rakitskii). For an attempt to briefly summarize the position common to many of the Soviet socialists, see D. Mandel, "A Market Without Thorns: the Ideological Struggle for the Soviet Working Class", *Studies in Political Economy* (Ottawa), no. 38, Autumn 1990, pp. 30-36.

25. *Trud*, December 30, 1990.

26. Soviet liberals oppose "common human values", that supposedly predominate in "normal" (capitalist) societies to the "class values", which allegedly inspired Stalinism. This has prompted one Leningrad socialist to quip that the "common human values" of the liberals must surely be dollars.

27. L. Radzikhovskii, "Kapitalizm v otdel'no vzyatoi kvartire", *Nedelya*, no. 48, November 25, 1990, p. 7.

28. V. Dudchenko and A. Karpov, "O vozmozhnykh posledstviyakh naibolee ochevidnogo i pryamogo puti k privatizatsii", Septem,ber 2, 1990 (unpublished document). The author's are leaders of the Leningrad social democrats. Karpov is a delegate to the Leningrad Soviet and a member of its economic reform commission.

29. O. Savel'ev, "Politicheskaya situatsiya v Leningrade", August 25, 1990 (unpublished document); O. Savel'ev, "Obsluzhivanie demokratii", *Informatsionnyi byulleten' Sotsial-demoraticheskoi assotsiatsii* (Leningrad), no. 24, September 1990. This account is also partly based on conversations with social-democratic leaders.

30. See D. Mandel, "Revolutionary Reform in Soviet Factories: Restructuring Relations between Workers and Management", *Socialist Register 1989*, London: Merlin Press, 1989, pp. 102-29. On the miners' movement, see T. Friedgut and L. Siegelbaum, "Perestroika from Below: the Miners' Strike and Its Aftermath", *New Left Review*, 1990, pp. 5-32; David Mandel, "Rebirth of the Soviet Labor Movement: The Coalminers' Strike of July 1989, *Politics and Society*, vol. 18, no. 3, September 1990, pp. 381-404.

31. *Pravda*, February 8, 1990. This account is based mainly on interviews and a recording of the January meeting.

32. *Za sovestskuyu malotirazhku* (Moscow), February 5, 1990.

33. "Demokratisatsiya na proizvodstve: vlast' dela i vlast' . . . ch'ya?", *EKO*, (Novosibirsk), no. 8, 1990, pp. 85-102.

34. *Rabochaya tribuna*, June 15, 1990.

35. The view is widespread among workers that "those people" do not work. Another contributing factor is the wage reform that began in 1987 and under which the salaries of technical and administrative personnel have risen significantly faster than wages. V. Pavlov and I. Yurchikova, "Novye usloviya oplaty truda", *Sotsialisticheskii trud*, no. 8, 1990, p. 89.

36. "Demokratizatsiya na proizvodstve. . .", p. 96.

37. *Rabochaya tribuna*, August 15, 1990.

38. *Rabochaya tribuna*, June 15, 1990.

39. A. N. Shkulov, "Na potustoronnnei traektorii", *EKO*, no. 8, 1980, pp. 108-9.

40. *Rabochaya tribuna*, December 8, 1990.

41. *Nasha gazeta* (Novokuznetsk), no. 33, October 2, 1990.

42. P. Funder Larsen, "La Confédération du travail", *Inprecor* (Paris), no. 312, June 26, 1990, pp. 9-12 and B. Ikhlov, "Neklassovyi vrag", *Rabochii vetsnik* (Perm'), no. 5, May 1990, pp. 4-7.

43. This was noted, for example, by V. Golikov, chairman of the Kuzbass Union of Workers' Committees, in his report to the Fifth Conference on September 29-30, 1990. See *Nasha gazeta*, no. 33, October 2, 1990.

44. This is based upon conversations and on the unpublished proceedings.

45. *Kazanskii rabochii* (Kazan'), no. 2, July 1990.

46. People close to the (official) Union of Workers of the Coal Industry claimed that the minister favoured the creation of a new trade union in order to split the workers. While there is probably some truth to this, most of the delegates to the Miners' Congress that founded the new union were of the opinion that any further attempts to reform the old union would be futile.

47. A summary of this programme appeared in *Komsomol'skaya pravda*, September 29, 1990. For an analysis of this programme and a comparison with the USSR government's "Basic Orientations for the Stabilization of the Economy and the Transition to a Market Economy", see A. Kolganov, "Doloi nomenklaturnyi kapitalizm!", *Dialog*, no. 17, November 1990, pp. 41-8.

48. *Nasha gazeta*, no. 33, October 2, 1990.

49. The editors of the popular weekly *Argumenty i fakty* rejected, without any explanation, an article by one of their reporters about these telegrams. This perhaps has something to do with the fact that five members of the editorial committee are deputies in the Russian parliament, which adopted the 500-Day Plan with only one opposing vote, even though few of the deputies had seen more than a brief summary of it.

50.   *Rabochaya tribuna*, September 25, 1990.
51.   *Komsomol'skaya pravda*, October 4, 1990.
52.   *Rabochaya tribuna*, October 21, 1990.
53.   Personal communication. The Confederation of Labour was founded by the Congress of Independent Workers' Organizations and Movements in Novokuznetsk in May 1990.
54.   From the unpublished protocols and personal conversations. At one point, Golikov tried to reassure the Donbass miners, saying that Kuzbass had helped the British miners during their strike; why think that they would not help their Donbass brethren?
55.   According to the bulletin of the Workers Group in the Yaroslavl' Popular Front, "Many intellectual democrats talk of the need for a union of the democratic intelligentsia and the workers. It sounds nice. But what they mean in practice can be seen from the example of the Yaroslavl' Popular Front. [. . .] They rejected from the very start the idea that the Popular Front should seek a social base in the workers and they observed with gloomy apprehension from the sidelines the activity of the Workers' Group. The Popular Front not only did nothing for the organization of Yaroslavl's workers, but it simply does not want the creation of real workers' and really independent workers' organizations. [. . .] They mouth off about 'common human interests' and toss out stupidities from the tribune to the effect that 'the class approach leads to genocide'." From *Listok Rabochei Gruppy* (Yaroslavl') reproduced in *Rabochaya tribuna*, November 7, 1990.

      For analyses of the debates at the Congress of Independent Worker Organizations and Movement on this issue, see P. Funder Larsen, "La Confédération du travail", *Inprecor* (Paris), no. 312, June 26, 1990, pp. 9-12 and B. Ikhlov, "Neklassovyi vrag", *Rabochii vetsnik* (Perm'), no. 5, May 1990, pp. 4-7.
56.   *Rabochii vestnik* (Perm'), no. 5, May 1990, p. 11.
57.   For a brief discussion of the ambiguous self-management provisions of the 1987 law, see D. Mandel, "Revolutionary Reform. . .", p. 110.
58.   *Rabochaya tribuna*, December 6, 1990.
59.   *Sobstvennoe mnenie* (Togliatti), no. 7. 1990.
60.   "Demokratizatsiya na proizvodstve. . .", p. 85.
61.   *Rabochaya tribuna*, April 22, 1990. See also, R. W. Davies, "Gorbachev's Socialism in Historical Perspective", *New Left Review*, Spring 1990, pp. 22-3.
62.   Of the sundry liberal parties, Travkin's has made the most effort to court workers. Travkin himself, who rather dubiously claims he was once a worker (at present, he is a businessman and politician), regularly appears at large worker gatherings, spreading his message of primitive anti-communism. So far, he has had little success among the workers, who have generally been withholding their allegiance from all political parties.
63.   In December 1990, Gorbachev disbanded this largely symbolic advisory council, one of whose main purposes seems to have been to co-opt potential opposition. Yarin, a metallurgical worker, has been co-chairman of the anti-liberal United Front of Toilers. He liked to say that after 30 years at the factory, all the property he had accumulated was what he was wearing. As member of the Presidential Council, Yarin enjoyed a spacious apartment, trips abroad, a generous salary, and, of course, much official honour. It did not take him long to come around fully to Gorbachev's policies. The United Front of Toilers, whose fortunes have been flagging since its foundation in the Summer of 1989 (its worker support is quite thin), recently ousted Yarin. (According to Yarin, he resigned.)
64.   "Privatization" and "destatiation" (razgosudarstvlenie) are often used interchangeably in the Soviet Union. This confusion, of course, speaks loudly.

65. See note 47. The 500-Day Plan gives the work collective one month to propose a form of property for the enterprise, but the decision remains that of the state authorities. It also allows that 10% of the stocks "may be transferred" (this apparently also depends on the discretion of the authorities) to the enterprise for sale or transfer on preferential terms to members of the work collective (not to the collective as a group).

66. This account is based upon personal communications from participants and *Rabochaya tribuna*, September 9, 1990.

67. *Rabochaya tribuna*, December 8, 1990. Parts of this account are based upon personal communications. The still incomplete representation at this congress was explained by the organizational committee's limited resources. The original decision had been to invite delegates only from regional unions of work-collective councils. But since these had not yet been established everywhere, requests from individual councils were accepted. But the organizational committee still had no bulletin, and not all councils learnt of this change.

68. These are a mechanic-assembler from VAZ, an engineer from the new Elabuga auto factory, and the chairman of the work-collective council of the Moscow Kauchuk rubber factory.

69. *Rabochaya tribuna*, December 12, 1990.

70. Unpublished document.

71. Radzikhovskii, "Kapitalizm. . .". Of Popov, Moscow wags say that "he is capable, even very capable, indeed capable of anything".

72. I. Klyamkin, "Oktyabr'skii vybor prezidenta", *Ogonek*, no. 47, November 1990, p. 7. Klyamkin uses the term "rabotniki" (very roughly translated as "employees"), which is even less socially defined than "trudyashchiesya" (toilers), the term usually preferred by liberals. Use of the word "rabochie", workers, is generally shunned, since it might imply the existence of separate working class interests.

73. In the view of A. Kolganov, a Marxist economist at Moscow University, "the '500 Days' are based upon a bloc between the 'new rich' and the party-economic bureaucracy on terms dictated by the 'new rich'. The Union programme calls for a smoother, less painful path of transformation of the bureaucracy into 'new rich', naturally, on its own terms, not forgetting to toss a little something to the people so that it, God forbid, will not interfere in this process". A. Kolganov, "Doloi nomenklaturnyi kapitalizm", *Dialog*, no. 17, November 1990, p. 45.

74. E. Bérard-Zarzicka, "Quelques propositions pour une perestroika autoritaire", *Les temps modernes* (Paris), no. 523, February 1990, pp. 11-22.

75. *Komsomol'skaya pravda*, December 30, 1990.

76. *Trud*, December 2, 1990.

77. *Rabochaya tribuna*, December 8, 9 and 11, 1990.

78. *Rabochaya tribuna*, December 6, 1990.

79. *Ibid.*

80. *Rabochaya tribuna*, December 8, 1990.

81. For a French translation of this document, see *Inprecor*, no. 318, November 9, 1990. The signatories included representatives of the Socialist Party, the Green Party, the Confederation of Anarcho-Syndicalists, the Marxist Platform in the CPSU (which has since split), the Committee to Aid the Labour and Self-Management Movements, the Social-Democratic Party of the Russian Federation, and "Moscow Memorial". (The last two organizations have socialist as well as liberal currents.)

PERESTROIKA AND THE NEO-LIBERAL PROJECT

Patrick Flaherty

The time has come to stop swearing allegiance to the dogmas of the Marxist faith, and to return to common sense, universal human experience, and the eternal moral commandments which have not yet let the people down. Will we not find our salvation and a way out of the impasse in these?

Introduction

Abjurations of the Communist God that Failed have become a social ritual surpassing even an ostentatious religious revival and astrological consultations as diversions among the Soviet intelligentsia during the Summer of 1990. The above quote is a typical example of a published mea culpa in which the well-heeled author berates himself for not having sooner found the "courage of Andrei Sakharov" to denounce the cruelty and injustices of socialist totalitarianism. Even two years ago, a public statement of this kind whatever its political colouration involved risk and would have to be regarded as bona fide proof of the depth of the author's convictions. But after the rout of a decadent Right, such acts of public self-flagellation invite the charge that old opportunists are now seizing on new opportunities and making a second career out of leaving the CPSU. The article cited above was written by Oleg Bogomolov and entitled "I Cannot Absolve Myself from Guilt" [Bogomolov, 1990a]. The head of a leading Soviet think-tank on international affairs admitted the failure of his life-long endeavour to reform the system from within and announced his intention to resign from the party. This recantation would sound more credible if Bogomolov's institute did not provide a haven to influential policy intellectuals preaching a Russified form of Ordo-Liberalism with unmistakable authoritarian implications in its vision of a free market and a strong state. Bogomolov's sudden ideological conversion provides an extravagant example of the realignment now taking place within the dominant class as different fractions vie for power in a Post-Stalinist Soviet Union.

The ideological debates of the first stage of the Perestroika have been dominated by this sort of "socialist Friedmanism" which offers a

128

sweeping privatization of the economy and professionalized de-politicization of administration as the sovereign remedies to the Soviet economic crisis [Kornai, 1987, p. 25]. The many strands of Soviet neo-liberalism converge on at least a verbal acknowledgement of the self-regulating market as the paramount social institution and core institutional nexus of a "normal" society. During the Neo-Stalinist retrenchment of the early seventies, ginger groups of neo-liberal intellectuals were allowed to go on working at various academic think-tanks like Bogomolov's Institute under the protection of influential apparatus "uncles" such as Iurii Andropov who headed the KGB from 1967 to 1982. From these safe harbours, neo-liberal intellectuals were able to enter the reform struggle of the mid-eighties with the most coherent and well informed critiques of the old regime. As a result, their ideas took centre stage during the opening skermishes of the reform discussions. The expressed aim of the neo-liberals was to supplant the decadent Real Socialism of the Brezhnev era with what they at first coyly described as a "realistic socialism". With the Neo-Stalinist system collapsing under the weight of its own internal contradictions, many neo-liberals are no longer bothering to disguise their enthusiasm for a "capitalization" of the Soviet system. One Soviet journalist even paraphrased Nikita Khrushchev's famous promise to read: "Will the present generation of the Soviet people live under capitalism" [Bobrovskii 1990]? This article will try to answer this question by examining the political origins, social foundation, and ideological programme of Soviet neo-liberalism. My primary aim is to sift out of its programme those essential themes which prefigure the neo-liberal future, and assess its potential for becoming a majoritarian political project. The paper is divided into the following sections:

I.   The Political Sociology of Soviet Neo-Liberalism.
II.   Neo-Liberal Political Strategy.
III.   The New Inequality.
IV.   Social Policy.
V.   Employment Policy.
VI.   Working Class Integration and Self-Management.
VII.   Neo-Liberal Economics.
VIII.   Conclusion.

I. *The Political Sociology of Soviet Neo-Liberalism*
The Brezhnevian *Zastoi* or Stagnation attempted to arrest forces of change which had been set in motion long before the Neo-Stalinist retrenchment of the late 1960s. But despite all attempts at repression, a modern secularized society continued to push its way up through the thin crust of an exhausted and antiquated system. Increasing demands

on the administrative machinery fostered a structural differentiation whose most obvious outward manifestation was the fissioning of ministries and industrial branch offices from 37 in 1957 to 60 in 1974 and almost 100 by 1988 [Rossolov, 1989, p. 157]. The multiplication of bureaucratic structures and the expansion of existing agencies were propelled by a doubling of the operational paper flow of the apparatus from an average of 30 billion pages a year during the 1960s to 60 billion pages a year in the 1970s. Roughly 80 percent of all administrative activity is now devoted to the processing of techno-economic information which theoretically at least involves the reasoned evaluation of 10 quadrillion (10,000,000,000,000,000) individual economic or political signals a year. The exponential growth of the paper flow in the administrative network reflected a proliferation of social interdependencies which created the objective need for a qualitative transformation of the command-administrative system. The defeat of the first wave of de-Stalinization enabled a dirigistic administrative system pretending to an illusory omni-competence to endure long beyond the phase of relatively un-complicated extensive growth for which it was originally designed.

The Soviet Union underwent decades of a state-led economic modernization and social mobilization. During the Stalin era, social mobilization was largely sublimated into individual mobility across class lines into a rapidly expanding command-administrative power structure. But the country has not yet undergone a real political mobilization in which elite fractions and functional groups outside the oligarchical strata of the dominant class were permitted to organize their common interests into political programmes and campaign for popular support. Reform from above was effectively precluded during the Brezhnev era because it would have upset precarious political equilibria within a closed power elite. Clientelism instead of a greater degree of elite pluralism became the preferred means of arbitrating differences within the Soviet dominant class [Sapir, 1989, p. 146]. The Brezhnevian coalition sought to broaden its elite base by cooptation or the practice of absorbing into its ranks the upper strata of ascendant functional elites and some segments of the intelligentsia [Hankiss, 1989, p. 16]. Coopted elite strata enjoyed greater privileged access to material goods, enhanced social prestige, and perhaps even reinforced clout within their own institutional preserves. But their honorary status within the councils of power confined them to playing at best a purely advisory role in the actual policy-making process.

If the class nature of a society is defined by the principal means through which the surplus is extracted by the dominant class, then the predominant mode of production in the Soviet Union can best be described as a statist system where exploitation is mediated primarily through administrative processes. Economic and political power remains almost entirely predicated on a monopoly of state or public property which provides a "splendid cover for private appropriation" by an administrative class which can pass all the risks and liabilities along to the central authorities. [Dzarasov, 1990, p. 80]. The Brezhnev government fortified the neo-Stalinist system with a rampart of overlapping oligarchical, clientelistic, and nepotistic networks [Hankiss, 1989, p. 22]. This perimeter was in turn reinforced by a "corrupt interweaving" of venal party-state cadre and underground entrepreneurial elites who all seek to capitalize on the defects of a demonetized bureaucratic market [Hankiss, 1989, p. 25].

After an initial half-hearted attempt to become a rationalized consultative authoritarianism, the neo-Stalinist power structure settled down into another historical example of a degenerate *vincolismo*. Segments of a dominant class which had outlived their usefulness as far as optimal economic development was concerned, sought to preserve their political pre-eminence by walling themselves off as much as possible from ascendant social forces through elaborate forms of protectionism and sinecurism [Burlatskii, 1985, p. 143]. One example of the inability of the cooptative mechanism to absorb a critical mass of the upwardly mobile was provided in an article by an Omsk journalist. He complained that only 0.8 of the college-educated specialists working in the agricultural production of the region headed a production collective, while most of present managerial strata were the beneficiaries of apparatus nepotism [Shpakov, 1987]. The prevalence of these practices was evident in the warnings of a sociologist about the detrimental effects on social morale of political inbreeding where the "privileged strata of our society are increasingly reproducing themselves across generations, and thereby causing these strata to become even more closed" to talented and ambitious newcomers from other elite groups outside the charmed circle [Naumova, 1990, p. 9]. She faulted the nomenklatura old guard not only for its blatant corruption but also a suicidal "unwillingness to share its growing income with the middle strata entrepreneurs and skilled workers". As Brezhnevism slipped further into catalepsy and real wages stopped growing after 1976, the co-optative mechanisms gradually lost their ability to ward off the emergence of counter-elites both within the nomenklatura and outside it. Fundamental economic change was impossible without a sweeping reallocation of power within the dominant class and the re-ordering of the hierarchy of elites.

An Italian journalist described the "cold and determined anti-ouvrierism" that she had often encountered among reform-minded intellectuals in the Soviet Union [Rossanda, 1987]. In pre-revolutionary Russia, distrust of the *Nizy* or plebeian classes drove much of the national liberal intelligentsia into a de facto alliance with Tsarism. Liberal fears of a popular revolutionary animus were reflected most abjectly in the Westernizing ideology of *Vekhi* or Landmarks. A Soviet left-wing emigré noted how the liberal dissident movement of the 1960s and 1970s recoiled from the prevailing paternalistic Marxist orthodoxy towards an indiscriminate *Narodofobia* (demophobia) [Belotserkovskii, 1985, p. 108]:

> The worker was always the social base of communism or fascism. In the future Russia, we must drive them down below. To the galleys with them. Let them have television and other household conveniences but keep them down below.

The working class on the whole was perceived as a privileged social constituency of the Brezhnevian social contract and a silent majority of "lumpen-elements" which upheld authoritarian rule [Gordon, 1987, p. 2]. This objective alliance between the nomenklatura and the industrial working class was cemented by the "common pot" of a welfare state which enabled the right to integrate workers into its political base and repulse any attempt at reform [Lisichkin, 1987]. In light of this political sociology, the only alternative for realistic reformers was to place their trust in the lofty sensibilities of modernizing elites. Since Stalinism had such deep plebeian roots, a mass movement against the apparatus must be restrained from becoming a democratizing revolution because it would result in the empowerment of totalitarian mass man. This reasoning dictated that the political overthrow of the nomenklatura should be limited to a liberalizing circulation of elites and no more.

This liberal elitism had earlier been given a academic pedigree by Oleg Shkaratan during the reform debates of the late 1960s. The labour sociologist contended that as a result of the past fifty years of meritocratic natural selection, the scientific-technical intelligentsia and the most highly skilled strata of the working class had finally coalesced into the "social core" of a new collective proletariat [Shkaratan, 1970, p. 463-4]. At the head of this collective proletariat should march "those vanguards which by the breadth of their political horizon, by their specialized knowledge and implementation of this knowledge in the struggle for the construction of a new society, most fully express the demands of the scientific-technical revolution as well as the tasks of social progress". Shkaratan identified these ascendant functional groups as the main driving force of a second industrial revolution. The clear political implication of his analysis was that if the Soviet Union was to meet the challenge of a new era, the government had to shift its social base from a now genetically impoverished working class to a radically reconfigured inter-class alliance centred on the intelligentsia. Shkaratan's ideological daring earned him an official party reprimand and academic demotion from a Brezhnev government whose core vested interests felt themselves mortally threatened by even the mention of the possibility of such a coalition.

The disciplining of Shkaratan and a number of other liberal sociologists drove this techno-biological elitism underground, only to have it resurface again in forms both ominous and ludicrous. The seventies witnessed a flurry of genetically rationalized justifications of inequality and hierarchy which essentially repackaged the theorems of Western sociobiology under the rubric of a "highly humane socialist eugenics" [cited in Dubinin, 1980, p. 70]. The modishness of this Social Darwinism within some segments of the liberal intelligentsia prompted an internationally respected biologist to publish a critique of these tracts which spelled out their profoundly reactionary implications in every realm from primary school tracking to an even more punitive penal system [Dubinin, 1983, p. 184].

The social tensions giving rise to this eugenics revival came closer to the surface in an 1980 essay by Aleksandr Gorbovskii who maintained that the present composition of the Writers' Union was predetermined by the "genetic code" of its individual members [Gorbovskii, 1980]. The journalist was addressing the problem that many more sought entry into the "temple of culture" than there were spaces available, and the resulting friction was fueling an increasingly "furious row" between the biologically gifted and the common run of humanity. Gorbovskii advised those overreaching "unrecognized geniuses" to abandon their quest for entry into the "social elite. . . and cultural elite which if continued, would sooner or later doom them to disillusionment and a mental breakdown". The genetically plebeian were encouraged to accept the humble station in life preordained for them by their genotype, and resolve to excel as "pot maker, ploughman" or any other menial occupation deemed compatible with their unfortunate DNA inheritance. Gorbovskii was directing his remarks to the restive dissident fringe of Soviet literati who were trying to counterpose new iconoclastic standards to the orthodox canons of excellence.

In both its refined and vulgarized forms, this techno-biological justification of an inegalitarian status quo reflected a mounting concern within some elements of the Soviet elite over the volatile concurrence of rapidly diminishing opportunities for social promotion and the swelling ranks of "pretenders" seeking access to professional-managerial strata which were becoming increasingly self-replicating [Shkaratan, 1978, p. 187]. Shkaratan's meticulous scholarship sought to legitimate social power asymmetries by the biological rationale of cognitive class differences. Gorbovskii's absurd sociobiological tract rooted an eternal social hierarchy in a genetic imperative. The common thread in these and countless other examples is the search for politically credible exclusionary devices or a set of legal-rational mechanisms which enable a dominant class to maintain and reproduce itself while preserving popular legitimacy or at least acquiescence. In the Soviet instance, this potpourri of biological and meritocratic apologetics would serve as a justification of social closure in a system whose class structure is still gelling after having undergone decades of state-led accelerated modernization with unparalleled levels of upward social mobility. The Soviet dominant class developed out of a dirigistic political-administrative system and it has yet to fully emancipate itself from this anachronistic crucible. The struggle against the Stalinist system at the elite level was in part a derivative of the long-term process of class formation within a state-created dominant class which in increasingly greater numbers seeks to assert itself against the state which had originally brought it into existence. These obscure controversies of the past three decades were the first trickles of the neo-liberal intellectual current which has moved into the mainstream of the reform debate of the nineties. The neo-liberal project has quite deliberately set out to become the "ideology of new class formation" and the main political vehicle of the restructuring of a dominant class-in-itself into a dominant class-for-itself [Semenov, 1990, p. 35].

II. *Neo-Liberal Political Strategy*

Gorbachev has been described as both a product of the old command-administrative system and a "mutant" bred by the crisis of Neo-Stalinism [Chiesa, 1990]. The party General Secretary first brought to the centre of power a new generation of nomenklatura elites who had recently been directors of major industrial complexes. These "energetic technocrats" took office confident of their ability to turn a deteriorating economic situation around by increasing investments across all fronts [Gaidar, 1990]. But this attempt to modernize the neo-Stalinist system without altering its essentials soon proved to be a futile undertaking. The Gorbachev government was then forced to consider the possibility that the Soviet economy was mired in a structural impasse which could not be surmounted by blindly continuing to press ahead with the conventional remedies. At the January 1987 Party plenum, Gorbachev for the first time openly espoused a transition strategy that called for a change of "property relations" or significant redistribution of power resources within the dominant class [Pavlov, 1990].

If Gorbachev has succeeded in anything, it was his often stated promise to restore meaningful politics to an oppressively ritualized public sphere. The Supreme Soviet elections of 1989 and 1990 demonstrated his commitment not just to liberalize the old neo-Stalinist system but actually transcend a bankrupt institutional regime. The radicalization of the party modernizers was accompanied by a radicalization of the reform intelligentsia. At the beginning of the Perestroika, the political leadership of the Soviet intelligentsia was provided by the "children of the XX Congress" or those cultural figures whose political worldview was formed during the Khrushchev Thaw [Pavlova-Silvanskaia, 1990]. Most were strongly influenced by the ideas of the Prague Spring and expected a revived party to become the main protagonist of reform. With the faltering of the first stage of the Perestroika, the political initiative gradually passed to policy intellectuals no longer content with courting the new nomenklatura reform generation and dissident party members who rose to prominence during the intra-elite struggles of the past few years. Ambartsumov described this rapid emergence of counter-elites after 1985 as the "formation of a new stratum of the ruling class" which must be absorbed into the ranks of an incompetent and compromised old elite to rejuvenate the entire political class [Ambartsumov, 1990b, p. 45]. The academic viewed these incipient trends as a classic historical example of ideas and rhetoric running well in advance of inexorable changes in social structure and broad-based political organization.

A few Soviet analysts of the Perestroika have interpreted its central political dynamic as a form of "class formation" which has been gathering momentum since the 1960s [Go, 1990, p. 116]. Some neo-liberal partisans point to the early 1970s as that decisive juncture where the "bureaucracy transformed itself into a ruling class" and the neo-Stalinist system finally lost its adaptive capacity [Kiva, 1990b]. Others perceived a "fusion of professional and bureaucratic elites" leading to the consolidation of "completely impenetrable monolithic professional-bureaucratic structures" [Khromov, 1989]. The latter analysis more accurately depicts the cooptive alliances struck between different strata of the Soviet dominant class under Brezhnev as opposed to the polarization described by Kiva. But the price of this modus vivendi was the ability of an oligarchical old guard to abort the emergence of a reindustrializing technostructure from a fusion of party modernizers and technocrats. Brezhnevism embodied the successful attempt of post-Stalinist elites to adapt a faltering command-administrative system to their narrowly conceived class interests [Bogachev, 1990, p. 41]. By the early eighties, the self-destructive growth pattern of Brezhnevism made it impossible to sustain the old coalition and latent intra-elite tensions quickly resurfaced. Subsequent attempts to realign the nomenklatura across all levels of the power structure have convulsed both the party and the Soviet dominant class as a whole. The animosity of the neo-liberals towards Brezhnevian Old Corruption is fed by the long festering resentment of counter-elites within the Soviet intelligentsia against the stifling rule of tenured nomenklatura mediocrities, the yearly waste of production resources amounting to 20 percent of total GNP, and the squandering of incalculable developmental potential [Zaichenko, 1990, p. 70]. The breakdown of the established political equilibria within the dominant class has set into motion a new dynamic of inter- and intra-class conflict and alliances of which neo-liberalism is only one tangent.

The neo-liberals are seeking to replace the tactical ouvrierism of neo-Stalinism with Shkaratan's formerly tabu ideological claim that the "major part of the scientific-technical intelligentsia is the most authentic working class" [Sobchak, 1990, p. 32]. The prospect of rapid privatization and marketization is designed to "appeal first of all to the so-called middle class, people of middle income who want to become property owners (as well as businesspeople)" [Belousov and Klepach, 1990, p. 28]. The principal constituencies of the neo-liberals were identified as the "main personages of the market": private farmers, private industrialists, private financiers, and foreign businessmen [Sokolov, 1990]. General estimates of the size of the Soviet middle class range from 15-30 percent of the entire population or 43-86 million. But many sociologists warn that this figure is greatly inflated by the inclusion of many middle-level apparatchiki and manual labourers receiving premium wages which dilute the concerted political clout of these intermediate strata [Naumova, 1990, p. 9]. The prospective constituencies of neo-liberalism can actually be drawn more precisely. In terms of income and savings, the natural political base of neo-liberalism would centre on that roughly four percent (11 million) of the entire population with a minimum average per capita monthly income of 300 roubles who control 68.9 percent of total savings deposited in Soviet banks [Shverdlik, 1990, p. 27]. In particular, the core of this social group would be the super-rich 0.7 percent possessing 54 percent of all savings. These high-income groups have been growing rapidly since the beginning of the Gorbachev era with the number of those earning a minimum per capita 300 roubles a month increasing from 1.4 percent in 1985 to 2.7 percent in 1988 and 4.3 percent in 1989 [Valiuzhenich, 1990]. But even the most fervent neo-liberals put the maximum figure of those with sufficient capital to buy into privatized enterprises at 5 percent of the workforce (6.5 million) and probably much closer in reality to 2-3 percent (2.5-4 million) [Piiasheva, 1990b]. The bedrock of these social strata is seen to be the burgeoning cooperative movement which has increased fifteen-fold over the past two years to 250,000 ventures employing 4.8 million with an annual production volume of 40 billion roubles or 6 percent of total national income [Esipov, 1990]. These social strata have already furnished much of the financial backing for neo-liberal politicians and organizations. Despite their relatively small number, these entrepreneurial strata provide one of the few solid footholds in the magma of a formative post-Stalinist politics. Alongside these are the roughly 30-100,000 underground millionaires who made their fortunes in various forms of illegal activity during the Brezhnev era [Bondarev, 1990]. An unsuccessful August 1990 proposal by neo-liberal parliamentarians to grant a blanket amnesty to all shadow economy dealers, indicates their desire to incorporate this demimonde into their political base and become in effect their lobbyists within the halls of power [Kurashvili, 1990a]. To this must be added the roughly 20-30 percent of the six million state managers said by neo-liberals to be professionally and temperamentally fit for the rigours of a private market economy [Travkin, 1990, pp. 34-35]. The primary objective of the neo-liberal project is to create the conditions for the emergence of a "new social class — a class of property owners which makes a living not by the sale of their labour to the state but through their own entrepreneurial activity conducted at their own risk and liability to facilitate the growth of capital" [Zaslavskaia et al. 1990]. The longterm ambition of neo-liberal strategists is to forge these few million nascent commercially oriented interests into the energized core of a "bloc of the most dynamic fractions of various social groups seeking the free realization of their lofty professional and cultural potentials" [Starikov, 1990, p. 41]. Their intention is to draw the main battlelines not between classes but within them by pitting the most enterprising elements in all social strata against a marginalized "bloc of stagnant social groups" which for whatever reasons do not buy into the neo-liberal vision of an opportunity society.

The tactical acumen of the neo-liberals was evident in their ability to snatch for their own reform project the ideological mantle of "left-wing" which has by far the greatest popular resonance in Soviet political discourse, and force all genuine socialist alternatives onto the defensive [Kurashvili, 1990a]. But this deft manoeuvring also suggests the difficulties that the neo-liberals expect to encounter if they attempted to sell an unadulterated programme of recapitalization to a society steeped in what they deem a crude levelling political culture. Some political commentators are sceptical of the ability of explicitly liberal bourgeois parties to broaden their political base in a society where the middle class is so small, and mainly confined to trade and distribution rather than production [Maliutin, 1990]. A more detailed sociological study predicted that the neo-liberals would never be able to extend their support beyond a "relatively small vanguard of highly skilled and motivated workers, and well-organized collectives (no more than one-third of all working people according to the most optimistic estimates)" [Sukhotin, 1988, pp. 16-19]. In plumping for a minimum tripling of present income differentials, the neo-liberals give no thought to the possibility that by raising the apex of the growth coalition, they are precariously narrowing the social base of reform [Koriagina, 1990].

This line of argument is rejected by some neo-liberal luminaries like Vasilii Seliunin who contend that the main social base of Gorbachev's left-centrist strategy is the "poorly politicized strata of the population" [Seliunin, 1990, p. 198]. This means that the majority consensus for a gradualist market transition is extremely soft, and its generally passive supporters could be expected to acquiesce if not assent when presented with the fait accomplis of a neo-liberal economic shock therapy. Even some radical sociologists such as Sergei Kara-Murza concede the possibility that the neo-liberals could become a majoritarian political force by offering a chance for individual personal enrichment even if it is necessary to accept the sacrifice of social welfare guarantees, egalitarian ideals, and the "casting out of society of that 20 percent of the population who are losers" [Kara-Murza, 1990, p. 49]. The ignominious demise of the old regime has presented the neo-liberals with a unique historical opportunity to exploit a popular loss of confidence in complex collectivist solutions and large public institutions to mobilize a sufficiently large bloc of Soviet society against the suddenly very vulnerable traditional radical egalitarian value matrix of social solidarity and the welfare state [Zupanov, 1983, p. 13]. By adopting the old Russian proverb of "Better a terrible end than terror forever", the neo-liberals are mounting an effective appeal to the apocalyptic mood of a people being worn down by political disappointments and economic deprivation [Danilov-Danilian, 1990, p. 5].

During the past year, many neo-liberals have obviously been further emboldened by the rapid collapse of the neo-Stalinist regimes in Eastern Europe [Sogrin, 1990]. No longer content to make tactical alliances with the reform wing of the CPSU, they began to openly identify Gorbachev and the party-state modernizers as their main adversary, and launched an uncompromising "struggle against ideologies". After the Spring of 1990, the main axis of the political battle began to shift from the apparatus versus the people to one pitting the open or dissimulating proponents of recapitalization against those advocating a non-capitalist third path [Kurashvili,

1990b, p. 18]. At a minimum, these militant neo-liberals would like to see a frontal assault on the collectivist institutions and mentality underpinning the old regime, and do not eschew "dictatorial" methods for achieving these ends [Piiasheva, 1990a, p. 95]. Many of them take as a strategic model their imaginings of the Thatcherite campaign against the British welfare state. A neo-liberal maximalist confessed her fond hope that a future Russian state would retrace the steps of the Adenauer government in postwar West Germany:

> Economic liberalism in the coming period, the banning of communist ideology, the conducting of an All-Russian process of repentance which culminates in the conviction of all the *ringleaders* at least posthumously, . . . the burial of Lenin's ashes, the sweeping of all socialist-communist symbolism into a museum, and the unleashing of all the entrepreneurial initiative preserved in our society [L. Piiasheva cited in R. Medvedev, 1990].

The historical confidence of these advocates of free markets and a strong state is premised upon the conviction that they like their Western counterparts have "hooked into" a global wave of decentralization brought on by the informatics revolution and the increasing diversity of the various social sub-systems [Stepin, 1990].

Other neo-liberals are far less sanguine about their immediate political prospects. Aleksei Kiva warned Yeltsin and other inexperienced neo-liberals that they greatly over-estimated the depth of their popular support across the country and their ability to assume power immediately. [Kiva, 1990c]. The historian counselled his colleagues that the construction of new democratic parties and the democratization of the CPSU must be conducted in tandem. Otherwise, the turmoil resulting from a premature political polarization would be conducive to the emergence of radical grassroots organizations which have no ties to the old power structure. The crucial difference between Eastern European events and the Soviet political scene is that relatively mature and tested oppositions were ready to fill the power vacuum left by the fall of dictatorial regimes in the former instances while no comparable democratic forces could yet step into the breach left by the complete disappearance of the CPSU [Shevtsova, 1990a]. Shevtsova urged the neo-liberals not to judge their strength by the size of demonstrations because the real political arbiter of the Perestroika will be the silent majority of "working people not inclined to go to demonstrations" which the neo-liberals have ignored up until now [Shevtsova, 1990b]. A profound lack of confidence in the durability of popular support for a proposed economic shock therapy is evident in the refusal of neo-liberals to submit their proposals to referenda which could conceivably provide a reform government with a badly needed credit of trust. This reluctance to put their ideas to a vote demonstrates the continued presence of an enormous social gulf between reform elites and the working class. Like the pre-revolutionary Russian bourgeoisie, the neo-liberal intelligentsia obviously does not know what to expect from the workers and has no confidence in its own ability to retain political control over a mobilized citizenry in the heat of a democratizing revolution. The more intrepid pin their hopes on the emergence of charismatic political figures who could parlay a victory in parliamentary elections into a plebiscitary mandate for the implementation of neo-liberal reforms [Aleksashenko, 1990, pp. 18-19]. In the face of these problematic political realities, even the most politically aggressive neo-liberals are beginning to have second thoughts about their leap into freedom. The failure of the Supreme Soviet to ratify the Shatalin plan in September 1990 forced many neo-liberal ultras to mute their rhetoric because the diffidence of Soviet parliamentarians genuinely reflected the fears of their constituents. Even a monetarist Jacobin like Nikolai Shmeliov now conceded that if the Soviet Union was to introduce a Polish-style shock therapy with a 25-30 percent fall in living standards, "there would be a danger of a social explosion" and so the Soviet Union "must resolve its problems by other less painful methods" [Shmeliov cited in Baczynski, 1990].

The one certainty amidst all the flux is that the final political face of a post-Stalinist Soviet Union will be shaped by the "resolution (moreover not so much legislative as factual) of the question of property" [Mau, 1990, p. 36]. Under the old regime, the "production-administrative apparatus" formed the linchpin of the governing coalition, and the neo-liberals had to dispossess these hegemonic elite groups whose power was rooted in monopoly control of state property [Kochega, 1990, pp. 48-49]. The neo-liberals are already voicing concern at the ease with which representatives of the old nomenklatura "are transplanting themselves" into the mixed or private sectors, and thereby reconstituting their power base on a new capitalist foundation [Rumiantsev, 1990]. Other neo-liberals play down these fears by asserting that the nomenklatura is mutating within and undergoing a rapid process of restratification. According to this conciliationist view, the opposition to reform emanates from a secondary complex of unregenerate bureaucrats and predatory underworld figures united into a *Bandocracy* of corrupt vested interests rather than the entire nomenklatura. This compromise wing believes that the neo-liberals can find receptive audiences among those segments of an internally divided nomenklatura which have confidence in their "business, commercial, and managerial abilities, and seek the elimination of the state monopoly and the complete privatization of property" [Radzikhovskii, 1990]. In the view of one neo-liberal economist, the party nomenklatura is now undergoing a process of bifurcation into a "managerial class already allotting to itself the most advantageous positions in the new commercial structures and a relatively small group of ideologues uniting around the Russian Communist Party" [Naushul, 1990]. With a Mandevillian cynicism, he perceived the rapacity of junior- and middle-level nomenklaturshchiki setting up their own industrial consortia and banks as no more reprehensible than the attempts of "democratic circles" to stake out their own claims in the Klondike of privatization. This conflict closely parallels a debate within the Mazowiecki government over the "enfranchisement of the nomenklatura" in Poland [Bugaj, 1990]. The neo-liberal wing of the Solidarnosc coalition perceives the old nomenklatura as a prime source of primitive capital formation whose evolution over time into a facsimile of Western finance capital should be encouraged. Their Soviet counterparts are also maintaining that marketization can only be completed after "all the most energetic and influential members of the nomenklatura are relocated into the new structures", and the reconstruction of the dominant class along these lines provides the swiftest path to marketization despite the fastidiousness of some neo-liberal purists [Naushul, 1990].

The most optimistic of the neo-liberal conciliationists assert that Gorbachev and the nomenklatura modernizers will involuntarily end up playing the same role as Janos Kadar and the Hungarian party reformers [Bogomolov, 1990c]. In opening the way to a liberalizing marketization, they will eventually be forced to relinquish authority to the dynamic social forces that their actions had inadvertently unleashed. The neo-liberal mayor of Moscow urged his colleagues to seek out alliances with that "part of the apparatus which recognizes the irresistibility of change" [Popov, 1990a]. He reasoned that the various local party apparatuses together constitute an "enormous social organism" which possesses indispensable knowledge of the unofficial inner workings of economic administration [Popov, 1990b]. Equally important for Popov was the realization that foreign lenders would not grant financial assistance to a neo-liberal government which did not have firm control over the army and the police. This circumstance made a "left-centre coalition" with Gorbachev a sine qua non for any movement towards a market economy. Popov was sure that this Grand coalition at the federal level would reflect a multiplicity of evolving coalitions with differing configurations of forces at all rungs of the Soviet political hierarchy. The mayor pointed to the increasingly cordial relations between the predominantly neo-liberal Moscow city council and the urban party committee as an example to be emulated across the country. Far from launching an indiscriminate attack against the bureaucracy,

Zaslavskaia emphasized that her reform wing was trying to win over the most competent segments of the apparatus service elite to the side of a neo-liberal Perestroika [T. Zaslavskaia cited in Hoehmann, 1988, p. 547]. The clamorous personal rancour accompanying the current realignment of power within the Soviet dominant class has caused most observers to lose sight of the fact that all the major contenders, including the neo-liberals, are "creatures of the very same nomenklatura" sharing the same class umbilical cord rather than dissidents who were subjected to serious persecution under the old regime [Kagarlitskii, 1990b].

Even Boris Yeltsin would admit that only "tactical differences" now came between Gorbachev and himself, and the Russian Federation President made known his readiness for a dialogue which would lead to the consolidation of a left-centre coalition [Yeltsin, 1990]. Despite the vituperation on all sides, the most likely outcome of this factional wrangling is the contemporary equivalent of a "compromise between the crown and new political elites" along the lines of British constitutional evolution where modernizing elements of the establishment gradually broadened the ranks of the politically enfranchised oligarchy into a more polyarchical power structure or pluralism of elites [Novak, 1989]. One Soviet academic speculated that the current crop of neo-liberal "muckrakers" and populists would soon give way to a "new generation of political figures who are technocrats" and much more capable of mastering the political processes unleashed by the collapse of neo-Stalinism [Shevtsova, 1990b]. The relative stability of the transition will hinge on whether the nomenklatura and the social groups represented by the neo-liberals are two distinct social classes with irreconcilable interests or in fact contingents of fresh social forces pushing their way up from functional elites and entrepreneurial elements into the centres of power and becoming the new core elements of the dominant class by supplanting the nomenklatura old guard? If the social affinities between the nomenklatura modernizers and the professional-managerial strata prove sufficiently strong, the Perestroika will culminate in the consolidation of a new form of technostructure emerging out of a more complete interpenetration of state managerial cadre and a formative entrepreneurial bourgeoisie.

III. *The New Inequality*

At present the neo-liberals are probing the generational and functional divisions within the diverse strata of the dominant class and a new anti-egalitarianism is the wedge being used to open wide these fissures. The neo-liberals flout orthodox hypocrisy by insisting that "elite groups are needed everywhere" and "they will arise spontaneously and transform themselves into a mafia-like force" if their role is not acknowledged and properly organized [Moiseev, 1988, p. 187]. The campaign against the purported levelling policies of the Brezhnev era is designed to appeal to widespread material discontent within the professional-managerial strata. Long festering frustrations pervaded an article published in an influential literary weekly by Aleksandr Sevastianov who complained about young workers making 300-350 roubles a month as busdrivers after a subsidized six-month training course while the pay scale for tenured academics peaked at 400 roubles [Sevastianov, 1988]. The journalist traced the source of the problem to the democratization of education and the over-production of intellectuals because previous governments had insisted on maintaining academic affirmative action for working class youth which brought about a "devaluation of intellectual labour". Sevastianov sought to debunk the prevailing egalitarian educational theory by alleging that the "creation of equal conditions for all ran counter to the laws of nature" and a biologically determined distribution of talents. Government educational policy must be predicated on a recognition of the fact that both the "cultural milieu and the genetic situation within the families of the intelligentsia are now most conducive to the emergence of the next generation with a higher creative potential". The reproduction of a "intellectual elite" was to be assured through the consolidation of institutional mechanisms like early rigorous educational tracking, a network of highly selective universities, and a fundamental overhaul of laws on inheritance. Sevastianov like most neo-liberals adamantly opposes educational reform measures which would mandate equal access for all to top quality, diverse, and free schooling at every academic level [Kagarlitskii, 1990a, p. 71].

Nor is Sevastianov voicing eccentric or marginal opinions. Even a party liberal of unquestionable integrity like Pavel Volobuev could write of the "genepool of our people" being diluted by the purges and the war [Volobuev, 1988]. As a remedy, the historian demanded the overhaul of an educational system founded upon "romanticized notions about the boundlessness of talent in our people". A whole generation of Soviet professional-managerial cadre have been profoundly alienated by a Brezhnevian socialism which redistributed income between the middle-income groups and the working class as the price of preserving social peace. The resurgence of a puerile eugenics is fuelled by the revanchist sentiments within these strata which the ideologues of the new inequality are trying to mobilize in the service of a neo-liberal Perestroika.

The neo-liberal reformers are intent on chipping away at the parasitic ascribed privileges and immunities incorporated into the old nomenklatura system with its conspicuous perks like the "army of chauffeurs", special stores, and endemic graft [Drozd, 1988]. But the neo-liberals seek to replace Stalinist Old Corruption with a rationalized inequality aimed at broadening the scope of meritocratic productive privilege which is viewed as the key to effecting an elite renewal. Zaslavskaia defended the new inequality with the argument that the removal of all nepotistic barriers would create an "equal opportunity. . . for youth from all social groups to enter the complex, interesting and socially prestigious professions" [Zaslavskaia, 1986, p. 63]. Instead of Khrushchev's sporadic efforts to overcome the social division of labour and Brezhnev's limited affirmative action, Zaslavskaia championed a strict meritocracy which would do away with the remaining collectivist rules of exclusion on the basis of social origins, ideological rectitude, or political connections. Rutkevich brushed aside the objections of leftist scholars that this nominally meritocratic educational policy would only further diminish the already vastly "unequal chances" of working class children in competition with the progeny of the elite for academic and professional advancement [Rutkevich, 1986, p. 16]. The prominent sociologist justified the extension of this acknowledged necessary evil with the all-purpose dialectical alibi of the thirties that the "use of social inequality in the role of a lever for the advancement of social equality, arises out of the general logic of the development of socialism". But another academic cut to the real nub of the debate when she offered a favourable assessment of the Chinese abandonment of worker and farmer educational affirmative action as the necessary price to be paid for concentrating limited intellectual resources on urgent priority targets [Bonevskaia, 1986, p. 132]. This new inegalitarian ideology has implications far broader than the temporary exigencies of a conjunctural crisis. Soviet neo-liberals share the tacit assumption of their Western counterparts that the age of a qualitative democratization has finally drawn to a close if this means any pretence at narrowing the gulf between social elites and the subaltern classes through education. In their view, a technologically determined realism dictates that class divisions can only become more unbridgeable in an age of laissez-innover intensive growth.

In addition to greater social differentiation and meritocracy, the third ideological component of the neo-liberal salutary inequality is a renewed cult of professionalism which presupposes that the professional-managerial strata will be the driving force behind intensive growth. Zaslavskaia writes of the need for younger managerial cadre to acquire a greater capacity for "self-supervision based upon a high degree of professionalism" [Zaslavskaia, 1986, p. 63]. Another sociologist described the model administrator as an individual who displayed "enormous competence, personal autonomy, sensitivity, independent judgement — in short everything which can be concisely defined as professionalism" [Ianovskii, 1986, p. 5]. A party ideologist derided the young Marx's vision of transcending the social division of labour as tantamount to an attempt to "destroy the individual personality" and called instead for the dissemination of a "lofty professionalism" as the only reliable road to maximum productivity [Tsypko, 1989]. This veneration of professionalism reflects the cohering class consciousness of the activist vanguard of cadre of upwardly mobile elites seeking a rejuvenation of the political class. Professionalism can serve as the crusading creed of those politically conscious segments of a dominant class which has undergone a thorough internal functional realignment while becoming largely self-regenerating and attaining elite status through regularized institutional channels. These insurgent elites share a common political profile moulded in the crucible of what one Soviet sociologist terms the "prestige" colleges [Rutkevich, 1986, p. 16]. The positive side of this cosmopolitanism within the Soviet dominant class was evident in the remark of a neo-liberal spurning the tribalist appeals of the right with the response that he "had more in common with a Kazakh, English or Jewish intellectual than an ethnic Russian bureaucrat" [Sevastianov, 1988]. The negative side is a pretentious gentility which utopianizes the pre-revolutionary past in mourning the waning of "deference towards educated individuals" and the "weakening of the church" as an instrument of social control [Ryvkina, 1989, pp. 30-31].

The ultimate aim of the neo-liberal campaign is to rehabilitate social inequality as a permanent rather than transitory feature of a "normal" society, and make egalitarian aspirations seem perverse or quixotic. An internal government document submitted to Gorbachev by neo-liberal advisors in early 1990 conceded that the postulation of an eventual equal distribution of power in the official ideology had skewed popular aspirations in the direction of a "society contaminated by an egalitarian psychology and the aggressive rejection of all manifestations of individualism, independence, personal initiative, and the successes which are bound up with this" ["Political Note", 1990]. Neo-liberal apprehensions about the political immaturity of the Soviet people mask their realization that economic restructuring for the vast majority of the Soviet people will result in the substitution of one form of domination and exploitation for another probably more onerous at least in the short run. The dissemination of an aggressive possessive individualism and other de-solidarizing strategies are designed both to unite receptive strata of the dominant class around a revindicative programme and fragment potential working class opposition by appealing to younger workers who can take advantage of the opportunities for self-reliance and individual advancement under the new system. The new inequality could thus become the ideology of a managerial revolution which legitimates itself as a hierarchy of competence certified by academic credentials and meritocratic promotion.

IV. *Social Policy*
The outlines of the ideal polity of the neo-liberals are adumbrated in their diagnosis of the current crisis and their prescriptions for dealing with it. The neo-liberal project is to Brezhnevism what Thatcherism was to Butskellism: a radical uncompromising assault on the social contract which underpinned the demobilized political consensus of the old regime. Zaslavskaia identified the main drag on the Soviet economy as an overly generous welfare state which was built up over the past three decades. A battery of welfare entitlements had resulted in the "slackening of administrative and economic compulsion for energetic labor in social production" [Zaslavskaia, 1986, pp. 62-63]. A sellers' market for labour had fostered the rise of a "system of *paid* protection for the individual which allows many to live "tolerably without exerting themselves too much. . . and obtaining additional income from the black market". In the neo-liberal view, the laudable social welfare achievements of the statist system have been transformed into fetters because an overly indulged working class is no longer being policed and disciplined by basic economic deprivations. Dzarasov complained that the Soviet system lacked the arsenal of economic whips needed to stimulate gainful labour because "nobody sleeps under a bridge" in this country and there was no "polarization of property" as in the West [Dzarasov, 1988]. The gist of the neo-liberal critique is that the Brezhnev government went too far too fast in freeing the Soviet people from the precariousness of modern industrial existence.

As a remedy to stagnation, Zaslavskaia proposed the strengthening of work incentives to restore a "personal interest in hard efficient labour" [Zaslavskaia, 1986, pp. 62-63]. A social wage judged overly generous had to be pared down to a basic subsistence minimum where consumption above this level would be entirely dependent on personal disposable income. Critics of an "overloaded" welfare state target what they describe as an excessively high minimum wage, a make-work job structure, huge social welfare subsidies, and a broad range of unpaid social services [Bim and Shakin, 1986, p. 65]. Popov alleged that the present one-third of earned income being channelled into the social wage, was undercutting the productive incentive of the most dynamic strata of the population, and the Soviet people must be made to realize that the "social consumption fund is not synonymous with communist distribution. . . nor an indication of proximity to communism" [Popov, 1987, p. 78]. The neo-liberals are right to charge that regressive financing of social services through indirect taxation and the prevalence of informal hierarchically determined access, combine to ensure that 80 percent of total food subsidies goes to the top 20 percent of the population [Kiselev, 1990, p. 61]. But their proposed solution is to end all food subsidies and allow prices in a situation of massive pent-up demand to skyrocket. Fixed state prices on basic goods provided the "sole anchor" of the old economic mechanism ensuring at least that the roughly eighty million Soviet citizens living at or below the minimum subsistence level did not go hungry [S. Nikitin, 1990, p. 13].

Zaslavskaia was the first to publicly urge the state to adopt a social policy founded on the recognition of the existence of politically conscious "classes" and "professional categories of employees" with frequently conflicting interests [Zaslavskaia, 1986, p. 62]. This belated acknowledgement of social heterogeneity is prompted by an awareness of the structurally induced slowing growth rate which will make it impossible for the state to continue raising living standards across the board as it has done since the mid-sixties. As a result of the budgetary squeeze, the state can no longer afford to pursue the "aim of an equivalent increase of the measure of satisfaction of all elements of the social superstructure". The Gorbachev government had to learn that it is a discriminating differential distribution of material benefits which "makes a social policy a social policy", and the state must choose the prime beneficiaries.

Zaslavskaia declared that the first test of the Gorbachev government's reformist mettle would be a "reordering of the wage structure which was radical in principle" [Zaslavskaia, 1986, p. 62]. Industrial workers were told to brace themselves for the restoration of "deep" wage differentials to reverse two decades of levelling [Sapritsiants, 1987, p. 97]. Only a decade ago, the dean of Soviet sociology was extolling the "convergence" of the wages of the intelligentsia and industrial workers as proof of the nation's inexorable advance towards a classless society [Rutkevich, 1977, pp. 79-80]. Today, he is citing the same figures to indict a twenty year pattern of discrimination against the "socio-professional groups" [Rutkevich, 1986, p. 17]. A new wage policy free from the encumbrances of a progressive income tax would be used to distill out of the professional-managerial strata the "new entrepreneurs" who are ready to ride the wave of the informatics revolution [A manager cited in "Editorial", 1988]. The core of the neo-liberal project is a Stolypin wager that a status revolution bringing power and remuneration into line with demonstrated talent, will propel the Soviet Union into a new technological age.

Shmeliov declares that the current debate around social policy turns on the question of what role should be afforded to the acquisitive instincts, i.e., "the striving of the enterprising and energetic individual for personal success" within the framework of the new economic mechanism [Shmeliov, 1989, p. 147]. Greed has become the opiate of most would-be tribunes of the professional-managerial strata because the market appeals to the "real living individual and their natural interests" while socialism addresses only the "idealized individual" [Levikov, 1988]. The advent of a highly stratified consumer society is prescribed as the only practical means of dynamizing a stagnant economy.

Greater wage differentials and the dissemination of an ideology of possessive individualism is also designed to break down troublesome informal group solidarities standing in the way of an optimalist economic rationality and thereby leave the individual worker less capable of resisting the "manipulation" of management [Rakitskii, 1988, pp. 5-9]. The object is to shatter the levelling dynamic and sever the power linkages between the right and the unskilled strata of the working class coopted into its political base.

V. *Unemployment*

An important rubicon of neo-liberal economic reform will be the Soviet government's embrace of the principle expounded by Shatalin that "socialism is not philanthropy automatically guaranteeing everyone employment irrespective of his or her ability to do the job" [Shatalin, 1986, p. 63]. Liberals in Hungary and Poland have long advocated the introduction of a competitive labour market because it would subject the working class to the supremely effective disciplinary force of impersonal economic coercion and provide the perfect lubricant for a decentralized new economic mechanism. However in the Soviet Union, the subject of a wholesome dose of permanent unemployment was raised only once in the press during the Brezhnev era. In the midst of a zero-growth slump in 1980, Gavriil Popov proposed that "we must limit the right to work" to allow greater managerial flexibility and provide a spur to individual productivity [Popov, 1980]. But the suggestion was ignored by the government and sparked no public discussion. Considering the severity of the crisis, the unwillingness of the Brezhnev leadership to permit at least some academic debate, indicates just how important the government believed the full employment pledge was to the established political consensus.

The enshrinement of the full employment principle in the Soviet Union issues from a cooptive corporatist social contract and the lack of any stimulus to the intelligent use of labour power. Despite being rooted in an enormous waste of human and material resources, the official commitment to full employment in the Soviet heartland underpins a battery of informal defensive adaptations of Soviet workers to a system which grants them job security in exchange for political passivity. Glasnost has now enabled the neo-liberals to press Gorbachev openly to prepare the country psychologically and institutionally for the impending redundancy of "millions of low-skilled workers" [Zaslavskaia, 1986, p. 70]. The more honest admit that the minimum 15-16 million slated to lose their jobs, will not easily be integrated back into a stunted service sector [Zaslavskaia, 1987]. By early summer 1987, Shmeliov was railing against the "economic damage caused by a parasitic confidence in guaranteed jobs" [Shmeliov, 1987, pp. 148-149]. The leading Soviet monetarist economist blamed "excessive full employment" for a host of social ills ranging from poor labour discipline to low production quality and the scourge of alcoholism. Shmeliov urged the government to consider the manifold therapeutic advantages of a "natural level of unemployment" and a "comparatively small reserve army of labor", could bring to a socialist political economy. By his calculations, roughly 25 percent of the labour force or more than 30 million workers are potentially redundant [Shmeliov, 1990]. Another neo-liberal economist estimated that "over-full employment" was directly responsible for labour productivity being 30 percent lower than it would otherwise be in an economy which used joblessness to prod greater output [Malmygin, 1990, p. 49]. Many managers have eagerly welcomed the broadening of their prerogatives in the areas of firing and lay-offs because the "whip of unemployment" would increase their leverage over the work force [Shirokov, 1989].

A significant level of concealed unemployment particularly among minorities has always existed in the Soviet Union. Reliable estimates put the current jobless rate at 6-10 million (5-8 percent of the workforce) concentrated for the most part in the Central Asian republics [Zaslavskii, 1990, p. 8]. The real issue at stake in this controversy is whether a "natural" level of unemployment should be accepted as an official instrument of state economic policy? In any economic restructuring, the hardest hit will be the 45 million workers (two-thirds of whom are women) now employed in low-productivity manual occupations who stand a good chance without remedial measures of falling permanently into the "peripheral strata" of a new segmented labour force [Penkin, 1990, p. 89]. Zaslavskaia frankly expresses her approval of such a development which would place the whole of the working class in "harsher economic and social conditions" imposed by fierce labour market competition, the difficulty of obtaining retraining, the fear of demotion, and the loss of social status [Zaslavskaia, 1989, p. 232].

Many neo-liberals echo Friedrich von Hayek's demand for the complete extirpation of what he deemed natural but self-defeating human propensities towards cooperative solidarity and democratic participation [Kara-Murza, 1990, p. 46]. By this reasoning, the notion of social justice is proscribed as incompatible with the efficient operation of the free market and the exercise of individual freedom. The object of this ideological offensive is to subvert incrementally or frontally the social wage whose tenacious normative supports are woven deeply into the popular political consciousness. This would result in the disaggregation of the working class into the more ambitious younger segments of the labour force and the older strata inured to what the dean of Yugoslav neo-liberals calls the "radical egalitarian value matrix" [Zupanov, 1983, p. 13]. The neo-liberals are bent upon abolishing the de facto veto power of the official trade unions over state economic policy as it is incorporated into the Brezhnevian social contract by eliminating a labour shortage which enables workers informally to "dictate" better wages and benefits than they deserve by a strict optimalist accounting [Popov, 1980]. As in their polemics against welfare state coddling, the neo-liberals are motivated by a de-integrative anti-collectivism aimed at atomizing the working class and stripping individuals of group protection by placing them in an economic situation where they cannot afford to keep faith with each other. The acceptance of chronic mass unemployment as a constituent element of a restructured economic mechanism would serve at best to fragment Soviet society into an economically polarized "Two-Thirds society" along the lines of Western neo-liberal capitalisms [Sabov, 1990]. A society where "the ruble must be placed at the centre of everything" would be most amenable to the rationalizing initiatives and discipline of modernizing professional-managerial strata whose ascent is championed by the neo-liberals [Shmeliov, 1989, p. 130].

VI. *Working Class Integration and Self-Management*
Most neo-liberals demonstratively drew the boundaries of democratizing reform at the modest government-sanctioned experiments intended to introduce some measure of industrial democracy into the enterprises. One survey revealed that 79 percent of managers would welcome administrative decentralization but an even larger number interpreted the notion of economic democratization entirely in terms of a "stiffening of discipline" in production [Torkanovskii, 1988, p. 52]. One factory administrator complained in an interview that "musicians are not elected by ballot", and

equally precious managerial talent should not be subjected to the caprices of an electoral campaign [Editorial, 1987]. Neo-liberal academics have sprung to the defence of enterprise directors wary of self-management constraints in asserting that "professionalism and the personal qualities required by a manager, will have difficulty winning a majority vote" [Sokolova and Manuilskii, 1988, p. 25]. Popov spelled out the real issues at stake in this dispute when he wrote that the self-management principle interpreted too broadly, could lead to a "Fourierism" in the factories and the advent of a new age of "mediocrity" [Popov, 1988, p. 108]. Fourierism is a standard coded allusion to the concern prevalent among managerial cadre that the workers were taking the self-management provisions in the Gorbachev enterprise legislation far more seriously than its authors originally intended. The neo-liberal economist wanted industrial democracy limited to a pacifying pseudo-participation which can cool out the tensions arising from a painful transition to a new political economy. Popov and his colleagues feared that a continuation of these early trends on the shopfloor could lead to a substantive production democracy being constituted spontaneously from below which would prevent the most capable managers within the Soviet elite from taking charge of a reindustrializing economy. These first scattered stirrings towards the self-empowerment of the labour force sent neo-liberals in search of alternative means of incorporating the working class into the reform coalition as loyal but fully subordinate partners.

The neo-liberals are seeking to overcome working class resistance by offering marketizing reform in conjunction with self-management narrowly defined as employee stock ownership. Aganbegian acknowledges that the Gorbachev Perestroika would "vanish into oblivion" like all previous reform bids if the government fails to win the committed support of a large segment of the working class [Aganbegian, 1988, p. 5]. But the only incentive offered to his trade union audience was employee stock ownership and profit sharing, which he promised would play a central role in the second stage of reform. One manager who pioneered this form of worker inclusion groused that it was virtually impossible to fire workers under the old system because the trade union local would come automatically to their defence [Nikitin, 1988]. The beauty of the new shareholding system in the eyes of its neo-liberal sponsors was that it pitted the more industrious segments of the workforce against the slackers "together with management in a battle for democracy and high quality". The neo-liberals are trumpeting this "direct participation of the workers and the engineers in the income of the enterprise as one step towards a realistic socialism". But this Realistic Socialism is obviously designed to shield an administrative monopoly of control over the enterprise surplus from the encroachment of factory councils and restrict self-management to "only one right for the workers — the right to make a dividend" if the firm turns a profit [Vavilov, 1988]. One radical economist complained that this pseudo-participation amounted to nothing more than workers being compelled to make a risky involuntary loan to their enterprise management without any real change in the basic power relations within the factory. Not surprisingly, surveys consistently reveal that no more than 6-8 percent of the working class are prepared to purchase stock in their own enterprises as compared with one-third of managerial personnel [Melikian, 1990b]. Many neo-liberals have responded to this shopfloor resistance to their transparent designs to insulate managerial prerogatives by calling on the Gorbachev government to introduce these measures "through force" if necessary [Popov, 1990a].

Aleksei Kiva warned neo-liberal intellectuals against their habitually "scornful if not contemptuous view of the working class as inert, amorphous, and servile executors of the will of the apparatus" [Kiva, 1990a, p. 202]. This arrogance is most apparent in an alliance strategy which apart from some obvious feints, largely ignores the political significance of the "roughly 75 percent of the employed population who are not property owners but workers on the staff of large enterprises, firms, scientific organizations, the government apparatus etc." [Abalkin, 1990]. The belief that only an "emancipated capital" can become the demiurge of economic rationalization, has caused many neo-liberal strategists to give short shrift to the crucial problem of how to incorporate non-entrepreneurial strata into a cohesive new growth coalition [Seliunin, 1990, p. 202]. Iaroshenko expressed the hope that the eventual pluralization of Soviet society into a welter of ethnic, cultural, sport, and other private civic organizations would become the "mortal foe of a society of economic and political monopolies where the individual is a member of the work collective and thus also of the trade union, communist party, Komsomol, queues for housing and a car and so on" [Iaroshenko, 1990, p. 141]. The submergence of long predominant "Production divisions" in a splintered social identity could then be relied upon to check the rise of a powerful cohesive labour movement. The national model once again is Poland where the socially atomizing effects of shock therapy are said to have induced workers to "tie their fate no longer entirely to the success of the trade unions", and thereby eliminate the working class as a collective political actor [Aleksashenko, 1990, p. 18].

Neo-liberal dogma canonizing private property is directed not against a bankrupt neo-Stalinist conception of state property but to preempt the exploration of any possible intermediary forms lying between private and state ownership [Bugaj, 1990]. Many neo-liberals were anxious to shift all the blame for the disastrous repercussions of market decentralization onto the first tentative experiments in industrial democracy which are held responsible for the breakdown of administrative coordination and worsening disproportions in the economy [Berger, 1990]. At most, neo-liberals suggest that worker participation in management may be broadened to include some representation on the board of directors of individual firms [Grigoriev, 1990]. But factory collectives should under no circumstances be given any voice in deciding such critical issues as the selection of the production programme, prices, investments, or loans. The main fear is that an institutionalized worker majority in self-managed firms would mindlessly veto any technological innovations which threatened to trade off increased productivity for a reduction of the labour force. By opposing worker self-management, the neo-liberals are trying to limit the Perestroika to a managerial revolution which replaces the administrative monopoly of the apparatus with a new administrative monopoly of profit-oriented technocrats. This academic dispute could take on real urgency somewhere down the line because the latest comprehensive surveys of shopfloor opinion reveal that even after the first disappointing experiments in industrial democracy, a larger majority now supports at least some worker imput into the running of the enterprise (30 percent) or complete authority in key decision-making (57 percent) [Melnikov and Kvasnikova, 1990, p. 38].

V. *Neo-Liberal Economics*

Most neo-liberals no longer camouflage their desire to move the Soviet Union into the "rapids of a capitalist or, more precisely, a normal society" [Ambartsumov, 1990, p. 39]. Much of the neo-liberal polemic still evokes the utopian imagery of an anarcho-capitalism replacing politics with omniscient markets which would naturally appeal to people who have known only the oppression of an authoritarian statism and not the impersonal cruelty of the market. This sentiment was exemplified by the remark of a group of neo-liberal economists that the "power of money over people is more expedient and moral than the tyranny of a bureaucrat interposing himself between the manufacturer and consumer, and usurping the right to determine what the former should produce and the latter consume" [Medvedev et al. 1990, p. 63]. Hayek has become the "idol" of market economists seeking an antithesis to the status quo rather than an alternative while the remainder put Friedman on a pedestal for his success in orchestrating the "stabilization of the American economy and the celebrated Reaganomics which enabled the United States to overcome its serious economic difficulties, lessen inflation, and strengthen the dollar" [Sogrin, 1990; Popov, 1989, p. 140]. A first-class economist like Popov is obviously being disingenuous in presenting Reaganite Military Keynesianism as evidence of the efficacy of neo-liberal economics but references to Reaganism and Thatcherism in Soviet political discourse actually serve as convenient coded metaphors rather than a summons to borrow literally from their examples. For all their propagandistic salutations to the market, Soviet neo-liberals remain vague in their technical writings about the type of market that the Soviet Union should move towards: competitive, monopoly, oligopoly, or monopsonistic. Moreover, they studiously evade the fact that the "market can embody the most disparate economic power relations" and never spell out their conception of what the optimal correlation might be [Bogachev, 1990, p. 19]. Aleksandr Zinoviev, went further and charged that the refusal of Soviet specialists to offer a realistic analysis of the market confirmed his suspicion that the "idea of the market plays less an economic role than an ideological or political one" in combatting the right [Zinoviev, 1990]. The emigre novelist voiced grave doubts about the feasibility of reform programmes based upon the projections of parrots who had quickly mastered new words rather than scholars who had undergone a carefully considered change of heart.

In their academic articles, the top neo-liberal economists share with the rest of the Perestroika coalition a recognition that the post-Stalinist Soviet economy will remain predominantly oligopolistic and even monopolistic in its overall structure. Popov envisages the winnowing process of the socialist market eventually yielding a rationalized "centralism of the oligopolistic type" [Popov, 1987, pp. 62-63]. The Moscow University academic compared the operation of this multi-sector economy to Joan Robinson's notion of "imperfect competition" in which the oligopolistic primary sector of the economy would serve as the intermediary between the secondary sector and the market. The neo-liberal economist has in mind a future Soviet industrial system which strongly resembles the Japanese model with a primary sector of large conglomerates flanked by a secondary sector of small and medium-sized firms. Popov brushed aside the more naive anarcho-liberal celebrations of the market to single out Japan as the country which has proven itself most capable of adapting to the scientific-industrial revolution through its "mighty bloc of centralized influences". Popov agreed that a broader role for the market will be essential for easing deficits in the consumer and service sectors but market forces alone could not serve as the "longterm foundation of the powerful economic leap of a great power at the end of the century". The Soviet state must try to emulate the Japanese developmental model in using the "power and might of the centre for the acceleration of technological reconstruction". Neo-liberals may be loudly demanding the "elimination of arbitrary central intervention" but they are also discreetly reaffirming that the "state is the instrument of accelerated development" whose macro-economic co-ordinating activity is integral to the survival of the Soviet Union as a great power. All major factions of the Soviet power elite are in accord that the omnicompetent modernizing state of the thirties is obsolete in an advanced industrial economy. From an overextended command centre, the state would be redeployed into a "strategic organ of scientific-technical progress", the patron and defender of emerging motor branches against vested sectoral interests [Popov, 1988a]. Despite their polemical wrangling, all the major ideological contenders for power in a post-Stalinist Soviet Union share the conviction that restructured Soviet economy must be driven by large oligopolistic firms under state macro-economic guidance with a low level of military spending.

The much vaunted "500 Days" programme authored by Stanislav Shatalin and a group of neo-liberal economists during the Summer of 1990 has been properly described as a "manifesto for the complete capitalization" of the Soviet Union but it was obviously never designed to provide operational guidelines for reform [Kurashvili, 1990, p. 17]. The best proof of the logical incoherence of the crash marketization manifesto was Shatalin's impromptu decision to appropriate unaltered the social welfare provisions of the much reviled government programme and tack it onto his own when the 500 Days package came under attack in the Soviet parliament for its obliviousness to such concerns [Bushkevich, 1990]. Even some neo-liberal economists were dismayed that the preposterous timetable drawn up for the privatization of state property bore all the earmarks of the spurious Brezhnevian "campaign" style which augured that the momentum behind the drive would soon wane after the sponsoring power elite faction had realized its ulterior objectives [Anulova, 1990]. Shatalinomics only made sense if its original rationale was political and not economic.

The most avid neo-liberals have been warning all along against the "illusion of a soft landing" during the transition to a capitalist market economy [Pinsker, 1990]. The leading theorist of the Russian Christian Democratic Party, Boris Pinsker, stressed that the "synonym of a soft landing is the long coexistence of the two economic systems and the two hierarchies of economic and political authority: a competitive market and a party-administrative system". Economic dualism would thus perpetuate a political dualism, and compel the neo-liberals to share power with establishment elites whose authority is grounded in the state sector. The debate over the 500 Days programme took place against the background of a massive wave of old-line ministries and state industries privatizing their own assets and retaining control firmly in the hands of the old nomenklatura [Bobrovski, 1990b]. The greatest fear of the neo-liberals is that the "old nomenklatura will set itself up comfortably" in the new state-regulated market economy with most of the old apparatchiki acquiring ownership of privatized government assets and the rest running the state regulatory agencies [Shifrin, 1990]. The 500 Days Programme would have decentralized legal control of these assets to the various republican legislatures and consequently preempted this wave of what the neo-liberals rather incongruously term neo-Bolshevism or the controlled metamorphosis of state functionaires into "capitalists" [Karpinskii, 1990]. The shock therapy was ostensibly designed to usher in an economy of perfect competition without which all reform efforts were said to be futile. But the real aim was to sever all the vital power linkages within the nomenklatura economy. Soviet neo-liberals expect that a wave of bankruptcies would expedite the transfer of state assets into private hands. Like many Eastern European neo-liberals advocating a *politique du pire*, they anticipate that the collapse of the economy into a chaotic shambles resembling War Communism will facilitate a "great leap into privatization", in much the same way the Bolsheviks supposedly attempted a leap into communism [Bugaj, 1990].

The controversy surrounding the 500 Days programme was also a political offensive by parliamentary neo-liberals striving to take advantage of growing popular discontent with the Gorbachev government. The champions of the "500 Days" programme were intent upon forcing Gorbachev to abandon his preferred mediating role between the emerging Third Estate and the metamorphosing nomenklatura, and commit his presidential authority unequivocally to their hidden agenda. Yeltsin believed his leverage over Gorbachev during the Summer of 1990 was sufficient at least to put on the table the demand that a new government be selected on a "parity basis" with himself choosing half of the ministers including the prime minister [Yeltsin, 1990]. This would effectively have reduced Gorbachev to a latter-day Ramsay MacDonald presiding as a figure-head over an aggressively neo-liberal government. For the past three years, Gorbachev has been trying to forge a Berlinguer-like left-centre Historical Compromise which would prevent the bipolarization of the country into antagonistic camps and above all preclude the formation of a reactionary centre-right bloc. Gorbachev's acquiescence to the neo-liberals would have derailed the attempt of the party modernizers to edge the reform process towards a neo-corporatist solution which entails an institutionalized incomes policy and tripartite negotiations between the government, managers, and organized labour. One of the authors of the 500 Days Plan complained that "the interference of politicians in the business of economists has reached such a scale that the plans of economists cannot be translated into reality" [Grigorii Iavlinskii cited in Rytov, 1990]. Only a shock therapy in the view of Iavlinskii could make a neo-liberal programme politician-proof or, more accurately, democracy-proof. The real object of the Shatalin Plan was to preempt the emergence of other social partners becoming represented in the formulation of economic policy. The authors of the crash marketization programme never intended to remove the state from the economy but rather ensure that its essential regulatory role would be entirely subordinate to neo-liberal control because their reform strategy was not amenable to compromise.

The advocates of a shock therapy subscribe to Hayek's categorical rejection of gradualist reform strategies which would give opposition forces time to regroup, and eventually soften or even reverse a punishing deflationary programme. The massive unemployment brought on by shock therapy would not only ease budgetary pressures but also atomize potential working class resistance to a neo-liberal restructuring. The assumption is that when faced with the imminent threat of joblessness, "most of the working class will avoid trade union struggles and arrive at a deal with entrepreneurs including feudal collective contracts or black market contracts" [Kara-Murza, 1990, p. 47]. The more candid architects of the 500 Days Programme dispense with the soothing public rhetoric in articles addressed to elite audiences, and assert that the Soviet Union must "pass through a stage of primitive capital accumulation with all its social consequences" [Iasin, 1990, p. 11]. The underlying premise is that the Soviet government should create a political economy where the incentives for capital accumulation are completely unencumbered by such "socialist" restrictions as a progressive income tax and child labour laws. Soviet neo-liberals are beguiling their audiences with the imagery of an advanced industrial capitalism while refraining from divulging that this ideal cannot be achieved without first passing through the historical antechamber of "classical capitalism" with all its privations for the vast majority and the loss of the modest social welfare achievements of the old regime [Kurashvili, 1990b, p. 17].

The preliminary aim of privatization is to create a broad stratum of people with a proprietary stake in a new economic order. Out of these first beneficiaries of the de-nationalization of state property will eventually be distilled "responsible competing capitalists" who can push aside inept nomenklaturshchiki seeking to reconstitute their social power on a new economic foundation [Radzikhovskii, 1990]. The technical variant of privatization incorporated into the Shatalin Plan was designed to give away for free the absolute minimum of state assets while selling the rest as dearly as possible [Melikian, 1990a]. The secondary aims of this approach were to soak up excess disposable income and bring goods hoarded as insurance in enterprise inventories onto the market. But the paramount objective was to "create real owners who will invest their resources in the enterprises". If fully implemented, the Shatalin Plan would have transformed the Soviet economy into three sectors with the first two comprising a rationalized state sector and a realm reserved to private enterprise [Artsishevskii, 1990]. The crucial growth sector would be a third joint venture sphere combining state participation with private and/or foreign capital.

When originally fleshing out his grand vision of the 500 Days Programme, Mikhail Bocharov mentions almost in passing that the government in the third stage will permit a "deep recession in the basic branches of the economy" lasting no more than 150 days [Bocharov, 1990]. Like other neo-liberals, the parliamentarian omitted even the most general prognosis of the social costs of this economic surgery. It was first left to conservative economists to float entirely plausible estimates that average purchasing power would shrink by 42-50 percent with workers in the state sector taking the brunt of the recession [Shchipantsev, 1990]. But subsequent parliamentary discussions have forced neo-liberal theorists to put some of their cards on the table. Bogomolov for the first time gave a hint of the neo-liberal estimates of the cost of a deflationary shock when he urged that the government ensure that the average decline in purchasing power would in no case exceed 25 percent [Bogomolov, 1990b]. Estimates of the possible unemployment level have ranged from 15-40 million (11 to 31 percent of the labour force) depending on how stringently a tight fiscal policy is enforced. At the outset, the new autonomous trade unions in the mining industry had been among the most enthusiastic boosters of the 500 Days Programme. But this was before the disclosure that the immediate cut-off of subsidies to the coal industry would result in the shutdown of 120 pits [Shprygin, 1990]. Neo-liberals observed sarcastically how miners' organizations which had only yesterday been calling for the immediate introduction of market relations, now did a complete turnabout in demanding continued state subventions and guaranteed supplies [Zhagel, 1990]. A union leader admitted that his membership "had begun to waver" after the neo-liberals finally spelled out the social consequences of their programme and the magnitude of the jobs reduction which would follow [Azarovskii, 1990]. When the time finally came to approve the 500 Days Plan in parliament, even the most radical deputies displayed what was charitably described as a "certain lack of resolve", and the chamber finally abdicated responsibility for drawing up the transition strategy to Gorbachev [Abdulleev, 1990].

The most vulnerable aspect of the 500 Days Programme was its gratuitous assumption that market relations will spring up automatically as soon as the existing administrative networks are annihilated [Danilov-Danilian, 1990]. Among others, Bogomolov has drawn the lesson from the Polish experience that a shock therapy will result in a cascading collapse of production and the branches suffering the most will be those in essential consumer branches [Bogomolov, 1990c]. Even some neo-liberals are warning that a shock therapy in the fragile Soviet economy would only lead to the complete breakdown of all remaining supply and sales linkages, precipitate more production stoppages, and foment a backlashing popular demand for the return of dirigistic compulsion. The main danger posed by a shock therapy is the economy finally bottoming out at a dangerously low level following a "long depression" caused by an uncontrolled deflationary vicious circle of collapsing demand and cuts in production [Belousov and Klepach, 1990, p. 24]. Others warn that the overriding priority given to fiscal stabilization by a halving of total state investment, would lead not only to mass unemployment but the closing of loss-making enterprises which produce goods vital to the economy [Piiasheva, 1990b]. If the reform government was serious about effecting fundamental structural shifts in the economy, it would have to transfer investment to growth branches, especially the consumer goods and service sectors, to absorb the unemployed created by the scaling back of the basic industries [Penkin, 1990, p. 88]. The monetarist strategy of slashing the budget deficit at any price, ignores the need to set in place an active labour policy and stable anti-inflationary mechanisms during the transition. By implication, the neo-liberals seem set to rely upon the only other means of checking inflation: longterm mass unemployment.

The other tacit premise of the neo-liberal transition strategy is a "reliance on God's holy help or more precisely the import of foreign capital" [Belousov and Klepach, 1990, p. 24]. Maidanik scorned those neo-liberals who "were striving with the passion (and naivete) of neophytes to get into the First World" [Maidanik, 1990, p. 88]. The political scientist in particular criticized them for approaching the transnational financial institutions of the North as if they were benevolent "socialist" entities and not coldly calculating capitalist concerns quite ready to preside over the "Latin-Americanization of yesterday's second world". Another Soviet academic cited Immanuel Wallerstein's admonition that countries seeking to enter the international division of labour, will have their longterm fate determined far more by what they are able to export rather than what they can import or produce for the domestic market [Usmanov, 1990, p. 143]. In the view of Sergei Usmanov, the intellectual poverty of Soviet neo-liberalism is most glaringly on display in its omnibus response to the tough technical questions of the economic transition with vapid assurances that "the West will help us" or "only the West can save the Perestroika". The neo-liberals assure their audiences that the hardships of the privatizing transition can be alleviated by the largescale import of consumer goods financed by foreign credit to off-set domestic shortages [V. Popov, 1990, p. 36]. But the resulting foreign indebtedness would also irrevocably box the Soviet Union into an IMF austerity programme and a domestic fiscal policy favouring a neo-liberal growth strategy and the ratcheting of capitalism into the national economy.

The more serious neo-liberal economists have been trying to restrain the romantic enthusiasms of some members of their camp by pointing to global experience which indicates that a maximum of 10 percent level of annual privatization is the optimal rate [Veger, 1990, p. 23]. This ceiling meant that there was no chance of cutting the size of the state sector to a "civilized" 30-40 percent of production in two or three years as many proposed [Anulova, 1990]. Aleksandr Nekipelov sought to dispel the prevalent "illusion" that the private sector would rapidly become the motor force of the economy because even under the best of circumstances, the entrepreneurial sphere would remain dependent on the state sector for the next 15-20 years [Nekipelov, 1990]. Others were dubious about the feasibility of attempting to implement a far-reaching privatization in a situation of explosive political instability and the almost complete absence of reliable market ties [Danilov-Danilian et al. 1990]. Belousov and Klepach were certain that private enterprise in a chaotic unbalanced economy would naturally gravitate not towards productive activity but the speculative realm of "trade intermediation and deals with fictive capital" or stockjobbing [Belousov and Klepach, 1990, p. 27]. It was most likely that the primary beneficiaries of a crash marketization would be well-connected basic industries who have virtually insuperable competitive advantages over the consumer-oriented branches which would be again relegated to the status of "outsider" [Galparin and Ursov, 1990]. The market would dictate that development follows the path of least resistance. In an unbalanced economy, this would place a premium on the continued expansion of energy and raw materials branches to keep pace with increasing waste in the domestic economy and the exportability of their product [Belousov, p. 23].

Iasin conceded that a shock therapy would lead to unprecedented levels of unemployment lasting at least one to two years, and this policy could only be sustained by a government which enjoys phenomenal popular support or a "harsh dictatorship" [Iasin, 1990, p. 14]. Maidanik speculates that the most realistic neo-liberals are those who publicly endorse the need for a return to capitalism "along a peripheral authoritarian course in declaring their liking for the Pinochets of this world" [Maidanik, 1990, p. 88]. Some neo-liberals frustrated by Gorbachev's reluctance to crack down hard on social disorder, contend that Western capital would actually welcome a military coup and this would facilitate the influx of foreign investment [Sokolov, 1990]. They see in a badly divided Soviet military a stratum of younger modernizing elements blooded in Afghanistan which seek to establish a "well-equipped and trained army of professionals", and therefore would be willing to preside benignly over an authoritarian variant of marketization as the only means to this end. These economic liberals regard political democracy as an obstacle to recapitalization at this stage, and point to a world experience which purportedly demonstrates that the smoothest transitions from a "socialized economy" were carried out under the auspices of a military regime as in Greece, South Korea, and Chile. No parliament can protect new property owners from the "class hatred of lumpenized mobs". Only the army could safeguard the "creation of new property owners in defending their property by military force from the vicissitudes of the transition period". Popov gave his own imprimatur to this neo-liberalism at gunpoint when he declared that capitalism could best be introduced into the Soviet Union by an enlightened authoritarianism closely resembling the postwar American occupation regime in Japan which dismantled the Zaibatsu and cultivated the necessary preconditions for the introduction of democracy [Popov, 1990a]. Bogomolov also alluded directly to the Chilean "variant of a market without democracy" as a successful method of administering neo-liberal medicine [Bogomolov, 1990b]. The academic warned that tough market reforms created an explosive juxtaposition between elite reformers and the working class majority because the old regime satisfied the basic needs of the people even if it was at a very elementary level. The social costs of deflation were likely to stir up widespread resentment among a people unused to the impersonal hardships of a capitalist economy, and this could only be overcome by an "inevitable concentration of power and anew curtailment of democracy". Bogomolov gave assurances that this resort to "authoritarianism is only a problem of the transitional period and not a permanent alternative" but he left no doubt that the neo-liberals would look to modernizing praetorians as their insurance policy in the event economic reform triggered widespread popular resistance. Kiva blamed the neo-liberals for harming their own cause by trying to "dictate to the people something that they were not ready to accept" [Kiva, 1990d]. But instead of looking to intelligent generals, he urged neo-liberals to throw their support to a plebiscitary form of rule being sought by Gorbachev in late 1990 as the best hope for the transition to a market economy. The historian reasoned that the country was not yet sufficiently mature for democracy, and could not escape an "authoritarian stage". But he sought to ensure that Gorbachev becomes the enlightened despot who could engineer the integration of new alignments of interests and power into a viable developmental bloc. Kiva wanted party modernizers to continue serving as the "intermediaries between the declining and ascending social forces" in averting any frontal clashes. But the disintegration of the command-administrative system and the resulting diffusion of power raises the question of whether there actually does exist in the Soviet Union any political force with the effective authority to carry through such profound and complex reforms across this vast country in so short a period [Guerra, 1990].

VIII. *Conclusion*

Most analyses of the Perestroika share a common perception of the neo-liberals as the cutting edge of an all-conquering commercial advance which will enable capitalist influences to permeate and fundamentally transform Soviet society. These gloomy assessments on the part of radicals may seem worldly-wise and warranted in light of the destructive and creative chaos unleashed by the reform process and the setbacks suffered by the international left over the past decade. The principal aim of my analysis of Soviet neo-liberalism was to show why this anticipation of an inexorable recapitalization of the Soviet Union is the product of a facile pessimism every bit as un-justified as a shallow optimism. A post-Stalinist Soviet Union faces the immense task of not only transforming anachronistic political institutions but also inventing an economy capable of sustaining intensive growth [Shevtsova, 1990c]. The chief cause of the current social unrest and political drift is the struggle for power within the power elite after the dissolution of the Brezhnevite coalition, and this instability will continue until these battles are resolved. This power struggle is driven not just by petty factional wrangling but the broader process of class formation. The ongoing metamorphosis of state cadre and the emergence of new entrepreneurial elites promises to be a long, difficult, and tumultuous process. The success of the Perestroika from above will hinge on the ability of these elites to build a consensual political framework and weld together a cohesive growth coalition capable of acting through these new institutions. The least likely scenario at present would be that of any single factional combatant achieving sufficient political leverage to be able to carry through the Perestroika strictly on its own terms.

The possible future permutations of the Soviet reform process seem quite different if the lines between the various strata of the Soviet power elite are perceived as blurred and wavering rather than solid phalanxes arrayed against each other. Boris Kurashvili went so far as to characterize Soviet neo-liberalism as a political phenomenon which would quickly unravel following closer parliamentary inspection or after attempts to implement shock therapy provoked the "first broad wave of popular outrage" [Kurashvili, 1990a]. In the cold light of practical transitional difficulties, it is quickly becoming apparent that the notion of an experimental "third path" is not the figment of a sentimental imagination but an historical necessity for countries attempting to move from warped neo-Stalinist economic structures to a viable market economy of any kind [J. Sapir cited in Sachs, 1990]. For all his free market bluster, Janos Kornai's vision of the only feasible transition strategy from a command-administrative system to a capitalist economy, bears an uncanny resemblance to the market socialist models of the sixties despite it now being relabelled a "dualistic economy" for an age of triumphalist neo-liberalism [Kowalik, 1990]. The slowly unfolding Polish disaster and their own sinking popularity are impelling some neo-liberals to broach the possibility that the restoration of capitalism is a problematic endeavour because it is impossible to leap into an "integrated balanced economy created over centuries" [Pushkov, 1990]. Some are already resigning themselves to the likelihood that structural constraints and widespread egalitarian sentiments will be most conducive to the emergence of some novel malintegrated "hybrid" system resembling most closely a dependent bureaucratic capitalism.

After the cresting of their political offensive in the Autumn of 1990, the neo-liberals began explaining away the abortive "500 Days" Programme as the "infantile disorder of privatization", a rash attempt by ultras at ushering in the market from below which would have resulted in the nomenklatura or insurgent factory collectives gaining effective control of industrial assets [Grigoriev, 1990]. In response to these latest trends, prominent neo-liberals are already beating a hasty retreat from the political maximalism of the summer. The more prudent neo-liberals were always more partial to salami tactics instead of risky frontal assaults: "Cutting off the dog's tail by a little bit every day so that he becomes used to it" [Kara-Murza, 1990, p. 47]. Kliamkin interpreted Gorbachev's rejection of the Shatalin Plan and endorsement of a compromise variant as a victory for the neo-liberal camp which had earlier badly overreached itself politically [Kliamkin, 1990]. In the view of the Soviet political scientist, Gorbachev's alternative programme should be constructed as a grudging admission by the nomenklatura that it could no longer cope with the demands of providing sufficient food and consumer goods to the Soviet people, and must accordingly relinquish responsibility in these spheres to "all those who work in agriculture, light industry, and trade". The academic was confident that the neo-liberals could use this new political space to expand the social base of those forces demanding the extension of private enterprise to the rest of the economy. Kliamkin foresaw the Perestroika settling down into a symbiotic antagonism between the nomenklatura establishment and the burgeoning ranks of entrepreneurs with the latter gradually improving their position within the mesalliance to become the dominant partner. But it seems at least equally likely that this modus vivendi would encourage the forming of alliances across old increasingly artificial battlelines and the osmosis of upwardly mobile elites into a rejuvenated dominant class. If the present protean and amorphous character of Soviet reform politics allows the party modernizers to impose a Pax Gorbacheva on querulous elites groping for a mediated accord, the Perestroika would culminate in the dominant class being reconstituted on a new mixed economic foundation of state capitalism and private enterprise.

However this felicitous outcome for the Soviet power elite is by no means preordained. A government specialist on the mechanics of privatization raised the spectre of the auctioning process getting out of hand if resentful workers at the various enterprises took advantage of the denationalization of state property to transform industrial assets into "economically illiterate" collective property which was for them the clearly preferred outcome [Melikian, 1990a]. All segments of the Soviet power elite realize that the greatest threat to a successful privatization would be a "change of the attitudes of work collectives. . . towards state property" when they see it being handed over to new private owners who made their fortunes in official graft or the black market [Kurashvili, 1990b, pp. 36-39]. Kurashvili anticipated that after an initial period of mass confusion about the technical arcana of privatization, the Soviet people would quickly grasp that the "state apparatus is transforming itself into the owner of a significant portion of the national wealth and thus into an important part of a new ruling class". The resulting popular upheaval would foster the rapid growth of an "anarcho-syndicalist movement" spearheaded by the new independent trade unions which will attempt to ensure the transfer of state property to worker collectives rather than private owners. The most likely outcome of this confrontation, in Kurashvili's opinion, would be the neo-liberals moving forcibly to suppress the shopfloor revolts. The ensuing unrest would then open the way to conservative revanchism under the pretext of restoring order. The iconoclastic legal scholar has been among the most prescient observers of the political evolution of the Perestroika so his opinions deserve special consideration on this score alone. But as even Kurashvili admits, the great weakness of the Soviet right all along has been its inability to develop a coherent counter-programme for the salvaging of a foundering economic system. Given this vacuum, it appears more likely that the conservatives would use the repression of the Soviet labour movement to seek an open or tacit alliance with the neo-liberals which could work to their mutual advantage in creating more stable economic foundations for class domination. Kurashvili also raises the entirely plausible possibility of an impressive show of strength on the part of the labour movement, encouraging segments of the power elite, including Gorbachev, hitherto cowed by the neo-liberal ideological offensive, into going over to the real left. In short, the range of possible outcomes of the Perestroika is not as narrow as most Western accounts have drawn them. We can only be sure that the moment of truth still lies ahead and the Soviet Union is only now in the words of Kurashvili "drawing close to the denouement of one of the greatest dramas in human history".

REFERENCES AND BIBLIOGRAPHY

Abalkin, L. 1990. *Soiuz* [Union]. no. 43.

Abdullaev, M. 1990. *Soiuz* no. 38.

Aganbegian, A. 1990. *Sovetskie profsoiuzy* [Soviet Trade Unions]. no. 10.

Aleksashenko, S. 1990. *Mirovaia Ekonomika i Mezhdunarodnie Otnosheniia* [World Economy and International Relations] no. 7.

Ambartsumov, E. 1990a. *Narodnyi Deputat* [People's Deputy]. no. 9.

— — .1990b. *Dialog* [Dialogue], no. 11.

Anulova, G. 1990. *Izvestiia*. October 1.

Artsishevskii, L. 1990. *Vechernaia Moskva* [Evening Moscow]. September 8.

Azarovskii, G. 1990. *Komsomolskaia Pravda* [Komsomol Pravda]. October 4.

Baczynski, J. 1990. *Polityka*. October 27.

Belotserkovskii, V. 1985. *Samoupravlenie* [Self-Management]. Munich: Neimanis.

Belousov, A. and Klepach, A. 1990. *Dialog*. no. 14.

Berger, M. 1990. *Izvestiia*. October 23.

Bim, A. and Shakin, A. 1986. *Kommunist*. no. 15.

Bobrovskii, S. 1990a. *Komsomolskaia Pravda*. November 1.

— — .1990b. *Komsomolskaia Pravda*. November 20.

Bocharov, M. 1990. *Literaturnaia Gazeta* [Literary Gazette]. August 15.

Bogachev, V. 1990a. *Ekonomicheskie Nauki* [Economic Studies]. no. 2.

— — .1990b. *Znanie-Sila* [Knowledge is Power]. no. 3.

Bogomolov, O. 1990a. *Ogoniok* [Little Flame]. no. 35.

— — .1990b. *Zycie Gospodarcze* [Economic Affairs]. November 11.

— — .1990c. *Izvestiia*. November 23.

Bondarev, V. 1990. *Trud* [Labour]. August 9.

Bonevskaia, A. 1986. *Sotsiologischeskie Issledovaniia* [Sociological Studies]. no. 1.
Borodkin, F. ed. 1989. *Postizhenie* [Comprehension]. Moscow: Progress.
Bugaj, R. and Kowalik, T. 1990. *Zycie Gospodarcze* [Economic Affairs]. September 30.
Burlatskii, F. 1985. *Sovremennyi Leviafan* [Contemporary Leviathan]. Moscow: Thought.
Bushkevich, M. 1990. *Pravda*. September 23.
Chiesa, G. 1990. *L'Unita*. July 15.
Danilov-Danilian, A. et al. 1990. *Argumenty i Fakty* [Arguments and Facts]. no. 33.
Danilov-Danilian, V. 1990. *Znanie-Sila* [Knowledge is Power]. no. 5.
Drozd, V. 1988. *Literaturnaia Gazeta*. September 26.
Dubinin, N. 1980. *Kommunist*. no. 11.
— — .1983. *Shto Takoe Chelovek* [What is a Human Being]. Moscow: Thought.
Dzarasov, S. 1988. *Sotsielisticheskaia Industriia* [Socialist Industry].November 11.
— — .1990. *Sotsiologicheskie Issledovaniia*. no. 7.
"Editorial". 1987. *Izvestiia*. November 2.
"Editorial". 1988. *Pravda*. December 12.
Esipov, V. 1990. *Trud*. May 19.
Gaidar, E. 1990. *Pravda*. July 24.
Galperin, I. and Ursov, Iu. 1990. *Trud*. August 18.
Go, S. 1989. *Voprosy Ekonomiki* [Problems of Economics]. no. 12.
Gorbovskii, A. 1980. *Literaturnaia Gazeta*. June 4.
Gordon, L. 1987. *Sotsiologicheskie Issledovaniia*. no. 4.
Grigoriev, L. 1990. *Moskovskie Novosti*. no. 48.
Guerra, A. 1990. *L'Unita*. October 20.
Hankiss, E. 1989. *Valosag* [Reality]. no. 2.
Henzler, M. 1989. *Polityka*. September 2.
Hoehmann, H. 1988. *Osteuropa*. no. 7.
Ianovskii, R. 1986. *Sotsiologicheskie Issledovaniia*. no. 2.
Iaroshenko, V. 1990. *Movyi Mir* [New World]. no. 2.
Iasin, E. 1990. *Voprosy Ekonomiki* [Problems of Economics]. no. 7.
Kagarlitskii, B. 1990a. *Narodnyi Deputat*. no. 9.
— — .1990b. *Predislovie k Khaosu* [Foreword to Chaos]. Moscow: Unpublished Manuscript.
Kara-Murza, S. 1990. *Dialog*. no. 10.
Karpinskii, L. 1990. *Moskovskie Novosti* [Moscow News]. no. 46.
Kerimov, B. ed. 1989. *Problemy Partiinogo i Gosudarstvennogo Stroitelstva* [Problems of Party and State Organization]. Moscow: Thought.
Khromov, G. 1989. *Izvestiia*. August 22.
Kiselev, V. 1990. *Kommunist*. no. 8.
Kiva, A. 1990a. *Novyi Mir*. no. 3.
— — .1990b. *Izvestiia*. April 16.
— — .1990c. *Izvestiia*. July 19.
— — .1990d. *Izvestiia*. December 10.
Kliamkin, I. 1990. *Moskovskie Novosti*. no. 47.
Kochega, V. 1990. *Sotsialno-Politicheskie Nauki* [Socio-Political Studies]. no. 5.
Koriagina, T. 1989. *Literaturnaia Gazeta*. December 13.
Kornai, J. 1987. *Gazdasag* [Economics]. no. 2.
Kowalik, T. 1990. *Zycie Gospodarcze*. September 9.
Kurashvili, B. 1990a. *Pravda*. October 4.
— — .1990b. *Dialog*. no. 16.
Levikov, A. 1988. *Literaturnaia Gazeta*. December 14.
Lisichkin, G. 1987. *Literaturnaia Gazeta*. June 3.
Maidanik, K. 1990. *Mirovaia Ekonomika i Mezhdunarodnie Otnosheniia*. no. 10.
Maliutin, M. 1990. *Pravda*. June 13.

Malmygin, L. 1990. *Izvestiia Akademii Nauk SSSR*. no. 4.
Mau, V. and Starodubtsev, I. 1990. *Kommunist*. no. 11.
Medvedev, P. et al. 1990. *Kommunist*. no. 14.
Medvedev, R. 1990. *Pravda*. October 11.
Melikian, G. 1990a. *Rabochaia Tribuna* [Labor Tribune]. September 6.
— — .1990b. *Pravitelstvennyi Vestnik* [Government Bulletin]. no. 43.
Melnikov, O. and Kvasnikova, N. 1990. *Izvestiia Sibirskogo Otdeleniia Akademii Nauk SSSR* [Proceedings of the Siberian Division of the Academy of Sciences of the USSR]. no. 2.
Moiseev, N. 1988. *Novyi Mir*. no. 4.
Naumova, N. 1990. *Kommunist*. no. 8.
Naushul, V. 1990. *Izvestiia*. December 9.
Nekipelov, A. 1990. *Izvestiia*. October 6.
Nikitin, A. 1990. *Izvestiia*. November 8.
Nikitin, S. 1990. *Ekonomika i Organizatsiia Promyshlennogo Proizvodstva* [Economics and Organization of Industrial Production]. no. 6.
Novak, L. 1989. *Polityka*. April 6.
Pavlov, V. 1990. *Trud*. July 19.
Pavlova-Silvanskaia, M. 1990. *Izvestiia*. September 24.
Penkin, A. 1990. *Kommunist*. no. 15.
Piiasheva, L. 1990a. *Rabochii Klass i Sovremennyi Mir* [Working Class and the Contemporary World]. no. 2.
— — .1990b. *Komsomolskaia Pravda*. October 6.
Pinsker, B. 1990. *Literaturnaia Gazeta*. September 10.
"Political Note". 1990. *Le Monde*. January 31.
Popov, G. 1980. *Pravda*. December 27.
— — .1987. *Nauka i Zhizn* [Science and Life]. no. 9.
— — .1988a. *Ogoniok*. no. 33.
— — .1988b. *Voprosy Ekonomiki*. no. 10.
— — .1989. *Voprosy Ekonomiki*. no. 12.
— — .1990a. *Moskovskie Novosti*. no. 42.
— — .1990b. *Vechernaia Moskva* [Evening Moscow]. October 15.
Popov, V. 1989. *Voprosy Ekonomiki*. no. 12.
— — .1990. *Mirovaia Ekonomika i Mezhdunarodnie Otnosheniia*. no. 1.
Pushkov, A. 1990. *Moskovskie Novosti*. no. 46.
Radzikhovskii, L. 1990. *Moskovskie Novosti*. no. 33.
Rakitskii, B. 1988. *Voprosy Ekonomiki*. no. 10.
Rassolov, M. 1989. "Problems of Information-Gathering" in Kerimov, ed.
Rossanda, R. 1987. *Il Manifesto*. November 5.
Rumiantsev, O. 1990. *Soiuz*. no. 36.
Rutkevich, M. 1977. *Intelligentsiia v Razvitom Sotsialisticheskom Obshchestve* [The Intelligentsia in Developed Socialist Society]. M: IPL.
— — .1986. *Sotsiologicheskie Issledovaniia*. no. 3.
Rytov, Iu. 1990. *Pravitelstvennyi Vestnik*. no. 43.
Ryvkina, R. 1989. *Ekonomike i Organizatsiia Promyshlennogo Proizvodstva*. no. 1.
Sabov, A. 1990. *Literaturnaia Gazeta*. April 11.
Sachs, I. 1990. *Zycie Gospodarcze*. August 26.
Sapir, J. 1989. *Les Fluctuations Economiques en URSS 1941-1985*. Paris: EHESS.
Sapritsiants, G. 1987. *Politicheskoe Obrazovanie* [Political Education]. no. 1.
Seliunin, V. 1990. *Znamia*. no. 6.
Semenov, E. 1990. *Dialog*. no. 15.
Sevestianov, A. 1988. *Literaturnaia Gazeta*. September 21.
Shatalin, S. 1986. *Kommunist*. no. 14.
Shchipentsev, A. 1990. *Sovetskaia Rossiia* [Soviet Russia]. August 1.

Shevtsova. L. 1990a. *Izvestiia*. September 17.
— — . 1990b. *Komsomolskaia Pravda*. September 26.
— — . 1990c. *Izvestiia*. October 6.
Shifrin, V. 1990. *Vechernaia Moskva*. September 7.
Shirokov, V. 1989. *Pravda*. October 31.
Shkaratan, O. 1970. *Problemy Sotsialnoi Struktury Rabochego Klassa* [Problems of the Social Structure of the Working Class]. Moscow: Thought.
— — . 1978. *Promyshlennoe Predpriatiie* [Industrial Enterprise]. Moscow: Thought.
Shmeliov, N. 1989. *Znamia* [Banner]. no. 1.
— — . 1990. *Pravitelstvennyi Vestnik*. no. 28.
Shpakov, Iu. 1987, *Pravda*. December 28.
Shprygin, V. 1990. *Pravitelstvennyi Vestnik*. no. 45.
Shverdlik, S. 1990. *Ekonomika i Organizatsiia Promshlennogo Proizvodstva*. no. 3.
Sobchak, A. 1990. *Kommunist*. no. 1.
Sogrin, V. 1990. *Pravda*. June 6.
Sokolov, V. 1990. *Literaturnaia Gazeta*. September 12.
Sokolova, I. and Manuilskii, M. 1988. *Sotsiologicheskie Issledovaniia*. no. 1.
Starikov, E. 1990. *Kommunist*. no. 5.
Stepin, V. 1990. *Pravda*. January 22.
Sukhotin, Iu. 1988. *Ekonomika i Organizatsiia Promyshlennogo Proizvodstva*. no. 11.
Torkenovskii, E. 1988. *Kommunist*. no. 11.
Travkin, N. 1990. *Ekonomika i Organizatsiia Promyshlennogo Proizvodstva*. no. 3.
Tsypko, A. 1989. *Nedelia* [Week]. no. 11.
Usmanov, S. 1990. *Latinskaia Amerika* [Latin America]. no. 8.
Valiuzhenich, G. 1990. *Argumenty i Fakty*. no. 45.
Vavilov, A. 1988. *Sotsialisticheskaia Industriia*. December 7.
Veger, L. 1990. *Voprosy Ekonomiki*. no. 5.
Volobuev, P. 1988. *Sotsialisticheskaia Industriia*. October 16.
Yeltsin, B. 1990. *Izvestiia*. October 17.
Zaichenko, A. 1990. *Dialog*. no. 15.
Zaslavskaia, T. 1986. *Kommunist*. no. 13.
— — . 1987. *Sotsialisticheskaia Industriia*. February 7.
— — . 1989. "Perestroika and Socialism" in Borodkin, ed.
— — . et al. 1990. *Izvestiia*. October 25.
Zaslavskii, I. 1990. *Dialog*. no. 12.
Zhagel, I. 1990. *Izvestiia*. October 7.
Zinoviev, A. 1990. *Komsomolskaia Pravda*. September 15.
Zupanov, J. 1983. *Marginalije o Drustvenoj Krizi* [Marginal Notes on the Social Crisis]. Zagreb: Globus.

"REAL SOCIALISM" IN HISTORICAL PERSPECTIVE

Robert W. Cox

"It is not the business of the historian to award prizes for virtue, to propose the erection of statues, or to establish any catechism whatever: his business is to understand what is least individual in the course of events. . ."

Georges Sorel, *Reflections on Violence* (1906)

The death of socialism is affirmed everywhere today as a matter of common knowledge, from yesterday's newspaper to the neo-Hegelian "end of history" proclaimed by Francis Fukuyama,[1] and the neo-Burkian reflections on revolution in Eastern Europe by Ralf Dahrendorf.[2] The events of Eastern Europe are read as the definitive seal of closure upon something much broader than the regimes of "real socialism".[3] They signal the end of an historical project that had its origins in the response of nineteenth-century industrial society to the disintegrating impact of capitalism.[4] Or so it would seem.

Those who retain socialist convictions must treat the proclamation seriously, even in offering Mark Twain's rejoinder that it is greatly exaggerated. Two lines of argument are weak responses. One is that Soviet (or by extension, Chinese, or Cuban or. . .) socialism was never true socialism. It was from the beginning, or from some later stage, a deformation, a perversion, of the true thing. Like Christianity, socialism has never been tried. The other weak rejoinder is that the failure of socialism was the fault of evil men — Stalin in the first place and secondarily of a corrupted *nomenklatura*. A corollary of these arguments is the fragmentation of socialism into a multitude of quarrelling groups, each convinced of its possession of the "truth" of socialism.

Whatever validity there may be in these judgments on the failures of "real socialism", they are inconsistent with a socialist view of history and a socialist mode of reasoning. Socialism is both a project of society and a method of social and historical analysis — and there has to be some consistency between its two aspects. The project of society is not a Platonic intellectual construct given in advance which is to be put into effect by enlightened leadership of a mass movement being led towards the light. The project of society is itself a product of historical struggles which have to be understood as a conflict of social forces the precise outcome of which is never altogether predictable. Individuals and leadership groups are important, but must also be seen as the product of impersonal forces. All revolutions create opportunities for individuals whose aggressive and deviant proclivities would be controlled and repressed in a more stable social situation. We have the right to moral outrage at what these individuals may do, but we should not let this obscure the impersonal forces that unleash their vicious tendencies. Both lines of apology for the failings of "real socialism" forsake historical materialism to fall into the trap of idealism. They thereby endorse the death certificate of socialism.

The most serious present task of socialism is to analyse what went wrong and not to try to avoid the issue idealistically by defining it out of socialism. "Real socialism" was shaped and conditioned by the world into which it came and in which it developed. What were these shaping forces? What historical social structures may survive the débâcle of "real socialism" to be available for the making of the future? Which configurations of forces delineate feasible future options, including, perhaps, socialist options? These are pertinent questions for socialism today.

The impersonal shaping forces have operated at three levels: production, the state, and world order.[5] These three levels are conceptually distinct but interrelated in practice. Production creates the material basis for all forms of social existence, and the ways in which human productive efforts are combined in productive processes affect all other aspects of social life, including the polity. Production generates the capacity to exercise power, but power in the form of state determines the manner in which production takes place. The structure of world order, in turn, conditions the possibilities of formation and development of different forms of state and of production. Socialism as an historical experience arose from a particular crisis of world order. It aspired to be at the same time a system of political rule and of production. The organization of production lies at the heart of socialist politics.

Two intertwined historical processes affected the course of socialist development: (1) external constraints from the world order influenced the origins of socialist experiments, the course they took and their possibilities of survival; and (2) internal dynamics of socialist development generated new social forces with actual or latent conflicting interests and they raised new problems to be confronted. The socialist state faces both inward, attempting to reach a modus vivendi or historic compromise with the emerging social forces, and outward, attempting to secure the political space and the material resources required to confront internal demands. As Machiavelli long ago warned, the necessity of reforms can never be acted upon without danger, the danger being that the state may be destroyed before having perfected its constitution.[6]

Machiavelli also underlined the importance of events in demonstrating the necessity of reforms in the state. It is well, in our present context, to reflect upon the relationship of events to historical structures. Braudel expressed this relationship as a dialectic of duration, an interaction of the immediacy of events with the slower-moving structures of the *longue durée*.[7] 800,000 people massed in and about Wenceslas Square in Prague manifesting opposition to the government is a salient event. When they walk home or to work, structures reemerge, though the continuity of these structures may have been called into question. At one moment there is "the people". "The people" is not a structure but an unstructured energized mass, a moment when structures are suspended, only to reappear again. Structures are the means whereby we get from one day to the next, but events may shake and cumulatively may transform structures.

The historical dialectic of "real socialism" comprises four moments: (1) the military-political conditions requisite to survival of a socialist experiment initiated in relatively underdeveloped territories; (2) an organization of state and production shaped and reshaped in the context of this military-political struggle for survival; (3) the emergence of contradictions within this organization of state and production which block its ability both to produce adequately and to guarantee order; and (4) a struggle among internally-generated social forces over the restructuring of state and economy in which external forces also play an influential role.

The analysis which begins with the state of world order in which a socialist experiment becomes possible, proceeds to the internal dynamic of socialist development, to return again to the implications of the *dénouement* of the crisis of existing socialism for the world order and for the prospects of socialism in the larger world.

The primacy of the military-political

Survival was the categorical imperative of socialist construction after the Bolsheviks seized power in a collapsing Russian state during the autumn of 1917.[8] The subsequent collapse of the Central Powers and the limited willingness or ability of the victorious Western powers to sustain a long civil and interventionist war on Russian territory provided the conditions of inter-state relations in which the Soviet state could establish itself. The first socialist revolution gained a precarious existence because the world military-political balance was not propitious for its suppression. Western statesmen, fearing an advance of the revolutionary movement through Europe, settled for a defensive strategy.

The military-political factor thus was dominant in the initial stages of the socialist experiment. This factor remained dominant in subsequent socialist revolutions. They all occurred in economically backward societies in conditions of internal military débâcle and armed struggle and of external hostility to the socialist project. The political, economic, and at times military, forces of the developed capitalist world have been mobilized to harass, destabilize and defeat efforts to consolidate socialist revolutions. Where the socialist experiment was supported or imposed from without, as in Eastern Europe following World War II, the military-political configuration was again dominant.

External pressures have the effect of privileging those internal forces that appear effectively to respond to them. External opposition to established socialist regimes, whether or not intended, whether or not justified, provoked responses from the socialist leaderships in the realms of foreign policy, production, and the form of state that have nothing intrinsically to do with the socialist idea *per se.*[9] Real historical socialism, in other words, has not been the gradual putting into effect of a socialist idea. Real socialism has grown through an historical dialectic with the forces of world capitalism within the framework of the inter-state system. Socialism has internalized the marks of this dialectic.

Two models of state and production emerged from the Bolshevik experience both of which have lived on to influence the shapes of historical socialism. One is War Communism; the other, the New Economic Policy (NEP).

War Communism was the creation of military necessity, though some Bolshevik leaders saw a virtue in it independent of necessity. Its characteristics were economic autarky; requisitioning and rationing rather than market allocation in a money economy; nationalization of industry as a preemptive strike against private capital and foreign control; the reconstituting of trade unions as agencies of labour discipline and labour control; the militarization of labour as an obligation to perform national service with administrative allocation to jobs rather than allocation through a labour market. Under War Communism administrative coercion replaced market coercion.

The NEP was also a creation of necessity; and some other Bolshevik leaders saw virtue in it independently of its necessity. The limits of War Communism were demonstrated by the Kronstad rising in the navy in March 1921 and by peasant resistance to the exactions from the rural economy. The NEP was, in the phrase of Lenin's collaborator, Ryazanov, "a peasant Brest-Litovsk", a necessary surrender and concession to the country's most numerous class and the one on which the revolution had to depend for physical survival. [10] The characteristics of the NEP were reliance upon market forces and material inducements to peasants to increase agricultural supply; encouragement of foreign trade and foreign investment; and emphasis on increasing industrial productivity.

Two foreign policies corresponded to the two models of economy. The policy of world revolution threatened from within the capitalist states which menaced the beleaguered autarky of War Communism. It aimed at transforming the inter-state system away from its identification with a capitalist world order. But when the Soviet Union sought to establish economic intercourse with the outside world in the interest of repairing wartime damage, the strategy of world revolution became dangerously provocative. The NEP required a normalizing of the Soviet Union's relations in the inter-state system. Soviet security would be best assured if Russia were to appear as a state like other states, not one bent upon transforming the structure of world power. A strategy of taking advantage of divisions among the capitalist powers and of encouraging economic relations with those which were willing would serve to gain a pause for internal recovery better than one that united capitalist powers in hostility to Soviet survival. The Soviets negotiated trade agreements with Britain and several other European countries and made a secret treaty with Germany for mutual assistance in developing the military strength of both powers.

The military factor was also influential in the organization of production. The workers' militia concept and the Red Guards expressed the intial form of revolutionary military organization, just as workers' soviets constituted the initial form of production organization. Both were changed into a disciplined hierarchical mode of organization in the testing ground of armed conflict. The Red Guards might be effective in gaining control of major cities; they were ineffective in waging a war against organized military forces over vast distances. The Red Army was constituted along classical military lines, incorporating many regular Russian officers who were placed under the surveillance of political commisars. Similarly, the workers' soviets were displaced by a hierarchical system of management in which many former owners and "bourgeois experts" paralleled the roles of czarist officers in the army. The pressures of war initially foreclosed any experimentation with alternative modes of production organization, either as the spontaneous outgrowth of working-class action or as a planned introduction of socialist ideas. This initial impetus became institutionalized in *edinonachalie* or the system of one-man-management which survived through the NEP in large-scale industry to become integrated into the central planning of the 1930s and after. Capitalism had achieved the highest development of productive forces through hierarchical management structures of industry. The Bolsheviks took over and developed the model of the capitalist labour process for its organization of industry.

The Stalinist "revolution from above" was a return to the War Communism model, more fully institutionalized as a systematic organization of state and production. The state was centralized and, along with the Party, subjected to police power. A new "people's intelligentsia" was recruited to manage state and economy, learning on the job through trial and error to construct and operate a central planning system. The new cadres, who displaced the purged "Old Bolsheviks" and the residual pre-revolutionary "bourgeois experts", depended exclusively on service to the autocrat in the manner of the prebendary Muscovite czardom of the sixteenth century.

It is possible to understand the features of this system of power without attributing it altogether to Stalin's personality. The coercive-repressive character of the system flowed from the political power struggles within the Party that preceded it; from the spillover of coercive practices from grain seizures and forced collectivization; from the use of coercive discipline in the formation of a new industrial working class of ex-peasants (which in comparative historical terms concentrated the coercion of the British enclosure movement into a single decade); and from a world environment perceived as hostile to Soviet survival and thus as requiring a forced pace of industrialization to prepare the military basis for resisting the inevitable attack.

Revisionist history has challenged and rejected the Stalinist arguments for the policies imposed from 1929 through the 1930s. It questions the economic efficacy of the collectivization of agriculture, and the reality of the external threat, and charges that Stalin's military purges weakened rather than strengthened Soviet defences.[11] These matters are not in dispute here. My point is that, wisely or unwisely, necessarily or unnecessarily, the Soviet system in its form of state and production as well as in its armed force was shaped in the consciousness of military threat. Soviet socialism was the product of the world system — a capitalist dominated system — as much as of internal political forces. The whole responsibility cannot be attributed to the personality of Stalin. Revolutionary situations give opportunities for power to personalities who would be excluded in more stable times — to both utopian visionaries and perverse jailers. We should not ignore the circumstances by explaining everything in terms of the individuals. Nor is it useful to speculate about what might have been. (Suppose

Bukharin had won out over Stalin.) Counterfactual histories can never be refuted because they cannot be tested. They are the stuff of idealism rather than of historical materialism.

Coercion consolidated the new system of power. It survived the Nazi onslaught during World War II and maintained its momentum during the post-war decades. But coercion left its impact on a very large part of the population whose surviving friends and familymembers had bitter cause for grievance against Stalinist rule. This suppressed anger would find expression when the pressure of authority slackened and it would be supported by others dismayed by the historical record and hopeful for a more open society.

The Chinese revolution followed a different pattern in its organization of production, but one which was also shaped by its rather different military experience. China's revolutionary military power was built up after the Long March in the remote rural zone of Yenan. It was ad new kind of army, adapted to the conditions in which it came to exist. The army lived in symbiosis with peasant communities and engaged in a guerrilla type of warfare. These conditions, very different from those of the civil war following the Bolshevik revolution, shaped the revolutionary theory and practice of the Peoples Liberation Army long before it moved to occupy the coastal cities in the final stages of revolutionary war.

The PLA was organized for production, side by side with the peasantry of the zones it controlled. The leadership type it cultivated was the versatile head of a guerrilla unit who was required to assimilate fully the goals of the struggle and then to improvise autonomously in carrying them out. These characteristics defined the Chinese model of the cadre. It carried over into the organization of civilian production as a tendency to rely on ideologically assimilated leadership at all levels — an assimilation recurrently revised through "rectification" campaigns — together with relative autonomy of work groups and coordination through committees rather than line hierarchy.

In effect, two models of production organization were rivals in China following the establishment of the People's Republic. One was the model just mentioned which was a product of the experience of revolutionary war. The other was the Soviet model of one-man-management under central planning. Just as the Bolsheviks took over the only available model of industrial management — the capitalist model — so the Chinese leadership had as the most obviously available model, the Soviet one. Furthermore, in the first phase of the People's Republic, China's leadership depended heavily upon Soviet aid to develop industry, particularly in the Manchurian region. The implantation into that region of the Soviet model led to a struggle that was both political and industrial, in which the Soviet model and its supporters were defeated.

This victory was more than an assertion of an indigenous Chinese way. It was also the proclamation of a heresy in relation to Soviet Marxism: the doctrine that production relations, not productive forces, could spearhead revolutionary change. It was furthermore, an affirmation that the Chinese way would be more relevant than the Soviet way for economically backward Third World countries which, like China, did not dispose of the numbers of technically trained staff required to manage central planning and industry in the Soviet manner.

As a corollary to the primacy of the military factor in shaping the forms of state and production in "real socialism", the military have had a prior claim upon the resources of socialist societies. Since socialism has come about in relatively poor and less developed societies whose leaders have felt compelled to prepare to resist a military threat from much wealthier capitalist societies, it follows that they have consistently allocated a higher proportion of their total product to the military.

One consequence is that in order to undertake any large-scale measures of structural economic or political reform, the socialist state requires both a relaxation of the external threat and a shift of resources from military to civilian production. From the 1960s onward, the socialist countries confronted the issue of reform, as the structures of production brought into being during the earlier phase of defence of their revolutions produced declining increments of growth.

The challenge from the capitalist world, military in form, was economic in its consequences, whether it confronted the Soviet Union itself or a small peripheral aspirant to socialism. The arms race during the Reaganite phase of Cold War was too much for an unreformed economy to sustain; and efforts to keep up with the arms race blocked economic reform. The "low intensity" conflict maintained by the United States against the Sandinista government in Nicaragua was directed primarily against economic targets and local economic leadership, while requiring the Nicaraguan government to abandon economic and social investment by putting its resources into the military. The Sandinistas made a strategic withdrawal by abandoning power in elections carried out in conditions of war weariness and economic collapse. The Soviet Union, reminiscent of the NEP period, made an about shift in foreign policy to acquiesce in US and Western European concerns, to seek technological and financial assistance from the capitalist world, and to devote more attention to internal structural change.

The social structure of accumulation

It is commonly asserted today that socialist central planning has been an unmitigated disaster. In the context of this general condemnation, some appraisal of the balance of achievements and failures of central planning seems a necessary prelude to any consideration of future options.

Socialist revolutions confronted two basic problems. One was to give work to all who were able. The socialist state took responsibility for the sustenance and welfare of its citizens, and determined to mobilize the whole of society into the production process. Even those who could not produce their keep would add something to the social product upon which everyone depended.

The other basic problem was to break the agricultural barrier to expanded development. Since socialist revolutions occurred in peasant societies, it was necessary to raise agricultural productivity in order to be able to shift employment to industry and to finance industrial development.

By and large, socialist economic organization went a long way towards resolving these two problems. In doing so, "real socialism" created the human resource for economic development in backward societies: an educated public whose health was adequately cared for and amongst whom the basic necessities of life were more equitably distributed. The human costs of these achievements were great, especially in the collectivization of agriculture, in police repression, and in the casualties of war. As these costs were in part determined by internal political decisions, responsibility for pain and suffering can be directly attributed to political leaders. But was the cost more terrible than the suffering caused by the impersonal market forces of capitalist industrialization? There is little basis to conclude that it was, though the socialist experience was compressed into a shorter space of time.

The success of socialist growth did, however, manifest diminishing returns in virtually all the countries of "real socialism" from the mid-1960s. There is, of course, much scope for quarrelling over the quantitative figures for growth rates. The pattern, however, seems clear enough. Return on investment of about 20 percent of national income during the first Five-Year Plans of the 1930s was high, as high as or higher than growth rates during the peak periods of growth of the major capitalist countries. These high growth rates continued during the reconstruction of the post-World-War-II period, not only in the Soviet Union but in the other countries practising central planning. These growth rates began to decline from the 1960s through the 1980s. Higher investment ratios produced lower and lower increments of growth. [12]

During the same period, those areas in which socialism had produced its greatest achievements also began to manifest problems. The quality of health services deteriorated. There were recurrent shortages of basic consumer goods. There was a growing mismatch between skills produced by the education system and job opportunities. All of these factors built growing frustration into society.

These developments coincided with changes in deep social structure. In the first phase of revolution, the Party confronted a crumbling and disarticulated pre-revolutionary society. This is the phase Gramsci called the war of movement. The old structures of political authority were quickly swept aside because they had weak support in the old-regime society. The Party was able to take the initiative to create new social structures. By the early 1930s, new directing cadres, the "people's intelligentsia", assumed the functions of a ruling group. They were not a class in the sense that they were not a self-perpetuating group possessing power as a group. Rather they were an agglomeration of individuals whose positions of authority depended on their loyalty and effectiveness. They worked in conditions of extreme personal insecurity.

In a subsequent phase, however, civil society gradually reemerged. This new form of civil society was in large measure the result of the ways in which the revolution had become institutionalized in the state and in production. In the Brezhnev period, the tension and personal insecurity of the ruling cadres was relaxed. Not only the small leadership group but also the much larger stratum of officials and managers in Party, state and economy felt more secure. Their access to forms of relative privilege was guaranteed. The chances of their children to accede to the status of their parents was enhanced. The *nomenklatura*, in other words, was becoming a stabilized ruling class.

The lower echelons of Soviet society were also settling into a more permanent stratification. The era of rapid transformation of ex-peasants into a new industrial working class had passed. Two strata of workers emerged. An upper stratum was closely integrated into the economic system, with more permanent stability and privilege; and a lower stratum was less firmly attached to the organizations of production. A new large service-sector was staffed substantially by women workers. The better-off agricultural workers were becoming assimilated to the status of industrial workers, while the less-well-off rural population remained more disadvantaged than urban residents.

Similar trends affected the populations of the Eastern European countries. The cycle of initial suppression of civil society, followed by its emergence in a reshaped form has been common to all the countries of "real socialism". In China, Mao twice launched an offensive against what he perceived as the challenge to the continuity of revolution from a renascent civil society — first in the Great Leap Forward, then in the Cultural Revolution. But by the 1970s, the war of movement in China was spent and the Party came to terms with the existence of civil society.

The revival of civil society modified the role of the Party. It could no longer play the role of active shaper of a passive social mass. The Party's new role became that of mediator between social forces and state power. The Party's ultimate goal in this phase was to achieve an "historic compromise" whereby the most articulate elements of civil society would acquiesce in its continuing rule in return for a substantial degree of toleration of their own autonomy.[13] The contradictions in the emergent civil society were either internalized within the Party, leading to intra-Party conflict, or they erupted outside the Party where opposition was more vulnerable to repression.

The historic compromise consecrated a social structure of accumulation. Socialist societies accumulate like capitalist societies for the purpose of investment and growth. Both capitalist and socialist societies grow by extracting a surplus from the producers. In market-driven capitalist societies, this surplus is invested in whatever individual capitalists think is likely to produce a further profit. In socialist societies, investment decisions are politically determined according to whatever criteria are salient at the time for the decision-makers, e.g. welfare or state power. The social structure of accumulation is the particular configuration of social power through which the accumulation process takes place. This configuration delineates a relationship among social groups in the production process through which surplus is extracted. This power relationship underpins the institutional arrangements through which the process works.[14]

To grasp the nature of the social structure of accumulation at the moment of the crisis of existing socialism in the late 1980s, one must go back to the transformation in the working class that began some three decades earlier. The new working class composed largely of ex-peasants that carried through the industrialization drive of the 1930s and the war effort of the 1940s worked under an iron discipline of strict regulation and tough task masters recruited from the shop floor. During the 1950s a new mentality reshaped industrial practices. Regulations were relaxed and their modes of application gave more scope for the protection of individual workers' interests. Managerial cadres began to be recruited mainly from professional schools and were more disposed to the methods of manipulation and persuasion than to coercion. The factory regime passed from the despotic to the hegemonic type.[15]

The historic compromise worked out by the Party leadership

included a social contract in which workers were implicitly guaranteed job security, stable consumer prices, and control over the pace of work, in return for their passive acquiescence in the rule of the political leadership. Workers had considerable structural power, i.e. their interests had to be anticipated and taken into account by the leadership, though they had little instrumental power through direct representation. This arrangement of passive acquiescence in time generated the cynicism expressed as: "You pretend to pay us. We pretend to work."

The working class comprised an established and a non-established segment. One group of workers, the established worker segment, were more permanent in their jobs, had skills more directly applied in their work, were more involved in the enterprise as a social institution and in other political and civic activities. The other group, the non-established worker segment, changed jobs more frequently, experienced no career development in their employment, and were non-participant in enterprise or other social and political activities. The modalities of this segmentation varied among the different socialist countries. In China, it was more explicitly institutionalized.[16] In the Soviet Union, it was more a question of job relations, attitudes and behaviour.

Hungarian sociologists discerned a more complex categorization of non-established workers: "workhorses" willing to exploit themselves for private accumulation (newly marrieds for instance); "hedonists" or single workers interested only in the wage as the means of having a good time; and "internal guest workers" mainly women, or part-time peasant workers, or members of ethnic minorities allocated to the dirty work.[17] In practice, labour segmentation under "real socialism" bore a striking similarity to labour segmentation under capitalism.[18]

This differentiation within the working class had a particular importance in the framework of central planning. Central planning can be thought of in abstract terms as a system comprising (a) redistributors in central agencies of the state who plan according to some decision-making rationality, i.e. maximizing certain defined goals and allocating resources accordingly; and (b) direct producers who carry out the plans with the resources provided them. In practice, central planning has developed an internal dynamic that defies the rationality of planners. It has become a complex bargaining process from enterprise to central levels in which different groups have different levels of power. One of the more significant theoretical efforts of recent years has been to analyse the real nature of central planning so as to discern its inherent laws or regularities.[19]

Capital is understood as a form of alienation: people through their labour create something that becomes a power over themselves and their work. Central planning also became a form of alienation: instead of being a system of rational human control over economic processes, it too became a system that no one controlled but which came to control planners and producers alike.

A salient characteristic of central planning as it had evolved in the decades just prior to the changes that began to be introduced during the late 1980s was a tendency to overinvest. Enterprises sought to get new projects included in the plan and thus to increase their sources of supply through allocations within it. Increased supplies made it easier to fulfil existing obligations but at the same time raised future obligations. The centrally planned economy was an economy of shortages; it was supply constrained, in contrast to the capitalist economy which was demand constrained. The economy of shortages generated uncertainties of supply, and these uncertainties were transmitted from enterprise to enterprise along the chain of inputs and outputs.

Enterprise managers became highly dependent upon core workers to cope with uncertainties. The core workers, familiar with the installed equipment, were the only ones able to improvise when bottlenecks occurred. They could, if necessary, improvise to cope with absence of replacement parts, repair obsolescent equipment, or make use of substitute materials. Managers also had an incentive to hoard workers, to maintain an internal enterprise labour reserve that could be mobilized for "storming" at the end of a plan period. Managers also came to rely on their relations with local Party officials to secure needed inputs when shortages impeded the enterprise's ability to meet its plan target.

These factors combined to make the key structure at the heart of the system one of management dependence on local Party cadres together with a close interrelationship between management and core workers in a form of enterprise corporatism. From this point, there were downward linkages with subordinate groups of non-established workers, with rural cooperatives, and with household production. There were upward linkages with the ministries of industries and the state plan. And there was a parallel relationship with the "second economy" which, together with political connections, helped to bypass some of the bottlenecks inherent in the formal economy.

Several things can be inferred from this social structure of accumulation. One is that those constituting its core — management, established workers, and local Party officials — were well entrenched in the production system. They knew how to make it work and they were likely to be apprehensive about changes that would introduce further uncertainties beyond those that they had learned to cope with. Motivation for change was most likely to come from those at the top who were aware that production was less efficient than it might have been, and who wanted to eliminate excess labour and to introduce more productive technology. (Those at the core of the system had a vested interest in existing obsolescent technology because their particular skills made it work.) Motivation for change might also arise among the general population in the form of dissatisfaction with declining standards of public services and consumer goods; and among a portion of the growing "middle class" of white collar service workers. The more peripheral of the non-established workers — those most alienated within the system — were unlikely to be highly motivated for change. There was, in fact, no coherent social basis for change but rather a diffuse dissatisfaction with the way the system was performing. There was, however, likely to be a coherent social basis at the heart of the system that could be mobilized to resist change.

Economic reform and democratization

Socialist systems, beginning with the Soviet Union, have been pre-occupied with reform of the economic mechanism since the 1960s. The problem was posed in terms of a transition from the extensive pattern of growth that was producing diminishing returns to a pattern of growth that would be more intensive in the use of capital and technology. Perception of the problem came from the top of the political-economic hierarchy and was expressed through a sequence of on-again off-again experiments. Piece-meal reform proved difficult because of the very coherence of the system of power that constituted central planning. Movement in one direction, e.g. granting more decision-making powers to managers, ran up against obstacles in other parts of the system, e.g. in the powers of central ministries and in the acquired job rights of workers.

Frustrations with piece-meal reforms encouraged espousal of more radical reform; and radical reform was associated with giving much broader scope to the market mechanism. The market was an attractive concept insofar as it promised a more effective and less cumbersome means of allocating material inputs to enterprises and of distributing consumer goods. It was consistent with decentralization of management to enterprises and with a stimulus to consumer-goods production. The market, however, was also suspect insofar as it would create prices (and thus inflation in an economy of shortages), bring about greater disparities in incomes, and undermine the power of the centre to direct the overall development of the economy. Some combination of markets with central direction of the economy seemed to be the optimum solution, if it could be done.

Following in the tracks of the reform movement came pressures for democratization. These came from a variety of sources: a series of movements sequentially repressed but cumulatively infectious in East

Germany, Poland, Hungary, and Czechoslovakia; the rejection of Stalinism and the ultimate weakening of the repressive apparatus installed by Stalinism; and the consequences of the rebirth of civil society and of the historic compromise allowing more autonomy to the intelligentsia. The two movements — perestroika and glasnost in their Soviet form — encountered and interacted in the late 1980s. Would they reinforce each other or work against each other? We do not yet know the answer.

Some economic reformers saw democratization as a means of loosening up society which could strengthen decentralization. Some of these same people also saw worker self-management as supporting enterprise autonomy and the liberalising of markets. Humanist intellectuals tended to see economic reform as limiting the state's coercive apparatus and as encouraging a more pluralist society. For these groups, economic reform and democratization went together.

Other economic reformers recognised that reform measures would place new burdens on people before the reforms showed any benefits. There would be inflation, shortages, and unemployment. The social contract of mature "real socialism" would be discarded in the process of introducing flexibility into the labour market and the management of enterprises. The skills of existing managers would be rendered obsolete, together with those of many state and Party officials engaged in the central planning process. Anticipating the backlash from all these groups, the "realist" reformers recognised that an authoritarian power would be needed to implement reform successfully. Without it, they reasoned, reform would just be compromised and rendered ineffective, disrupting the present system without being able to replace it. [20] The economic Thatcherites of real socialism would become its political Pinochets.

The initial effects of both economic reform and democratization have produced some troublesome consequences. Relaxing economic controls towards encouraging a shift to market mechanisms has resulted in a breakdown of the distribution system with a channelling of goods into free markets and black markets, rampant gangsterism, and a dramatic polarization of new rich and poor. This is hardly surprising, since many of those who had any previous market experience had been involved in the often shady activities of the second economy. The relaxing of political controls gave vent to conflicts long suppressed, mobilizing people around ethnic nationalisms, various forms of populism, and, at the extreme, right-wing fascist movements. Furthermore, the outburst of public debate, while it has severely shaken the legitimacy of the Soviet state and its sustaining myths, has also demonstrated its inability to come to grips with the practical reorganization of economy and society. The reform process has itself made things worse, not better. (One Soviet journalist in the United States summed this up by observing that while the radical-leaning municipal council in Leningrad debated for months whether or not to change the city's name back to St. Petersburg, the shops became more and more empty.)

The legitimacy of "real socialism" was destroyed by Stalinism and the anti-Stalinist backlash. Civil society is reemergent but its component groups have not achieved any articulate organized expression. This is a condition Gramsci called an organic crisis; and the solution to an organic crisis is the reconstitution of a hegemony around a social group which is capable of leading and acquiring the support or acquiescence of other groups. What does our analysis of the structure of Soviet society tell us about the prospects of this happening?

There are three distinct meanings that can be given to "democracy" in the context of the collapse of "real socialism". One is the conventional "bourgeois" meaning of liberal pluralism. It has a strong demonstration effect, particularly in Eastern Europe. Liberal pluralism has a history and many examples. Two other meanings arise out of socialist aspirations.

One is producer self-management. It has been expressed in spontaneous action by workers in many different revolutionary situations — in the original Russian soviets, in the Ordine Nuovo movement of northern Italy in 1919, in workers' control of factories during the Algerian revolution, in the works councils set up in Poland following the events of 1956, and in factory movements in Hungary during the 1956 revolution and Czechoslovakia in 1968. These experiences were all short-lived. The only long experience with worker self-management is the Yugoslav one and, despite continuing debate, it cannot be considered persuasive. There is a strong point about producers being able to determine their own conditions; but there is also evidence of a tendency for such experiences, assuming they survive repression by a higher political authority, to turn in the direction of self-serving corporatism.

The other socialist meaning is popular participation in central planning. No historical experience can be cited; it would have to be invented. And yet it is perhaps the most attractive prospect in the spirit of socialism. Alec Nove suggested a form of compromise between democratic planning and producer self-government: consumers would decide what to produce; producers would decide how. [21]

Georg Lukács wrote a text that was posthumously published in Hungary as *Demokratisierung Heute und Morgen*. [22] Rejecting both the Stalinist past and the liberal concept of democracy, he speculated about the conditions in which a democratization of socialism might be possible.

A first condition was a reduction in socially necessary labour time that would shift the balance in human activity from the realm of necessity to the realm of freedom. Society would have to be able to produce sufficient to satisfy the necessities of material existence without absorbing all the time and effort of its people. This condition is recognised also by others who have thought about the problem. Kornai posited that sufficient slack in production would be necessary to undertake reform in an economy of shortage.[23] Bahro argued that a state of "surplus consciousness", i.e. the existence of a margin of time and effort over and above the satisfaction of basic wants, was requisite for the pursuit of "emancipatory interests" as an alternative to the "compensatory interests" of consumerism.[24]

The next condition would be a coalition of social forces upon which the structure of democratic socialism might be based. At this point, Lukács' prescription becomes obscure. Like Bahro and like Gorz in the West, he did not, in this last phase of his thought, look to the workers as the leading social class around which democratic socialism could take form. He spoke rather of liberating the "underground tendencies" hitherto repressed. The Party could, he hoped, reconstitute itself to achieve this.

This was a hope inspired by the reform movement led by the intelligentsia in Czechoslovakia in 1968. It had a brief revival again in the GDR during the time Neues Forum and similar groups were building the popular movement that overturned the Honecker regime. The project lives on for now in the Soviet Union, though its plausibility is diminished. The Party is an object of cynicism and the idea of socialism no longer has a secure basis of legitimacy.

Two other routes towards democratization in recent Eastern European experience have been, first, a movement from outside a moribund Party led by an independent workers' movement to which an intelligentsia attached itself (Poland); and second, an enlargement of scope for independent decision-making in the economy through a strategic withdrawal by the Party from direct control over certain aspects of civil society (Hungary). Both of these routes now in retrospect seem to be leading towards a restoration of capitalism. The former GDR shows a third route to capitalism: total collapse of the political structures of "real socialism" and full incorporation of its economy into West German capitalism.

For the remaining countries of "real socialism", options for the future can be grouped broadly into three scenarios. Each of these should be examined in terms of the relationship of the projected form of state and economy with the existing social structure of accumulation.

The first scenario is a combination of political authoritarianism with economic liberalization leading towards market capitalism and the integration of the national economy into the global capitalist economy. In its most extreme form, this is a project favoured by some segments of the intelligentsia who recognise that a "shock therapy" in the Polish mode will be necessary to carry through privatization and the freeing of market forces; and that dictatorial powers will be needed to prevent elements of existing civil society, notably workers and segments of the bureaucracies, from political protest and obstruction in response to the bankruptcies of enterprises, unemployment, inflation, and polarization of rich and poor that would occur as the inevitable accompaniment to this kind of restructuring. This is the option encouraged by the Western consultants pullulating through the world of "real socialism" as the whiz-kid offspring of private consulting firms and agencies of the world economy. It is encouraged by the revival of von Hayek's ideas in Eastern Europe and by the mythology of capitalism and of a pre-environmentalist fascination with Western consumerism.

More moderate and mature political leadership might hesitate before enforcing the full measure of market-driven adjustments upon the more resistant elements of civil society. The compromise envisaged by this leadership would likely be a form of corporatism that would aim at co-opting core workers into the transition to capitalism, separating the more articulate and more strtegically placed segments of the working class from the less articulate and less powerful majority. The enterprise-corporatist core of "real socialism" 's social structure of accumulation would thus lend itself to facilitating the transition to capitalism.

Some intellectuals have entertained the possibility of a transition to capitalism combined with a liberal pluralist political system. This vision most probably underestimates the level of conflict that would arise in formerly socialist societies undergoing the economic stresses of a transition to capitalism in the absence of a corporatist compromise. The choice then would become which to sacrifice, democracy or the free market? The historical record, as Karl Polanyi presented it in *The Great Transformation*, suggests that democracy is first sacrificed but the market is not ultimately saved. This setting was, for Polanyi, the opening of the path towards fascism; and some observers from Eastern Europe raise again this spectre as a not unlikely outcome of the social convulsions following the breakdown of "real socialism".[25]

The second scenario is political authoritarianism together with a command-administrative economic centre incorporating some subordinate market features and some bureaucratic reform. This would leave basically intact the enterprise-corporatist heart of the existing planning system, which would also constitute its main political roots in civil society and its continuing source of legitimation in the "working class". China seems to be following this route; and the "conservatives" of the Soviet Union (with the backing of influentials in the military and the KGB) could also be counted among its supporters. The long-term problem for this course would be in the continuing exclusion of the more peripheral segments of the labour force from any participation in the system, though these elements might be calmed in the short run if the revival of authority in central planning were to lift the economy out of the chaos resulting from the removal of authority in both economic planning and political structures.

The third scenario is the possibility of democratization plus socialist reform. As suggested above, this could take the form either of producer self-management, or of a democratization of the central planning process, or conceivably of some combination of the two. Of the three scenarios, this one, with its two variants, is the least clearly spelled out. One reason for this may be, as David Mandel has suggested, that the power of the media in the Soviet Union has been monopolised by the adherents of the first two and especially by the radical market reformers. [26]

Self-management has been claimed by both economic liberals and socialists. It has lost ground among the liberals without noticeably gaining conviction among socialists. Some of those economic reformers who once thought of self-management as a support to economic liberalization, now appear to have drawn back from this option. [27] Nevertheless, from a socialist perspective, the possibility must remain that self-management in the absence of some larger socialist economic framework is likely to evolve towards a form of enterprise corporatism within a capitalist market, i.e. the moderate variant of the first scenario.

The position of workers in relation to these three scenarios remains ambiguous and fragmented. In this there is a striking resemblance to the position of workers under capitalism since the economic crisis of the 1970s. The same question is to be raised: does the unqualified term "working class" still correspond to a coherent identifiable social force? The potential for an autonomous workers' movement was demonstrated in Poland by Solidarnosc; but in the hour of its triumph that movement fragmented. The Soviet miners' strike of July 1989 revived the credibility of a workers' movement; but it has not definitively answered the question.

Projects for managing and reorienting the working class that emanate from members of the intelligentsia are more readily to be found than clear evidence of autonomous working-class choice. David Mandel reports that the Soviet government tried to channel the miners' strike towards demands for enterprise autonomy, only subsequently to abandon self-management as part of market reform. [28] Academician Zaslavskaya, in the internal Party Novosibirsk Report that was attributed to her authorship, prescribed a planned reorientation of worker attitudes:

> ". . . it is in the interests of socialist society, while regulating the key aspects of the socio-economic activity of the workers, to leave them a sufficiently wide margin of freedom of individual behaviour. Hence the necessity for directing behaviour itself, i.e. the subjective relationship of the workers to their socio-economic activity. Administrative methods of management are powerless here. The management of behaviour can only be accomplished in an oblique fashion, with the help of incentives which would take into account the economic and social demands of the workers and would channel their interests in a direction which would be of benefit to our society." [29]

Some economic liberal reformers, no longer interested in self-management, entertain the notion of collective bargaining by independent trade unions as a counterpart to a capitalist economy.

Workers, it seems, may not have very much of an active initiating voice in the reform process. They may continue as previously to be an important passive structural force that the reforming intelligentsia will have to take into account. Their attitudes might be remoulded over time as Zaslavskaya and others would envisage. For the present they are, as a structural force, likely to remain committed to some of the basic ideas of socialism: egalitarianism in opportunities and incomes, the responsibility of the state to produce basic services of health and education, price stability and availability of basic wage goods. (In this respect, they would have to be classified, in the new vocabulary with which perestroika is discussed, as "conservatives".) Workers like other groups are critical of bureaucracy and irritating instances of privilege. These are the basic sentiments that future options for socialism could most feasibly be built upon.

World order and the future of socialism
The state of the world system now seems singularly unpropitious to a socialist future anywhere. The United States remains the strongest military power, though it is moving into the same kind of difficulties as beset the Soviet economy — declining rates of productivity, high military costs, and an intractable budgetary deficit. US military power serves as enforcer for deregulation and unrestricted movement of capital in the global economy. The financial mechanism of the global economy disciplines all countries except the United States whose

deficits continue for the moment to be financed by other countries, notably Japan. Third World countries as well as countries of "real socialism" insofar as their external economic linkages grow are subject to the policies promulgated through the main agencies of the global economy — the IMF, World Bank, OECD, G7 etc.

This phase of apparent unification of military and economic power behind a capitalist structure of world order is, in the sweep of history, necessarily transitory, though none can say with certainty how long the transition may last or towards what future structure of world order it may tend.

An underlying dynamic is at work in the global economy that gives some indication about possible futures. Its present manifest effect is globalization in production and in finance sustained by US military power. The further consequences of this globalizing movement are also predictable: more acute polarization of rich and poor within the global economy; and lines of social cleavage that will cut across boundaries thanks to the restructuring of production and to world migratory movements, transforming the geographical core/periphery structure of the past into a social core/periphery structure.

This polarization is likely to proceed apace before it provokes a concerted response because it generates a segmentation of peripheral social groups rather than a clear global class cleavage. The segmentation of the more disadvantaged groups will likely form around various distinct identities — ethnic, religious, nationalist, and gender identities, in particular. These distinct identities may find new grounds of unification. Islam, for instance, can become a metaphor for Third World revolt against Western capitalist domination. In this respect, the situation of countries of "real socialism" is not different from that of other countries. The same global tendencies are at work.

The long-term challenge to socialism will be to bridge these various identities so as to arrive at a common understanding of the global economic forces that place all of them in a subordinate position. Bridging identities means preserving them, while allowing them to develop their distinctive personalities by removing the causes of their subordination. This socialism would have room for diversity — for mutual support in the pursuit of distinct projects of society.

Two tendencies apparent at present may open opportunities for the rebirth of socialism. One is the decline of hegemony in the global system. This undermines conviction in the legitimacy of the principles upon which the globalization thrust is grounded. The cloak of common values becomes a transparent veil revealing the dominance of power, not the impersonal functioning of the order of nature. Such events as the collapse of the GATT negotiations and the mobilization by the United States of military intervention in the Persian Gulf contribute in different ways to the erosion of global hegemony.[30]

The other tendency, not unrelated to the first, is toward a world of economic blocs. Insofar as this would imply a decentralization of power, it could give room for diversity in projects of economy and society. The balance of social forces is different in Europe, in East Asia, and in North America. Opportunities in social struggle will be different in different parts of the world. The survival and transformation in some form of "real socialism" is conceivable in this context. The struggles going on in the Soviet Union and China towards the definition of a new project of society could have a longer range importance not just for those countries.

Effective containment or limitation of the central military enforcer of the present global economy will be a necessary condition for any devolution of power or economic decentralization in the world system. This can happen only through internal resistance within US society combined with external resistance, perhaps in parts of the Third World that reject the IMF medicine and the US-dominated "new world order". For the future, the Gramscian war of position becomes the appropriate strategy for socialist construction, most particularly in targetting the heartlands of capitalism, but carried on in coordination with movements in the Third World and in the countries of "real socialism". The struggle will be at once internal and global.

NOTES

1. The National Interest (US), Summer 1989.
2. Ralf Dahrendorf, *Reflections on the Revolution in Europe* (New York: Random House, 1990).
3. The cumbersome and redundant term "actually existing socialism" became current in English-language discourse, after the publication of the English translation of Rudolph Bahro's *The Alternative in Eastern Europe* (trans. by David Fernbach, London: NLB, 1978). It applied to those social formations shaped since the Bolshevik Revolution by Leninist and Stalinist types of political parties and by economic central planning. This term now seems outdated as well as cumbersome since the continuing "actuality" and "existence" of this type of formation was placed in question by the events of 1989 in Eastern Europe. Gordon Skilling suggested to me that a more accurate term is "real socialism" (from realsocialismus). "Real socialism" both designates a concrete historical phenomenon (whether past or present) and avoids confusion with measures introduced by social democratic and socialist party governments in capitalist social formations. The quotation marks signify a borrowed term designating an historical phenomenon open to critique, which the author does not consecrate with the meaning of a real essence.
4. Karl Polanyi, *The Great Transformation* (Boston: Beacon Press, 1957).
5. I use here the framework for analysis applied more specifically to capitalism in Robert W. Cox, *Production, Power, and World Order: Social Forces in the Making of History* (New York: Columbia University Press, 1987).

6.   Machiavelli, *The Discourses*, Book 1, Ch. 2.
7.   Fernand Braudel, "History and the social sciences: the longue durée", in Braudel, *On History*, trans. by Sarah Matthews (Chicago: University of Chicago Press, 1980).
8.   I have not included footnoting for factual or historical information in this article. Such footnoting, if carried through consistently, would result in a series of appended essays on each point of historical interpretation or evaluation — a distracting encumbrance in what is intended as an essay in theory rather than in historical research. Critics need no encouragement to strike where the shield is down.
9.   R. W. Davies in a recent article points out that the three major principles of the nineteenth-century vision of socialism — common ownership, democratic management, and equality — were all either rejected or drastically modified in the construction of the Soviet model of "real socialism". "Gorbachev's socialism in historical perspective", *New Left Review*, 179, January-February 1990.
10.   E. H. Carr, *The Bolshevik Revolution 1917-1923*, Vol. II (London: Macmillan, 1952), p. 278. Lenin's longer phrasing was: "Only an agreement with the peasantry can save the socialist revolution in Russia until the revolution has occurred in other countries."
11.   There is evidence that collectivization, far from enabling agriculture to contribute a surplus to the state during the First Five-Year Plan, actually drained resources from the non-agricultural sector through the need to supply agricultural machinery. The chief aim of collectivization was probably to break the power of the peasantry — the power of a social force independent of the state to determine what grain to produce and what to sell. Stalin was prepared to incur loss of production to gain state power over agriculture. As in the sphere of control over the military, Stalin's policies opened a period of extreme Soviet vulnerability to outside attack. He must have gambled that the depression in the capitalist world would deter aggression while Soviet power was being consolidated. This opening of vulnerability has to be read in the context of a speech in 1931 in which Stalin declared (*Works*, Vol. 13, pp.40-41):"We are fifty or a hundred years behind the advanced countries. We must make good this distance in ten years. Either we do it, or we shall go under." Ten years later, Germany invaded the Soviet Union.
12.   CMEA figures showed an average annual rate of growth in aggregate output for the USSR from the early 1930s to the beginning of World War II of 16 percent. This was about twice that of capitalist countries during their boom periods of development, e.g. the United States during the second half of the 1880s, Russia in the 1890s, or Japan between 1907 and 1913. During the years following World War II, the USSR and the Eastern European countries maintained annual growth rates of industrial production in the range of 10 to 16 percent with investment ratios somewhat in excess of 20 percent of national income. The most backward (Bulgaria and Rumania) grew the fastest during the 1950s and 1960s. From the 1960s on, high and even increasing investment ratios began to yield lower rates of growth in industrial production. Soviet industrial growth averaged 13.2 percent annually in the 1950s, 10.4 percent in the 1960s, and 8.5 percent in the 1970s, while the investment ratio had risen from 23.9 percent in the 1950s to 29.5 percent in the 1970s. The combined rate of growth in national income (measured in (measured in Net Material Product) for the USSR and Eastern European CMEA members declined steadily from the mid-1960s. From a rate of 10 percent annually in the 1950s, it dropped to 7 percent in the 1960s, and 5 percent in the1970s (6 percent in the first half of the decade and 4.2 percent in the second), down to about 2 to 3 percent in the early 1980s. These figures do not appear disastrous compared to the economic performance of some major

capitalist countries during the years of economic crisis, but they contrast markedly with earlier socialist performance and indicate a trend towards stagnation. The editors of *Monthly Review* (March 1990, p. 12) cite Soviet Academician and Gorbachev economic adviser Abel Aganbegyan to the effect that the official figures for 1981-85 are flawed because of a failure to take account of hidden inflation, with the inference that in that economic period there was practically no economic growth. (Sources for the above figures include Silviu Brucan, "The strategy of development in eastern Europe", IFDA Dossier 13, November 1979, for the historical comparisons; Alec Nove et al. *The Eastern European Economies in the 1970s*, London:Butterworth, 1982, p. 215; A. Bergson, "Soviet economic slowdown and the 1981-85 Plan", *Problems of Communism* 30, May-June 1981; and T. Colton, *The Dilemma of Reform in the Soviet Union*, New York: Council on Foreign Relations, 1984, p. 15.)

13.   The concept of "historic compromise", borrowed from the lexicon of the Italian Communist Party (compromesso storico), was applied to this phase of "real socialism" by George Konrád and Ivan Szelényi, *The Intellectuals on the Road to Class Power* (Brighton: Harvester, 1979), esp. pp. 185-187.

14.   I have taken the concept of social structure of accumulation from David Gordon, "Stages of accumulation and long economic cycles", in Terence K. Hopkins and Immanuel Wallerstein, eds. *Processes of the World System* (Beverly Hills, Calif.: Sage, 1980), pp. 9-45. My use of it focusses more specifically on the relationship of social forces, whereas Gordon uses it more broadly to encompass e.g. the institutions of the world economy. I have applied the concept to the capitalist world economy in Cox, *op. cit.*, Ch. 9.

15.   The terms are taken from Michael Burawoy's use of Gramsci's concept of hegemony. See Burawoy, *The Politics of Production* (London: Verso, 1985).

16.   William Hinton, *Fanshen* (New York: Vintage Press, 1966), p. 287 called the formal categorization of people as workers or peasants (with correspondingly different rights and responsibilities) a form of "hereditary social status". Industry in China was also organized on a core/periphery basis in which core enterprises employing established workers had satellite enterprises employing peasant-workers, and core enterprises could also employ teams of temporary peasant-workers in their main plants alongside established workers but with lower pay and benefits. The "iron rice bowl" of permanent job tenure and buyuan system whereby a worker is entitled to pass on his job to a qualified family member are Chinese counterparts to the social contract of Soviet post-Stalinist practice.

17.   See Hungarian Academy of Sciences, Institute of Economics, 1984, Studies 23 and 24, *Wage Bargaining in Hungarian Firms.*

18.   One study covering capitalist countries that comes from an International Working Party on Labour Market Segmentation, is Frank Wilkinson, ed. *The Dynamics of Labour Market Segmentation* (London: Academic Press, 1981).

19.   Prominent among those who have opened up this line of theoretical enquiry are Wlodzimierz Brus, *The Economics and Politics of Socialism* (London: Routledge and Kegan Paul, 1973); János Kornai, *Economics of Shortage* (Amsterdam: North-Holland, 1980) and *Growth, Shortage and Efficiency: A Macrodynamic Model of the Socialist Economy* (Berkeley: 1982).

20.   The positions of various groups in Soviet society with regard to reforms are reviewed in R. W. Davies, "Gorbachev's Socialism", *op. cit.*

21.   Alec Nove, *The Economics of Feasible Socialism* (London: George Allen & Unwin, 1983), p. 199.

22.   Budapest: Akadémiai Kiadó, 1985. I am indebted to Dr A. Bródy, Director, Institute of Economics, Hungarian Academy of Sciences, for drawing this text to my attention. It proved to be difficult to trace a copy of it.

23. János Kornai, *Anti-Equilibrium. On Economic Systems Theory and the Tasks of Research* (Amsterdam: North-Holland, 1971).

24. Rudolph Bahro, *The Alternative in Eastern Europe* (London: NLB, 1978).

25. E.g. Milan Vojinovic, "Will there be a palingenesis of extreme rightist movements". Paper presented for the conference "After the Crisis", University of Amsterdam, 18-20 April 1990. Ralf Darendorf, while arguing the possibility of capitalism with liberal pluralism, is also concerned by the possibility of a fascist revival, *op. cit.,* pp. 111-116.

26. David Mandel, " 'A market without thorns': the ideological struggle for the Soviet working class", *Studies in Political Economy*, 33 Autumn 1990: 7-38.

27. R. W. Davies, *op. cit.,* p. 23 reports this of e.g. Aganbegyan.

28. *Op. cit.,* p. 18.

29. Novosibirsk Report, 1984. Trans. published in *Survey 128* (1): 88-108. Quotation from pp. 95-96.

30. There is a substantial literature about the decline of hegemony, mostly American. Much of the debate is about whether or not there has been a relative decline of US economic, financial, and military power. More basic to the question of hegemony, in a Gramscian sense, is the extent to which the principles of world order on which the Pax Americana has been based are broadly shared, especially among the more powerful capitalist countries. Susan Strange (e.g. in *States and Markets* London: Pinter, 1988, pp. 235-240) argues that US power is still relatively great, but that the United States has misused its power in narrow national interests by following unilateralist policies. I would agree in large part with her assessment, but consider this trend in policy to be an indication of declining hegemony. There is a formally hegemonic aspect of the United Nations Security Council decisions in the Persian Gulf crisis; but since in brute fact they express a temporary coalition put together by diplomatic arm-twisting and side payments rather than a basic consensus on global order, this too must be considered an indication of US dominance rather than of hegemony.

THE ROOTS OF THE PRESENT CRISIS
IN THE SOVIET ECONOMY

Ernest Mandel

I

There is a near-consensus among economists and political ideologues today in the world that the present crisis of the Soviet economy expresses the historical failure of central planning. All those directly or indirectly influenced by the neo-liberal/neo-conservative school, in the first place the Austrian school of von Mises — von Hayek and Milton Friedman, who identify central planning as applied in the USSR and Eastern Europe with socialism, triumphantly add: socialism is for ever dead and buried. And the most historical and theoretically minded among them remind us constantly: "We told you so." They refer to the century-old debate between the neo-classical school and marxist socialists of many creeds around the question: can any economy not guided by the market work with a minimum of efficiency? They now claim that history has definitely shown them to have been right from the start in that debate. [1]

We reject all these statements and claims as empirically not proven and theoretically mistaken. Socialism never existed in the USSR, Eastern Europe, China, Cuba or anywhere in the world. Socialism cannot exist in one country or in a small number of countries. It can only exist in the leading industrial nations taken in their totality or near-totality.

What developed in the USSR and similar systems were societies in transition between capitalism and socialism, i.e. postcapitalist societies submitted to the unrelenting pressure of the capitalist system and the capitalist world market, military pressure, political pressure and economic pressure. Furthermore, for specific historical reasons neither unrelated to that pressure nor purely reducible to it, power in these societies was usurped (with the partial exception of Cuba) by a privileged bureaucracy, which by its concrete policies and the social consequences they engendered, made significant advances in the direction of socialism impossible.

So the only conclusion one can draw from the disaster which befell these societies is not that socialism has failed but that Stalinism, i.e.

bureaucratic dictatorship, has failed. People belonging to the political/theoretical tradition which I represent among others can say at least as emphatically as the neo-liberals (and certainly more than the social-democrats and neo-social-democrats): we told you so. For we have been predicting this crisis for decades. And we can convincingly show that the concrete policies which led to that crisis and the collapse of Stalinism in Eastern Europe in no way represent directly or indirectly a "logical product" of the theories or political projects of Marx and even of Lenin. They were conceived and implemented in a complete break with the ABC of Marxism, again an analysis not made now post festum but decades earlier.

With regard to economic organization, the question seems to boil down to a definitional, i.e. semantic dispute. The neo-liberals/neo-conservatives, and their social-democratic/neo-social-democratic hangers-on, proclaim that "the command economy" (others call it "barracks communism") is the only possible form of central planning.[2] They claim that central planning is impossible without huge bureaucracies. These are supposed to be the only possible "mediators" who could try to replace the market as forces determining preferences and allocation problems between "millions of products". But this substitution is considered doomed to be qualitatively less efficient and less "workable" than the mediation through the market.

Socialists on the contrary contend that bureaucratic planning is but one of the possible variants of central planning, as the capitalist market economy is but one variant of the market economy.[3] Democratic planning based upon articulated self-management and pluralistic, multiparty political democracy, is perfectly conceivable and workable. That is what "Marxian socialism" was all about and remains all about: the rule of freely associated producers as Marx states it (we would say to-day: freely associated producers/consumers/citizens).

Nothing that has occurred in Eastern Europe, China or the USSR presents any evidence against that hypothesis. Many trends of producers/consumers/citizens' behaviour in the East, the West and in the more developed parts of the South, show that more than ever this "third model" represents the line of the future, that history is moving in that direction, though in a contradictory way ("two steps ahead, one step backward"; sometimes "one step ahead, two steps backward") and in a much slower rhythm than Marx and his followers assumed in the past.

But whatever may be the value of a still largely speculative debate about what the future will show, what has today a very concrete content is a discussion of what really happened in Soviet society and in the Soviet economy, and what is really happening there right now. This is a debate turning not around speculations but around an analysis of facts, (facts taken in their totality and their context, not fragmented, isolated and arbitrarily selected). In that debate, the Marxists represent the scientific tradition and use scientific methods of empirical verification and falsification. Their neo-liberal opponents appear as stubborn dogmatists, who oppose value judgements and unproven axioms to deny all those aspects of reality which do not conform to their schemas.

II

What is strikingly apparent in practically all defenders of the axiom "central planning implies a hypertrophy of the state and thus of bureaucracy" is the reified approach to economic analysis on which it is based. "The plan" is presented as an anthropomorphic entity which operates with an implacable logic of its own.[4] Marx, at the end of *Capital*, vol. III, ironically suggested that you cannot meet in the street Mr Capital and Mrs Land and shake their hand. We must likewise ask the question: can you meet Mr Plan in a coffee-bar and offer him a drink?

An essential revolution which Marx introduced into economic analysis is the relentless effort to discover *relations between human beings and human social forces* underlying relations between human beings and things or institutions. Another similar revolution — the so-called materialist interpretation of history — consisted in searching for and discovering the material interests which, in the final analysis, explain the attitudes and actions of these actors on the historical scene, at least regarding basic problems and conflicts. This is why, let it be said in passing, there is no "purely" economic analysis in Marx. It is always a socio-economic analysis. Economic trends and "laws of motion" always assert themselves through actions by specific social groups.

"Planning", like "economic laws", like "the state", are not timeless phenomena, eternally equal to themselves. They are always specific to given historical situations and limited in their relevance to these situations only.

Soviet central planning therefore is not "planning in general". It is planning introduced by a ruling bureaucracy, in order to consolidate and extend its power and privileges. It will be shown that characteristics of economic organisation and management, which are not in any way congruent with any "general logic of planning" but which are contrary to such a logic, put their marks, their contradictions and their crisis-dynamic on the way Soviet planning developed from the beginning of the first Five Year Plan.

The objection is sometimes raised: is it not the switch from the NEP to generalized central planning which inevitably engendered a hypertrophied bureaucracy, rather than a hypertrophied bureaucracy which bureaucratically centralized (i.e. state-managed) planning?

In fact, the establishment of the bureaucratic dictatorship — the "Russian Thermidor" — occurred prior to the First Five Year Plan, not after it. It dates back to 1923 if not earlier. A tremendous apparatus of state and party functionaries controlling, under Stalin's Secretariat central control, all key aspects of social life in the USSR, existed prior to the turn towards forced collectivisation of agriculture and over-accelerated industrialization.

Certainly, these new economic policies extended the dimensions, power and privileges of the bureaucracy. But far from contradicting our thesis, this confirms it. We contend precisely that the specific forms of Soviet central planning had that extension as their main social purpose. Because the bureaucracy was in power and used power to further its interests, planning was introduced under such forms as to serve these interests.

Again, the question has to be decided on the basis of a concrete analysis. No logical argument can be advanced to prove that the massive deportation of hundreds of thousands of wage earners, — the so-called "oukazniks" — for absenteeism corresponds to the "logic of planning". If it did, how can one explain that it was not introduced in any Eastern European country simultaneously with planning (we don't know whether we should say: with the exception of Rumania)? Was the monstrous Gulag system an expression of the "logic of planning"? In what way? Aren't these criminal moves by the Stalinist bureaucracy notable expressions of a specific need to atomize, terrorize and condemn to passivity a working class still characterized by a level of class consciousness determined by the victorious socialist October revolution?

The biggest disaster which befell the Soviet Union in 1929-1931 was the forced collectivization of agriculture. Its consequences on livestock and meat production were felt for 25 years. Its effects on the workers' standard of living and on the peasants' mentality lasted longer. But in what way can one say that these were results of central planning? If so, why didn't they occur or were rapidly abolished in Yugoslavia, the GDR, Poland, Hungary under conditions of central planning? Was their duration and their disastrous effects in the USSR not a result rather of a political dictatorship of extreme ruthlessness, in which any form of dissent was suppressed through terror? How can one prove that such extreme forms of political arbitrariness, which made any rapid correction of the erroneous decisions of 1929-1931 impossible, were in any way necessarily congruent with central planning, when this very regime disappeared even in the USSR after the death of the tyrant, while central planning continued?

In the analysis of what occurred under Soviet planning we have therefore to distinguish carefully what are likely to be features of planning in all its possible variants, and what is due to the specific social forces and interests, and the specific historical situation, in which Soviet planning was introduced. A similar method is used by Marx in vol. I of *Capital*, where he carefully distinguishes general features of commodities and of commodity exchange, from features specific to capitalist commodity production, i.e. commodity production with the use of wage labour as a decisive feature of the economy.

III

How can we define "planning in general"? Planning is a system of economic organization, of resource allocation, based upon deliberate, conscious *a priori* choices determining the key trends of economic development. The words "determining the key trends" are decisive here.

Capitalists, and certainly big capitalist monopolies, do a lot of planning inside their enterprises and even in whole branches of production and exchange. But they do not have the power to decide in a conscious way how the economy and society will develop in its totality in the medium and long term. These trends will be imposed upon them "behind their backs", by objective laws — in the final analysis the law of value mediated by the oscillations of the average rate of profit and the deviations therefrom — parallel to the way they are imposed upon the mass of wage-earners and all other sectors of society behind their backs.

Behind the incapacity of capitalists to determine in the medium and long run the trends of socio-economic development, and the capacity of "planners" to do just that, lies *a qualitative difference in control over the social surplus product*.

Under capitalism, which can only exist in the form of "many capitals", i.e. of competition and private property leading to competition, such control is always fragmented. No absolute monopolies can exist. Central planning is only possible if society, under whatever political form (including extreme despotism) actually exercises such widespread monopoly, or delegates such control over the social surplus product, through the abolition of competition and private property.

Central planning equals *a priori* allocation of economic resources. But as long as we are not living under full-scale communism, with a generalized saturation of satisfaction of needs for goods and services for the final consumers, resources are relatively scarce. So planned conscious allocation of resources always implies a deliberate choice of priorities. The realization of these priorities can only be implemented at the price of not satisfying other needs.

Exactly the same thing happens in a market economy. No neo-liberal economist or ideologue will deny that a market economy functions under conditions of relative scarcity of economic resources. This implies that the satisfaction of the demand for certain goods and services always leads to less satisfaction of the demand for other goods and services — if not complete non-satisfaction. In a market economy, unevenly divided income and especially unevenly divided wealth entail that the satisfaction of the demand of rich people and of large firms will be achieved at the expense of the demand of the mass of the wage earners, not to speak of the demand of the impoverished.[5] From that point of view, we are justified in speaking of "market despotism", in the same way as the critics of Stalinism are justified in speaking of "state despotism" in the USSR.

In both cases, the priorities in the use of scarce resources are determined by social forces and institutions behind the backs of the mass of the people concerned. Only in a system of democratic planning based upon articulated self-management would these priorities be decided in a democratic way by the mass of the people concerned.

While the "planning authorities" can actually decide priority allocations of scarce resources in whatever way they choose to do — including in an arbitrary and irrational way — they cannot overcome the relative scarcity itself and one of its main consequences: the unavoidable coincidence of "overinvestment" in those sectors chosen as priority sectors, and of "underinvestment" in the non-prioritized sectors. But in a complex modern economy characterized by a high degree of interdependence between all main branches of the economy and all main sectors of social activity, i.e. characterized by a high level of objective socialization of labour, the iron laws of reproduction, as first laid bare by Marx, inevitably assert themselves.

You need metals, electricity, and machine tools, in order to produce rockets, space craft, or pipelines for exporting gas. You need relatively well-fed, well-clothed and well-housed workers in order to produce these "priority goods" with a minimum of efficiency, especially when they have to use more and more sophisticated and costly equipment to assure that production.

But rockets, sputniks, tanks and Kalashnikovs do not contribute to the production of metals, power plants, machine tools, food, clothes and workers' housing. So if you "overinvest" excessively in the first production run, and "underinvest" excessively in the second range of products, from a certain point on even your output of "priority goods" will start to stagnate. Subsequently it will even decline. No terror of Stalin, no boasting by Khrushchev, no benign neglect by Brezhnev, no cajoling by Gorbachev, could prevent these crises from developing.

In other words: central planning can function with a relatively high level of efficiency only inasmuch as a *certain minimum of proportional development between all main branches of the economy and sectors of social activity*[6] is realized, maintained and up to a point perfected. When these proportions are negated through arbitrary "overemphasis" on prioritized sectors, seeds of crisis if not of slow disintegration are implanted in the system.

Neo-liberals again retort with apparent triumph: this is precisely so because a planned economy does not possess in the market a built-in mechanism to correct such disproportions. "Free enterprise" does.

Factually this is not true. "Free enterprise" produces disproportions and waste on a huge scale, probably similar in extent to that of bureaucratic planning. These disproportions are "corrected" through the market by means of even bigger waste and outright destruction of resources. This is what economic crises, massive unemployment of human and mechanical resources, are all about.

In fact, two conclusions can already be drawn from this first general approach to the problem of Soviet planning.

First that it is wrong to represent it as "totally" or even "basically" inefficient. It isn't. Nothing in the history of the Soviet Union allows such a judgement. It is based upon a misrepresentation of what really happened.

In all those fields where the bureaucracy chose priority goals, these were by and large implemented. The Soviet Union did build nearly from scratch a heavy industry which transformed a semi-agrarian backward country into the second industrial power of the world. It built a weapons industry which enabled it to defeat Hitler in the second world war (compare that to the performance of Tsarist Russia in the first world war and Japan in the second world war). It equalled the USA in spacecraft during a whole period. It developed the diffusion of classical world culture on a mass scale unprecedented in any major country of the world, including the USA, Germany and Japan. It educated more scientists than the whole of Western Europe plus Japan.

One can discuss whether these priorities were correctly chosen, what were the reasons for their choice, whether other choices would have been more meaningful, what were the costs endured (sometimes tremendous and absolutely out of proportion to the relative importance of a given prioritized goal). But by and large, the superiority of planning showed itself in the capacity of the system to realize those prioritized goals it had deliberately chosen.

Second, the excessive weight of these priorities in overall planning goals led to an excessive number of underdeveloped branches and sectors, i.e. to built-in disproportions, which created from the start economic and social deficiencies which co-determined the general dynamics of the Soviet economic and social system as a whole. The failures of bureaucratic "planning" are as much part and parcel of Soviet reality since 1928 as are the undeniable achievements in prioritized sectors.

The end-result of the interaction between what functioned and what did not function under Soviet bureaucratically centralized planning was overdetermined by two key factors: the existence inside the country of huge reserves of manpower, raw materials and "virgin soil", which could be mobilized and introduced into the system with relative ease, "regardless of cost"; and the possibility of borrowing with relative ease advanced technology from the imperialist countries. [7]

When these environmental contributions were generally positive, the average rate of growth of the Soviet economy was on average high — much higher than that of the imperialist countries. Stalin and Khrushchev could have the illusion that they would "catch up and surpass" the USA. This period is correctly called that of extensive growth of the Soviet economy.

But from a certain moment, the environmental contributions turned into environmental constraints. Now the hour struck for turning from extensive into intensive growth. Reserves declined. Natural resources became depleted. Stepping up the skill, training and motivation of workers became more important than just bringing young people from the countryside into factories as semi-skilled labourers. Technological change in the West became more and more accelerated. Keeping up with it in antagonism and not cooperation with imperialism became more and more difficult. [8]

Moreover, and of particular importance, Soviet society could less and less free itself from the desire of at least tens of millions of consumers to imitate the consumption pattern of the richer capitalist countries, with all the positive and negative aspects of that pattern. In that respect, the unification of the world market in the forty years after World War II, coinciding with a long expansive wave of the international capitalist economy first, and a still limited impact of the subsequent declining long wave later, exercized a strong pressure upon the Soviet economy and society, in sharp contrast with the advantages the USSR drew from the fragmented world market of the twenties, the thirties and the early forties.

Deep inter-imperialist rivalries prevailed under the latter conditions. A lasting imperialist alliance substituted itself to those, with inter-imperialist rivalries operating within that alliance.

IV

From the first Five-Year Plan onwards, Stalinist-bureaucratic planning was characterized by fundamental disporportions:

1) The disproportion between allocations to heavy industrial and to "department III" expenditure (armaments and administrative expenditure)[9] on the one hand, and allocation of resources for mass consumer goods and services on the other hand. The second category of expenditure was first drastically reduced in absolute terms. It then increased in absolute terms during half a century, with the exception of the war years. But in relation to the sum total of available resources, it was qualitatively lower than under the NEP and remains so till today.

While the intention of the "planners" might have been to maximize investment and the rate of growth in this way, this continuous and sometimes extreme curtailment of mass consumption did not result in significantly higher rates of growth, contrary to a myth widespread among many economists and ideologues in East and West, including socialist ones.

We explained long ago why this was not the case. Consumer goods and services for producers (workers and toiling peasants) are indirect producer goods. When they are continuously below expectation, producers become unmotivated. Their output remains constantly below what was expected from a given mass of means of production introduced. A huge mass of "controllers", i.e. economic "policemen/women", i.e. lower and medium-rank bureaucracy has to watch over them constantly. Hence the tremendous increase of non-productive expenditure. Hence the reduction of expected growth in productive investment, side by side with the relative reduction in consumer outlays.

As we formulated it elsewhere: the key for understanding bureaucratically centralized planning does not lie in a hypertrophy of department I.[10] It lies in a hypertrophy of department III.[11]

2) The disproportion between the allocation of resources (outlays) for industry on the one hand, and allocation of resources for services on the other hand. It is difficult to globalize information in this respect. But we believe that we are not wide off the mark if we estimate that outlays for the modern tertiary sector were and remain in the USSR roughly around half of what they are in the West and the semi-industrialized countries of the "third world" as a fraction of the GNP (of total annual outlays). In practice this means a tremendous

and chronic underdevelopment of the transport system, of the distribution system, of the system of storing and of the repair (and spare parts) systems.

3) A chronic underdevelopment of reserve stocks, i.e. a tendency to use all currently available resources for increasing current annual output.

4) A systematic underdevelopment of investment in agriculture as compared with investment in industry, the only exception being investment in some agricultural raw materials for industry like cotton. It is true that this disproportion began to be partially corrected much earlier than the other ones, immediately after Stalin's death. But the corrections were limited and often inconsistent. They led, however, to an impressive growth in agricultural output.

These disproportions had increasingly perverse effects upon the Soviet economy and society taken in its totality. Their interaction explains most of the basic ills of the system of bureaucratically centralized planning, and the way they tended to spread like malignant tumours.

The underdevelopment of the service sector meant that an increasing part of current production did not reach its intended final destination, was wasted and lost for the planned economy. A dramatic example is that of potatoes. The USSR produces four times as much potatoes as the USA. Yet 75% of these potatoes do not reach the final consumer. They rot on the fields, rot in open railway cars waiting days if not weeks before getting unloaded, cannot be adequately stored when they reach cities, etc. Another similar example is that of chemical fertilizers.

The underdevelopment of stock, reserve inventories and generally margins of flexibility in the use of available resources led to a chronically discontinuous flow of raw materials and spare parts to productive units. Production was therefore often curtailed if not interrupted during part of the month; efforts to fulfil the plan were feverishly stepped up in the final part of each month (the period of so-called "sturmovtchina").

Food and consumer goods shortages had a disastrous effect upon workers' morale and motivation and led to a productivity of labour much below expectations by the "planners", as well as much below that of capitalist production units using similar techniques.[12] Again, exact aggregation of these differences is extremely difficult. Our rough estimate would be that, for similar technologies, USSR productivity of labour is around 50% of the American level in industry and below 20% of American productivity of labour in agriculture.

Under capitalism, demotivation of direct producers is partially compensated by the pressure of unemployment and the fear of un-employment. The noncapitalist nature of the Soviet economy is most strikingly revealed in the fact that this whip did not work for nearly half a century (even Stalin's terror could not really replace it). So demoralized and demotivated direct producers became a permanent, near-structural feature of bureaucratically centralized planning.

The combined perverse effects of all these disproportions were so all-permeating and so vast that society in its near-totality, Stalin's terror notwithstanding, started to develop spontaneous reactions in order to limit the rot. The very pressure for fulfilling planning goals operated in the same direction. Confronted with chronic discontinuities in supply, as well as chronic shortages of stocks (inventories) at central level, managers systematically built up hoards of supplies and resources including manpower. "Unstocking" at centrally planned levels was thereby compensated by "overstocking" (overhoarding) at plant level, one could even say over-compensated.

Chronic shortages of food made available through the collective and cooperative sector of agriculture led to a rebirth of private food production, all intentions for completely collectivising agriculture notwithstanding.[13] Insufficient and inefficient "official" distribution of food led to the revival of legal and illegal private distribution networks (black market). Arbitrary access by the bureaucracy, including its lower ranks, to given categories of consumer goods and services, led to a widespread "grey" market, i.e. barter of goods and services on a "scratch-my-back-and-I'll-scratch-yours" basis. This rapidly spread from food distribution to distribution of different industrial consumer goods. Hence it spread to illegal output of these goods, as long as the used techniques were relatively simple and the illegal appropriation of raw materials and tools likewise.

In that way, a whole private system of "informal" economy developed side by side with the planned economy. Some observers estimate that it adds 20-25% to the official GNP.[14] The key purpose of the middle ranks of the Soviet Nomenklatura and the new "middle class" of the USSR is to legalize that black and grey market and informal economy through *perestroika* and privatization/marketization.[15]

So the perverse end-effect of excessively centralized planning with huge built-in disproportions, is the emergence of a vast non-planned, uncontrolled sector of the Soviet economy. The conclusion is clear: the Soviet economy is not a fully planned economy. It is a partially planned and partially unplanned economy, a quasi-planned or semi-planned economy. The USSR is not only suffering from too little political democracy and too little market relations.

It is also suffering from too little planning. More real efficient planning is only possible with significantly less disproportions, which is only possible with qualitatively more democracy and self-management, and, in addition, for a long transition period, more control through the market. [16]

V

The economists in charge of drafting the successive Five-Year Plans were of high quality. The same remark applies to some of the initiators of the so-called Liberman-Kosygin reforms from the early sixties on. They were certainly aware of most if not of all the deficiencies of bureaucratically centralized planning as sketched above. The question therefore arises: how could it happen?

There is no monocausal explanation of what went wrong with Soviet planning right from the start, and why its dysfunctions gradually increased. But in the chronological and logical chain of causes and consequences, a common denominator can be discovered: the nature and the interests of the Soviet bureaucracy as a relatively autonomous ruling social layer in the USSR.

This was in the beginning an essentially conservative layer, intent upon enjoying a calm and undisturbed existence, after the violent upheavals of revolution and civil war. Stalin gained the upperhand in the inner-party faction fight against the Left Opposition first, the United Opposition later, by catering for that bureaucracy's needs.

He therefore opposed any serious acceleration of the pace of industrialization, any serious reduction of the part of the social surplus controlled by the kulaks and the petty and middle bourgeoisie (Nepmen). His faction as well as the supporters of Bukharin disregarded the warnings of the Opposition about the kulaks' growing capacity for a delivery strike of grain surplus, which could put feeding the city and the army in jeopardy. They rejected the rather mild cure proposed: a gradual stepping up of industrialization, in the first place in order to assure the building of tractor plants; the financing of these initial steps of industrialization through a tax on high incomes and a radical reduction of administrative expenditure; a turn towards the gradual development of producers' cooperatives in agriculture, based upon a higher technology than that of private farms, and ensuring therefore for the poor peasants who would join them voluntarily from the start an increase in their standard of living; an elimination of unemployment and an increase in real wages in order to increase the morale, motivation and active involvement of workers in ensuring economic growth.

When the delivery strike by the kulaks finally occurred in the winter 1927-1928, [17] the Stalin faction and the bureaucracy reacted in a panicky way. They jumped practically from one day to another from complacency towards the kulaks towards harshest repression, from "industrialization at a tortoise pace" to industrialization with dizzy rhythms. An investment effort serious planners had projected to be spread over ten years, now suddenly had to be implemented within a time-span of four years. A general overextension of efforts, a radical tautness in the allocation of all available resources, a fanatical concentration on attaining plan objectives regardless of cost, became the rule. Hence the priority given to physical indicators in the general formulation of often contradictory planning objectives. Hence the increase of waste at all levels of economic life.

The argument of "imminent war danger" (the defence of the beleaguered bastion) was largely invented by the Stalin faction to justify the crushing of all opposition and dissent in the 1927-1932 period, especially when a huge famine and economic crisis resulted from the disaster of forced collectivization of agriculture and Stalin's prestige in the party apparatus began to decline. After Hitler came to power in 1933, the war danger became quite real. It increased pressure for prioritizing heavy industry and armament industry developments far from the traditional industrial centres of the Donetz, Moscow, Leningrad, the Ukraine and Western Russia, again regardless of any growing disproportions in the economy.

Serious theoretical mistakes contributed to these excesses. Around Strumilin, a whole school of "voluntarists" arose, denying the existence of objective economic laws in the transition period. Other economists, some of them of Menshevik origin, genuinely believed in the "law" of priority development of heavy industry in order to ensure long-term accelerated economic growth. [18] This "law" is derived from an erroneous two-sector model of production/reproduction instead of a three-sector one. Maurice Dobb stubbornly defended the same mistake for decades in the West, but he was by no means the only one.

The disastrous social consequences of the panicky measures of 1928-1932 provoked a social crisis of major dimensions, besides sowing the seeds of long term economic dysfunctioning. The two main classes of Soviet society, the working class and the peasantry, witnessed a traumatic decline in living standards. As a result, both classes became demotivated with regard to elementary economic efficiency. Increasing output and productivity of labour could not be based under these conditions upon conscious involvement and even the material self-interest of these classes. Only the material interests and the strictest monopoly of authority in the hands of the bureaucracy became the motor for fulfilling the plan. Thereby, power and privileges of the bureaucracy as opposed to those of the mass of both the workers and the peasants, became rigidly institutionalized throughout the economic system and society as a whole. Stalin's total political control at the top crowned a complex system of levers and incentives to ensure a minimum of operability of the planned economy which was thereby, from the start, a form of planning managed by the bureaucracy in the interests of the bureaucracy.

But a basic contradiction arose out of the combination of bureaucratic planning and bureaucratic management geared to the material self-interest of the bureaucracy. Bureaucratic planning over-emphasized the realization of planning goals in physical terms. Income increments of the bureaucrats depended upon fulfilment and overfulfilment of the plan. But under conditions of taut and over-stretched resource-use and discontinuous flows of supply, the closer the plan goals came to the actual maximum capacity of output of a factory, the more difficult it became to fulfil or slightly overfulfil the plan, and the lower became the total income of the "economic" bureaucracy. So a permanent tug-of-war set in between the "central" layers of the bureaucracy (sometimes called the "political" layers) and the economic managers. The latter became systematically inclined to build up hidden reserves of resources at plant level. The former were constantly on the look-out for such "hidden resources for additional investment" (additional growth).

An absurd system of rampant disinformation arose. Information about productive capacity at plant level was systematically wrong, i.e. below reality. At the "centre", it was systematically considered as such, and arbitrary "additions" were added to projected output figures. This led to the hiding of still more reserves, and to still more dismissal of information coming from below by the central authorities.

Whereas the constant flow of information, unhampered by private property and competition, is one of the great potential advantages of a planned as compared to a "free market" economy, bureaucratic planning and the bureaucracy's material self-interests produced a system of permanently unreliable information, which even the obligation of filling out literally billions of control and checking forms a year could not basically correct.

During an initial phase, the bureaucracy as a large social layer (at least its top and middle layers, i.e. several millions of households) had an obvious self-interest in building a broad industrial basis in the country. You cannot have several million cars and apartments, endowed with millions of electro-domestic equipment, without large-scale automobile, steel, machine building, electrical equipment, power stations industries. But once that layer, which concentrated all political and economic power in its hands, had reached a certain saturation of consumer demand, its attitude towards economic growth began to change. It again reversed to its initial conservatism:

"anything for a quiet life". Increasingly, it became demotivated for speeding up, not to say optimizing economic efficiency.[19] The system became one of generalized irresponsibility, to quote the former Stalinist prime-minister of Hungary, Andres Hegedus.[20]

Caught between the unbreakable inertia of a huge bureaucratic machine on the one hand, and a largely atomized and demotivated mass of workers and peasants still unable to replace bureaucratic mismanagement by generalized producers' self-management, the system gradually ground towards stagnation. The rest is recent history.

This sad story in no way implies that democratic planning based on articulated self-management has been condemned as impracticable or undesirable by the Soviet experience. Its case stands as it stood in the past. Intellectual and moral arguments in its favour remain convincing. But the last word has to be said by practice.

NOTES

1.   We deal more in detail with that debate in the last chapter of our book "Power and Money. A General Theory of Bureaucracy", London, Verso, 1991.

2.   Underlying some of the formulations in that respect is a form of myopic conservative prejudice: everything which does not exist cannot exist. With the same "logic" one could have stated that slavery was the only possible form of large scale agricultural or handicraft production (in the 1st century AD); that monarchy was the only possible form of government (in the 14th and 15th century); that parliaments could only be elected without universal franchise (in the 18th century) etc. Yet slavery finished by being abolished. Republics appeared while monarchies disappeared in their majority. Universal franchise ended by becoming general in all countries opting for a parliamentary system. Not to see what is developing without being already realized is a form of ideological colour-blindness often based upon wishful thinking: you don't see what you don't want to see.

3.   Market economy based upon small independent producers, who have direct access to their own means of subsistence (land) and their own means of production, is structurally different from a capitalist market economy in which such access is denied to 80-90% of the population.

4.   A radical example in that respect is offered by the Belgian economist Gérard Roland, in his interesting book *L'économie politique du système soviétique* (Paris, 1989). He presents the Soviet economy as ruled by "indicator values" i.e. the gross output targets set for enterprises. How can "indicators" rule over human beings?
      Do they fall from the sky? Aren't they the product of humans? Shouldn't one say that some human beings, social layers, use indicator values to rule over other human beings?

5.   A good example is that of housing under contemporary capitalism. In the richer countries, millions are still homeless and waiting for cheap apartments, while in the meantime millions of "second residences", often unoccupied during most of the year, have been built. In the poorer countries, hundreds of millions are homeless or dwell in miserable shantytowns and slums, while the rich have villas built for them which equal those of the richest countries, and the super-rich live

in estates and luxury compounds which more than 99% of even the richer countries' inhabitants cannot afford.

6. The allocation of relatively scarce resources for education and health, just to give these two examples, is decisive for the long term development of any country, including the economic one.

7. The economic crisis of the thirties made it profitable for German capitalism first, USA capitalism after that, often in competition with each other, to export modern machinery on a large scale to the USSR. The relatively slow pace of technological change didn't create any problems of successive waves of technological innovation in that period for the Soviet economy.

8. The stepped-up arms race since the beginning of the cold war, and especially since the sixties, exercized a growing pressure on the Soviet economy. As the GNP of the USSR was only 50% or less of the GNP of the USA, similar or equal arms expenditures meant a burden of double the size on the Soviet economy compared to the burden of the arms race on the USA economy.

9. In an adjusted tri-sector system of reproduction, department III includes all those goods and services which do not reenter the simple or expanded reproduction process. These are distinct from department I goods, raw materials, energy and machinery (tools) for simple and expanded reproduction, and of department II goods: consumer goods and services reconstituting and expanding labour power.

10. This is the wrong assumption of, among others, the Cliff school of adherents to the theory of "state capitalism" supposedly existing in the USSR.

11. This is again ignored by Preece and Unsal, who correct Feldman's two sectors model by building an ingenious three sectors' one, in which the third sector represents machine-tools and like goods (during means of production). Goods not entering reproduction are ignored in an unrealistic manner, "Science and Society", pp. 32-3, 54-4.

12. One should however consider that, from the point of view of the worker, and of human development, the slower work rhythm in Soviet factories is not something *per se* negative.

13. This is one of several phenomena which prove that, at least in its extreme form, the theory of "totalitarianism", i.e. the allegedly total control of Stalinism over society, was as incorrect as a similar allegation about Nazi Germany. In fact, there was a significant saying among people in Stalin's time: "blat" (i.e. connections) are stronger than Stalin.

14. This might on the other hand be considered a simple correction of the many excessive output figures contained in official statistics, so that the GNP, including the 25% output of the shadow economy, would be roughly equal to official statistics not including the informal sector.

15. Widespread criminalization of the private sector of the economy developed in the last 10-15 years, side by side with increasing growth of the informal and market operations. The mafia became a permanent feature of Soviet economy and society.

16. Leon Trotsky summarized his views about a cure of the ills of bureaucratic mismanagement in the following formula: "Only through the interaction of these three elements, state planning, the market, and Soviet democracy, can the correct direction of the economy of the transitional epoch be attained." (The Soviet Economy in Danger", in: *Writings of Leon Trotsky*, 1932, p. 275.)

17. See in that respect among other sources E. H. Carr and R. W. Davies: *Foundation of a Planned Economy 1926-1929, Volume One — II*, pp. 698-701. Stephen F. Cohen: *Bukharin and the Bolshevik Revolution*, pp. 278-280.

18. This was especially the case of Feldman, one of the fathers of the first Five Years plan.

19.   The saddest example in that respect is that of the tens of thousands of
      scientists enthusiastically engaged in creative research and in building a model
      "communist city" in Akademgorodok near Novosibirsk, just to become
      completely demoralized by a decline in their standard of living combined with
      the increase in material privileges of their superiors, and generally their
      subordination to a rigidly hierarchical system of science management.

20.   It has been alleged that the bureaucracy rules the USSR, like Western
      capitalists, in order to assure "production for production's sake". In the first
      place, this isn't an adequate description of the way capitalism functions any-
      where in the world. The correct formula is: production for profits' sake.
      Capitalists are not interested in unprofitable output. They ruthlessly curtail out-
      put when this serves the profit motive. In the second place, there is not the
      slightest indication that Soviet managers or even the Soviet bureaucracy in its
      totality is motivated or even interested in the last decades by maximizing, not to
      say optimizing output. All evidence revealed since the beginning of *glasnost* —
      indeed already initially revealed in the sixties — shows the opposite: a growing
      indifference towards overall economic performance, at plant level as well as at
      macro-economic level.

PRIVILIGENTSIA, PROPERTY AND POWER

Daniel Singer

The upheavals of 1989, propelling a playwright to the presidency in Prague and intellectuals from Solidarity into ministerial offices in Warsaw, have revived the old question about the function performed by the *intelligentsia* in the societies of central and eastern Europe. The question is controversial, since this *intelligentsia*, generally considered as bullied, gagged and hence the main victim of the Soviet system, is described by, say, Alexander Zinoviev, as gutless, submissive and, actually, a pillar of the regime. For Konrad and Szelenyi the intellectuals are a class in the making on the road towards power, while for Rudolf Bahro they are the main agency for a possible transition to socialism.[1] And these differences are not only the result of the ambiguity of the concept itself — the *intelligentsia*, in the narrow sense of the term, being perceived as an intellectual elite dedicated to a more or less radical transformation of society and, in a wider sense, as including all those whose labour is more mental than manual, those who went beyond the secondary school, the "educated tribe" to borrow Solzhenitsyn's rather contemptuous definition.

Thus, the subject is a complex one and we can only touch upon it here. We shall approach it through Russia not only because *intelligentsia* as a concept was conceived in the Tsarist empire, but also because what happens in the centre weighs heavily on developments in the periphery: without *perestroika*, without a Gorbachev giving up the Brezhnev doctrine, Havel would not have become president nor Mazowiecki prime minister. Once we have seen through the example of the Soviet Union that the *intelligentsia*, far from being uniform, can perform several roles, we shall stop for a brief spell in Poland, where the intellectuals first contributed to the revival of a labour movement and where they are now trying to resurrect the *bourgeoisie*. Finally, we shall try to see what lessons can be drawn from these upheavals here, in western Europe, where *commitment* was already out of fashion among intellectuals even before the funeral of Jean-Paul Sartre.

The notion of the *intelligentsia* as a separate social stratum appears

211

in the second and third decades of the last century.[2] It is not surprising that this idea was born in the Tsarist empire nor that the concept became widely used there in the second half of the 19th Century. Whereas in western Europe there was a certain correspondence between the spread of education and the development of capitalism, in Russia there was an obvious discrepancy between the two. The newly educated, finding no outlets, were naturally enough inclined to question society, to seek models beyond national frontiers, to be non-conformist. True, Russia, too, had its doctors, its engineers, its mandarins in the service of the established order, its nostalgic writers and reactionary politicians. Nevertheless, the *intelligent* was generally perceived as a dissenter, a radical reformer and, with the turn of the century, as more or less socialist (the French equivalent, at least in terms of perception, leads from the dissenters at the time of the Dreyfus case to the *intellectuels engagés* of Sartre's day).

In 1917 the revolution revealed that reality was less radical than the reputation. If a fraction of the *intelligentsia* joined the Bolsheviks and another was ready to collaborate with them, the majority emigrated either literally or metaphoricallly. Yet it was under Stalin that the bell tolled for the old *intelligentsia*. Under his reign, to dissent was to commit suicide and the critical spirit, unconcealed, was a passport to Siberia. But, at the same time, Stalin needed badly plain engineers and not only "engineers of the soul". He eliminated the *intelligentsia* in the narrow sense of the term and mass produced it in the broad sense. In this second function he was only a link in the chain. The cultural revolution, inaugurated in 1917, altered the figures altogether. According to Soviet statistics, on the eve of the revolution, among people employed in the economy only 200,000 had more than a secondary education; by 1960 they were 12 million and to-day their number can be estimated at some 40 million, that is to say almost a third of the labour force.[3]

Thus to use the term *intelligentsia*, without further precision as to its definition, can be as misleading as the utilization of the "tertiary sector", or of white collar, is in some western analyses: the truly privileged and the real ruling class are conveniently dissolved within a loose mixture including millions of people having very few privileges and no power whatsoever. Besides, this huge body is put together using as a criterion the diploma and not the function exercised in society. Out of the 40 million mentioned above, roughly 23 million went on studying for a couple of years after secondary school: about half of them came out of technical colleges and work in industry; this biggest group is followed by teachers without a university degree and junior staff in management and accounting. Even if these non-commissioned officers of the army of labour are excluded, the remaining 17 million are very far from uniform: about 30% among them are teachers, mainly women teachers and thus not surprisingly poorly paid, while over 40% are engineers and those among them who work in production only differ from the technicians because they do have a degree. But under the same headings one also finds academicians, heads of big firms, high-ranking technocrats and powerful party dignitaries. Still, while this diversity must always be kept in mind, the fact remains that the huge quantitative change has altered the social role of the *intelligentsia*.

With the first liberalisation after Stalin's death, the so-called *thaw*, the new *intelligentsia* recovered its former· function. In countries where diverse interests and aspirations have no directly political outlets, the intellectual in general and the writer in particular thus reappear as witness, spokesman or prophet. There is, however, a fundamental difference with the past. The *intelligentsia* is no longer necessarily progressive. Socialism having been identified with the established order, with the "really existing" regime, the *intelligentsia*, or at least a large part of it, is literally backward looking, hankering after an idealised capitalism or, nostalgically, after an even more distant past. During the Brezhnevian "era of stagnation" this tendency gained ground throughout eastern Europe and in Russia, too, as could be seen through the growing success of Solzhenitsyn. (Incidentally, to refer to the restoration of capitalism in that part of the world should not be taken to mean that these countries were previously in any way socialist.)

The second and crucial phase of liberalisation, the period of *glasnost* allowed the *intelligentsia* to play a progressive part. Only the true "watchdogs" of the regime — the censors, the prosecutors, the jailers, the keepers of the orthodoxy — were really opposed to the extension of the frontiers of freedom. Doubtless, an important section of the party apparatus wanted to prevent the Soviet people from recovering their memory because a reminder of Stalin's crimes was damning for the regime. Nevertheless, with a professional stake in the battle, the *intelligentsia* taken as a whole was in the vanguard in this struggle and in this first period expressed the superior interests of the entire society.

It is only at the next stage, the stage of the economic *perestroika* and restructuring, that the *intelligentsia* began to defend its own privileges and to fight for new ones; it is only then that it revealed its own inner divisions. The contrasting interests were only now being crystallised, the main protagonists still advanced in disguise and the various postures, therefore, remained ambiguous. Yet it was already possible to distinguish, admittedly in a rather schematic fashion, three main divisions, or rather the three temptations, of the Soviet *intelligentsia*.

The first was linked with the apparatus. Gone were the days when important functions were filled by the so-called *praktiki*, workers whom the Party trusted and who were learning their trade on the job. Now the *apparatchik* himself had a higher education: most often he was a graduate engineer. In addition to the servants of the organs of coercion and propaganda mentioned earlier, the conservative coalition included the many functionaries of ministries and other bodies of the central administration who were directly threatened by dispersion as well as those among the industrial managers whose position and privileges were linked with the preservation of a system in which all the decisions flowed from the top. Finally, the majority of the party apparatus itself was for the preservation of as much as possible of the old system of management because the control of the economy gave to the party secretary the supreme command at all levels.

The spokesmen of that conservative coalition have rapidly grasped that it was not very wise openly to defend the interests of the *nomenklatura*. Hence, they now parade as the protectors of public property against the new robbers and, since their privileges are more discreet than those of the *nouveaux riches*, as the defenders of the downtrodden. Since the advocates of the market now take the West openly as the model, the conservatives play unscrupulously on the most jingoist Great Russian feelings which, incidentally, have not been stirred by *perestroika* but simply revealed by *glasnost*. This alliance between the unrepentant neo-Stalinists and the reactionary nationalists, sworn enemies of the revolution — a curse imposed on the Russian people by "cosmopolitans" (since one cannot really speak of the Bolshevik Revolution as a "Zionist plot") — is actually less paradoxical than it might appear at first sight.

The noisiest, though not necessarily the most numerous, is what might be called the potential *priviligentsia*. It includes, among others, factory managers and economists, high ranking engineers and doctors, successful writers and journalists. Alll of them treat *perestroika* as a transfer of privileges and power from the *apparatchiks*, whose main virtue was their faithful obedience, to themselves, whose main quality is allegedly their competence. This self-proclaimed meritocracy is, and even more was, allied to the reformist or Gorbachevian wing of the apparatus, which embarked on a journey towards a market economy without really knowing where it was going to lead.

To begin with, the *priviligentsia*, too, dissimulated its posture. It used average incomes, heavily downgraded by the low salaries of the predominantly feminine staff in schools and hospitals, to prove the poor fate of the intellectual workers. By now, it has plucked up courage and asks openly for a very wide range of salaries, for different housing for the rich and for the poor, for a two-tier medicine or education. Admittedly, the frontiers are not clearly fixed and the foreign observer gets lost the more easily since this *priviligentsia*, represented in the Soviet parliament by the so-called *Democratic Platform*, is usually described in the Western press as "the Left". It is a symptom of the propaganda of our times that it is enough to be in favour of unemployment, of private property, of striking inequality to be proclaimed progressive. In the earlier phase, the *priviligentsia* could still be described as waging a democratic struggle for freedom. By now, the adjective has become highly doubtful. As privatisation and the introduction of a ruthless market meet growing popular resistance, the preachers of that school change their sermons. They now begin to advocate an authoritarian regime, at least for a transitional period until the market economy is consolidated (and this may lead to most unexpected shifts in alliances). Altogether, the *priviligentsia* speaks more and more as a class in the making, fighting not only for privileges, but also for power and property. [4]

So far we have mentioned the two sections of the *intelligentsia* linked to the two fractions of the ruling class, the former *apparatchiks* and the new *managers*. The budding socialist opposition is the third section: it is potentially the most numerous and is the true heir of the old *intelligentsia*. One finds it in the clubs spreading in Soviet towns, in research institutes and universities. It is not put in the limelight either by Soviet propaganda or by western correspondents and, above all, it is still searching its own way. It tries to establish links with the proletariat, notably through the striking workers. It admits the need for incentives at work but would like to insert them in a fundamentally egalitarian project. For the sake of transparence it accepts the provisional necessity of a market, yet simultaneously refuses its tyranny. It wonders how to socialise state property and how to render planning democratic. In short, it must reinvent democracy at all levels to render its project realistic. If one adds that it is by now vital to insert the economy into nature and that the Soviet Union has a terrible lag both in this and in the movement of women's liberation, the task facing this New Left is tremendous. The new socialist opposition is, for the time being, no more than the embryo of a movement.

Which of the three tendencies is likely to find itself on the winning side? The *intelligentsia* linked with the old apparatus seems to be in the least comfortable position: if the party leadership finally resigned itself to *perestroika*, it was because the former system of economic management, and hence of government, was no longer workable. The *apparatchiks* could, nevertheless, stand a chance should the so-called reformers, in their arrogance, precipitate a popular upheaval at a time when the socialist opposition is still unable to provide an outlet for such a movement. The *priviligentsia*, on the other hand, is clearly in the lead; at this stage, it dictates the pace of *perestroika*. But it runs the risk of being split into two. Gorbachev's followers favour a gradual, controlled transition. They wish to carry along as much of the party apparatus as possible and, above all, they want to avoid a confrontation with the workers, the inevitable first victims of the economic reform as it is conceived. On the contrary, most members of the *Democratic Platform* wish to rush the reform through and damn the consequences. They tend more and more to speak with the impatience and self-assurance of a future class-for-itself. Finally, there are the modern heirs of the progressive *intelligentsia*, handicapped by the discredit of the very idea of socialism, identified in the popular mind with the *ancien régime*. Their chance, on the other hand, is connected with the transformation of Soviet society, with the spread of education, with the connecting role, for instance, the technicians can play between the workers and the graduate engineers. The technical and professional *intelligentsia* is by now too numerous to be bribed in its entirety. Since it can no longer be tempted by the promise of "singing to-morrows", it must be given the feeling, like the workers themselves, that it is gaining a genuine say in shaping its destiny both at the workplace and in the society at large. A late starter, the socialist opposition is not necessarily a loser in this historical race.

History, however, is not predestined. It is a developing process. The nationalist stench emerging from the pores of east European societies infects the atmosphere and darkens even the image outlined here. Yet, essentially what I have been trying to convey is simply the intensification of the class struggle in the Soviet Union, the gradual crystallisation of conflicting interests. Even if these conflicts are still expressed in a confused and often ambiguous fashion, they are intense enough to break into pieces the myth of a united *intelligentsia*, revealing instead its deep divisions and its contradictory potentialities.

*   *   *

To follow the "organic intellectual" of a class in the making, it might be more helpful to turn to Poland where the conversion to capitalism is the openly admitted objective. Since, previously, Poland was the ground chosen for an alliance between the intellectuals and the workers, it is worth studying the present position against its historical background, even if the latter is sketched here very roughly.

The collaboration between the *intelligentsia* and the proletariat was no Polish peculiarity given from the start. When in 1968 the Polish government beat up the students in Warsaw, the workers did not come to their rescue. Two years later, when the workers conquered in blood their *veto* power over the government's economic policy, it was the turn of the intellectuals to be absent; the students from the Gdansk Polytechnic symbolically refused to join the striking workers on the march. One had to wait until 1976 for all this to change. The government then tried to get back the concessions it had granted, but was forced to give up the idea by the scope and sweep of the workers' response. Thwarted, it nevertheless tried to seek revenge through repression. It was then that a small group of intellectuals offered to the victimised workers its financial, legal or journalistic help. The creation of the KOR, Polish initials for the Committee for the Defence of the Workers, marks a date. It shows how intellectuals, even when not very numerous, can play a historical role if they are linked with a genuine social movement.

This collaboration grew. Four years later the same drama was re-enacted on an incomparably wider stage when, in front of an amazed world audience, the strikers of Gdansk conquered what at the time seemed unthinkable in a "communist" country, namely the right for the workers to have a genuine and independent representation. There again the intellectuals were in the service of the workers within an experts' committee already presided over by Tadeusz Mazowiecki, the future prime minister. This relationship between the *intelligentsia* and the proletariat was to persist throughout the first phase of *Solidarity*, when the new labour union represented nearly 10 million members. When in the autumn of 1981 there was a question of compromise with the authorities what was at stake was a project recognising the current political imperative of geography, and granting therefore to the Communist Party the control of the Lower House, but allowing at the same time for a Senate dominated by the workers, representing on the national scale the self-management committees encouraged at that time by Solidarity.

This idea of dual power came to nothing. The Polish CP was ready to share power with the Catholic Church, not with the proletariat. Its reply came on December 13th with the military coup of General Jaruzelski. Technically a success, this *coup* broke the resistance in the factories, though not sufficiently to drag the workers into an economic reform. When after seven years a new series of strikes began, the authorities grasped the vanity of their efforts and, with

Gorbachev now in power in Moscow, resigned themselves to a dialogue. In the meantime, however, while the power of Solidarity in the factories was being broken, press, propaganda and, hence, the *intelligentsia* were playing an increasing part in the resistance movement. When it came to talks and elections, in 1989, the relationship within Solidarity was thus turned upside down. This time the intellectuals claimed to express the "superior interests" of society and the workers were treated as electoral fodder. This change was rapidly reflected in the programme of the new government headed by Solidarity. The self-management slogans and the egalitarian aspirations were quickly forgotten and replaced by a primitive gospel of capitalist accumulation. To reduce the rate of inflation and stabilise the *zloty*, the new Minister of Finance did not hesitate to precipitate a slump, to cut real wages drastically and allow unemployment to soar. If privatisation did not proceed any faster it is because one cannot sell off the whole of Polish industry to foreigners (who, in any case, are not particularly keen); because domestic buyers must still be somehow created and profitable firms prepared for the market. The political revival of the bourgeoisie precedes its economic restoration as a class.

The intellectuals are not the only ones to blame for what is happening. The whole leadership of Solidarity must take its share and none more than Lech Walesa. The IMF-sponsored programme of transition to capitalism at breakneck speed was introduced by Solidarity in office but backed by Solidarity — the labour union. True, the workers were bewildered and even ready for sacrifices. Yet had they fought simply for the right to be more exploited, were they ready for sacrifices without any counterparts? It took a man they trusted to convince them that there was no alternative and this is the sense in which Walesa is more responsible than Mazowiecki for the distortion of the class struggle in Poland. Now that he has been elected President, he will no longer be able to put the blame for the trouble on the government. It is to be feared that he will try to divert mounting discontent through McCarthyist witchhunts, the search for scapegoats and other irrational solutions.

The worst is never sure. More generally, it seems less useful to speak once again of betrayal than to ask oneself why a Tadeusz Mazowiecki, once a left-wing Catholic (connected with the then relatively progressive review, *Esprit*), became the Prime Minister who introduced Thatcherism into Poland; why Jacek Kuron, the veteran of so many battles, was his alibi as a Minister of Labour; why Lech Walesa himself, once a symbol of the fighting revival of the working class, is now the champion of its non-resistance? Stalinism is no longer sufficient to explain all this metamorphosis. This final ideological descent, this complete acceptance of capitalism as the only possible alternative, giving up the search for any other way — all this coincides with the last phase of the so-called "era of stagnation" and the beginning of the *perestroika*.

In Poland all this brought about an interesting transition. The rejection of "communism" is total and it ensured the victory of Solidarity in 1989 and the election of Walesa as president the following year. Popular gratitude towards those who had delivered them from the *ancien régime* was such that the Mazowiecki government could proceed with its ruthless economic policy for about a year without major social upheaval.[5] But already then the workers were no longer treating Solidarity as a trade union defending their interests; at its congress, in April 1990, the organisation claimed 1.9 million members, roughly five times less than its membership at the height of its power nine years earlier. True, the memory was sufficiently strong for Walesa to be elected president. Yet how long will the workers consider even his government as their own?

The *intelligentsia* itself, despite the presence of its representatives in office, is not in a comfortable position either. While the price of paper climbs and state subsidies vanish, the writer, the artist, the actor, fed up with the bliss of party monopoly, discover the virtues of the cultural market at its most savage, without the cushion provided by prosperity and the fat of the foundatijons. It is the turn of the professional and technical *intelligentsia* to experiment with the burdens of insecurity. How much time will be needed for all this to have political consequences?

The restoration of capitalism, not to be confused with a few privatisations in England or France, is an unprecedented venture and, in any case, it is unwise to extrapolate without reflection. Each country has its peculiarities. All that can be ventured for the area as a whole is that an entire new period of awakening and disillusion will be required before a resurrected Left is strong enough to cast aside the hackneyed beliefs which are now paraded as the latest gospel. All that I would dare to suggest is that this confrontation with budding capitalism is more likely to take place earlier in the birthplace of a genuine revolution than in countries where it was an imported product. Meanwhile, both the collapse of these regimes and their clever identification with socialism allow our propaganda at its most triumphant to proclaim that capitalism is eternal.

*   *   *

In the long or even medium run the upheavals in eastern Europe may well have the opposite effect from the one presently expected. The final dismissal of the absurd identification of socialism with the

Soviet tank or the Russian concentration camp, the ultimate collapse of a "model" that has for many years been no more than a bogey, the need for the western labour movement to face its own problems and the impossibility of accusing western rebels of being "foreign" agents — all this should contribute to the resurrection of socialism. Maybe it is this prospect which drives our propaganda to insist so heavily on the absence of any alternative and on capitalism as the end of history. With, for the time being, a great deal of success.

In France the last twenty years will figure in history books as marking the spectacular elimination of the influence of Marxist thought (of which a good part, under the impact of Stalinism, was, it must be admitted, sterile).[6] But they will also confirm the wisdom of the Marxist maxim that the ruling ideology is the ideology of the ruling class. Who could have imagined, on the morrow of May 1968, when the established ideological structure seemed shaken, that twenty years later France would have two million unemployed and virtually nobody would question the validity of the capitalist system? Doubtless, the nature of the economic crisis, attacking the strongholds of the labour movement, had a crucial impact on this evolution. But the ideological battle itself was not without influence and, within its framework, the so-called *operation gulag* carried out by the *nouveaux philosophes*.

Not because of its intellectual content. The very idea of these latter-day Christopher Columbuses discovering the Soviet concentrationary universe in 1975 was perfectly ridiculous. The dish they served was entirely imported: a drop of Hayek, a few slices of Popper, a good dose of Solzhenitsyn and the whole seasoned with the anti-totalitarian sauce. The only French contribution was that of its hawkers (to compare the rubbish produced by the Glucksmanns and other Bernard — Henri Lévy with *The God That Failed*, published thirty years earlier, is to realise that the passage of time is not always the equivalent of progress). As a political and advertising campaign, however, it was quite a different matter. It was important that imagination should not get involved with power. It was necessary to persuade the young generation that, while to rebel individually might be just, to act collectively in order to change society can only lead to the *gulag*. The "thirty glorious years" of capitalist expansion over and unemployment revealing once again the true face of capitalism, it was vital to prove that any alternative was "concentrationary". Such a message would not have been accepted at the time coming from, say, Raymond Aron; "children of May 68" were needed to do the dirty job. Sponsored massively by the media, the message got through. It helped the regime to consolidate. It contributed to the failure, or rather the abortion, of the attempt by the Socialists to tackle the foundations of existing society. (The French Left got back into office in 1981 without the backing of a vast social movement and at a time when the Right had gained complete ideological hegemony.)

This inability of the western Left to carry out a "break" has, in turn, influenced the political climate in eastern Europe, strengthening there the conviction that between capitalism and "really existing socialism" nothing can be invented. Historians will show one day how the reactionary currents in the two halves of Europe reinforced one another. The *operation gulag*, destined mainly for western countries with strong Communist parties, looks very modest when compared with *operation "end of history"* now being performed on the world scale to convince everybody that there is no way out of capitalism.[7] Admittedly, a spectacular collapse of several regimes lends itself better to such exploitation than a book by a witness, however eloquent.

May be the campaign is too triumphant. There are signs that some of its more subtle promoters are changing their tactics, partly because they can now afford it and, partly, because they are themselves troubled by the wave of jingoism, xenophobia and antisemitism rising in the East. To accept that the capitalist market, if needed, be introduced in an undemocratic and even authoritarian fashion is one thing; our freedom-loving press knows only too well how to look away in the circumstances. Yet, without a serious threat of revolution, one does not take a Le Pen for ally. The second reason to correct the range is that too heavy a fire runs the risk of being counter-productive. The pseudo-hegelian creed of Francis Fukuyama — presenting capitalism as the culmination of history — sounds like a provocation, a challenge. It may be preferable, now that the main message has been spread, to play more on the subconscious, to speak less of capitalism, to stress the possible democratic improvements in our market economy and law-abiding society. The accent, if not the policy, may be to-morrow closer to social-democracy than to Thatcherism. It is this middle-of-the road appearance and semblance of objectivity that we must now prepare to unmask.

While myths collapse, names change and the confusion is at its highest, it is not easy in the West either to define what the Left stands for to-day. The Left can only be rebuilt around a new project. It is better off without models, particularly without one it should never have accepted as its own, but it must also draw the lessons of the bitter heritage. It must rebuild its project in the light of present reality, taking into account the new structure of the working class (with its many women and immigrants), the growing number of white collar workers, the new role played by science in production. The Left must reinvent democracy at all levels if it wants to speak of planning once again. It must remember that, absorbed by the electoral map, macho in mood and productivist in outlook, it has proved unable to understand and to integrate the three movements which in this last quarter of a century have fundamentally questioned our world: the revolt of the students, women's liberation movements and the green growth of the ecologists. And we could continue with the challenge of nationalism or the internationalisation of the economy on the world scale. Hence the task is as immense as it is urgent. And yet there is a prior duty. All projects will come to nothing if the bulk of the people become convinced that one cannot change, merely refurbish, our society. In the *Kulturkampf* now being fought all over the globe the dividing line among the intellectuals is clear. On the one side are the upholders of the established order who, whatever their labels, accept capitalism as the ultimate horizon and, on the other, the heirs of the *intelligentsia* in the original sense of the term who, resisting the tremendous offensive, are preserving the Promethean spirit. One side stresses the eternity of capitalism, the other — the permanence of revolution.

NOTES

1. For A. Zinoviev see particularly *The Yawning Heights*, Random House, NY, 1979; G. Konrad and I. Szelenyi: *The Road of Intellectuals to Class Power*, Harcourt Brace Jovanovich, NY, 1979. R. Bahro: *The Alternative in Eastern Europe*, NLB, London, 1978.
2. The word itself appears in the 1860s, probably for the first time in the writings of the novelist P. Boborykin. The literature on the subject is rich. For a recent study of the Soviet *intelligentsia* see B. Kagarlitsky: *The Thinking Reed*, Verso, London, 1988.
3. Projection based on figures for 1987 taken from *Narodnoye Khozyaystvo SSSR v 1988 g.*
4. American readers could see a perfect example in an article published in *The NY Review of Books* on August 16, 1990. Entitled "Dangers of Democracy" it was written by Gavriil Popov, the new mayor of Moscow. In it, the darling of the liberals complained that ". . . now we must create a society with a variety of different forms of ownership, including private property; and this will be a society of economic inequality. There will be contradictions between policies leading to denationalization, privatisation, and inequality on the one hand and, on the other, the populist character of the forces that were set in motion in order to achieve these aims. The masses long for fairness and economic equality. And the further the process of transformation goes, the more acute and the more glaring will be the gap between those aspirations and economic realities." What lessons does he draw? "The first conclusion from the analysis I have been making is that we must speed up changes in the forms of ownership. The second is that we must seek new mechanisms and institutions of political power that will depend less on populism."
5. Mazowiecki paid the price in the presidential poll, where he came a poor third in the first ballot behind a completely unknown Stan Tyminski, a local boy who allegedly had made a fortune in America. Mazowiecki's defeat was not due to his honesty. It was due to the consequences of his economic programme, but also to the ideology coupled with it. If your main message to the people is "enrich yourselves", no

wonder that some of them then vote for a hero from a soap opera and Stan Tyminski was a figure from a poor man's *Dallas*.

6. Must one first clear the ground? Some of us thought that there would be no socialist resurrection without the destruction of the Stalinist model and no socialist or revolutionary revival in France without the destruction or the total transformation of the French CP. The negative, however, does not necessarily give birth to the positive.

7. The theoreticians of totalitarianism claimed that the "empire of evil" and its satellites were immutable, that it was a hell from which there was no exit. Instead of self-criticism they have produced a transfer: it is now capitalism which is a system from which there is no exit.

This text, translated by the author, was originally written for the *festchrift* for Olivier Revault d'Allonnes, professeur of the Philosophy of Art at Paris 1 (Sorbonne), author, inter allia, of *La création artistique et les promesses de la liberté; Musiques, Variations sur la pensée juive; Plaisir à Beethoven.*

FOR A SOCIALIST REBIRTH: A SOVIET VIEW

A. Buzgalin and A. Kolganov

What country is this we are living in? Do you call this socialism, if yesterday hundreds of thousands or millions of people — mainly communists — were sent to the camps and today tanks and armoured personnel carriers appear on the streets of our towns? Is this socialism when you can't even buy ordinary shoes and milk — let alone a video or pork — in Uglich, Nizhnii Tagil, Arkhangelsk or Astrakhan? Do you call this socialism, where a veteran worker has to get by on 70 or perhaps 100 roubles a month, but young foreign currency dealers and prostitutes can make hundreds, or rather thousands of roubles a day? Do you call this socialism, if hospitals and kindergartens look like barns, but the 'servants of the people' notwithstanding all the criticism, still 'serve the people' in marble palaces. Do you call this socialism?

Any social drama is difficult to submit to sober scientific analysis if you are one of its actors. When one of the two ruling world social systems melts away like last year's snow in a few months, when Poland, Hungary, Czechoslovakia and the rest don't even want to be called *Peoples'* republics, let alone socialist, when a once monolithic (to outward appearances, at least) block of communist and workers' parties of the socialist countries collapses like a house of cards, when. . . When all this becomes reality, it can make you feel like burying your head in the sand of domestic problems, or repenting of former errors and joining a rag-bag band of home-grown monarchists and liberals in the Requiem for socialism.

Anybody interested? Well, we aren't at any rate. Like most Marxists, we want to get to grips with understanding the crisis afflicting socialism and the world communist movement. It cannot be simply reduced to food shortages and a loss of faith in the ruling parties (essentially the fault of the corrupt elite and the party-state apparatus) of the so-called socialist countries. The problem lies deeper. It is now increasingly obvious that the production relations, economic mechanism, the politics and ideology of Stalinist-Brezhnevite society left the key tasks of today — the mass introduction of the technology of the scientific and technical revolution, a civilised and comfortable standard of living and socio-political and cultural freedoms — unanswered.

This, we repeat, is obvious. But the question is: does this mean in principle that socialism never had, and never will have a better answer than that 'civilised' part of humanity, which now seems to have such an unassailable lead on us?

Indeed we have just posed the readers and ourselves not one, but several questions at once. One: What sort of society are we living in, and can we consider 'real socialism' a practical embodiment of Marxism, and on the basis of its crisis judge one section of humanity's road to socialism and communism to have failed? Two: Have Marxism and the socialist idea completely discredited themselves as a scientific and objective programme for the creation of a new society? Three: What prospects do the countries of 'real socialism' have of escaping from the crisis, and where do we go from here?

1. *What Sort of Society?*

Socialism is a society built for and in the name of humanity, a society whose mission is to provide welfare and all-round development for every. . . Yes, what the USSR, Poland, North Korea and Yugoslavia have today bears little resemblance to that bright ideal. So where are we living? In a country of state feudalism with its universal hierarchy, castes, social barriers and administrative coercion? Or is this simply a bastard social and economic system without parallel in world history? And what do the socio-economic systems of the other 'socialist' countries represent — for the present or for the future? What did we fight for? For what cause did millions of party members, workers and peasants go to their deaths at the hands of noble Russian (and also British, French, Japanese and American) defenders of civilisation on the fronts of the Civil War? Why were the millions of those who were repressed by their fellow citizens convinced of the rightness of the ideas and cause of socialism? Why did the children of those shot by Stalin hurry off to join the fight against fascism in Spain (rather than the rockers or the punks)? Why were the collective farms and Soviet power restored in the areas controlled by the partisans, and the women and children literally worked to death? Why, only thirty years ago were most of us so keen to go into space, to the virgin lands and to Bratsk, rather than to become well-heeled playboys? Why do those returning from war in Afghanistan value the support of friends above everything else and why are they prepared to fight for justice?

Why is this happening in a country where the government has lied itself black in the face for decades, and a monstrous web of corruption and an all-pervading morass of bureaucracy have doomed the people of a great power to freeze in conditions comparable only to developing countries? Why?

The answer is not simple, but there is one. Because our history resulted from playing out a terrible and monstrous contradiction, which gave birth to both the achievements and the decay of new-born socialism. At one end were those of us who fought for seventy years to build socialism with our own sweat and blood. At the other were those who by their apathy, fear and indolence saddled us with a band of outright criminals and dealers in red tape sincere only in their enthusiasm to suppress everything living. So where are we living? Is this a socialist country, or isn't it? And what sort of a socialist country has a standard of living lower than that of Taiwan?

Have you ever seen children deformed by polio? One leg longer than the other, arms sticking out in all directions, heads on one side, hardly even able to speak? Is this a human being? Stand him next to a gorilla and compare their viability. There's no question about it. Or is there? Our socialism, hardly yet born and or able to stand on its own two feet, was stricken with a terrible disease of bureaucratic trans-formation. Yes, there were reasons: the child was weak and the environment was hostile. Yes, today we are barely alive, and hardly know what to put right first in order to sort out which way to go, what to do, and how to do it.

There are many who would prefer to put this sick child out of its misery. After all, the experiment was a failure, its legs wont support it, its arms are useless and it's got the head of a zombie. . . some people maybe, but not those who put their own soul, heart, work and blood into the life of that child.

We have certainly built a strange society. It has everything: — a semi-feudal hierarchy, state capitalism with monopolies and a bureaucracy hiring dispossessed workers, and the embryonic 'bits and pieces' of socialist relations, which were deformed almost before they had sprung up, and survived in this terrible distorted form for decades.

What gave this monstrosity its strength? Maybe it was the strength of the totalitarian and bureaucratic system, subordinating everything to itself, distorting our lives and our ideals alike.

2. *Only Communists Can Discredit Communism*

And we have. We have discredited the greatest achievement of the human mind — the idea of the Communist future of Mankind, the idea of the unification and emancipation of the workers. We have discredited it, drowning it in the blood of the Stalinist purges, in the empty phrasemongering of Khrushchev's promises, and the swamp of Brezhnev's stagnation. We have discredited the ideas for which people like Bauman, killed by a Tsarist secret police agent, Sacco and

Vanzetti, sentenced to the electric chair by the democratic State of America, Allende and Jara, shot by Pinochet's worshippers of private property all gave their lives.

We have discredited many of socialism's values on what is virtually a world scale. With our own hands (correction: the hands of Stalin, Yezhov, and Beria are not the hands of the people) we wiped out the Comintern, both directly by purges, and indirectly, by the fight against social democracy and our flirtation with fascism. With our own hands (and these were our hands and nobody else's — the hands of bondsmen who dumbly tolerated the trampling of the ideals of our country and the ideals of socialism) we laid the way for our country to become the image of the 'evil empire' of totalitarianism and suppression of the individual.

During a public debate our colleague V. I. Danilov-Danil'yan justly remarked that during the twenties and thirties a well educated and cultured Englishman or Frenchman was as afraid of admitting his sympathies for the capitalist system as virtually the majority of the elite intelligentsia of the USSR or Poland are now of confessing to a belief in socialism. . . It's alright nowadays to bewail the passing of Russia the Great (Lithuania, Moldavia, Georgia), of (My God) civilisation, even the innocently murdered Nikolai Ivanovich (who called him 'bloody' — he was such a nice, well-educated man, and he was so fond of Russia) but words like 'marxism', 'socialist revolution' and 'Communism'. . . sorry, these are a bit unfashionable and not quite the thing in civilised society.

You can get as worked up as you like about this (and we must admit that we do!), but the worst of it is that these judgements are in many respects correct. Our generation has never seen any other form of socialism than that of the corrupt power of the Rashidovs and Churbanovs, and knows no other marxism than the demagogy of Brezhnev and Suslov. For decades they lectured us on the advantages of developed socialism, swore loyalty to the ideals of Leninism. . . and lied. Lied in what they said and lied in what they did.

And what did *we* do? We just sat there and listened. We repeated the lie at meetings. Worse, we even believed some of it. At first we believed blindly that this lie really was the ideal of socialist marxism. Now we are ready to believe blindly. . . in what? Strange as it may seem, the same thing — that the ideals of socialism and marxism are lies, dirt and blood.

Whose fault is this? Those who humiliated us — the government, the Party, the paid ideologists and their lackeys from the social sciences?[1] But however true that may be, the guilty are among us too — those who did not hold senior posts, did not take bribes, did not speculate, did not sing the praises of developed socialism at meetings (and how many of us 'without sin' in this respect) but in doing so kept quiet and maintained 'well-paid sycophants and lovers of sinecures' (K. Marx)[2] — those who now sit and wait a new mafia — consisting of the banking aristocracy, speculators and their willing or unwilling ideologists — to humiliate them once more.

But still, much is changing. We've thrown off our slumbers and keep asking ourselves 'why can't we live like they do over there if we clearly can't go on living the way we do over here?' Over there they've got things to eat, things to wear, somewhere to live, and all of this without any queues. Sounds good? It certainly does. And if you look at Sweden, they've even got a Social-Democratic government and live under what virtually amounts to socialism. What more could you want? We'll organise everything like that and live like. . . Yes, how? Like they do in Sweden? Or like they do in India which also has a market, and a mixed system of property, and democracy?

3. *Does 'Civilised Society' have disadvantages, and should we be afraid of them?*

Our erstwhile choruses of 'Shame!' at meetings and in books about 'their' way of life just a few years ago has given way to the still more unanimous 'Hooray' which we now raise on the same subject at meetings and in newspapers.

Suppose we take a sober look at the West? No, we're not trying to present opinion as objective analysis. Let us just mention the diametrically opposite views of two acquaintances who were in the USA at the end of 1989. Let us begin with perhaps the only thing on which our colleagues agreed. The level of domestic and industrial technology is more than ten years ahead of ours. But at this point there is a surprising divergence of views. One goes into endless raptures at the variety and beauty of all the things around you: the dozens of different types of wineglasses and tumblers in a bar; the eight different knives and forks that civilised man uses to eat scrambled eggs; the genuine art that one sees in any shop window, which, he feels, must have taken a talented artist over one hundred hours. The other, an art specialist, with a certain latent diffidence of a man given to quarrel with the obvious facts, has his doubts: does one have to waste the time and genius of an artist in order to present Her Majesty the Product to the customer? No, art in everyday life is all very well but. . . And (continuing his impressions) the bondage of the 'businessman' who has to put in 8-12 hours of hard work every day to. . . earn enough to pay for a flat, car and suit befitting his status and to be able to relax in the sauna or the club (where, however, one should also not miss any opportunity to talk business). The business centre of New York consists of thousands of identical stony-faced office workers. Such is the opinion of the art specialist.

His opponent, on the contrary, is in love with the rhythm of business life; he came to make deals, and what a welcome he got. Villas, swimming pools, tennis. . . And the food!. . . Of course, there are the homeless, but they are just the layabouts — its the businessman who really counts.

But a new objection breaks in upon these encomiums. Perhaps the homeless, the unemployed, the Hare Krishna Temple and the Hippies are a mute and unassuming opposition to the satiated business life of the majority? Yes, the minority (though not everybody) in the USA or Europe can get welfare benefits and free soup; society is prepared to feed its dissidents providing they don't stand in the way of business — but doesn't this hint at the enslavement of Western man — not by a despotic state, but by 'business', by 'the organisation' by 'things'. No doubt many, on reading this, will choke with rage: there's damn all in the country to eat, nothing to wear, and you go about. . . We'll leave aside the fact that most of our enthusiasts of Western lifestyles are quite decently dressed and in no danger of starvation. Let us ask ourselves — do we want to work several times harder than we do today? Do we want to vote for the redundancy of two thirds of our fellow workers? Do we want real competition with our neighbour, our friend and our colleague? Do workers, rank and file engineers, doctors and teachers in the USSR want that? And what will they get from 'Swedish reforms?' — a civilised European lifestyle or a 'New India' with a rampaging mafia and inter-ethnic wars to boot?

We will more than likely live in this 'civilised' society in very different ways. Those who in the notorious years of stagnation stashed away. . . it's hard to say how much; if in Uzbekistan alone the mafia of Rashidov, Adylov and their ilk managed to appropriate several thousand million, then for the Union as a whole, these sums must be of an order of magnitude greater (indirect data suggests that our mafia controls maybe 30, maybe 150 thousand million roubles, and its total annual wage bill is several thousand million roubles). So these people stand to gain a fair bit from the transition to the market and the mixed economy.

Those who believe in striking while the iron is hot[3] and argue that it is immoral to count the money in other peoples' pockets will not do so well, but they won't do too badly either.

But how will the tens of millions of pensioners and more than 100 million factory workers, peasants and office workers fare, those whose basic income is a pension of 70-100 roubles per month or a wage of 200-250 roubles, if prices at the market, cooperatives and shops with the KKOP[4] sign are already putting every family essential beyond their means? Isn't competition supposed to bring prices down? Then why is it that in Poland and Yugoslavia prices, far from falling, are rising at crazy rates?

Perhaps we'll all start making money like cooperative members and smallholders? But if so, why is it that in countries where this has been going on for more than a year, the real wages of workers have not risen for several years? Why is it that the vast majority of our workers have no wish to join cooperatives, and the peasants don't want to become smallholders?

Why is all this happening? Why did even the 'Chinese miracle' run out of steam? Perhaps because what we are trying to learn from the West is the market and economic organisation which ended in the Great Depression of 1929-33, rather than the prosperity of the eighties? Perhaps because, having lost capitalism's habits of cruelty and vigour, and having introduced state monopoly capitalism, we have got all the drawbacks of capitalism, but are unable to reap any of its benefits.

DIGRESSION ONE:

The Swedish Model is unlikely to do us any good.

As a small theoretical digression let us consider the idea that the introduction of the 'Swedish' model of economic organisation is likely to bring abundance to this country in the near future. The opposite is more likely: it will condemn a large part of the present generation to the contradictions of life in an economy trying to break into the ranks of the new industrial countries by means of rampant exploitation of the workers by cultivated bureaucrats, technocrats, graftocrats[5] other crats (rather as in South Korea in recent decades).

Argument No 1: Abstract and methodological considerations: The highly efficient economic and socio-political mechanism of modern Sweden is the result of centuries of the organic growth of capitalism. Capitalism in the 20th century has made painful progress (and in most countries is still doing so) toward the rule of the pluralistic and 'humane' model which we usually call 'Swedish'. Yes, painful! The right to live under capitalism with a 'human face' has been purchased with the lives of millions — workers, peasants and the intelligentsia. Those who were killed or tortured in Germany in 1918, in Hungary in 1919, in Austria in the thirties, those who fought world fascism throughout the thirties and forties, those who were not afraid to fight the witch hunts and racism of the boom years of the turn of the forties and fifties. The 'human face' of capitalism has been bought by the energy of strikes, the outbursts of the 'new left', and the determination of the pacifists and the 'greens'.

The result? — the new face of capitalism. From the socio-economic point of view this face represents the development of an intricate complex of transitional production relations, including elements of a new — socialist — system. For us, this idea is important primarily because when we look at modern capitalism, we can see quite clearly the features of. . . our future socialist production relations!

Argument No 2: (decoding the above abstractions). The modern market and mixed property relations is not a naive, balanced, hundred-year-old competition where purchasers quietly decide which goods are cheaper and better, and producers bend over backwards to please the consumer. It may look like that superficially, but deeper down. . . Deeper down it is a complicated assemblage of highly organised economic relations involving the plan, social security, the market, and much else. The main 'secret' of the success of modern capitalism is even more deeply hidden — a working class which is highly organised, highly skilled — and, most important, able to stand up for its interests. And today these are not just machine operators, but also those who sit at computer terminals, serve customers and grow wheat. They have strong organisations — trade unions, consumer associations, 'greens' and so on. The workers spent decades of blood and sweat fighting to create them, going hungry during strikes and dying on the barricades. They can keep working at rates which we (and that means all of us) maintain only at the end of the quarter. They have been schooled in centuries of capitalist labour discipline, and the work ethic has entered their flesh and blood. Do we have workers like that?

And this is not all. Modern Sweden and Austria also have a highly cultured ruling elite (the 'financial oligarchy'), who have learned from both their own mistakes, but mainly from those of others, not to push conflicts too far, not to get carried away with their pursuit of power and wealth, and not to make an exhibition of themselves. This elite has succeeded in raising several generations of high-class managers; it did not stand in the way of, but on the contrary promoted the formation of a democratic, civilised system of state power, and of a social consciousness giving the political and ideological pluralism needed for everyone to be able to say and even do what they liked without in so doing going beyond the bounds of 'civilised society', at the top of which stood this elite. Could our home grown businessmen, economic administrators and officials follow such a policy, brought up as they are in an atmosphere of delight in red tape, corruption, theft, systematic petty barter and self-deception?

Let us now leave aside theoretical arguments and ask ourselves an odd question: do we really want to live like the Swedes or the Austrians, the Americans or the Japanese? Well of course we all want our own house, plenty of good food, fashionable clothes, a video and two cars per family. We want holidays in the Bahamas and weekends in Monte Carlo. . . but let us repeat. . . do we want to work like the Japanese worker or American engineer? And another, perhaps rather naive question: how happy is he, this average Swede or American, so full of the good things in life?

It is hard for us at the moment to imagine how anyone could be unhappy when they can buy whatever they like — from comfortable shoes to cars that don't break down. But why does one get this sense of boredom from the best Western films and novels? Why the mass suicide and drug addiction? What makes our emigres in well-fed America so unhappy — do they just miss the Russian countryside, or is it the cruelty of their comfortable well-fed world?

Il'ya Ehrenburg remarked in his memoirs that in the twenties and the fifties we did not envy the West; instead the West envied us. What did they envy us for? Our well being? We had no such thing. Because we knew why we were living, perhaps? Because we weren't afraid of putting out a hand to our neighbour and saying — comrade? Or the fact that the word 'our' had a real meaning for us — if only partially — and meant more than the word 'mine'?

No, it didn't last long. . . The enthusiasm of the twenties gave way to the concentration camps of the thirties, the romanticism of the fifties suffocated in the stifling atmosphere of the sixties and seventies. . . Which makes all the more surprising the viability of those embryonic elements of socialism, which live on in many of our hearts, although one would have thought the cynicism and lies which have ruled us for decades would have caused general revulsion to the very idea of socialism.

And lastly. Haven't you ever felt a lump come to your throat when you read about the young Kibal'chish[6] who refused to betray military secrets to the accursed bourgeois? Haven't you ever wanted to break out of this aimless life and be there, alongside that boy, knowing that all you have to do is to stand your ground for the day and survive the night?

No, it isn't like that now. The real enemy is now not on the other side of the barricades, but right here among us, in our indifference and passivity. But we are sorry for people who laugh at these lines, because it means only one thing; the decades of lies, falsehood and speculation on the ideas of socialism have defeated the Communist in you (never mind whether you are a party member). But perhaps you never were one? Well then, our apologies, but the rest of this is not for you. And not because it is a 'military secret' but because it will cause you only growing irritation and anger. However, anger is better than nothing, and we are prepared for polemics.

4. *What Sort of Tomorrow do we want?*

Well, what is to be done? Where do we go, if the price of the market and mixed property threaten to be the rule of the graftocracy and new contradictions to add to the old ones? Back to Stalinism, perhaps? 'Defend ideals, long live the firm hand, universal state control, bring everyone down to the same level, and power to the bureaucracy'?

Economists and journalists (with very rare exceptions) have been trying for almost five years to bang it in to the heads of Soviet people that there is only one alternative; Stalinism or NEP, coercion or the rouble, the bureaucrat or the market — there is no other way.

Isn't there?

Before answering this question let us stress one thing. The point is that the real scale of problems facing our country is immeasurably greater, and the problems themselves more complex than shortages of meat, milk, housing and fashionable clothing. We have to prove that our system and country, having endured the tragedy of the Cult of Personality (and of the Non-Personality) and having been stuck for decades in the swamp of stagnation can solve the main problem of modern times (and not just of modern times but of all world history) better than the cultured and highly experienced West or East. That problem is the overcoming of social alienation, the socio-economic liberation of man (not just from exploitation, but from the power of money and the bureaucracy), the transformation of all of us from 'tim'rous beasties' into masters of our own lives and country.

In order to attack these problems, we need far more radical answers and changes much more far-reaching than those taking place at present. But we must confess that precious few of the conditions needed for these changes and answers exist.

So, do we fold our arms and settle for half-measures? Or maybe we should roll our sleeves up and start fighting for those conditions (not forgetting of course the 'Minimum Programme', which we may use as a starting point as long as we are not confined by it).

DIGRESSION 2

The Scale of the Changes

If what we have said about the scale of the changes which have begun are not to look like empty phrasemongering, we must allow ourselves a certain analogy.

THE HIGH RENAISSANCE

In the renaissance of human culture, belief in the greatness and power of Man, the Personality, and the Individual supplanted submission to dogma. That is how we see that age from 500 years away. Most of the people of the 14th, 15th and even 16th centuries saw things quite differently.

Medieval man was quite unlike like you and me. He felt himself to be a member of a social body rather than an individual or separate personality. A person was a member of a town workshop or guild, or a village community, or a family if he was a nobleman, and this sense of belonging was virtually the foundation of his life.

And such a person was unable to believe that the nobleman and the serf, the townsman and the peasant could be equal. Such an idea contradicted the whole of life and the experience of centuries, and how could you live if you did not know which family, town, or community you belonged to? To take away from medieval man the hierarchy of social estates meant the destruction of all social values, of all concepts of good, evil and nobility (a synonym for 'noble birth') and poverty (which was the lot of the 'third estate').

And then came the turning point. Gradually, affecting only individuals at first, then as the slogan of great revolutions came the great march of change. Hereditary power is no more — instead one is free to make one's life in the world of 'honest' trade (we should note that the exploitation of hired labour, since it does not contravene the law of value, is also part of bourgeois equality).

These changes brought immense progress, but they were long and painful. Rational economic man took his place upon the earth, motivated primarily by economic, monetary profit. In a few short centuries, from a historical point of view, these stereotypes penetrated our affairs, consciousness and way of life so completely that to question them seems an attempt to subvert natural and eternal human values. Not just to the man in the street, but also to high-powered economists and talented journalists.

And so mankind is faced with a new qualitative leap. This too is reaching the end of its days. And this was not only predicted by Marxism. It has been sensed by Western philosophers, sociologists, economists, even writers and artists. And so, in bringing this digression to a close we conclude: Some sort of turn or leap is needed. But where to?

Where to indeed? What sort of renewed socialism do we want? What must we, and more importantly, *can* we do. What do we want tomorrow's society to be like?

The answer could be simple — an antitotalitarian (the slogan of 1989/90 "Antitotalitarians of the World Unite" is not just a joke), civilised (here in quotes) country belonging to the highly developed human civilisation of the turn of the 21st century and. . .

And here we might add 'socialist' and underline it, notwithstanding well-nigh universal distrust of the word, in many respects rightly identified with the institutions of Stalin and Brezhnev. Why socialist? Because the history of mass socialist workers' movements, from the naively utopian (and sometimes reactionary) communes of the Reformation, through the mass workers' movement of the turn of the 20th century to modern leftwing social democracy has gradually worked out a system of objectives which are inseparably bound to the concepts of socialism and communism. The slogans have been repeated in various forms for centuries: the economy should be in the hands of those who work, their work should be the work of free people, incomes should be earned, and distribution should be fair and equal.

19th Century theoretical studies and our own experience have shown that these slogans may conceal a system of barracks equality and the freedom of the concentration camp. Thus we should not reject these studies and experiences, but arm ourselves with that theory and practice of the Communist movement which has not and will not lead to the barracks, but to a society where the free development all will depend on that of each individual.

Words, Words. . .

Haven't we had enough of these high sounding words without you starting. . .

Maybe. We want to give these fine words more meaning by formulating a system of principles for the future society which both you and me (or at least a lot of us) need, but which will remain on paper if the power of the bureaucracy survives. We did not invent this system; it was born of the sufferings of 19-20th century Marxism (though let's not confuse it with our textbooks on philosophy and political economy), it is based on analysis of the few new (and we venture to say, socialist) social relations which have emerged and survived in Western Europe and Japan, and it proceeds from a critical reevaluation of the tragedy of the world socialist system.

The essence of this strategy of social renewal is the gradual but decisive abandonment of traditional industrial society based on the power of the bureaucrat and (or) the market, in favour of free workers' associations, and has as its aim the mandatory and general prioritisation of social and humanitarian objectives. In this case, we are not simply talking about making the economy the servant of human needs. The problem is larger than that. If we fail to concentrate the major and decisive share of our economic, political and ideological resources and efforts on the rebirth and creation (i.e. co-operative creation) of the new man, we shall not be able to feed the country, and will not be able to get scientific and technical progress started again.

Civilised Japan, which is decades ahead of us, was one of the first to understand this, and, having reoriented a poor, demoralised and war-ravaged country towards science-intensive technology and the 'human factor', in the space of ten years outpaced the United States, which had been the dominant power for decades.

This is nothing to do with us, someone will say. We can do without the luxuries, as long as we have the essentials. Really? In the later works of Lenin the phrase about a 'system of free cooperators', comes up with increasing frequency but on virtually every page Vladimir Il'ich, with one foot already in the grave, literally cries out that it is the cultural revolution, education, civilisation, training, control of 'all the riches which mankind has created' that we needed above all else. And this was the literally (not figuratively) starving Russia of the early twenties. . . And the Bolsheviks made many starts along that road. In the twenties and early thirties I. Ehrenberg, L. Feuchtwanger, B. Shaw, V. Mayakovskii and R. Roland rejoiced sincerely and not without reason at this spiritual rebirth, in which there was a place for everyone — Khlebnikov and Gaidar, Akhmatova and Fadeev.

We do not want to idealise this period — its development was contradictory, and it ended in tragedy. The point we are making is different. It is absolutely essential that we finally realise the economic imperative of the scientific and technical revolution: production must either be subordinated to mankind or degenerate.

The long term tasks in this area are:

Firstly, decisive social and state support for innovative systems of upbringing and education encompassing the entire educational system, including kindergartens and nurseries, various types of upbringing and instruction aimed at young people, continuing education, and civic education and communication skills for adults right up to homes for the elderly. Tasks and methods must not be decided in the private offices of the state or sponsors. All that is needed is to give people who want to deal with these matters what they ask for; money, materials and information, and the opportunity to initiate large scale experiments. In such cases the role of the administrative apparatus will be extremely simple: to act as genie to the innovators. Don't get in the way and don't ask them to prove this or that is necessary or to submit the necessary papers. It is your job to fill in the papers, to find the money and ways and means for them to get their work done. Don't fret about whether these people are wasting the 'country's money'. We have so few innovators — and we have wasted so much money! If we added up the demands of innovators in the area of upbringing, communication and education they would initially total hardly more than a few hundred million roubles, perhaps a few thousand million — which is about the price of two or three nuclear submarines.

Secondly, a key problem will be to regenerate the capacity of our citizens for cultured, human communication and dialogue, to nurture the development of people who can overcome mutual alienation, and to create the circumstances which will make that possible. What are the specific components of this problem, and what must be done? The same ones: to find, support, and if necessary publicly exalt the people who have persevered in building the house of human communication in the face of block-headed petty bureaucrats and cynical, pragmatic remarks about these 'day dreamers'. Who are these people? Take a look around you — somebody may have been trying to set up a workers sports club for years, despite repeated evictions from unwanted basements, someone else in a dusty factory rest room has been trying to get theatre and poetry lovers together. . . Yes, these people may seem eccentrics, romantics, idealists today. But there are already millions of them, notwithstanding all the booing and hissing from all sides. Every country in the pragmatic West has several thousand such clubs. Suppose we give general public and state support to this new medium of human communication and culture and make it our second highest priority? And suppose we put these 'eccentrics' in control of thousands of millions of roubles and make the officials and economic administrators the instruments of their will (initially perhaps as part of an All Union Programme of State and Public Culture)?

Thirdly, the rebirth of our society is unthinkable without a new attitude of partnership towards nature as a cultural value instead of just a 'source of valuable chemical raw materials'. And here we need a single state and social system of programmes, organised finance for recreation and, most important, the creation of a new human attitude to nature. How will this be done and who will do it? The 'greens' maybe. In the West and in Japan they have achieved a good deal, as maybe they will do here, as long as they are not obstructed, but instead given financial assistance, organisational facilities, and independent scientific centres working for the environmental movement and so on.

And a further, more 'traditional' aspect of the humanisation of society: the adoption of a social policy which encourages the development of creativity, of scientific, educational, artistic and communicational skills. An essential element of this is radically to raise the science (or creativity) intensiveness of industrial technology and to accelerate the growth of industries which provide predominantly creative employment. We emphasise that this is not so much a matter of reconstructing factories where the machine minder will become the robot minder, but of the national structure of economic reconstruction, of phasing out traditional industrial technologies and developing those areas where we still stand some chance of participating on equal terms in the world market (certain aspects of fundamental and applied science etc.).

The problem is, however, that to reorient society towards priority development of science and culture[7] we need a new environment — one of social and personal emancipation. The new man must be civically conscious and cultured, not just well educated. The new social organisation of science will take the form of non-departmental, open, competitive, and democratically organised teams of scientists.

Such types of group (associations or *unions*) can and must become the established organisational forms of any creative social activity — education and upbringing, science and art, nature conservation and the organisation of communication.

DIGRESSION THREE

A few words on the mechanics of making social priorities

All this is so fascinatingly (or revoltingly, depending on your attitude) novel, unusual and even Utopian. And there are continuing fears that these romantic experimenters will take the last crumbs from our already meagre table for their pet projects and drive busy economic administrators, businessmen and leaders mad with their empty chatter and senseless projects. Haven't they heard of the economic crisis?

No, no and again No, because we are not talking of indulging the ramblings of isolated eccentrics, but of new principles for organising the work (and creativity) of millions of people.

What organisation is this? We have in fact already sketched its outlines. At the top, sovereign Commissions of the USSR (or Republics etc.) Supreme Soviet with control of finances, material resources and administrative staff, taking decisions on projects prepared mainly by social movements and associations. Scientific expert services and an administrative apparatus will work on a competitive basis to the order of these commissions and organisations, and will help to set up the work of mass social organisations, associations and societies (environmental, creative, educational etc.). The Soviet government will give power and resources to associations of 'eccentrics'[8] but only after scientists (non-governmental organisations, open to criticism and working, we repeat, as experts) have given a provisional go-ahead, and the Commissions of the Supreme Soviet have ratified these plans. The professional staff should be subordinate to and paid by lower associations. The administrative apparatus should preferably be organised as consultative service agencies providing administrative and other services on a paid contractual basis, rather than as permanent professional organs of social associations (in which form they will very quickly become the bosses again, as did the Soviet executive committees).

The aim of this system is very simple; to bring people together so that they can create themselves a suitable social, cultural and natural environment. One of the most important related tasks is the protection of nature, culture and humanity from the arbitrary actions of bureaucrats, from pollution by rational technocrats concerned only with short-term gains, and from their witting or unwitting allies among the 'simple people'.

Certainly, these programmes may seem pie in the sky from the point of view of material production, but they can only be realised given suitable reorganisation of politics and the economy. The question is — how.

5. Politics today must have Primacy over Economics

A condition for realising even the most perfect strategy — is the thorough political democratisation of society, beginning with freedom of conscience and other personal human freedoms, political pluralism, freedom of speech, press and assembly and other such attributes of civil society, but going beyond that. The price of a multi-party system might turn out to be the replacement of the existing dictatorship of the so-called communist party by that of a bloc of anti-communist or non-communist parties (in Eastern European countries, people of communist convictions are already being effectively expelled from scientific institutions and government offices, just as a short while ago those who did not share such convictions were expelled). What is the guarantee that several equally closed and privilege-ridden bodies will not appear in the place of single-party rule?

Our pluralist friends explain that parties will compete for power and therefore will fear losing the trust of the people. Really? But perhaps it will be simpler for them to pretend (unconsciously of course) to compete for power, whilst in fact sharing out spheres of influence and patronage.

So — down with the multi-party system and parliamentary games, and long live the wise and guiding hand of the Leninist Politburo, alone in its knowledge of all our present, past and future desires. The problem is not to reject traditional parliamentary democracy (we need it, but with us it has, exactly as Lenin predicted, become a talking shop and a stage for the collision of the ambitions of newly arrived professional politicians) but to make it a working democracy, a genuine, organ of popular power pervading the daily life of every home and work group, giving each of us a chance to participate directly in government at all levels, from the work group and the home to the country as a whole. How does one do this? Experience shows where the answer lies. The Soviets in the first years of our history and 'foreign' experience — the mass organisations of local self government and social movements of Western Europe, for example.

The political power of the people consists first of all of mass organs of self-government based on the workplace and the home; neighbourhood self management committees and consumer clubs at home, Worker Collective Councils at work — if they have managed to elect decent officers — or Workers' (Strike) Committees. The mass grassroots cells of neighbourhood and shop floor self-government are the indispensable foundations for deputies' efforts to control the administration, and not to be controlled by it. It is the base which can prevent the divorce of politicians from the interests of the people and their emergence as a new 'civilised' bureaucracy. It is the basis for tackling such prime issues as turning the local Soviets into real governing bodies dealing independently with regional infrastructural development (housing, health, culture, education, trade, services, and liberation from the dictatorship of government departments).

Secondly, the political power of the people is a flexible system of mass social movements involving the majority of population, dealing with political, social, economic, cultural and ecological issues. Freedom to create such movements, material and moral support from Soviets for those that work for the good of the people (and don't just waste time in talk), decisive judicial proscription of those which violate human, popular and constitutional rights — all these are by no means fantasy, but a precondition for the reawakening of the people.

Thirdly, there never was and never will be peoples' power while the system of privileges and subsidies to the leading levels of the party, state and other agencies remains intact. People are tired of lies. Open and honest declaration of what was appropriated by the bureaucracy, and the introduction of the principle of paying the administrative apparatus for work done — is absolutely essential before the people even begin to trust State and Party leaders. Moreover, the eradication of the system of secret distribution 'from above' will be an important factor in dismantling it 'from below', when everyone of us to a greater or lesser extent is bribed by government housing and off-premises retailing. [9]

Popular power presupposes grass roots mass involvement in the ideological struggle. Nowadays monopoly of the mass media by bureaucracy is giving way to its monopoly by professional politicians and journalists. . . Previously it was Brezhnev, Suslov, Rashidov and Co. who knew best what the people wanted; now it is Afanas'ev, Popov, Selyunin and their colleagues. The very few 'foremen' (or more accurately workers) of perestroika — for instance the Kuzbass, Donbass and Vorkuta Workers' Committees had no national platform, and still don't. The people who talk about their interests are the ones who are fighting for political power and influence in Moscow. Hence there can be no proper democracy without a guarantee that all sufficiently large, democratic and constitutional social movements and organisations will be given a platform in the national, republican and local media. The freedom of independent organs of the press is useful, but is not in itself sufficient, since it does not overcome information imperialism: the mafia of money will take the place in the media once held by the government mafia (he who pays the piper calls the tune).

6. *Self government and the Emancipation of Labour — Instead of the Power of the Market and the bureaucracy*

Where an administrative system rules, economic power belongs to the bureaucracy. The bureaucracy stand apart from and over the masses and is made up of privileged people. In a market economy, this power (in the simplest case) belongs to those with money. But how can one ensure that the workers retain economic power? At present we are trying to do this mainly by the breaking up of property; leasing of factories, workshops, contract brigades and private farmers on rented land. It is a simple method, allowing practical steps to be made towards putting people in control at their place of work, if not in the economy at large. Are such steps necessary?

As elements of perestroika — yes. But as a main principle of strategy they will not, in our opinion, live up to expectations. To return to small-scale collective and individual property at the end of the 20th Century is possible only in certain 'auxiliary' areas of the economy, as is the case in the West, which is ruled by highly socialised corporate property, controlled by the largest financial groups.

The strategic problem of socialism is something bigger than this — to put us all in control of the economy as whole. We tried once. It didn't work, did it? But we didn't try — that was the problem. Yes, we made a lot of proclamations. But what we did was something quite different. Under the banner of nationalisation and common property, we introduced bureaucratism and the alienation of the workers from property.

So what shall we do? We can start with taking power by workers, shopfloor engineers and factory economists, but we cannot leave it at that!

As people get involved with self management or organisation at their own enterprise, they quite quickly learn that the main problems in the fight against bureaucracy come from higher levels. On one side the persisting diktat of the Ministries and government departments, and on the other the embryonic market. The former need an obedient and efficient administrator who cares more about indicators than he does about the consumer or the collective, and who idolises the plan. The latter needs commercial secrecy and an enterprising leader and businessman with funds readily disposable and able to react flexibly to the state of the market. In both cases real self-management is more of a hindrance than a help. If any use is made of workers' initiative in these conditions, it will be at the brigade level, or that of the workshop at the most. Beyond that it's none of their business. [10]

Suppose we try a different approach? What if we raise the principle of self-management and of putting people in control of production to a higher level — regional, industrial (nowadays inter-industrial) or national? Utopia? At first glance, yes.

But let us take a historical analogy.

As soon as we mention self-management at the national economic level, everyone thinks of some super-Gosplan, inhabited by hundreds of millions of illiterate workers and housewives deciding by mass ballot which thirty-five million types of product to produce at which hundreds of thousands of factories.

A frightening picture, isn't it? Now imagine some believer in money and commodity relations approaching some Russian peasant or landowner in about 1698 and starting to explain that the future of their economy lies in the world market, paper money (or rather credit), shares, stockmarkets and so on.

What would our 'marketeer' hear in reply? More than likely, that he is suggesting assembling millions of people who can't speak, read or write each others' languages in one market place to create a fool's economy in which you'd have to journey thousands of miles to buy butter, bread or a decent axe (the world market). Isn't this the height of idiocy? Isn't this economic utopia?

But at the time a new, capitalist world order was being born. True, in Russia capitalism and the market fell victim to feudal arbitrariness and barter. But in England they were victorious. And this is not all. The point is that progressive socio-economic systems are never born without struggle (and hence temporary setbacks), be they the nineteenth century market and capitalism, or twentieth century self-government and socialism.

And now a brief consideration of self-government above the enterprise level. Let us begin with the first experiment, albeit a minor one. What did the workers of the striking Kuzbass factories do when they began to feel that their efforts to gain control of their own economic life were being frustrated by the enterprise, city and ministerial bureaucracy? They decided to unite and created city strike committees (renamed Workers' Committees when the strike was over). Why? In order to assist each other, to control the activities of the town authorities and the ministry and to prevent arbitrariness in paying wages, norm setting and capital investment.

This of course is only the first step. Or more accurately an attempt to take the first step. But if we rely on our own historical experience and look at the birth of new non-market non-bureaucratic social methods of economic regulation in Western Europe and Japan, we can draw the outlines of a new model. Its essence is *a compound of self-government, programme planning and the priority of social objectives.*

DIGRESSION FOUR

The basic units of the new management model

The first unit is a new mechanism for formulating strategic objectives, and the structure and essential proportions of the economy. These should be decided primarily by mass social organisations, and Commissions of the Supreme Soviet through commissioning related research from professional ´economists, and through national discussions, analysis of alternative drafts and decision making at Congresses of Peoples Deputies, and perhaps through referendums.

The second unit is a new principle for setting up organs of economic management — a change to 'voluntary centralism'. What does this mean? Roughly that producers and consumers, once they have formed voluntary associations will, on initiative from below, independently form the necessary organs of management which will then, as it were, assume the role of the market and help producer and consumer to find each other.

The third unit is a new type of relationship between producer, consumer and the centre — a change from bureaucratic decrees and market deals to a 'planning dialogue'. What would this be? An open procedure, democratically controlled by consumers, trade unions and environmentalists etc., for matching the economic interests of producers and consumers, supervised by the Soviet Government (its aim being to ensure that strategic plans are implemented).

Perhaps it is time to call a halt. What we have outlined is no more than a forecast or a hypothesis. Everything in it is new, untried and highly debatable. But the hypothesis is not without foundation. What is that foundation? To take only one example, the steadily growing role of trade unions, the 'greens', the consumer associations and other social organisations in the control of the Swedish and Austrian economies. And who do we have wrestling at home with such key economic problems as nature conservation? The ministries? Self financing enterprises? The cooperatives? Who is trying to stem the cultural and moral degradation — for example the need to preserve the cities, human kindness and compassion. So these aren't economic problems? If not then who are the main productive forces in society — men or beasts?

Real economic self-management is an absolutely essential (though not sufficient) condition for putting each of us in control of the economy as a whole, and of ensuring the prime precondition for real equality and freedom (irrespective of the contents of one's wallet) of all members of society.

Workers' power in the economy could turn out to be a new version of totalitarianism if it does not go hand in hand with their economic emancipation and with overcoming their alienation not only from property but also from each other, from their own labour, and in the final analysis from society as a whole.

Putting it in elevated theoretical terms this task coincides with the strategy of developing associated socio-economic creativity. Freedom as an 'unconscious necessity' is not adaptation to circumstances, or the ability to 'keep your head down' and act by common sense, since were this the case one would be bound to regard the freest individual as a conformist and philistine. Freedom is the opportunity for all, without domination of one by another, to cooperate in shaping life within the framework of its own laws.

Suppose we leave theory aside and deal with obvious and urgent problems. Today a resident of the Soviet Union, even if he is not a labour-camp inmate or a down-and-out can hardly be considered free to change his place of residence (registration), job (state housing, kindergartens etc.) or social status. The breakdown of semi-feudal forced labour, which begins with the director and head of the passport desk, and ends in the corridors of the Central Committee and the Council of Ministers — which are quite unknown to the vast majority of Soviet citizens — is essential to the emancipation of Soviet man.

A further condition is the guarantee of the genuine and equal rights for all to work according to inclination. This is much harder to achieve, since it comes up against the material and technical under-development of the economy and the widespread persistence of heavy, routine manual work. What is to be done? To begin with the simplest problem — guaranteed employment and opportunity to improve ones qualifications. Not 'unemployment at work' and the labour exchange for the unemployed, but well-run public and state systems of flexible employment, (financed by the state, trade unions and enterprises), when a person has advance warning about the phasing out of old skills and has the chance to acquire new ones.

An important condition for the emancipation of labour is the freedom of the workers to create unions and associations to defend their interests. Why? Because in a modern economy dominated by large systems (enterprises and associations) it is impossible to defend one's interests as an isolated individual. But workers can be enslaved by the unions themselves (witness today's trade unions), which is why it is so essential to be free to create alternative trade unions, and to preserve their open nature. [11]

But the question recurs — will the workers want to take on the burden of extra work involved in economic self-management; will they want, in other words, to be the masters of the economy? At the moment they don't. But soon none of us will have any choice — it will be a matter of the collapse of the economy by continuing down the bureaucratic road of perestroika, or the aggravation of social conflict during the birth of our 'Asiatic' market, or of settling down together to create a new economy, in which, with the help of scientists and specialists, we and not the officials will decide who will do what and how.

7. How Can We Re-Learn the Desire and Ability to Work?

We have to create a system of incentives for initiative and creative work which can break down the wall of apathy and passivity of the majority, and which will shift society from its present stagnation. This is the problem which socialism must solve if it is not to perish. In the last few years we have been browbeaten into believing that the only things which make people work are money and fear. There aren't any other incentives. We have tried fear, and we've had enough of it. To return to those times would be a crime. So what about the rouble?

Are our people, who on one hand have grown accustomed to indolence, yet on the other cling to the naive but stubborn conviction that our aim is a society of guarantees and equality, in such a hurry to elbow aside friend and stranger alike in pursuit of the big money? Yes, some workers are joining cooperatives; some peasants are renting land. But there are not many of them, and they encounter powerful opposition from their fellow workers, who are somehow reluctant to heed the journalists who argue that it is all a matter of the envy of the incompetent and idle for their 'enterprising' fellow worker.

Then what is the problem? Maybe that we are living not at the beginning of the 19th century, but at the end of the 20th century, when one of the main incentives is not merely what one earns, but the chance of a job with initiative, purpose and interest, in which one does not feel like an animal earning a day's pay at any price, but a person in their proper place, a member of a team for whom wages and pay increases are not an end in themselves but the means of living in a decent human fashion.

More Utopia? But suppose nevertheless we rely on two basic incentives — the freeing of initiative (self-management) and social justice (reward according to labour), and make that the basis for fighting passivity, wage-levelling and unearned income?

Yes, that slogan has been proclaimed many times, but has it ever been put into practice? How do we revive it?

First of all, we need a mechanism of social, grass-roots up, and therefore democratic and open control of matching measures of labour to measures of consumption — a slogan proclaimed by V. I. Lenin on the eve of the October revolution and revived under NEP. How does one implement such control? We have some experience. We need only recall Il'f and Petrov's portrait of the underground millionaire Koreiko, who was afraid to spend a rouble more than his wages for fear of drawing attention to his capital. There is a certain amount of experience in the West; systems of income declaration, mandatory registration of all large civil contracts (expenditures and purchases), the growing importance of cashless transactions, and in the longer term the changeover to electronic money.

Is it wrong to count the money in someone else's pocket? According to market ethics it is, since the most prized possession of the petty bourgeois is the contents of his wallet. But a mere hundred years ago it was wrong for most people to talk about the equality of the landowner and the peasant. Perhaps market morals are not eternal? But we are not suggesting the invasions of peoples' homes, simply giving someone specially empowered by public organisations the right to check your current account, just in case you 'forget' to pay your taxes. [12]

Another step, perhaps the most important is a *democratic and open decision on the norms, forms and methods (hourly paid rate etc.) by which a man is paid for his labour.* [13] This would be decided by the brigade — based on what it has earned — for the individual worker, by the workshop for the brigade, and by the enterprise Worker Collective Council for the workshop. And who will determine how much the enterprise has earned? The market? But that has already been divided and re-divided long ago by monopoly producers in league with the government bureaucracy, and would hardly be any different if left to its own devices. . .

Perhaps we should adopt a rather different approach, where the prices of key products, deductions from profits, interest etc. for an enterprise are not fixed from above by bureaucratic bodies but laid down by social organisations bringing together representatives of worker groups, consumer associations, environmental organisations, trade unions, etc. under the aegis of the Soviet Government using the assessments of non-governmental experts as a guide. Fantasy? The Austrian experience shows that it is by no means wholly so, since in that country social control of prices for certain goods is already a reality.

And now the last of these considerations on of what can and ought to be done to avert a deepening of the crisis. These phrases may be puzzling, since we are proposing the use of the latest organisational methods of state monopoly capitalism, including a highly organised modern market, as a major form of medication for the Soviet economy, to be administered once the socio-economic relations of socialism have been revitalised, and where necessary completely renewed.

DIGRESSION FIVE

In which the authors recall the sergeant's widow

At this point the authors ought perhaps to ask themselves whether they somewhat resemble that sergeant's widow, who gave herself a beating?[14] To spend all that time demonstrating the unsuitability of the 'Swedish' model, only to reach the conclusion that what is required is an identical economic mechanism. What has gone wrong? Is our reasoning faulty?

No, the question is one of clearly defining goals and means of economic development. It is one thing to strive to revitalise productive relations of socialism and to remake them where necessary along the lines on which they have germinated in Sweden and Austria, and on that basis to use the most progressive forms of the market and economic organisation of modern capitalism. It is quite another attempt to restore the market and a 'pluralist' economy lock, stock and barrel, thus dooming to lingering death the remaining fragments of socialist relations, ideals and convictions which still survive in our country and people. In the first case we are counting on the development of socialist relations, albeit weak and underdeveloped, but cleansed of distortions (and above all of those of bureaucratism) while accepting forms of modern capitalism as a temporary (perhaps even long term) expedient of economic development in order to 'turn the Russia of NEP into the Russia of socialism' (V. I. Lenin). In the second, we restore the capitalist system using 'bits and pieces' of socialism as supplements, means to an end, or just as a name.

One can deal with forms of property and the economic mechanism in a similar fashion.

Do we accept pluralism in property relations? Yes. But only after a debate on the economic authority of genuine, universally open associations of both producers, consumers, and organisers of production, for only this allows the debureaucratisation of State property and breathes socialist content into leasing and cooperatives, thus preempting their degeneration into groups of private traders.

Decentralisation and independence of collectives? Yes, but not so much by their separation as by the expansion of the rights and opportunities of worker collectives and other worker associations to genuinely participate in democratic national economic planning, using on that basis and as a means (and not as an end in itself) the instruments of the modern market.

True, one could do nothing, bury one's head in the sand and leave the democrats to talk about it (endlessly lecturing the world at large) and the bureaucrats who have at least learned something to take the decisions, but in that case the end will be upon us with catastrophic speed.

So the competition of objectives and social forces is now increasingly obvious. And the more proponents of 'pluralistic socialism' and 'reform of the apparatus' consolidate their position, the more pressing becomes the question that we 'mislaid' at the beginning of the article: are there any real opportunities for our country to adopt a third path which would allow it to rely on specifically socialist relations?

DIGRESSION SIX

Is a socialist revival possible in this country?

The only possible answer to that is yes. Not because we must keep faith with the martyrs of socialism, and not because to betray the tasks of socialist revival would be to spit on the graves of our ancestors, grandfathers and fathers. Feelings, however noble, should not stand in the way of discussion. We say yes, because we believe that socialism is still alive in our economic relations, culture, and in the hearts and minds of our people. It is mutilated, but not yet dead, and can still revive the country given democratic rights and workers' freedom.

Firstly, in this country (as distinct from most of the developing countries, with which we have become accustomed to compare ourselves) there are individual technologies (primarily in the defence and aerospace industries) which, though few in numbers are close to world levels, and, more importantly, there is a significant potential of unexploited research and design.

Secondly, and particularly in the natural and technical sciences, we have a working class and intelligentsia which has forgotten how to work, but has the potential for a rapid growth in initiative, quality and rate of work. (Sociological survey data show that on average 50-60% of the working potential of workers and 30-40% of that of scientists and engineers is actually utilised.)

The third and main point is that in order to make use of these reserves, we need conditions which only socialism can provide. The emancipation of labour and initiative means the chance to earn one's living at a job with a generally perceived outcome and purpose, secure in the knowledge that the products of one's labour will not be squandered by bureaucrats or appropriated by speculators, and that unemployment, social conflict and inequality will not be the price of greater efficiency at work. In many of us (especially if one takes workers and intelligentsia from the provinces and not the elite intelligentsia of the capitals), the remains of a former collectivism, comradeship and readiness for mutual aid (nowadays these words sound almost indecent), a dislike for the cult of money, a desire to do respected work, and a hatred of speculative income have not completely disappeared.

It might be said that if this is true, these people are hopeless cases of relapse into wage-levelling and general ideological deception, and we would agree that to a significant extent that if these socio-economic principles really have survived, it is only in a distorted and stagnant form. But what can one expect after twenty years of Brezhnev? Why do we believe that these feeble remains of socialism will 'work' today? But why did they 'work' after 20 years of Stalinism, when the 'thaw' with all its zigzags and excesses gave the country a unique economic and spiritual boost?

And now to the main point: one can only count on the survivals of socialism under one condition; that life convinces people that their work and initiative will not be wasted yet again. Many still wait for such assurance to be given 'from above'. But the pace of change is accelerating, and we are increasingly convinced that the 'powers that be' can at best only help; it is we that must act. Let us recall the great words of the proletarian anthem:

> No saviour from on high delivers
> No trust have we in prince or peer
> Our own right hands the chains must shiver
> Chains of hatred, of greed and fear.

8. *If I Don't, Who Will?*

Never before have these words been so topical. Today (or tomorrow at least) each one of us will have to decide whose side he is on, what he will fight for, and if he is going to do nothing, then what will be the human products of his apathy?

But the alignment of socio-economic forces (they have yet to become political groups) presents a complex picture.

The *bureaucracy* — a stratum of 'privileged persons standing above and apart from the masses' (V. I. Lenin) is largely preserving its positions, and is trying to monopolise its control of the economy and society. It is fairly obvious that new groups are arising among them;

the emergent reformist wing realises that the bureaucracy must periodically fight bureaucratisation in order to survive, cutting away the rottenest sections and allowing rational opposition, in order for dialogue to be possible, and to provide an object for public opinion. One should not, however, write off the 'old' wing, retired to the wings for a while but with some justification still thinking that it may yet be of service.

Does the bureaucracy enjoy mass support in this country? Undoubtedly. It comes from those who are afraid, too lazy or simply unwilling to 'pick a fight' and take up the difficult cause of self-government. It comes from those who still believe in the 'Good Tsar' in all the manifold forms of this belief: from those who favour the 'firm hand' who put their faith in the strength of the apparatus, to liberal heralds of presidential dictatorship, hoping that the hand of Gorbachev will curb the opponents of perestroika; from militant Russian chauvinists to the champions of 'saving ideals' at any price and by whatever means.

The socio-economic basis of these attitudes is a petty-bourgeois mentality born of the bureaucratic distortion of socialism — essentially the petty-bourgeois strata of the workers, who have 'sold' their status as masters of the socialist economy 'in exchange' for guarantees of a tolerable stable existence and freedom from the requirement to earn their pay. These include many office workers, former star workers now on the permanent staff, and if handouts are on offer, the lumpenproletariat and other declasse elements.

The advocates of bourgeois democratic pluralist socialism[15] are becoming increasingly visible. And we are not simply dealing with a group of intellectuals from the 'Democratic Union'. The point is that for various reasons the 'Swedish Model' presents the only genuine alternative to bureaucracy for a whole spectrum of social groups. Who, specifically? First of all those 'businessmen' for whom the market is the only place where they can show their paces. A section of them (the self-employed, small-scale cooperative members, and managers who lack confidence in themselves and their enterprises) are prepared to stop half-way, settling for the introduction of a commodity market and alliance with the liberal bureaucracy, guaranteeing them a normal existence by restraining the sharks of big business. But many of our 'businessmen' and their ideologists have already understood that a modern market must also be a market for labour, capital and securities, a market with monopolies (and anti-monopoly legislation), marketing and, most important, private (groups and shareholders') property.

These goals enjoy more or less active support from those who are prepared to work on their own initiative to earn (very) high incomes.

These optimistic workers, peasants and engineers are prepared to hand over part of the wealth they have created to 'businessmen' if this means an above average income. This is quite legitimate. Bureaucratism took away our control of the economy, and turned us into hired servants of the state, teaching us to trade submission for a meagre wage, so why not sell one's abilities for good money? (In academic terms this should be termed a petty-bourgeois, trade-unionist[16] tendency among the working class, or persons of hired labour in general.)

These goals also enjoy solid ideological support from that section of the non-scientific intelligentsia (publicists, writers, economists etc.) who did not completely sell their souls and pens to the bureaucracy in the days of 'stagnation'. And one can understand this support; the only democracy these people have ever seen is democracy 'Swedish style'; socialism and its ideals have been discredited by the rule of Stalin and Brezhnev, and so there would seem to be no other choice. Moreover there are selfish motives at the back of their minds: whatever comes of 'pluralist socialism' — whether the standard of living of Sweden or India, we creative people still live better (and in the manner that becomes us) since a good economist (or journalist or writer) earns almost the same in India as in Sweden, and, most important, gets paid in hard currency.

Finally, these goals will also be supported by those nationalist movements which are trying to throw off the bureaucratic tutelage of the Russian centre, and many of those who see the 'Swedish model' as the only alternative to bureaucratic dictatorship.

Perestroika and 'glasnost' have exposed the existence of previously almost unnoticed 'informal' socio-economic forces in society. Prime among these is the graftocracy — a coalition of organised crime with corrupt officialdom and bureaucracy, and the 'supply' and 'service' elements that closely support it, such as moonlighters, ex-convicts, down and outs and the unemployed — especially the youth of the labour-surplus regions — Central Asia and the Transcaucasus etc.

What are the real forces and aims of the graftocracy? Even one of its 'Godfathers' would be hard put to answer this question. We are inclined to assume as follows: On one hand, this social force clearly stands to gain from the adoption of any economic arrangement which allows them to wash the blood and dirt from the thousands of millions of roubles they stole during the 'stagnant' years by investing them in cooperatives, private enterprise, shares and other forms of 'business'. In this sense our 'Godfathers' are bound to support the 'pluralist' economy. On the other hand, the graftocracy has always lived 'in the pores' of the administrative bureaucratic system, growing fat on a distorted market and creating a network of corruption from bottom to top. In that sense the end of the rule of the bureaucracy is un-profitable to our 'mafiosi'. So?

So as a rule they will support (and partially initiate) the worst of all scenarios and go for the symbiosis of the asiatic market at the bottom with the dictatorship of the bureaucracy at the top. If the central authorities assist in this (as the Brezhnev government unwillingly or willingly did), they will look after it. If it starts to get in their way (as recently happened in Transcaucasia and Central Asia), they will fight it. . .

So to whom do the authors address their programme for the rebirth of socialism? The bureaucracy? The supporters of the 'Swedish model'? Or perhaps the mafiosi? No, we are deeply convinced that time will bring to the fore a stratum of the workers (and primarily the organised proletariat and the rank and file intelligentsia of the industrial centres) which, having started the fight for democracy against the bureaucracy, will not stop halfway and settle for a chance to work for and be paid (some better some worse) by clever 'Good Uncle Businessman' having made fun of stupid 'Wicked Uncle Bureaucrat'; those who will fight for the genuine emancipation of their labour, social justice, and control of the economy.

Why should they join this fight? Mainly because they are the ones worst squeezed in the vice of a contradiction one side of which is our desire to be in charge of our own lives through cooperation rather than competition. This desire has not been invented by the authors, it is the fruit of the socialisation of production and those remains of socialism which have survived by a miracle to this day. The other side of this contradiction is the complete alienation of the rank and file worker from the role of master of the economy and society.

And if today the main alienating force is the bureaucracy, then the workers, engineers and teachers will join the 'men of business'[17] and their ideologists in the fight for the overthrow of the administrative system, as the peoples fronts of Yaroslavl', Kuibyshev and others are doing today. But tomorrow (and to some extent today) they will learn that the cultured technocrat and businessman who has replaced the bureaucrat will still try (and what is more will try harder and more subtly) to turn the worker and engineer into wage slaves, slogging away like the Japanese for Indian wages.[18] Moreover the most likely outcome is not a radical turn to the Swedish model, but a coalition of liberal democrats and liberal bureaucrats retaining a stagnant transi-tional economy of the type in permanent crisis in the Poland of the mid-eighties. In these conditions the struggle for socialism will come to the fore.

9. *What can we do today, and how can we do it?*

We are well aware that today these suggestions for directing our society towards a cardinal reconstruction and the reorganisation of politics, society and the economy on a self-managing basis, and other strategic tasks may seem pure fantasy. But it is easy to 'bring them down to earth', and formulate them as things which any one of us can to today.

Task Number 1 (the simplest)

What causes us the most trouble at the moment? Shortages, probably. These can be eliminated very simply — by the introduction of so-called 'equilibrium prices', i.e. prices at which our enormous demand will equal our beggarly supply. If we start from the premise that the purchasing power of today's rouble is about twenty 1961 kopecks then it does not take much calculation to see that prices for high quality goods and foodstuffs will have to rise by several times. Do we want to solve the problem of shortages by high prices?

There is no single answer. Those who robbed the country of thousands of millions of roubles during the years of stagnation, those who today are making several thousands and even millions by exploiting shifts in a bureaucratically distorted market would say yes. They want to buy without queueing, even if prices are high — after all they've got the money. Those who living on a pension or an average Soviet wage (200-250 roubles per month) would probably say no.

What is to be done? Suppose consumers took control of the market for consumer goods and services, pitting the power of united consumers against the monopolistic prices hikes and quality falsification of producers? Who would carry out these functions? Primarily consumers' associations, supported by the trade unions, social organisations and the Soviets of Peoples' Deputies.

Is there any experience or precedent for this? At the moment very little, although the first consumers' associations have already been set up in a number of Soviet towns, and workers' control is already taking its first steps against the trading mafia. In many towns, representatives of the Peoples' Front are intervening usefully in the operations of distributive agencies. In the first decades of Soviet power we had the mass activity of voluntary and open consumer associations (involving most of the urban population), and there is the experience of similar associations in other countries.

What will our consumer associations do? They will defend their own interests. One can begin with monitoring prices and conditions of sale of goods and services. In the longer term one can tackle production regulation, dictatorship by monopoly suppliers, artificial shortages, secret departmental distribution and so on. Clearly the consumer associations themselves should become the organisers of public debate and decisionmaking on the question of rationing, and its application in practice.

But the main problems are problems of production rather than of distribution. For that reason our second and fundamental task is to take immediate and practical steps to put the working man in control of the economy.

How do you gain control of an enterprise? The authors have already written a good deal about this, turning to the experience of those collectives where real self-management is already a fact, and drawing on the practical work of the school of self-management which we organised on a voluntary basis at Moscow University. [19] The most simple step is to start taking decisions on questions of vital interest to workers and technical staff through the Worker Collective Council (or, if it is dormant, through Workers' Committees or Strike Committees). How should wages be paid, and what for? What should factory funds be spent on? How does one avoid Saturday working? People are prepared to sacrifice their own time and effort to solve these problems. But what if the director gets in the way? One can take extreme measures, such as bringing the question of his dismissal (or re-election) before a general meeting of the worker collective. There is a simpler method of making the bureaucratic director into a manager looking after the interests of workers and engineers in professional and literate fashion, which is to adopt a system already tried at enterprises in Moscow, Leningrad and Kaluga, where the bonuses and sometimes the basic salary of the director is fixed by the Worker Collective Council.

The *Third Question* which we can tackle today is to take practical steps to emancipate labour by creating independent trade unions or by reorganising existing traditional unions and radically purging them from below. [20] There is already some practical experience of this. In Lithuania, Latvia and several other regions the prototypes of new independent trade unions have already been created — the Unions of Workers. Their rules and programmes are highly democratic, and although the influence of traditional (Western-style) trade-unionism is noticeable, they give first priority to defending the workers. Who from? First of all (and in this lies one of the greatest differences between the new trade unions and the old bodies headed by the AUCCTU[21]) from today's employer-bureaucrats, from the enterprise director to the minister. In these programmes, prime attention is given to production self-management, going as far as decisionmaking on key questions of the life of the enterprise, and in the longer term to systems of flexible employment, opposing attempts to solve economic problems at the workers' expense (wage freezes while prices rise, unemployment, and backhanders for the administration and mafias through the cooperatives etc.). Similar unions are being set up by peasants, engineers and creative workers.

In regions where there have been massive strikes, workers adopted a somewhat different approach and have grasped real power through strikes. They have changed the composition and operation of existing organisations, reelecting the Worker Collective Council, Trade Union Committees and Party Committees. The organs of self management and the workers' committees of the Kuznetsk basin have joined together to form the Kuzbass Union of Workers. So the experience is there. It is up to us to act; participation in one of the new trade unions (or if there are none in your town or region) in their creation, the fight to renew the old organisations set up to defend the workers' interests — here is a workers' struggle which is open to all.

And lastly, the main thing — politics.

Today's *fourth task* is to consolidate the political forces which support complete and radical debureaucratisation of the country (this requires a coalition of all democratic forces, and its further development via a socialist alternative although clearly there are limits to cooperation with those in favour of a bourgeois model of the USSR). At the time of writing — the first months of 1990 — the democratic forces of the socialist alternative are small and poorly organised, but they exist. They consist of the marxist platform of the CPSU, the new socialists, and to some extent left wing social-democracy and certain other organisations and groups.

What is to be done? We have tried to answer this question in a general way in the previous section. And now a few words on how to start the practical fight for the revival of socialism.

Unless we unite, we remain powerless individuals. The first thing to do is to find comrades, like minded people and those who genuinely want to defend the workers' interests. The simplest way to do this is not to be afraid to talk openly to your friends in the canteen and the smoke room and at trade union and party meetings. Go to the meetings of the Worker Collective Council, the Party Committee or the Trade Union — you will probably find people with ideas there. Once you have found supporters, start agitation and propaganda among your workmates to promote energetic members of the collective who are dedicated to the workers' interests to the Worker Collective Council, Trade Union Committee and Party Committee. Those who genuinely defend the interests of the worker, engineers and enterprise economists ought to be in the majority in the organs of factory self management. Get the Worker Collective Council to resolve the vital issues affecting your workers and engineers — such as reorganisation of wages, norm-setting and social justice.

If you do not succeed in taking power at your enterprise by peaceful means, use the rights given to the workers by the Law on Labour Disputes.

Firstly create strike committees, (preferably at several enterprises), publicise your demands, but don't try to win yourselves privileges or get a few more crumbs from the half-eaten cake of our semi-bankrupt economy — such demands are unjust, and such strikes are doomed to isolation and failure. Put forward demands for management democratisation, the right to get on with the job without parasites and bureaucrats. If they don't grant your demands — don't be hasty, use all the possible peaceful means, hold a demonstration strike (for an hour or two) and remember that a strike in our conditions is a blow struck at your comrades. The strike is a political weapon of last resort, and is permissible only where and when the workers do not hold economic power.

If you succeed in protecting the interests of the workers at your enterprise — fight for more complex causes.

— help to organise and run consumer clubs and associations where you live, neighbourhood organs of self-government and environmental groups. The town consumer association will tell you how to set these up.

— join working groups promoting the election of promising representatives to the Soviets of Peoples' Deputies, using all legal forms of verbal and written propaganda and explanations of their manifesto. If such groups do not exist, or the way they work does not suit you, make it your job to create others.

— by the same methods ensure the support of progressive Party and Soviet leaders (if there are any) for the fight against bureaucracy in the administrative bodies of your enterprise, region or city.

— organise meetings with deputies from regional and town Soviets, representatives of town Soviets, trade unions, regional and town party committees, explain your aims to them, offer active assistance, and press for your programme using forms of mass agitation (meetings and rallies), the right to recall deputies, and mechanism of pre-term reelection of trade union and party leaders; if you can't get a peaceful dialogue going, or it produces nothing, hold peaceful meetings and demonstrations demanding the breakup of the bureaucracy.

— create primary cells of the CPSU marxist platform, or socialist associations of non-party members, and find ways of consolidating socialist democratic forces. Work out and implement practical programmes of action.

— get involved in mass democratic workers' organisations, trade unions, creative and environmental associations, city and oblast'[22] Peoples' Fronts, develop and explain your political objectives, find legal means of defending your interests in the struggle for socialism, join the supporters of the struggle for democracy, and distance yourself from those who prefer the piecemeal reform of the existing system and above all remember: the revival of socialism and the prospects for building communism are in your hands!

NOTES

1. However sad it may be to have to admit it, the overwhelming majority of economists, philosophers, historians and sociologists were directly or indirectly involved in this demagogy. . . Only rarely did anyone succeed in simply keeping quiet and getting on with his research.

2. Fair enough, not every one kept quite and did nothing. Dozens, hundreds of people kept up the struggle for socialism and against bureaucracy. Some of them are in poor health but still living; some are now dead. Living and fighting in conditions of abuse, sickness, prison, the mental hospital was not easy.

3. Here we have omitted an untranslated play on the Russian version of this saying 'Kui zhelezo poka goryacho' rendered by the authors as 'te, kto kuet zhelezo poka Gorbachev'. — Trans.

4. Kolkhoz cooperative. — Trans.

5. The authors coin the word bandokratiya (compare byurokratiya — bureaucracy). Banda in Russian means a band of criminals or gang. Bandokratiya denotes a powerful coalition of organised crime and local and national government and Party agencies (of which Uzbekistan was a supreme example in the days of Sharaf Rashidov, a close associate of Leonid Brezhnev). We have coined the term graftocracy to translate this. — Trans.

6. Kibal'chish — a fictitious childrens' Soviet folk hero — roughly the Soviet equivalent of the all American boy. — Trans.

7. We should point out in passing that the first (and very primitive) wave of such a mass social preoccupation with science and art took place at the turn of the sixties when practically every young person wanted to become a physicist or cosmonaut, read Yevtushenko and Voznesenskii and argued themselves to a standstill over physics and poetry.

8. These resources can be channelled by very flexible means, from finance through the State budget and compulsory contributions from economic organisations to voluntary donations by citizens and organisations.

9. A system whereby a retail organisation agrees to bring popular (and usually scarce) goods to an organisation's offices for exclusive sale to its employees. — Trans.

10. As is witnessed by established technocratic managerial tendencies in Yugoslavia, where they have been trying for more than thirty years to link the market economy to worker-management at the enterprise.

11. In describing a number of the problems of self management and liberation of labour we have drawn on the work of our colleague A. A. Auzan.

12. No, we are not calling for equality in poverty as the alternative to the right of all to become as rich as they like. Not to mention the fact that the market programme in Poland and Yugoslavia brought riches to thousands of millionaires, but virtual poverty to millions of workers (according to national figures, up to 20% of their populations are on the poverty line). We want to emphasise a different point; the aim by no means justifies the means. The road to riches

should not violate social justice, and wealth should be earned by one's own labour, otherwise it will not bring people happiness, and will cause only mutual alienation and conflict.

13. As a comment we should underline: today is witnessing a world wide introduction of qualitatively new incentive schemes — free time, work by inclination, through the organisation of collectivist relations at the enterprise etc. It would be no bad thing for us to learn from these, since the incentives are in principle socialist.

14. A reference to an anecdote in one of Chekhov's plays, in which a soldier's widow, having been the victim of physical assault, adds some self-inflicted injuries in the hope that they will improve her chances of obtaining redress against her assailant.

15. One may notice from Hungarian, East German and Polish experience that these forces, who start by fighting for 'pluralism', end up fighting communists, since they are seemingly carried far further down the road to capitalism than the 'pluralist model' presupposes.

16. The authors use the Russian, historically pejorative term 'tred-yunionistskii'. In orthodox Soviet marxist writing, this has traditionally denoted trade unions pursuing strictly economic goals, and thus doing nothing (in the view of such writers) to advance the cause of Soviet orthodox marxist socialism. — *Trans.*

17. In English, the term 'businessman' can represent the Russian word 'biznesmen' which is often used pejoratively. The Russian term used here is 'delovye lyudi', which stresses entrepreneurial energy and practical skills, and has no such disapproving overtones. — *Trans.*

18. The course of History is not simple. The elections in eastern Europe showed that the majority of workers may support a right wing bourgeois alternative if the socialist candidates discredit themselves again by a liberal-bureaucratic fight for power, and the right wing succeed in exploiting decades of discredited socialism and (economist) trade-unionist tendencies in the working class.

19. We have in mind the recommendations on development of self-management in worker collectives published by the *Znanie* Society (Moscow 1988) the journal *Sotsialisticheskii trud* (1989, nos. 3, 5, 9) and the newspaper *Komsomol'skaya pravda*, 16th January 1990.

20. In this case the authors refer to the trade unions already in existence in the USSR, and not to unions of the more familiar Western type. — *Trans.*

21. All Union Council of Trade Unions — the ruling body of the Soviets 'official' trade unions. — *Trans.*

22. *Oblast'* — the largest administrative subdivision of a Soviet republic. — *Trans.*

MARKETIZATION AND PRIVATIZATION: THE POLISH CASE

Tadeusz Kowalik

Introduction

The fall of Tadeusz Mazowiecki's government — nearly as spectacular as its emergence — marks a break in the first stage of change of the economic system in Poland. The country which pioneered radical reforms now learns a pioneering lesson; its experience may be the lot of any country undertaking a profound change of its economic system.

According to both domestic and foreign observers, the government's fall and the collateral defeat of Solidarity will retard the processes of change in Poland as well as in all of Central and Eastern Europe.

The press reacted by criticizing the defeated government's elitism, its "inside" style of governing and insufficient information about its activities. Walesa and his camp were criticized for implicating Solidarity in factional fights, many of them personal.

These concerns must not be dismissed. But they do not touch the heart of the matter, and mistake the symptoms for the causes. In my view, the reason for the government's defeat is a recession of unprecedented dimension, caused by the economic stabilization programme (popularly known as the Balcerowicz Plan). Two contradictory value systems confronted each other: that of the population at large, and that of the "political class". The same discord surfaces in the present discussion about privatization.

Toward Economic Liberalism

The eighties witnessed a turn to the right in all of Central and Eastern Europe. Poland was especially well conditioned for a triumphal re-entry into the domestic political arena of free-market ideology and for its subsequent expansion, as well as for the accompanying conservative sentiments.

Three factors created favourable circumstances for the marriage of Polish economic liberalism and the ideology of political conservatism. The first is the exceptionally deep economic crisis, unharnessed from the end of the seventies, which compromised the economy of actually existing socialism in the eyes of the people in very obvious and tangible ways. It may be difficult to choose the lesser evil between some Communist governments' refusal to introduce any major reforms, and others' implementing only partial, half-way reforms. Most likely as the result of the latter option, Poland was the first country under Communist rule to achieve the "none" system (also referred to as "neither market nor plan"), which turned the economy into anarchy and made it the plaything of the most aggressive lobbies. The population's communal consciousness encompassed the system as a combination of compromised etatist absolutism and the inertia and inefficiency of the state and party bureaucrats.

The second factor is the unquestioned spiritual leadership of the Catholic Church, traditionally conservative. The dusk of Communist ideology was also the return of triumphant Catholicism, especially after a Pole became Pope. Incidentally, it is notable that John Paul II's influence in Poland is limited and selective. It is well known that the Pope made a heroic attempt to position the Church's social teaching to meet the challenge of the Third World countries. His encyclicals, especially *Laborem Exercens* and *Solicitudo rei Socialis* include pointed criticism of both the Communist and the capitalist systems. These Church documents, however, did not become guidelines for the Catholic prime minister, nor for his economic team who derived their inspiration from the laissez-faire conservatism that had reemerged in Anglo-Saxon countries. The heroes of economic policy became Ronald Reagan and Margaret Thatcher, whereas intellectual nurture was provided by conservative American neo-liberals. In the 1980s, the Polish economic imagination was shaped by Rose and Milton Friedman (their *Free to Choose* was published at least twice by the underground printing presses), by F. A. Hayek (his well-known pamphlet *The Road to Serfdom* became especially popular), by L. Mises, George Gilder, Michael Novak, and others. The relative laxity of the Polish authorities in issuing passports made it possible to travel and to study abroad, to receive stipends, etc.

The frequent conversion of intellectuals from Communism to extreme economic liberalism was reinforced by the absence of a non-Communist leftist tradition in Communist countries. The non-Communist left suffered the greatest repression, and for many years it found few supporters, whether in Poland or abroad. The West European social-democrats (the British Labour Party included) are much to blame for assuming the false strategy of appeasing the Communists and attempting to cooperate with them. This tactic naturally excluded cooperation with the opposition groups that attempted to restore the democratic left. It also caused the

Solidarity movement in Poland to oscillate to the right, especially as the very diversified movement won the support of many conservatives — even though at first it was dominated by egalitarian and participatory ideals — so that the outbreak of freedom in the summer of 1989 meant first of all freedom for conservative neo-liberalism.

Tadeusz Mazowiecki's Solidarity government at once declared that its aim was to create a privately-owned market economy modelled on the highly developed Western economies. It thus dispensed with the obsolete "Round Table" agreements, signed in the spring of the same year, which were a continuation of the Gdansk Agreements of the summer of 1980, as well as of the Programme for a Self-Governing Republic accepted by the First Solidarity Congress.

The sudden change of programme without a previous public debate was possible in the ambience of public enthusiasm and widespread confidence in "our government". This was to have serious consequences after some time had elapsed.

"Shock Therapy"
The term was popularly applied to the economic stabilization programme, best known as the Balcerowicz Plan.

When the new people came into power, there were many circumstances favourable for implementing such a "shock" operation; most important of these were a depressed market and rampant inflation.

Shortly before the end of the Communist rule and in the initial stage of the already evident severe recession, the last Communist cabinet liberated — without proper preparation — the prices of foodstuff. This created a wave of price increases, as inflation became hyperinflation (in the fall of 1989 prices went up 20-40% per month). It was therefore necessary to revert to radical action, and economists generally agreed that hyperinflation could only be tempered by an operation that to a certain extent had to be a "shock therapy". The open question was whether the counter-hyperinflationary operation was to become part of a larger programme of systemic changes. The government chose this option, drafting and implementing a programme of rapid transition to a market economy.

An important part of this "shock" operation, which was intended to be not only a radical abatement of inflation but also a leap into a market economy, was the concept of stabilization endorsed by the IMF and the World Bank. It must be emphasized that the deflationary and export-led recipe typically prescribed by the IMF and the World Bank bear effects that are much more shocking in economies that have no market mechanisms than in already existing market economies. This is so because in the post-Communist economies there are no "natural" adaptive mechanisms which could absorb the shock of a sudden change.

Furthermore, Jeffrey Sachs, the new cabinet's main advisor, was a typical product of the American success story, who saw everything as simple, and who believed that wishful thinking was all that it takes! History? Tradition? What is that? People are not accustomed to market-directed behaviour? All that is needed are sufficiently strong material incentives, and the rules of the game will enforce pro-market activity. The same thinking is represented by the Nobel-prize winning Milton Friedman, who recently tried to persuade our Establishment that Poland ought not to imitate the present American economic model which is polluted by "welfarism", but to pattern our economy on real free-competition market, the kind the United States had one hundred years ago.

Let us remind ourselves that the conservative-liberal argumentation of "Americans" (the term, in quotes, is intended to include representatives of the aforementioned international organizations in the broadly defined North American Establishment) was supported by the "conditionality" of Western aid.

At the "outbreak" of freedom and independence, numerous social circles were persuaded that Poland would not be able to battle the severe economic crisis unless the West offered assistance; and of course, the condition for the granting of aid was the assent of the international institutions, which made their loans contingent on a number of qualifications.

Balcerowicz presented the first draft of his plan in Washington. The Polish authorities never concealed the fact that they often acted under pressure from the IMF and the World Bank. No doubt, it must have been possible to negotiate with their representatives; but it is difficult to know whether the Polish side exploited these possibilities. Both the unofficial information circulating in spheres close to the government, and a comparison of declarations made by the Polish economic ministers with the doctrine and the practice of the IMF and the World Bank, suggest that the views of the Poles closely resembled those of the "Americans".

Moreover, the political scene in Poland was unfavourable to the reduction of conditionality and to the attenuation of the shock of change. From the very beginning the government strove to create the impression that matters of economy were controlled by professionals (the government's representatives' favourite word), or by experts, but not by politicians. The prime minister himself modestly declared he could not presume to comprehend those matters and that he had entirely to rely on specialists. This strengthened the laymen's conviction that the stabilization programme was a matter that should be handled by professionals.

Popular opinion was that the economy should be more or less independently managed by professional economists. This was a reaction to the excessive politicization of the economy by the Communist regime. Furthermore, Poland has a weak tradition of public pressures exerted on the government and the parliament by non-governmental social organizations. On the one hand, the establishment of a Solidarity government caused the movement to abdicate its role as trade union.[1] On the other hand, the sudden fall of Communist rule paralyzed (especially after the bloody events in Rumania) the other trade union (more precisely a federation of unions), which was accused of closely collaborating with the Communist authorities. Thus, there were no partners who would demand negotiations. Finally, Lech Walesa, then the greatest authority in socio-political matters, accepted the Balcerowicz Plan in advance, even before its details were known, apparently convinced that control of "our" government was unnecessary.

As a result, the Balcerowicz Plan — potentially one of the major political decisions made in recent years — was tacitly accepted without so much as an attempt to present to the population its far-reaching consequences.

What was the shock? The main target of the anti-hyperinflationary operation was the elimination of an excess of ("empty") money from the market by the sudden liberalization of prices and limiting the rise in wages (partly accomplished in the second half of 1989).

The state-regulated prices of energy were drastically raised, which resulted in the sky-rocketing of the prices of all products. In the first month of the plan's implementation, prices rose not by the 40-45% predicted by the government, but by 80%. Only 30% of the rise was compensated for, because the index figure for January was 0.3. In the following months, only one fifth of the price rise was compensated by indexation. The real value of wages in the first few months dropped by more than a third, or even by 40%, according to some opinions. Because the Polish products were not competitive on the international market, the extreme dive in employees' buying power resulted in a disastrous decline of production output. Industrial production of the state-owned enterprises fell by 30% in the first half of 1990, and production fell by even more in food processing and light industry. Production in the private sector did not fall, but neither did it show signs of expanding. The private sector is still small (a few percent), and its rise does not bear much effect on the overall level of production.

The interest rate, unexpectedly raised and definitely too high, was another factor which exerted a dismal effect on trade and agricultural production, which naturally was a long production cycle.

Social Costs

The results of the Balcerowicz Plan are ambivalent. On the one hand, inflation has been curbed (although it is still high: in the last three quarters of 1990 it was 70-100%, thus one of the highest in Europe). Because of the sharp drop in the population's purchasing power, shortages were also curbed in some markets, and in others altogether eliminated. For example, the foodstuffs market is oversupplied and farmers complain about difficulties in selling their produce. Throughout the year, the rates of exchange of Western currencies have remained almost invariable (internal convertibility has been introduced).

These are the undisputed achievements of the Balcerowicz Plan. On the other hand, the price of this shock therapy was also high in terms of negative phenomena that it will be hard to eliminate. Many economists are anxious that the present recession, without precedent in post-war Europe, may easily become a lasting stagnation or a depression. Last summer, some symptoms of revitalization appeared, but they were few, weak and short-lived.

Equally disadvantageous is the restructuring, or the modernization of the economy through liberalization of prices and the introduction of tight money policies (subsidies reduced radically, credit expensive and difficult to obtain). The authorities assumed that stabilization of markets and the creation of a high demand barrier would force enterprises to strive for greater efficiency; it was hoped that they would attempt to overcome the barrier by reducing costs and implementing cheaper means of production. The enterprises that failed to do so were supposed to go bankrupt. Unemployment would improve work discipline, raise the quality of products, etc.

These expectations were only partially realized. A very high degree of industrial concentration in Poland — high even by American standards — caused the state-owned enterprises to behave like monopolists. These firms can afford to increase prices for their products to cover any expenses, and they prosper even when their output goes down. Their financial situation did not deteriorate in the present recession. Sociologists and economists noticed in many enterprises at least a potential risk in work discipline: absenteeism is lower, employees are more concerned with keeping their jobs. However, the managers often cannot (or do not try to) use this increased work potential. Only in a few enterprises has work discipline improved. The same situation is reflected in the low quality of products and their limited variety, which also have not improved.

Unemployment must be looked at separately. The liberal economic team of the government expected that in a short time the so-called unemployment on the job (also known as disguised unemployment) would radically decrease. It was assumed that the rules of the market would force the state-owned enterprises to rationalize employment both by limiting unnecessary positions and by restructuring. Yet, there are few signs that such strategies have been implemented by state-owned enterprises. First, the market has not yet eliminated all inefficient enterprises. There were almost no bankruptcies in the past year. Second, the wages are so low that they do not represent a big fraction of the overall costs. A one-third decrease in production resulted in a 10% reduction of industrial employees. Moreover, this reduction does not accompany modernization or innovation. Sociologists suggest that it is a purely bureaucratic policy of fitting the number of employees to the recession-caused drop in productivity (compared to the level of production, disguised unemployment is greater now than it was a year ago). [2]

Thus, the shock therapy applied by the government does not resemble Schumpeter's *creative destruction*, a crisis as a break-through to economic and technological advancement. Equally ineffective are the appeals and the threats which some ministers address to the managers of state-owned enterprises (one of them told a group of managers: you act like bureaucrats in a command-directed, distributive economy. Apparently, the present recession is not big enough for you).

Thus it seems that besides the naive faith in a market that would "take care of itself" (which is not the case even in developed capitalist countries), two false assumptions underlay the Balcerowicz Plan.

The first was a belief that, despite the unfavourable structure of industry, liberating prices and implementing tight money policies would result in competition that would then naturally enforce market rules. However, this did not happen, nor could it happen. Monopolistic behaviour, far removed from the ideal of free competition, hindered such a scenario. Some feeble signs of increased efficiency of some state-owned enterprises are no harbinger of greater efficiency on the level of the national economy.

The Market and Tradition

The other false assumption is ahistoricism, or neglect of the influence of tradition, and of spiritual and material culture.

The official propaganda often speaks of a "return to normalcy", or a "return to Europe". These terms are supposed to suggest that before the "Communist violation", Poland had been a European country with a privately-owned, market economy, and that privately-owned property in a free-market, capitalist system had been the norm there. Yet that was not so. The majority of the population lived and worked in rural areas, in conditions akin to a natural economy. The modern capitalist sector was not only small, but also linked with the state; Polish capitalism was etatistic by its very nature.

A change in the socio-professional structure and a demographic transformation took place under Communist rule. However, this modernization of population cannot be identified with a readiness to accept the rules governing a market economy, or a universal ability to adapt one's behaviour to such economy. Communist rule or the Communist system were not the sole obstacles to adopting such behaviour. Among European countries, Poland had never been very advanced in either market economy or "market society". Further more, Poland has lost in the war the two most enterprising minorities: the Jews and the Germans. Then, the displacement of millions of people from the villages to the cities under Communist rule took place in a highly bureaucratized economy. Even agriculture, which, paradoxically, became more market-oriented than it had been before the war, did not compel competition-oriented economic behaviour; such development was hindered by the shadow of a paternalistic-bureaucratic umbrella.

As far as patterns of social advancement under Communist rule are concerned, these were mostly continuations of the old ways rather than their negation. As before the second world war, the ideal career was that of administrative official — not that of entrepreneur, or trade dealer. For these reasons among others a transition to a market economy in Poland must take time. The aforementioned factors are usually noticed by historians and sociologists, but ignored by economists, especially those of "American" orientation.

Here are a few quotations from a book by a well-known Polish sociologist:

> The slogans calling for a departure from socialism, which seem to have greatest appeal, are those encouraging decentralization, freeing economic activity from bureaucratic straitjacket, releasing new energies driven equally by the idea of free choice and a wish to get rich. Let us remember that such and similar appeals were voiced in the 19th century by positivists. They were also repeated in the inter-war period. Each time the results were only limited. In the period between the two world wars the press accused the young generation of seeking employment with the state, which was less paid but more stable, rather than turning to private entrepreneurship. . . The new coalition government [of T. Mazowiecki — TK] feels obliged to create conditions favourable for entrepreneurship and to remove obstacles to individual initiative and drive. Yet in my view the conflict between lingering elements of socialism and new political ideas will continue long into the future. . .[3]
> . . . It is relatively eas(y) to change legal acts, ideological declarations, institutional statutes, but it must be remembered at the same time that society can be said to have changed only when each and every one of its members has changed his way of thinking and doing things, his habits and his work patterns, his sense of duty, values as well as his sensibilities and perceptions on what is natural and what is

not in a given community. . . A considerable number of Poles will consider it natural that Mazowiecki's government will bring us all that socialism promised. Only he will do it faster, more efficiently, and in greater quantities. [4]

These words were written in the fall of 1989. A year later, Tadeusz Mazowiecki suffered a spectacular defeat as a candidate for the presidency. He received fewer votes than an unknown stranger from Canada and Peru. He interpreted these results as a decisive rejection of his political and economic programme. Disappointed and bitter, accusing the other candidates of giving in to populism, he resigned with his cabinet. The future will show whether the new government will draw similar conclusions and abandon the "great operation" (as top politicians refer to it) of hasty imposition of a market economy and adopt instead an historical-evolutionary approach.

Meanwhile, the situation was used dexterously by Stan Tyminski, who returned to his homeland after twenty years of emigration with a book (*Swiete psy* — Holy Dogs), ruthlessly critical of the government for its "stagnant" politics. In Theses for his economic programme we read:

> The present situation is like seeing a film I had already seen in Peru a few years ago. The film starts after a year of economic program designed to stop inflation, but which has the effect of restricting economic growth. I know how the film ends and I could tell you how it ends. But I don't want this ending to happen in my own country. . . The level of production in Poland fell by 30% in 1980. Ten years later this situation has repeated itself. We can't let production fall by 30% again next year. . . Poland is a victim of an international economic war. [5]

It is interesting that the candidate attracted votes by promising easy wealth, but he was very cautious in referring to privatization. [6]

It is also notable that both candidates in the second round of the elections advanced isolationist sentiments. Only a year ago Walesa travelled in the West, and tried to persuade Western businessmen to invest in Poland and to buy Polish enterprises. He used to say that he would "internationalize the Polish economy". Yet now he speaks a different language: "Let us give Poland to the Poles, instead of selling it off to Americans who want to close down 75% of the firms and to dismiss people."

Contrarily to Tyminski, however, and paradoxically, Walesa enters the political arena with the slogan of radical acceleration. In the political dimension, the intended meaning of the slogan is clear: it voices a desire to fight the former nomenklatura and to cleanse the power apparatus of Communists. But in the economy? What could acceleration mean here? And what do his electors expect? It is not easy to answer this question. The numerous contradictory promises and general programmatic declarations allow everyone to interpret "acceleration" as they like. Perhaps it is possible to make the generalization that the majority of Walesa's electorate expects a quick improvement in their lives.

A look at the social composition of Walesa's constituency indicates a pending conflict. He was supported on the one hand by those eager to proceed with the privatization and with erecting a basis for a capitalist economy (one of Walesa's ideologues called him a Thatcherite), who expect a significant lowering of taxes, and on the other hand by those most hurt by the Balcerowicz Plan, that is, the unemployed and those in danger of losing employment, retired pensioners, the activists of employees' self-management, who may hold Walesa by his promises to them, the supporters of employees-owned stock companies, the enemies of nomenklatura companies, who expect that Walesa will quickly deal with these companies. A long-term symbiosis of the two groups is quite unthinkable.

Recession and Privatization

For a number of psychological and economic reasons, the severe recession is not favourable to privatization.

The aim of the stabilization plan was a radical limitation of the excess ("empty") money, which aim was realized times over, resulting in a radical drop in the population's savings. The savings would only suffice to purchase a small fraction of the capital presently owned by the state (some economists assess the private savings to be no more than 1.5% of the value of state capital). Therefore, if privatization were to be based on domestic resources, and if sales of property were to be on a level approximating the real value of state capital, then even with much credit support the process would take several decades.

Moreover, the recession evokes a defensive behaviour, as opposed to expansive entrepreneurship. Most people are interested in maintaining their standard of living and rebuilding the level of their savings rather than in long-term investments. Additionally, inflation is still high, and there is uncertainty as to whether enterprises will indeed be forced to increase their efficiency; thus widespread reluctance to capitalize one's savings in investment is natural.

The most significant factor is perhaps distrust in the privatization programme created and implemented by the mainspring of the present recession: the government. Confidence in Poland's national economy depends on confidence in the government.

All in all, the Balcerowicz Plan only partially and perhaps even to a negligible degree prepared the way for privatization. The government's policy, which hardly extended beyond the implementation of the stabilization plan, also did little to improve initial conditions for privatization. I have in mind here the government's attitude to the so-called nomenklatura companies and the employees' self-management movement, as well as the latter's concept of employees' stock companies. (I will not analyze incentives for foreign capital, though here, too, the government's efforts were meagre.)

The Controversy Over Privatization

The economic stabilization plan was also left to the "professionals" by public opinion, which noticed too late that the plan was highly political in character. However, the situation of privatization is very different, as it has from the very start been regarded as a socio-economic problem. Everything concerning privatization is the subject of endless public debates. Although a privatization bill had already been passed in July 1990 and another act established the position of the Minister for Property Transformation (henceforth referred to as MPT) and defined his prerogatives, only the legal aspects of the so-called "small" privatization have been clarified (concerning small production plants, shops, pharmacies). In order to illustrate the divergent paths of privatization it is enough to quote one opinion of the victor in the presidential elections.

As is well known, the aforementioned legislative bills give many prerogatives to the government, which (especially the MPT) initiates and organizes the privatization process. The government designated five big firms for the initiation of "big" privatization. This is how Walesa reacted:

> Educated by Communism, we built plants for political reasons. Now, as children of Communism, we obey the same principle while moving in the opposite direction, we want to "politically" privatize factories. This is a mistake. We are supposed to create favourable conditions, but the cleansing work is to be done by the economy itself. Kuczynski [the MPT — TK] or Balcerowicz issues a decree that these or those seven or eight plants are to be privatized. That is ludicrous. The situation needs to be turned around. Seven or eight military factories should not undergo privatization for strategic reasons, but the rest? We should define the rules and let the economy do the rest. Political decrees are unthinkable. I am against them, because their thinking is marked by the old style.[7]

Walesa also repeated his former idea that "Plants ought not to be shut down, but new plants must be created."

Both Walesa's first and second opinions link the privatization process to the selective activity of the "economy", which probably means rules of economic competition, and to a social attitude of entrepreneurship. It is difficult to predict whether the government's surrender of its initiating function would indeed result in faster, spontaneous privatization, as Walesa sees it. At this point in time, Polish society's economic imagination is far from embracing rapid privatization.

This is evident from sociological studies conducted at twenty state-owned firms shortly before the passing of the privatization bills. Here is the concluding opinion:

> The majority of employees give limited support to the governmental privatization programme — especially as it concerns their own factories. . . Too many unknowns among the potential advantages of privatization make them reluctant to participate in "de-etatizing" their work places. Their distrust of privatization is also caused by their passive attitudes and the long-standing expectation that the state should take care of their material, housing, and educational needs. . . Attitudes of apathy and waiting are most characteristic among employees of the enterprises. [8]

Lech Kaczynski, one of Walesa's associates in his capacity as the Solidarity trade union leader, expresses a similar opinion of society's attitude to privatization. He says: "Privatization is a difficult problem, contrary to the majority of people's idea of justice." This convinced him to support Walesa's candidacy for presidency, because Walesa ". . . is a politician closely related to the plebeian strata of our society and who can provide a protective screen for this great operation. It is necessary to acquire the workers' support for this difficult process, which is in their long-term interest." [9]

What are the socio-psychological obstacles to privatization? What are the reasons for reluctance on the part of employees of state-owned enterprises?

Let us refer to another sociological study. In September of 1990 the Public Opinion Research Centre conducted a survey on privatization. The answers to questions about the general principles of privatization suggested that privatization was socially accepted. As many as 74% of respondents expressed their assent. Moreover, nearly half of them believed that privatization proceeded too slowly. However, answers to other questions reflected bitterness about the process and scepticism about its effects. Respondents assessed negatively privatization's effects in boosting efficiency and in improving their own economic standing. Only 27% hoped that their own situation would improve in two or three years, and 22% that the national economy would improve during that time. As many as 35% of respondents did not expect improvement of their individual situation in the next five years, and 40% did not expect an improvement in the national economy in that period. Nearly one-fifth of all respondents expected their own situation to improve only after ten years.

Thus the majority of Poles do not link privatization with improvement of their own economic standing or the national economy in the foreseeable future.

Equally interesting and distant in principle from the general support of privatization were the answers concerning the criteria of future privatization. Respondents were asked which of the following criteria should be decisive: maximum economic efficiency; avoidance of discrimination against anyone in particular; or avoidance of the creation of a new privileged group. 30% selected the first criterion, 37% the second, and 29% the third. The respondents were also asked which method of privatization they preferred: vouchers given free of charge by the state which could be used to purchase stock of any of the privatized enterprises, or sales of stock (for cash or credit) first to the employees of a privatized enterprise and then to outsiders. The majority chose the latter procedure: sales to the employees; they refused the government's gift!

The concluding comments of the study were: "The government's intention of concentrating on efficiency as the main criterion and goal of privatization, coupled with disavowal of the concept of the employees' stock companies, may meet with social resistance. This is so because in the popular opinion, effectiveness depends on employees' stock ownership.[10]

Employees' stock ownership is an intermediate form between collective and private forms of ownership, or a form of group ownership. One could ironically conclude that Poles universally support privatization (74% answered in the affirmative), on the condition that it is quite different from regular, actual privatization. Similarly, some say that everyone in Poland is for the market, provided the state will guarantee them work, housing, and social security.

Employees' Stock Ownership
The workers' sympathy towards the employees' companies (as opposed to joint stock companies) requires explanation.

The beginnings of popularity of the employees' companies were in the summer of 1989, when Mazowiecki's government declared its intention of creating a privately-owned market economy patterned on highly developed Western countries. The declaration was followed by others, generally received as aimed at dismantling the employees' self-management.

The latter institution's name, present in most state-owned enterprises thanks to a bill passed in 1981 and resulting from negotiations between Solidarity and the Communist government, must not be taken literally. "Self-management of the workforce", despite this official name, never possessed full managing power but meant participation in the enterprise's management, limited in its capacities by numerous legal regulations and the hierarchical structure of Poland's industry. Furthermore, according to experts, only 20% of employees were active and ready to participate in management.

Nevertheless, the announced intention to remove the mostly formal participatory prerogatives of the employees was taken by many workers — especially by the legalized Association of Activists for Employees' Self-Management — as an instance of injustice and a challenge. The move was unexpected, because it was contrary to the Round Table agreements (February-March 1989), which promised the removal of any restrictions imposed on the workers' self-government during and after the period of martial law. Reassured by those agreements, the self-management activists undertook to design a self-managing enterprise in the new political situation, expecting that favourable conditions for this form of management were finally close at hand.[11] Soon they found that the governmental policy was headed in the opposite direction, and that it was unfavourable to employees' self-management. After initial protests, the activists observed that the openly capitalist option found support with international financial institutions. As a result, some self-management activists became persuaded that employees' management scares away foreign investors.[12]

In these new conditions, some of the activists attempted to adapt the postulate of employees' participation to the altered external conditions. They were assisted by proponents of the American ESOPs (Employees Stock Ownership Plan): Louis O. Kelso, who formulated this form of ownership, and his supporters. In a short time, many publications attempted to popularize this concept in Poland. Special groups were formed to tailor the American, and then also the British ESOPs, to the specific Polish conditions. The goal was to protect participatory rights of the employees, which were to be especially significant in the transitory period during which the employees would own too few shares to control the firm solely on the basis of ownership. The problem had special import in view of the prospect of the many years that property transformations of state enterprises were to take, with the very meagre savings that the employees had at their disposal.

At first the government categorically rejected such concepts. Credit assistance was refused to the first Polish ESOPs, as was permission to form the first employees' companies. As a reaction to those clearly unfriendly gestures on the part of the government (especially its representative for property transformations), a number of employees' councils, their national representation and the aforementioned Association issued a number of protests and declarations critical of the government, and even demanded its resignation.

The National Representation of Employees' Self-Management in Gdansk addressed a "legal question" to the Constitutional Tribunal: whose property is the capital of state-owned enterprises? The basis for this question was created by the last Communist government, which (in February 1989) divided the enterprise's capital into the part owned by the State Treasury and consisting of the founding fund, on which was imposed a special tax called the dividend, and the capital raised by the enterprise, or the enterprise fund. This led to the presumption that only the founding fund was subject to sale, while the enterprise fund was by definition the employees' property, and as such need not be purchased by them.

Public debates concerning employees' ownership, as well as the stamina of self-management activists, who countered the government's privatization plan with their own participatory proposals, resulted in a privatization bill which admitted the possibility of creating employees' companies. The battle today is for sufficient credit assistance and for the removal of other obstacles to creating such companies. The popularity of this form among workers forced the government to surrender some ground. The present phase of the debate suggests that the idea of employees' companies is again threatened by a new concept of property transformations, involving the free distribution of coupons.

The new concept involves a probable one-time distribution of stock to employees of state enterprises. The act of embourgeoisement or appropriation, turning workers into owners by giving away easily resaleable stock, is intended on the one hand to win their sympathy for the idea of privatization, and on the other to create a basis for a capital market. The prices of free stock would most likely be low when resold, which would facilitate their concentration.

Rafal Krawczyk, the main proponent of this concept, does not hide his conservative-liberal intentions (his present career began with a failed attempt to establish a branch of the Washington-based Heritage Foundation in Warsaw), or his enmity towards employees' participation or any other form of non-private ownership.

> It is a paradox that a philosophy originating with the liberal-conservative idea of a free market, private property and free competition as the basis of healthy democracy, led to conclusions that — at first sight — may seem populist and egalitarian. This is obviously misleading. The whole concept is subservient to a single goal: swift restoration of the free market in the national economy. . . The problem is that the great operation of transforming the national economy — and also the whole Polish society — into a pro-market one, with all its consequences, cannot be accomplished by the government only — no matter how pro-market it is — but it requires social participation. [13]

Krawczyk won the support of some self-management activists who did not notice — at least not immediately — the anti-participatory edge of his concept.

In the United States, ESOPs are used by conservatives to weaken the trade unions' position. In Poland, ESOPs —as a seemingly more radical form of group ownership with *en masse* appropriation — are intended to counteract deeply ingrained participatory and egalitarian tendencies. However, the "class" interest is the same in both cases.

Following the "great operation", Krawczyk clearly predicts a "policy of concentrating capital", facilitating the transfer of stock beyond the firm, special progressive taxation, bankruptcies, etc., all this to change the initial egalitarian distribution of property — a change affected to a certain extent by the employees themselves. At the same time, Krawczyk writes very openly: "Obviously, the idea of workers' self-government is only an instrument of transition to a stock ownership system. . ." [14]

Very active in the presidential campaign, Krawczyk suffered a defeat. Yet, it is significant that the post of the Minister of Property Transitions in the Walesa-created cabinet was given to Janusz Lewandowski, who for a long time has voiced a similar concept of popular appropriation. It is a logical continuation of Walesa's idea of giving away money cheques, with which shares in privatized enter-prises might be purchased.

It is hardly possible to expect that such paper-bureaucratic rather than actually privatizing operations can lead to a privately-owned market economy that would be more rational than the present one. The situation illustrates the difficulties that arise in the creation of such an economy, contrary to the expectations of the majority of Poles.

Pathological Privatization
Although privatization begun by the Mazowiecki cabinet is in an initial stage, the process of special forms of privatization widely called "pathological" has already quite a rich history. It started in 1987 as a part of the so-called second stage of economic reform and took place under the last two Communist cabinets (of Messner and Rakowski). The essence of this new stage consisted in recognizing changes in ownership relations as an equally important (beside marketization) part of reforms. Many legislative changes clearly aimed not only at the expansion of the private sector onto so to speak "nobody's land" but also at the transformation of existing state property. It has become very "fashionable" to create different types of companies. While joint-stock companies were not numerous as yet, those of limited liability have been mushrooming.

The Rakowski cabinet considered these companies as the most suitable form into which the state firms should be transformed. According to the draft Programme of Structural Adjustment, published in July 1989, all state firms were to be transformed into joint-stock companies within half a year's time. These companies were to remain state property (since most of their assets would be owned by the state).

The intention of this Programme was rather clear: to get rid of self-management bodies and to strengthen the power of the state administration. As the Communist government collapsed, this programme was not implemented. Thousands of companies, however, were created formally outside the state firms, but on their fringe, and dependent on their equipment and personnel. This process was labelled "pathological privatization" or "enfranchising the nomenklatura". In a similar way, some of the state firms were formally transformed into joint-stock companies, usually by either breaking the law of exploiting its loopholes.

These companies mushroomed not in the least because their form was superior to the existing forms of business organization. Decisive factors were the following:

— the actual taxation burden could be lessened, making it possible to pay higher wages;
— the number of high-salaried posts could be increased;
— self-management bodies could be debarred from decision-making;
— higher profits could be achieved by monopolizing the supply of scarce commodities.

Generally, these companies have become the source of excessive profits, and thus fuelled inflation, severed the established links of co-operation, etc. Very often, directors of the state firms were simultaneously members of the board of directors of these companies and many top *apparatchiki* and their families took part in this procedure. As more than a half of the number of the state firms' managing directors have been actively involved in that procedure, the phenomenon is common enough to be regarded as the most typical feature of the decadence of real socialism, or a form of post-Communist primitive accumulation of capital.

Although this way of privatization had glaring features of pathology, and was outrageously resented by ordinary people, the judgment of it by many intellectuals was rather favourable. Arguments are often advanced that the process amounts to abolition of state ownership and fosters accumulation of capital. This view, quite popular among the Polish economic liberals, seemed to be shared by the Solidarity government, which tolerated too long this way of destruction of the state sector.

The social costs of this process, however, are enormous. Many people got accustomed to treating any programmes of privatization, which are beyond their control, as stealing national wealth. This sentiment was noticed by the politicians and exploited by them in the presidential campaign: "Today ownership transformation is being blocked by society's conviction, that the new owners (small and big ones) will become people of the nomenklatura. I fully understand that the problem is difficult from the legal point of view. But without solving this problem. I forecast very little progress in privatization." [15]

Alternative Scenarios for the Future

The above mentioned difficulties in implementing the stabilization programme, and in the privatization of the state sector, do not exhaust, of course, the full list of tensions and conflicts with which the process of the "great transformation" is fraught in Poland. Just these two problems, however, seem to be decisive. For this reason one should focus on them in making an attempt to outline imaginable scenarios of systemic transformation over the next few and more years to come.

Two main scenarios seem to be most probable.

1) The programme of full-blooded capitalism will be implemented "by taking a short cut", as some like to call it. Members of the power elites (even those who otherwise would opt, though in abstract terms only, for the social-democratic variant, often express their conviction that Poland must go through the stage of "primitive accumulation". The former nomenklatura, capable of creating "political capitalism" (J. Staniszkis), would become a driving force, a kind of substitute for the middle class.

Although the current Balcerowicz Plan has many features of just this, the 19th century model (and its author himself seems to reckon little with social resistance), I do not believe in the success of this programme. Poland has not maintained (never had) powerful entre-preneurial traditions and the social forces interested in such a model are meagre. On the other hand, the tradition of the workers' move-ment, of class struggle, and finally of participation in management, was rich and continues to the present day. After all, it should be remembered that it was industrial workers who abolished the Communist power. It is not difficult to foresee that just these factors will shape the future social framework for institutional changes. The alternatives that are likely to arise are that after a period of hoping in vain for a marked improvement in economic performance, after making the first attempts at privatization, after exhaustion of Walesa's charisma, the government will either have to retreat or resort to authoritarian methods of enforcing the new order. This second outcome, however, will only delay and possibly aggravate an open conflict.

2) Mazowiecki promised at least twice the creation of the "social market economy" (which was also included in the economic programme of an opposing coalition called the Alliance of the Centre).

Walesa on the other hand made an important concession benefitting the employees' companies, and he also promised to curb unemployment. These pronouncements are thus far only words. In the changed political constellation, however, they may happen to be the point of departure towards some combination of features of the Swedish, Austrian and West-German models. If the sufficiently influential social groups such as trade unions, self-management movement, etc.) were convinced and won over to institutionalized "cooperation" rather than institutionalized "conflict", then such a modus vivendi would make "learning by doing" and mutual adjustment of different social groups with different vested interests possible.

We are speaking, of course, about a process which assumes evolutionary development, full employment and a comprehensive social policy programme, going beyond the present concept of limited protection of the poorest groups. Only then would it be possible to check how effective group forms of ownership are on a large scale, and to put different forms of employees' participation to the test.

NOTES

1.   Criticized for not taking energetic measures to make the Solidarity Trade Union stronger, Lech Walesa has said: "We will not be on equal footing with Europe if we create a strong union which would oppose the reforms." P. Lewinski, "Ile zytrzymacie?" (How much can you stand?), *Tygodnik Solidarnosc*, September 6, 1989.

2.   G. Gesicka, "Komisje zakladowe NSZZ Solidarnosc wobec bezrobocia" (Factory Committees of the Solidarity Trade Union and unemployment), *Studia i Materialy*, April-September, 1990, Warsaw.

3.   J. Szczepanski, *Poland: Facing the Future*, University of Warsaw, mimeo, p. 136.

4.   *Ibid.*, p. 135.

5.   S. Tyminski, "Tezy Programu Gospodarczego", (Theses of the Economic Programme), *Gazeta Wyborcza*, no. 262, November 10-11, 1990.

6.   *Ibid.*

7.   L. Walesa, an interview, *Zycie Warszawy*, no. 268, November 17-18, 1990.

8.   M. Jarosz, "Robotnicy o prywatyzacji" (The workers on privatization), *Polityka*, September 8, 1990.

9.   L. Kaczynski, an interview, *Tygodnik Gdanski*, no. 40, October 7, 1990.

10. B. Dr., "Opinie i nastroje, Poparcie bez zrozumienia" (Opinions and Attitudes, Support without understanding), *Zycie Warszawy*, no. 243, October 18, 1990.

11. M. Groszek and P. Roszkowski, "Przedsiebiorstwo panstwowo-samorzadowo-pracownicze. Zalozenia koncepcji uspolecznienia wlasnosci panstwowej" (The state-self-managed-employees enterprise), *Zmiany*, no. 1, 1989.

12. The vice-president of the Association for Self-Management Activists and Member of Parliament Andrzej Milkowski has put it bluntly: "We are a bankrupt state and as such we have to comply with the conditions which are dictated to us. In that situation the self-management system in its present form

may prove to be impossible to defend." A. Gutkowska, "Samorzadnosc miedzy realnym socjalizmem a neoliberalizmem" (Self-management between really existing socialism and neo-liberalism), *Zmiany*, no. 22, 1989.

13.   R. Krawczyk, "Wielka przemiana, Upadek i odrodzenie polskiej gospodarki" (The great transformation. The collapse and rebirth of the Polish economy), Warsaw, 1990, pp. 163-64.
14.   *Ibid.,* p. 152.
15.   L. Kaczynski, as in note no. 9.

FROM WHERE TO WHERE? REFLECTIONS ON HUNGARY'S SOCIAL REVOLUTION

Peter Bihari

There is a revolution going on in Eastern Europe. That much is known for sure. Perhaps it can also be said that some form of capitalism is evolving in Eastern Europe. Everything else is uncertain. We do not even know exactly what kind of systems collapsed, let alone what are those being born. From socialism to capitalism? From what kind of socialism into what kind of capitalism? There is no doubt that the change in political regime in 1989/1990 was a milestone within a revolutionary process. But it was not its beginning and even less its end.

I. *FROM WHERE?*

Socialism: Ideal and 'Actually Existing'
For socialists, the equality ideal of socialism means that no individual social group exercises systematic control over other social groups. In the positive sense this means that the members of society — directly or through their representatives — themselves organize their social life. From the economic aspect this implies production subordinate to the universal purpose of society as a whole and not to the particular purposes of some specific social group.

Many believe that the reason for the failure of the East European socialisms was the lack of democracy. Others attribute failure to the low performance of the economy. The performance of the economy, however, was also diminished through the lack of democracy. Common property and democracy are not two independent attributes. One is the economic, the other is the political aspect of society's self-organization. Common property is democracy in the economy; democracy is common property in politics. That is to say, socialism if it is to mean true social self-government, the "free society of associated producers", can only be based on democracy and public ownership.

The countries of Eastern Europe started out on the path of establishing public property and democracy, of establishing social self-organization in 1945. The expropriation of private property was,

279

however, followed not by the development of the self-organization of society but by a peculiar combination of social subordination and self-organization hitherto unknown in history. The development of Eastern Europe represented a specific degeneration of socialism.

Essentially, the expropriation of the surplus by private interests was terminated but production controlled by the needs of the community did not come into being. Neither the community, nor any of the social groups became the systematic beneficiary of the net product. A part of the consumption of the state and party bureaucrats did represent a socially uncontrolled expropriation of the social surplus for private purposes and to this extent this was similar to the characteristic relations of capitalism. But the extremely limited communal nature of the ownership relations of the East European economies was related basically not to the excessive consumption of bureaucrats. The lion's share of the surplus eventually flowed back to the direct producers through an irrational and inefficient mechanism of income re-distribution, in the form of production subsidies, investment grants and welfare benefits in cash or in kind. (In Hungary, the social wage amounted to some 25-30 per cent of real wages, and 60-70 per cent of enterprise investments were financed by non-enterprise sources.) Far too often it flowed not to where it would have been expected on the basis of the rational utilization of resources or social needs.

The decision makers were unable (perhaps even unwilling) to expropriate the surplus products for themselves. But what the state/party bureaucracy did was to withdraw the decisions related to the use of the surplus (the *process of accumulation*) from the scope of control by society. It was this decision-making process that the state/party bureaucrats expropriated. A closed group of decision-makers cannot have knowledge of the entire scale of needs, not even if they want to have that knowledge. Under these conditions, the decision-making fora that could have mediated actual social requirements did not function (in fact, did not come into being in the first place), thus resources could not be allocated according to actual social needs. Even if we assume that the decision-making elite allocated resources aiming at the optimalization of the social output (and also considered subjective aspects such as equitability and fairness) the result could not be other than sub-optimal in a system which either *en bloc* excluded those concerned from the process of accumulation or permitted participation in it only occasionally and in the form of secret deals.

Cui prodest? According to the habitual argument, the over-centralization of the process of accumulation can be explained by the endeavours of the decision-making elite expropriating the social surplus, by their lust for power coupled with privileged consumption.

Yet the question is much more complicated than this. *Ab ovo*, the decision-making elite was not a unified bloc. Moreover, it must be admitted that during the history of actually-existing socialism, *no* coherent democratic socialist economic programme, *ever came into being*. It existed only as an abstract ideal and not as a practical alternative. The practical choice has always (at least ever since Imre Nagy's "new line" of 1953) been between the centralization of accumulation and subjecting it to control by market forces. This was still a version of socialism (insofar as the market was to be advanced without private owners or with a private sector playing only a subordinate role), but it was an alternative that bespoke a weak, incomplete, minimal socialism.[1] One can take a stand against this "minimal socialism" (for profit-oriented production) from the platform of "maximal socialism", that is, from that of the abstract theoretical requirements of social ownership, pointing out the limitations of the ideal models of market reforms. But one can also attack it in a hypocritical manner, using socialism only as a pretext, aiming in fact at preserving the decision-making powers of "degenerate socialism". Both these considerations were present in anti-market political actions in Eastern Europe. The forces taking a stand for the protection of socialism merged with those protecting their own powers and, although starting from totally opposed points of departure, they united in attacking those advocating "minimal socialism". Thus, they involuntarily collaborated in keeping the irrational accumulation system of degenerate socialism alive so long.

The permanent isolation and weakness of those advocating social ownership as against the market is indicated by the fact that practically there were no political movements, intellectual workshops or practical experiments that would have endeavoured to supercede actually-existing socialism in a socialist manner. Especially from the mid-sixties, socialists advocating public ownership pointed to the inherent limitations of the system that could be established by way of market-based reforms, with good reason. Their criticism was even more justified by the fact that the elements that would have opened the way for a capitalist type of development of the market reforms have always been present in the ideological tenets supporting the market reforms.[2] What is more, the advocates of market socialism received considerable intellectual support from the representatives of a capitalist restoration who, although without free political scope, nevertheless were present. Many of the present representatives of the transition to capitalism took part in the preparation of the most important decisions as government advisors, as members of party committees, as the "reform economists of the reform era". During this period, the advocates of "maximal socialism" landed on the same platform with the group that expropriated decisions on accumulation; while the representatives of "minimal socialism" were thrown in the same camp with the latent forces of capitalism. Both proved to be ill-formed alliances.

It is obvious today that the criticism directed against minimal (market) socialism expressed by the advocates of maximal socialism (and here the author of the present study does attribute a measure of self-criticism to his own words) was frequently doctrinaire. Their point of departure was not real life, not the practically existing possibilities, but abstract theoretical requirements. Today it seems that they thereby helped conserve a greater evil than market socialism. Moreover, since what was conserved could not be upheld forever under the given economic-political constellation of forces, the defenders of maximal (democratic) socialism indirectly contributed to the political annihilation of any socialist alternative. An unbiased examination might have led to the conclusion that weak socialism is worth more than degenerate socialism or a primitive capitalism.

To be sure, weak socialism was just one of the possible outcomes of the market reforms. Irrespective of the subjective intentions of the proponents, depending on the social constellation, market reforms can give rise to, or can become combined with social movements that will lead to the restoration of private capitalism (to a social revolution). And that is precisely what has happened.

In retrospect it seems that the period during which market socialism could have evolved into a stable, non-capitalist system, lasted from the early sixties to the beginning of the seventies. This historic opportunity was missed. The economic-political bases of the system were still strong enough to manage a transition that would have obviously been concomitant with a major shock including un-employment, inflation and major income disparities. At that time the system did have sufficient political support to have made the political burdens of transition manageable. The advocates of maximal socialism partly did not realize the necessity for such a severe compromise and so they could also not see its timeliness. Those who did acknowledge this necessity were not strong enough to enforce the changes. The practical and theoretical attempts made at the correction of the system — such as the Kosygin reforms in the USSR, or the "new mechanism" in Hungary — did not lead towards the democratization of the process of accumulation, of the planning system or towards drawing ownership under true social control (maximal socialism). Nor did they result in the breaking of the power of the bureaucratic apparatus by way of the market reforms (minimal socialism). Due to the pseudo-reforms introduced, the closed circle of decision-makers was extended: certain groups were drawn in to the decision making process. The technique of decision-making was also changed by the introduction of more flexible plan targets or, in Hungary, by mandatory plan indicators being replaced by informal contracts. But this did not amount to a really major change. Market reforms overstrain the system unless it is an economically and politically stable one. In the eyes of the decision-makers, however, the more stable the system, the less such reforms can be justified and socially supported. The art of politics lies in catching the historic moment when the need for the reforms is sufficiently pressing but the forces bursting the system are still weak. But the majority of Eastern Europe's socialist politicians were hardly adept at the art of politics, and the rest had good reason to fear the impact of the reforms on their bureaucratic power. So everything remained as it had been, while the crisis grew ever deeper.

A Revolution that Preceded the Revolution

Beginning with the mid-seventies, economic and political tensions piled up and strained society to such an extent that the urging of the market reforms led not to market socialism but to social revolution. A significant part of the socialist forces did not recognize this and, *bona fide*, assisted in or actively took a part in the preparation of the capitalist market economy.

By the mid-seventies, an acute structural crisis evolved in the economy. Keeping low efficiency enterprises employing a large labour force artificially alive undermined, to a dangerous degree, the income-generating capabilities of the entire economy. As a result of the deteriorated income-generating capabilities of the economy, it was less and less possible to ensure the usual growth of real incomes. The economic policy-makers tried to secure additional resources and the usual growth rate of the living standards by way of external leverage. This step seemed reasonable in view of the loans available on favourable conditions in the international money markets. It also seemed like a humane decision that the country's leadership accorded first priority to increasing living standards. *Under the conditions of the given system*, however, the external resources could not be used any more efficiently than the internal ones. (The problem was further aggravated by the fact that a significant part of the inputs of manufacturing industry came from the dollar markets, while a significant part of its exports went to the rouble market.) This foretold the development of an external liquidity crisis and the elimination of any chances of economic growth or the improvement of the standard of living for a long period of time. With the cynical support of some liberal economists, the leadership that took the living standard objectives seriously walked guilelessly into the trap leading to the annihilation of the system.

By the end of the 1970s, the debt-trap closed on Hungary: internal resources proved to be inadequate to generate coverage of the debt service. Debt repayment was possible only through new borrowing and a net withdrawal of resources. The debt crisis provided a singular opportunity to the leading capitalist powers for asserting their strategic and political objectives in the East European region.[3] They made good use of this opportunity. As a result of the cool calculation of the creditors, from the early 1980s loans were always available just to the extent that they were sufficient to avert the direct collapse of the economy, but no more.[4] This further aggravated the domestic crisis: real incomes began to decline, the additional resources needed for re-structuring were not accessible, and the political legitimation of the leadership was completely worn away.

The dependence on loans ensured that the creditors were able to penetrate economic and political decision-making. The main creditors were directly incorporated into the Hungarian decision-making structure. (The IMF's representative in Hungary was one of the leading officials of the economic Cabinet and a member of the Central Committee of the communist party). Access to loans was conditional upon strict terms which directly or indirectly included the *determination of the prices of certain products, giving certain positions to certain persons, taking political measures.* In fact, these terms and conditions contained the surrender of the system. A significant part of the dictates and agreements was reached not in a public manner, recorded by protocols, but *via* informal discussions behind closed doors, over dinner and tennis parties. Often, a pointed remark would suffice. The degree of dependence was such that it was enough for creditors to put their lips together for Hungary's leaders to dance. Those measures were in most cases cloaked in the illusion of rational economic (or political) decisions. As a result of the successful deployment of the credit-gun, all important decisions related to the economic policy and to the modification of the socio-economic regime fell under the decisive influence of the creditor banks, governments and financial centres. This was not simply one of the antecedents of the 1989-1990 revolution; this was the turning point in the failure of any kind of socialism. From this point on, even rudimentary public ownership was no more than mere illusion. From then on, the direct producers did not only have no say in the use of the surplus, they also had to give up a part of the surplus in favour of the creditors. (While the debt service between 1980 and 1989 exceeded the amount of the loans taken out, the country's debts nearly doubled.) Directly or indirectly, the creditors decided on the use of a large part of the retained surplus. Thereby the Hungarian economy — irrespective of its form of ownership — has in fact become part of the capitalist economic order.

On the surface, the change of political power took place only in 1989-1990. Most of those, however, who possessed direct political power in the last stage were themselves advocates of the private ownership-based market economy (although some of them called this formation "democratic socialism") and took the most important steps in preparation for the actual establishment of such a system. There were no major differences between the views of those newly in power and those losing it in 1989-1990 as far as the model of society to be achieved was concerned. The change of political power constituting the actual turning point took place *gradually and continuously* from the early eighties. [5]

In the early eighties, when the economy was desperately balancing on the brink of direct collapse, radical market reforms and (initially partial, then more and more comprehensive) democratization measures were introduced. Appealing to the obvious crisis and enjoying the effective support of the external and internal representatives of the private ownership-based market economy, the disciples of market socialism seemed to grow in power. (Rezsö Nyers was returned to power, the reform-spirit of 1968 was re-awakened.) The adjective "socialist" in the slogan "socialist market economy" lost its meaningful content: its function was only to ensure political palatability for the establishment of the market economy. Willy-nilly, the representatives of weak socialism assisted in the passing over to capitalism. By that time, the reforms did not stabilize socialism anymore. The reforms undertaken produced no economic results whatsoever, but the reform ideology (praise of the profit principle, elevating individualism to the rank of a value in itself, denial of the rational economic role of the state) devastated even the remnants of the political legitimation of the system. *By the mid-eighties, the Hungarian economic crisis became irredeemable* internally. Parallel with this, the political reserves of the system were fully exhausted. Democratization (governed, on the part of some, by miscalculated tactical steps and by exceedingly well calculated ones on the part of others but certainly not by some kind of awakening to the nature of "true socialism") by then provided the means for the expression and organization of mass dissatisfaction against the system. Thus, a full-scale political crisis evolved, leading to a change of political power in the spring of 1990.

In view of the nature of the economic problems and the threat of the deployment of the credit weapon, stubborn resistance to creditors or attempts to halt the erosion of power by resolute means could have plunged the country into an economic and political catastrophe. The helplessness, the concessions one after the other and finally the virtually voluntary handing over of power to the forces supported by the creditors was partly rooted in this state of affairs. The fact that "maximal (democratic) socialism" had no coherent economic programme, that there was no adequate model for the economic arrangements of socialism, hit back again.

In Hungary, it was argued for a while whether the crisis was of external or internal origins. The system based on the expropriation of the process of accumulation is a system encumbered with serious inefficiencies, with severe deficiencies of political democracy and of social ownership. Nevertheless, the limitations do not render economic growth, modernization or the improvement of living standards within the framework of the system impossible, as was proved by the Hungarian experience of the 1960s. The fact that the economies of Eastern Europe lagged behind the private capitalist economies, that the technological gap widened between them, are phenomena characteristic of not the entire history of the system and they are valid not in all comparisons. The historical time period of 40 or 70 years is not sufficient to evaluate the actual potential of the system. The deficiencies of the system of accumulation, the constraints on its efficiency do not provide sufficient explanation for the disruption of the Hungarian (or East European) system. The failure of the system can only be understood if the inherent limitations of the system and the external and internal economic, political and strategic conditions and struggles are *jointly* taken into consideration. It is obvious today that it was the joint effect of the irrational system of accumulation and the financial-economic dependence on the West continuously increasing from the mid-seventies that led to the failure of socialism in Hungary. The internal system of accumulation wasted resources by using them suboptimally. International capital, on the other hand, withdrew significant resources from the economy, making good use of the debt burden resulting from the country's financial dependence. It was able to subordinate economic (and, to some extent, political) decision-making to its own interests. In the last analysis, international capital strangled the system of degenerate socialism by exploiting its economic power.[6]

II. *WHERE TO?*

With the change in political regime in 1989-1990, the first stage of a long social revolution came to an end.[7] The nature of political power did change, but not yet the nature of society. The transformation of the entire institutional and ideological structure of the state, of the social class structure, of the operational system of production and the economy, the relations of production and of the norms of human co-existence is just beginning.

Irrespective of the change of regime, the economy is in a position that it can remain operational only at the cost of extremely severe social sacrifices and the fundamental support of the creditors. [8] Struggles will shape the character of the new society about to be born: whether it will be *democratic or dictatorial*. The same struggles will also determine whether Hungarian capitalism will be one of stagnation, collapse or of modernization; whether society will tread the path of social cooperation or extreme antagonisms. The outcome is open. Right now, the question is not whether *ultimately* and in principle private ownership and democracy can be reconciled. Right now the question is whether it is possible to get to a system based on private ownership from one based on state ownership under democratic political conditions; whether *this* historic endeavour can be accomplished within the framework of democracy.

The historical experiences available are not too promising: in general, capitalism was born under dictatorships and the example of the newly industrialized countries — South Korea, Chile — confirm this. In addition, Eastern Europe only has had short spells of democracy. Many refer to the example of post-Franco Spain, but that can hardly be a valid comparison, as there was no need of the most painful social surgery, namely, the establishment of a new class of owners. Is it possible to do things differently here and now? Perhaps it does make a difference to the world and particularly to Western Europe that Eastern Europe houses political democracy rather than dictatorship or unstable regimes.

But even this may be insufficient if the historic programme, the establishment of capitalism itself produces such social conflicts and shocks that the democratic institutions cannot manage. The institutional system of democracy is threatened not by the former ruling elite that lost its power, nor by the unfavourably affected working class. Democracy is threatened by capitalism itself. The social burdens concomitant with the transition are heavy: the elevation of certain strata takes place at the expense of others, at the cost of the absolute impoverishment of many. This is exacerbated by the existing economic crisis and by political passions. It may well be that at the end of the twentieth century, in Eastern Europe, capitalism can only be created through dictatorial means. Irrespective of whether or not the leading politicians of the present Government have an affinity to dictatorship, they may be forced into a dictatorial regime. If they are unwilling to succumb to this, the de-stabilized conditions can easily elevate others, more willing, to replace them.

New Administration, New Ideology

The present Government is justified in talking about a democratic change in power and of new state power of democratic origins. From the point of view of breaking the monopoly of economic and political decision-making, the *institutional and legal framework* at least does not contain institutions or rules that would impede the social control of the state. Indeed, its main elements had already been established through the self-reforming attempts of actually-existing socialism. There is a Government elected by universal suffrage by secret ballot responsible to Parliament, there is a Constitutional Court to guarantee constitutionality, there is a Supreme Audit Office, there is a political philosophy attributing high value to democracy, etc. The laws limiting the freedom of citizens, prohibiting the exercise of basic freedoms, were declared null and void. These are highly valuable, great achievements of the most recent period. Without all of these, a democratic state cannot exist.

History, however, amply shows examples of how popular movements based on the free expression of will still created dictatorial systems, and/or how the democratic institutions were turned into the instruments of narrow group interests. Democracy is a *practice* of politics aimed at bringing about a synthesis among social groups with different social interests and at preventing the exclusive power of any social group. From this point of view, Hungarian democracy is very fragile. The institutional system and the actual practice of politics are not synchronized. Hungarian society leads a double life: forces of democracy and anti-democracy are fighting one another. The result, for the time being, is a peculiar mixture of democratic and anti-democratic relations.

Life has never been grey or drab in Hungary; now it has become strikingly colourful. Innumerable new organizations, clubs, publications, public fora, all based on voluntary activity, have come into being. The scope of personal choice has greatly extended as far as political erudition and self-expression are concerned. These are, however, engulfed by a stream of petty accusations, hatred and lack of cooperation, covering everything from high politics to everyday life. The difference between the economic and political philosophies of the parliamentary parties is not so great as to justify the degree of animosity that has evolved between them. (*Every* parliamentary party shares the objective of the implementation of a private ownership-based market economy. Every parliamentary party advocates democracy and urges that the victims of the social changes be supported.) In addition to the lack of democratic traditions, this is also due to the fact that a number of new organizations would like to expropriate democratic institutions and to use them for the exclusion of minorities, of those having a different opinion. It is possible that what will emerge from this discordance will be an unstable "democracy" unable to come to a consensus or cooperate, governed by narrow party interests, a "Balkan Hungary" of petty reckoning and hatred. The democratic institutions are already frequently proving to be not the guarantees, but the instruments and fora of social division. Some of these institutions — particularly some of the institutions of economic democracy — function only in part; many important decisions are not even submitted to the democratic institutions and are made without granting a hearing to those concerned.

For the partisans of the old regime and even for those who used to enjoy higher positions in the past regime, the new system already presents certain dictatorial traits. They are being driven out of public life and their jobs through the means of awakening animosities, intimidation, denunciation, internal "cold war". Parallel with this, a wide range of senior and junior leading positions can be filled only under the condition of subscribing to a certain mentality — that of a "Christian-Hungarian" market economy — but mainly under that of loyalty to the new political power. It was in this spirit that the transformation of the direct state administration and the accelerated replacement of the entire managing and executive staff of economic and social institutions began.

Since the spring of 1990, the development of the executive apparatus of the new political power, the actual transformation of state administration and the replacement of the old staff with adherents of its own has been going on at a fast rate. These replacements have already reached the lower levels of the central administration. The new government did not wish to collaborate with a significant part of the old apparatus. Yet it did not have an expert staff of its own, having received strikingly little support from professionals, especially those with an expertise in state administration. Consequently, many people have been elevated to high positions in the civil service from total obscurity, without any professional experience. In 1948, it was workers without expertise who, on the basis of the principle of loyalty to the communist party, were put into executive positions in the economy, the army, the police forces and state administration. Now, in 1990, the same thing is happening, except the difference is that the high school teacher is made deputy to the Minister of Education, or the university lecturer is made deputy to the Minister of Defence.

The picture of the "squirearchic" Hungary of the past also emerges from the staff replacements so far carried out. A characteristic feature of these replacements is the exceedingly great role played by political considerations and personal relationships at the expense of professional considerations. Staff replacements executed for political and personal reasons by far exceed the extent and range needed for the establishment of the "necessary loyalty": what is happening is the conquest of the state at the expense of professional expertise. Traditional relations of personal dependence, patronage, mutual obligations and favours, elements of personal/political revenge can all be found behind the personnel changes made in the course of the transformation of both high and lower level civil service. It seems there is a petty, base contest going on even within the ruling parties for lucrative posts, for high positions in government, for giving relatives and friends fat jobs. Consequently, the professional standard of the civil service and its democratic character, its willingness to engage in dialogue with society, show a deterioration in comparison to the previous two decades.

The present regime defines itself as a right-of-centre system. Democracy, patriotic sentiments, Christianity, individual freedom and charity are the positive values to which the predominant ideology refers. The negative values include the rejection of dictatorship and of the idea and practice of "collectivity". The actual ideology permeating everyday life is a conservative nationalism mixed with anti-communism. In a number of its practical manifestations, this nationalism is of the culturally inward-looking kind, paranoid and arrogant. There are striking tendencies of racism and hatred of foreigners.

National problems are elevated above virtually all other social problems, or rather virtually all social problems appear in the guise of a national issue. Amidst the re-emerging prejudice against ethnic minorities, the national interests of Hungarians keep being presented as suffering from the discrimination of other nations: Hungarians belonging to the European civilization are allegedly threatened by non-Hungarians in and outside the country. [9] Stalin's fortress under siege is replaced by the thesis of the nation under siege. This nationalism is conservative not only because it increases animosity between nations, but also because of its domestic social role. Just as in Stalin's case, the threat from outside provides a basis of reference for the implementation of domestic political endeavours. Threatened Hungarians will have to defend themselves. And the best way to defend themselves is to rally round the national programme of the Government.

Nationalism is the main force that keeps the power-bloc together and links it to society. This ideology has credibility and actual support. Due to the undervaluation of national consideration earlier amidst a pseudo-internationalism, there are significant masses backing the Government's conservative nationalism. Yet this nationalism is also a general social straitjacket, containing within it the germs of a nation-based totalitarianism. The Government is the representative of the national interests hence whoever stands up for national interests will also have to stand up for the Government. That is how the programme of capitalism becomes a national cause, the programme of all Hungarians and the voluntary acceptance of the burdens concomitant with capitalism becomes a positive sacrifice made in the interest of the nation. The slogan of 1956 is valid in a twofold sense: "Whoever is Hungarian will side with us." In practice, however, the excluding sense of the slogan is also present: those who do not side with us are not Hungarians. Those who are not for the ruling party, are not true Hungarians. Every political action taken against the power-bloc, be that an article in a newspaper or a manifestation of the protection of workers' interests, is interpreted as an action against the nation, against society. Thus it was possible in October 1990 for political leaders to sing the National Anthem waving the national tricolour while condemning the demonstration of the taxi-drivers protesting the petrol price increases as a crime against the nation.

This nationalism, however, has still not addressed the gravest real problems of Hungarian sovereignty. Sometimes it seems that the politicians of the Government are more concerned about having the name of a street inscribed in Hungarian in the Hungarian-populated sectors of Slovakia than with handling the problems arising from the Hungarian economy being at the mercy of external forces. The Government has no clear-cut ideas on how to restore the country's economic sovereignty so fatally reduced due to the debt crisis. Nor, apart from the declaration of a few general principles, can any one see what the Government's intentions are in relation to foreign capital investment. It is simply not known in what areas, to what extent and at what terms the Government would encourage foreign ownership in Hungary.

The Revolution of the Social Structure

In the course of the past few years, J. K. Galbraith has warned many times that if Eastern Europe was to re-create the conditions of classical capitalism at the end of the twentieth century, it will be bitterly disappointed. On the other hand, Janos Kornai says that the only way to grow into modern capitalism is to do that in an organic way, that is, the classical stage of capitalism cannot be avoided. Both are right.

The new regime implies a new social class structure. The political annihilation of the old proprietors of political power as a power, is an accomplished fact. There is, however, no new ruling class born. This is a highly peculiar, transitory state of affairs in which *there is a capitalist state (or, at least, a state that proclaims the restoration of capitalism as its political programme), but there is no capitalist class.* Within the revolution of state structure and of consciousness, a political superstructure is evolving which has no supporting beams within the structure of society. It follows that this political power is quite shaky. It is only now, after the event, that the socio-structural revolution is beginning that will lead to the evolution of a stable capitalist class. It is now that it is to be determined, who shall partake of the new ruling class — and this can also stabilize political power.

The "capitalist class" is of course a generalization: it is the common denominator of certain competing social groups. The opportunity to become an owner on a small scale is more or less given, but the economic and financial conditions for the fast evolution of private ownership on a large scale are missing. To this extent, Hungarian political power is presumably going to rely on a petit bourgeois capitalist class in the foreseeable future. Even if the Government's plans are realized and within 3 years the share of state-held assets will be reduced to below 50% of the total from the present 90%, it is quite likely that the largest enterprises (making the highest losses) will continue to be state-owned for a long time.

As a result of the Government's economic policy opening the gates of private capitalization, many of the present small-scale entrepreneurs and wage earners will turn into owners on small or even medium scale. The personal savings needed for this are available and they can be supplemented by preferential loans provided by the Government. At the level of the present small owners, primitive accumulation of capital is taking place according to the classic rules: making large fortunes out of small ones, using all possible means. Economic policy and economic ideology place the emphasis on removing the barriers in the way of the free development of capital, rather than on institutionalized agreements to secure a cooperative relationship between capital and labour. One worker turned (small) factory owner expressed this with some exaggeration by saying in a newspaper interview that there is no need for a trade union, that the best trade union is the market itself. There are no moral constraints or unwritten rules limiting the endeavour to become rich; all means are permitted. This is happening within a culture in which written rules, contractual agreements have not had much of a weight or social value in the past; thus finding loopholes and evasion of the law have been all the more esteemed. Some of the luckiest, most aggressive new entrepreneurs could soon become owners on a large scale. Nevertheless, owing to the limitations of the financial capacity of this stratum, they cannot become the owners of the concentrated capital assets of the state within the foreseeable future. The question is not who the ice parlour on the corner belongs to, but who the dairy plant belongs to. To buy the dairy plant and the bauxite mine, the savings of the past are not enough, not even with domestic and foreign government loans. There are individual savings of several tens of billion forints against the state assets valued at several thousand billion forints. [10]

The formation of the class of large-scale capitalists in Eastern Europe will have to differ from the classic manner, primarily because large capital does not need to be created: accumulated capital is there, in a materialized form, held by the state. *There is capital, but there is no capitalist class to go with it.* The previous state had, more or less successfully, accomplished the task of the original accumulation of capital. The capitalist class will come into being by simply transferring the assets of the state into private hands. In this sense, there is neither original accumulation of capital, nor organic capitalist development. The historical situation does, however, show some traits of kinship with that of the classical capitalism to the extent that privatization at the end of the twentieth century leads to the coming into being of a new ruling class the same way as industrialization produced a new ruling class in the nineteenth century. The social role of the original accumulation of capital was not merely to create the physical assets, but also to select the ruling elite possessing economic power. At the time of classical capitalism, this went hand in hand with the creation of new bases of production. This will be omitted this time. Yet, the selection of a new ruling group will be no less dramatic and shocking than the one two hundred years ago. The conflicts could be particularly great because no clear-cut archetypes, social outlines of the new capitalist class exist within the inherited class structure of society. The merchant capitalists and manufacturers of the period of the West European original capital accumulation, or the land owners turning capitalists of Central Eastern Europe are missing here. *Based on their accumulated wealth, no social group is* ab ovo *predestined to constitute the new capitalist class.*

The epochal question today is what social groups and on what basis will have access to the presently accumulated state assets. Two points can be stated right at the outset. Firstly, a social fight is going to ensue for capitalization and for social elevation. Secondly, *capitalism is being formed in such a manner that the state is urgently "founding" its capitalist class* because, in view of the given state of the social structure and the economic power relations, this issue cannot be decided as a result of the "free economic selection of the fittest". Capitalization cannot wait until the small capitals that already exist or are being born are moulded into a capitalist class in a fair economic competition according to the rules of the market. Or, to make use of a Marxian paraphrase turned upside down, if we were to postpone the privatization of the large scale enterprises until the amount needed is accumulated as a result of the efforts of individual small entrepreneurs, Hungary would be characterized by the predominance of the state sector even in the first decades of the next millennium.

A class structure adequate to the new political system and concentrated economic power can be established only in an artificial manner, directed from above and from outside the economy. The representatives of the new political power speedily tried to find the positive (and negative) moral and other criteria on the basis of which certain individuals would be more entitled to have access to the state assets than others.[11] On the whole, however, the behaviour of the state in assisting the creation of a new capitalist class is not unambiguous and predictable. The groups that could be considered as in some way eligible to constitute the new capitalist class are not in fact eligible for political reasons; other groups, on the other hand, do not have a chance. It is the managers of state enterprises that stand in the focus of the public debates on capitalization.

The Government elected in the spring of 1990 came into power in an extremely difficult economic situation, but with a relatively strong political hinterland. In such a situation, economic rationality and the considerations related to upholding the operationality of the economy should urge the Government to co-operate with the managerial stratum. Their experience, their command of the technical skills required in large-scale undertakings, their knowledge of the market, of their foreign and domestic partners all provide strong grounds for this. Western investors have also learnt to appreciate the qualities of the Hungarian managers. The possession of business information, the knowledge of new business opportunities arising from existing business contacts, constitute an intangible capital that, although not appearing as purchasing power expressed in money terms, renders it possible that the existing managerial stratum could become the most successful capitalist class. There are many examples of managers who, making use of market freedom and the somewhat chaotic regulations, have played the assets of the state enterprise they managed into their own hands, well below their market value.

Trusting the favourable political climate in the early summer of 1990, the new government, pushed by its own right-wing, started off a campaign against the "communist managers" with the unconcealed intention to replace the managers with those who would be more in line with the interests of the new elite. As soon as this replacement is carried out, the prevention of the capitalization of the managers would not be expedient from the point of view of the powers that be. The political rationalization given to questioning the legitimacy of the managers was the consistent reckoning with the old regime. It was argued that the change of system could not be complete while the appointees of the old regime were still in place. (It was not taken into account that in the course of the past two decades, political considerations lost most of their validity in the selection of enterprise managers. Since 1985, directors in most enterprises have been elected by the so-called enterprise councils consisting of the representatives of the employees and of the managers. External actors had little formal or practical influence on determining the person of the executive.) According to the moderate wording of Prime Minister Antall, the Government seeks to have partners loyal to the new political power in the leading economic posts. To achieve this, the Government ordered that all enterprise managers be reviewed, that is, that they be subjected to a kind of political vote of confidence.

Managers were replaced first in those enterprises where they had during the old regime been appointed by the central government. (These are the largest undertakings, playing a key role in the economy.) The general experience of these centrally initiated replacements was that it was not the "communist managers" that were replacced by entrepreneur-technocrats but the other way round: semi-managers were frequently replaced by non-managers. The political dismissal of the managers inherited from the old regime is going on, but the new power has no technocrats capable of assuming manage-ment assignments. Consequently, many of the new enterprise leaders have little or no business experience or management skills. It seems that foreign capital is coming to view the ensuing insecurity and occasional fall in standards in an unfavourable way. [12]

The Government's endeavours to displace the old managers did not get very far in any case. Enterprise councils refused to confirm only some 25% of the old directors in their office. The general political atmosphere, local political vendettas, personal ambitions, and motives of individual revenge might have suggested the radical replacement of the old managers. The system of review through the enterprise councils, however, also gave a chance to an approach starting out from the actual economic-professional realities, as well as allowed those enterprise councils that had been the tools of the managers in the past to vote for continuity. The moderates in the ruling majority obviously reckoned with this possibility, too. Ultimately, the forces of destabilization were not strong enough to turn the majority of the enterprise councils against the managers.

The Government must now either make peace with the managers of the old regime and resign itself to the fact that they will constitute a part of the new capitalist class; or, by continuing to press for the replacement of the old managers, run the risk of considerable economic and political instability. The scandals around the forced dismissals, the demonstrations of sympathy for the dismissed directors, the resignation of many senior managers out of solidarity for the dismissed director can lead to the disintegration of the economy as much as the local campaigns and strikes against the "communist director". Only peace between the Government and the managerial stratum can give a chance for relative social peace and avoiding political-economic chaos. Some of the political forces in power may be inclined to make peace, having seen the results of the local elections and of the unsuccessful manager replacement campaign.

Yet the political risks of making peace are considerable. With inflation almost getting out of hand, collapsing traditional markets, a shrinking domestic market due to falling purchasing power, the Government will be forced to take restrictive measures that might make potential investors uncertain, might frighten off those who want to go into business. The Government has little chance of solving the crisis without external help, even with the most radical measures. If, in addition to all this, the Government were to realize that it has to rely on the experts of the past regime if it wants the economy to function, the small holders, the petite bourgeoisie who helped the Government into power in the hope of a speedily completed system-change and becoming rich fast, will certainly be disappointed because of the "compromises" of the Government. And this might open the way to authoritarian solutions permitting much less social resistance to the decisions of the Government. (The taxi-drivers blockade in October can be evaluated as a manifestation of this disappointment.) Political forces highly inclined towards such solutions are already present in Hungary. The extreme anti-communism of some could easily turn into the basis of a "consistent and all embracing change of systems", i.e.: dictatorship. The prolongation and eventual worsening of the economic crisis could give further impetus to those standing up against the moderates who dare to "enter into collusion with the communists" and increase the chances of the emergence of a "legitimate" dictatorship.

Who Pays the Bill?

The state of the economy has deteriorated since the change in power, with dramatically increasing unemployment and inflation getting out of hand. The prospects opened up for individuals by the developing market economy are counterbalanced by the significant worsening in the position of wage earners. Still, small ventures are sprouting up like mushrooms and these give a chance of speedy financial rise to many wage-earners as well. The question of *individual* life prospects is formulated by many as follows: setting up in business implies the possibility of rising socially and financially, while remaining a worker means uncertainty, deterioration of their present position and, for some social strata, actual impoverishment. In a society where the split between the well-off and the poor is widening by the hour, the question of who will be a winner and who a loser pervades everything. The experiences of setting up in business also reveal that is not merely a matter of free choice. The myth of the "worker-capitalism" of tens of thousands of flourishing small ventures entered by all who wish to according to their free volition, is beginning to be shattered. The free competition of performance capabilities is made illusory precisely by the unequal access to capital goods. As an entrepreneurial stratum is in the process of being established, a new wall, made up of the bricks of unequal possession of capital assets, is also being built around it. Only a few, and only under certain conditions, will soon be able to penetrate that wall. The self-sustaining, exclusive nature of the entrepreneurial sphere implies that the vast majority of the wage earners will be condemned to remaining wage earners.

In the present situation, the upcoming entrepreneurs can improve their own position only at the expense of the wage-earners. The economic crisis in any case implies a general reduction of real wages and a severe weakening of job security; the social transition, however, causes a deterioration in the position of the wage earners irrespective of the economic crisis. The creation of the capitalist class leads to the re-distribution of the current national income away from the wage-earners and to the weakening and, in certain cases, the closing down of the welfare institutions. A part of the social surplus product appearing in the form of the tax revenues of the state is used to support private enterprise. In this way, the social costs of the creation of the capitalist class is paid for through the reduced consumption of the direct producers. The reduction of real wages is not yet counter-balanced by the output increased through the better utilization of privatized state assets that could offset the disadvantageous effects.

A few illustrative examples could throw some light on the above statements. There are two conflicting economic policy priorities: in the economic crisis monetary policy should, in general, be restrictive; but it should be expansive where privatization is concerned. It follows that monetary policy has to restrict especially the outflow of money in the other spheres, particularly in the area of wage increases. The credit lines set aside for privatization reduce the amount of credit available for other purposes (thus also consumption). With a given average interest rate level, the preferential interest charged on the privatization loans implies higher interests on all other loans.

The change in ownership does not necessarily go with increased output and improved efficiency. Therefore the direct impact of the tax concessions promised and given in the interests of privatization is a loss of tax revenue. This, in turn, leads to necessary cuts in budgetary expenditures which results in the increased devaluation of the social benefits and the termination of certain welfare expenditures. It is not just that the real value of the welfare expenditures is decreasing; they also give preferences to different groups, in line with the predominant political values. Referring to the uncontrollably high expenditures of social security and to the intention of doing away with the privileges of the past regime, the Government terminated the supplementary pension granted to the families of the one-time "political martyrs". (Most of the beneficiaries had been persecuted by fascism or were widows of poets and writers of national fame abducted to the concentration camps.) Yet at the same time, the Hungarian POWs of World War II have been promised a supplementary pension as of 1991!

It is mainly the wage earners who are the most defenceless against inflation, generated in part also by privatization. Their defenceless-ness is also related to the fact that the conditions provided for the expansion of capital include not only a direct re-distribution of incomes, but also the weakening of the institutions of workers' representation. The Government has, in fact, driven the represen-tative organizations of the workers out of macro-level decision making; it operates the institutions of interest reconciliation only to prevent acute crises and has reduced consultations to a minimum in comparison with the previous period. The formal decision has been made to terminate the enterprise councils. This extinguishes a potential local institution of social partnership.

For most wage-earners, there is no alternative to a private ownership-based market economy. But workers have no organized political representation that would even be able to ensure at least that the burdens concomitant with capitalization be reduced to a minimum. The working class is lonely: it has lost its confidence in socialism, which is not surprising in view of the deficiencies of degenerate socialism, while all it gets from the new system is difficulties. Who can they trust? Perhaps they can hope that sooner or later, through spontaneous protest movements arising with the deteriorating living conditions, they will be able to organize themselves, to set up their own organizations and to outline a more cooperative system that could be an alternative to both capitalism and its Christian-nationalist, Hungarian version.

NOTES

1. Weak-incomplete-minimal socialism means that the immanent essence of socialism is unable to unfold. The indigenous social constraints resulting from the system of accumulation bar the way to social ownership and democracy. Unless we share the (neo)classical paradigm, according to which the free assertion of the particular interests is a precondition of the assertion of the public interest, the subordination of the social production process to particular, microeconomic interests (irrespective of whether particularity is embodied in self-governing communities, powerful company managers or individual capitalists) also implies the predominance and rule of the particular interest of the social groups expressing them. In social practice, this is embodied in the direct conflict between the profit objectives (and the social groups representing them) and the wage interests (and the social groups representing them), in the competition for the surplus. Through exercising the power arising from their monopoly in decision-making, the representatives of the profit objectives have a good chance of winning this fight. To this extent, weak socialism shares many of the characteristics of private ownership-based capitalism, even if they differ so far as the form of ownership is concerned.

2. In 1966, the party document endorsing the principles of the Hungarian economic mechanism, argued for the need for market reforms by reference to the self-regulating ability of the market. The idea of subjecting the state to real social control was not even raised in most of the tenets criticizing the role of the state.

3. A part of Hungary's debt consists of ordinary private bank-loans; another part of the debt, however, was borrowed from governments or from private institutes under strong government influence. Service on the debt rose from $1.9b. in 1980 to $2.6b. in 1985 to $3.4b. in 1989. The trade balance showed a deficit through most of the period. As a result of the additional loans taken out to repay the interest, the total debt of the country virtually doubled in these ten years.

4. The statement made by President Bush in the summer of 1989 in Budapest, according to which the United States would aid the market reforms and the upholding of the operationality of the Hungarian economy with a sum of $25 million, seemed almost like open cynicism. Hungary's debt at the time amounted to 700-800 times the sum offered.

5. In the 21-23 years preceding the change in power in 1989/1990, but particularly in the past 6-7 years, a great deal has happened in the establishment of the institutional and legal framework of a market economy. Hungary acceded to a number of international economic organizations and multilateral economic agreements (e.g. GATT, IMF); the issuing and commercial banking functions were separated and profit-oriented merchant banks were set up; the legal regulations pertaining to private economic activity based on the association of capital were enacted; the legal framework for transforming state enterprises into companies was put in place; gradually the central controllers were divested of virtually all property rights; several institutions of the capital market were set up (Stock Exchange, regulations pertaining to companies engaged in the purchase and sale of securities); the institutional system of unemployment benefits and re-training were established; a law was enacted to regulate strikes, etc.

6. The scenarios of the failure of socialism in Hungary and in Poland were very similar. If, however, the debt-trap is substituted by the arms race, the social crisis of the Soviet Union is also presented in a different light. The arms race — entered into by the Soviet Union partly due to its own decision and partly as a result of the long term political-economic strategy of Western powers — played

the same kind of major net resource withdrawing role as the debt crisis. Consequently, growth slowed down, the resources put towards the arms build-up proved to be too much of a burden in this inefficient, wasteful system and finally, at the time of the neutron bomb and Star Wars, the arms build-up could only be financed at the cost of a severe reduction of living standards. From then on, the unfolding of a full-scale political crisis was only a matter of time.

7.   Since the elections in the spring of 1990, Hungary has been ruled by a three-party coalition government. (The most powerful party in the coalition is the Hungarian Democratic Forum, the other two participants are the Smallholders Party and the Christian Democratic Peoples' Party.) The programme of the coalition parties focuses on political democracy and on the so-called "social market economy" based on private ownership. The private ownership-based market economy has no alternative for any of the organized political forces of significance. The electoral and social base of the governing coalition consists of the already existing entrepreneurs and small-scale manufacturers and the social groups aspiring or responsive to such values. It seems most of their votes came from these circles and from rural Hungary, especially from the rural intelligentsia representing traditional values (national identity, Christian values). Accordingly, the Government programme published in the summer of 1990 reckoned with several tens of thousand new small entrepreneurs by the end of the year. A career as a small entrepreneur, and the value system of the market economy, are popular among the workers, too. Without a large number of votes from the working class, the present coalition could not have come into power.

8.   With the given forces of production and irrespective of the nature of the system of accumulation, the export revenues that could at least prevent a further increase in the national debt cannot be produced. This circumstance is a major constraint on the functioning of the market economy about to be born. The conditions whereby the increase in national debt could at all be stopped could only be created through foreign capital investments of truly radical magnitudes. Lacking this, we can envisage the following scenarios: the new Hungarian market economy is going to writhe under the weight of the debt burden just like the previous system in the past fifteen years; the Government will be forced to re-schedule and the creditors will show understanding; the creditors will cancel some of Hungary's debt.

9.   In the summer of 1990, a one-time officer of the Horthy army (under the communist regime he had been reduced in his rank, but recently re-instated as General) said in Parliament — with the silent approval of government politicians — that the Hungarian army with its voluntary (sic!) war against the Soviet Union in World War II, was in fact defending the country and European civilization against the spreading of Bolshevism.

    A prominent representative of the leading party of the governing coalition wrote in an article that liberal Jewish intellectuals in Hungary are attempting to intellectually assimilate the nine-and-a-half million Hungarians.

10.   According to 1987 data, the household saving deposits (including the amounts saved for housing purposes, durable consumer goods, illness and old age) of the country amount to HUF 300 billion. The reduction of real incomes, the negative real interest rate and the inflation climbing higher year after year certainly do not encourage individual savings. The amount actually available for investment is only a fraction even of this.

11.   One of the governing parties came to be part of the coalition Government with an election programme stating that in return for the injustice suffered, the one-time smallholders and their heirs should be given back the lands that were taken away from them since 1947 without compensation.

12.   Recently, the Government appointed a performing artist to replace the director

(who used to be a member of the Communist Party and, according to some, was of Jewish origin) of a flourishing, profitable enterprise of international reputation producing and distributing art products. The most outstanding representatives of the artistic community protested against the unfounded, autocratic decision. Within a week, a leading multinational company that was about to set up a joint venture with the Hungarian enterprise in question with an investment of $15 million, rescinded the contract because of the change in management.

NICARAGUA: A REVOLUTION THAT FELL FROM THE GRACE OF THE PEOPLE

Carlos M. Vilas

for Anna

1. *Facts and perceptions*

The Sandinista Revolution inspired an abundant literature — although its quality was uneven. Analyses employing social science research methods and aspiring to reach a balanced view, stood side by side with texts that stressed the need for solidarity with a country suffering brutal aggression from the United States. The opening of Nicaragua's frontiers to anyone who wanted to come and see things for themselves created a situation in which thousands of people paid short visits and produced innumerable articles, pamphlets and books. Even academics with no direct knowledge of the revolution assumed their right to make assertions about the Sandinista revolution, its achievements and its limitations, on the basis of general ideas and *a priori* schemes.[1] But quantity did not signify quality, and often the pressure of solidarity, or the desire to figure in the bibliography on the subject, inhibited a more realistic and objective analysis of an extremely complex process plagued with specific problems as all revolutionary processes are.

The coincidence in time of the electoral defeat of the Sandinistas with the collapse of state socialism in Eastern Europe and the crisis in the Soviet Union allowed some to address the Nicaraguan events in terms of the same framework of meanings or at least as part of the same universal progress towards democracy[2] — a view that was ultimately supported by the self-serving discourse of some Sandinista leaders. Nevertheless, any observer who has been able to rise above the waves of opportunism and crude thinking that course through the majority of analyses of the problems of the current period will see that the two situations are entirely different. Apart from attempts to establish commercial, diplomatic and cultural relations with the contries of Comecon, there is nothing in the present or the recent past of Nicaragua — whether in its socio-economic structure, its political processes, the configuration of its social classes or its popular culture — that bears any relation to "actually existing socialism". In any event, the notion that Nicaragua had embarked on a "transition to socialism" was always a questionable hypothesis.[3]

The reasons for the electoral defeat of the Sandinistas have been discussed by the FSLN itself[4] as well as by other observers and analysts.[5] Their documents have addressed the multiplicity of factors that affected the election results, and which derive as much from the specific features of these elections and the conditions under which they took place as from their immediate national and international socio-economic and political context and the effects of nearly a decade of counterrevolutionary aggression.

I do not intend in this essay to rehearse those issues again; instead I want to address some broader aspects of the revolutionary process in Nicaragua, aspects which had begun to make themselves felt long before the elections of 1990, and which in fact conditioned the circumstances in which voting took place. I would stress in particular the fact that by the mid-1980s the revolution became bogged down in ways which I have discussed in earlier writings.[6] This was intimately connected with the war and the regional economic crisis, but also with the way in which both were dealt with by the leaders of the revolution. For they gave priority to strengthening alliances with employers' and landowners' groups at the expense of the organisational independence of the working masses, workers and peasants, and maintenance of their living standards. It was these sectors who bore the brunt of the war effort, both in terms of physical participation in the conflict, and of paying its socio-economic costs. There was not an equal distribution of effort across the whole of society — as the Sandinista leaders themselves acknowledged.[7]

The war and the confrontation with the United States government were taken out of their socio-political and ultimately class context, which had been explicitly recognised during the early years of the revolutionary process; Sandinista perspectives relegated social transformations and the central role of the masses to a secondary level.[8] In these circumstances, it became increasingly difficult for people to perceive the popular content of the political project which was the target of the counterrevolutionary assault. Even more importantly, the preference given by the government to reaching agreements with employers' groups and the international community, together with the unequal distribution of rewards and sacrifices between the elites and the masses, contributed to the dilution of many aspects of the popular democratic project that had defined the early measures of the revolutionary regime. In 1984, the FSLN won the elections despite the high intensity counterrevolutionary war, because there was a high intensity revolution under way which left no doubt as to what was at stake; in 1990 the elections were lost despite the fact that the armed conflict had diminished, for the revolution too had drawn back from the intensity of earlier years.

As the political and in particular the class content of the anti-imperialist struggle became less and less visible, that struggle was increasingly transformed into a conflict between governments sustained by the sacrifices of the masses — the dead, the wounded, the communities forced to resettle in new locations, the families divided against themselves —. Under these conditions, popular criticism of concrete aspects of government policy and of the behaviour of government bureaucrats, together with demands for an end to the war, coincided more closely with the political discourse of the opposition and were ultimately translated into votes against the Sandinistas. In the context of an increasing demobilization of the masses, the gulf between the rhetoric of the highest levels of the Sandinista government, who kept up a resounding anti-American rhetoric and continued to affirm the socialist direction of the revolution, and the content and actual achievements of government strategies and policies became an abyss.[9] The rhetoric reached the outside world and had an impact on the international scene, but the real character of the policies had its effect within the country. The gulf between the two helps to explain the high level of external solidarity which the Sandinista government enjoyed right up to the end, while a significant part of its internal support had been eroded. The surprise of many of the actors and the external observers at the electoral defeat of February 25th 1990 derives in large part from this divorce between reality and perception.

2. National liberation, democracy and social transformation

The Sandinista experience is testimony to the enormous difficulties faced by democratic and national liberation revolutions in peripheral, poor and backward countries, of passing from an antidictatorial phase based on broad alliances, to a phase of deep social and political transformations. The second phase involves a redefinition in popular class terms of the direction of the revolutionary process; it is a transition in which there is a close correspondence between the popular effort that is decisive in ensuring the political victory and the maintenance of the revolution, and the content and perspectives of the policies promoted by the revolutionary regime. These difficulties arise first and foremost from the structural characteristics of such societies, but also from the way in which they are addressed by the political organisations leading the process of change.

The principal factor is the particular class structure that has arisen in the underdeveloped capitalism of Central America. The polarisation of bourgeoisie and proletariat occurring in developed capitalism is weak in the agrarian societies of Central America, and the social structure is dominated by a large and highly differentiated mass of peasants, indigenous communities, seasonal labourers, and the urban petty bourgeoisie. The contradiction between the development of the productive forces and the structure of the relations of production which in Marx's view produced the conditions for the development of social revolutions is of little relevance to the majority of Central American societies. In any event, their revolutionary potentiality does not refer to the overcoming of capitalism, but rather to different modes of capitalist development and modernization. Furthermore, the contradiction previously referred to is articulated with others that do not necessarily arise in the sphere of production: the question of national liberation, for example, or the struggle to establish a democratic order. [10]

In these societies the working class is small, has little experience of organization, is still developing and continues to maintain strong links with the peasantry and the artisans; to say the very least, their capacity to lead the process of social transformation is problematic. In the context of the revolution the working class progressively gains political maturity, but this process occurs within the framework of alliances and conflicts with other groups and fractions that dispute their leadership of that process, though from an equally fragile position. The initial multiclass character of these revolutionary processes, based on the demand for democracy and national liberation, and the close articulation of democratic struggles with projects for structural transformation and a new relationship with the external world, turn the revolution into a theatre of internal tensions and confrontations between the social groups who participated in the struggle against the dictatorship.

In such conditions, the extension of democracy into the field of socio-economic relations and access to resources produces major tensions, aggravated by the vulnerability that is the result at a number of levels of backwardness and underdevelopment. The reciprocal weakness of the groups in conflict tends to generate a style of political leadership relatively separate from the direct social actors. The "vanguard" presents itself as the administrator of the interests of the popular classes until such time as they reach maturity; but in practice they take on the political role attributed to the fundamental social actors. The situation moves from one of leadership as representation to leadership as substitution. It is usually sectors of the urban petty bourgeoisie who assume that role, but in societies as backward as those of Central America, it is not uncommon to find elements of the bourgeoisie deeply embedded in organizations committed to social transformation and seeking to impose their perspectives and conceptions from within the camp of the revolution and the state.

To pass from a perspective that limits the revolution to the substitution of one government by another by non-institutional means, to one that looks to transformations in the class relations of political and economic power means that the struggle for democracy must penetrate the very social structure, with a consequent intensification of conflict between groups and sectors that had all participated in the revolution. The alliances that made a revolutionary victory possible later conspired against its progress towards more advanced stages of political and economic change. This combination of factors imposed on the revolution a slow and generally protracted development through time. [11]

On the other hand the global backwardness of the society, its low level of technology, the organizational inexperience of the workers and peasants, the monopoly of scientific and technical knowledge by small segments of the dominant classes, further called into question viability of alternative development strategies based on broad popular participation. You learn to participate by participating, but the process itself demands additional effort, overtime working, sleepless nights. Learning to participate is a slow business, and requires disposable time, a rare commodity given the urgent tasks imposed by increasing international tensions and above all the counter-revolutionary war. This often leads in its turn to an accelerated centralization of decision-making and a sharp separation between the leadership — where the presence of petty bourgeois and bourgeois elements may be particularly significant — and the masses, thus reproducing within the revolutionary camp a hierarchy of those who make decisions and those who carry them out. [12]

The second issue arises from changes in the international context of the Sandinista revolution. The victory of the FSLN in 1979 occurred in favourable external circumstances which gave the revolutionary regime broad and flexible economic and financial co-operation. As the pressures from the US government grew more intense, Nicaragua found strategic support for their programmes of social and economic transformation in the aid it received from the USSR, Cuba and other Comecon countries. Soviet military assistance provided the Sandinista army with material supplies which made a major contribution to the victory over the counterrevolution. When Mexico and Venezuela stopped supplying Nicaragua with oil, the USSR filled the gap.

The situation changed from 1987-88 onwards. The economic difficulties of the countries of Eastern Europe and the negotiations between the US and the USSR reduced the flow and the quantity of supplies, including military aid and the supply of oil. Finally the USSR decided to accept the North American strategy for a solution to the regional crisis which implied, among other things, the reentry of the "contras" into the Nicaraguan political scene and an end to the military activities of the Salvadorean guerrillas. On his visit to Nicaragua in October 1989, the Soviet foreign minister stressed the interest of the USSR in carrying out "bilateral monitoring" of the Central American crisis jointly with the United States.[13] At the end of the eighties the international space for processes of radical political and economic transformation in Central America was shrinking; in such conditions it was unlikely that the Sandinistas would return to their revolutionary perspectives of a decade earlier.

3. *Alliances, policies and tensions*

The FSLN believed that the struggle against the Somoza dictatorship would lead to profound transformations in property and power relations and in the articulation of new relations in the international system. Such a conception involved, among other things, a modification of the social and political alliances which had been the basis of the struggle against the dictatorship. It is clear that not all the groups and sectors who joined in that phase of the revolution were prepared to move from confrontation with the Somoza dictatorship to confrontation with the landowners and industrialists on whom the dictatorship had rested; nor did they share the FSLN's view of relations with the United States, the USSR, Europe or Cuba.

The early suspension of the revolutionary decrees providing for the nationalization of properties owned by the Somozas underlined how limited the anti-Somoza phase of the revolution had been, and how difficult it would be to pass from a simply institutional perception of the dictatorship to a socio-political one. It also demonstrated how far elements of the bourgeoisie, including many of those who had joined the struggle against the Somozas, had been involved with the dictatorship that the popular masses had just overthrown.[14] In this situation, a class perspective entailed high political costs, insofar as widening the confrontation with the Somoza dictatorship would threaten the social alliances that had provided the base for the final stages of the insurrectional struggle led by the Sandinistas.

The mounting conflict with the US government from 1981 onwards gave priority to the anti-imperialist, national liberation dimension of the revolution, but from a fundamentally defensive position. Without wishing to minimise the importance of the growing external articulations of the Sandinista regime with the USSR, Cuba and Comecon, and the practice of an active non-alignment, there is no doubt that defence against the counterrevolutionary war sponsored by the North American government became the central axis of an anti-imperialist project designed to ensure the survival of Nicaragua as an independent country; and this defence was to be conducted *on the basis of the*

social structure obtaining at that time, rather than by further transforming the socio-economic structure of the country in the interests of
the masses, hitting the local bourgeoisie and projecting the struggle
for democracy beyond the conventional political framework — as was
the case, for example, with the transition to socialism in Cuba.[15]

From 1984 onwards the Sandinista regime responded to the
intensification of economic and military aggression by seeking to
widen the social alliances on which it based itself, by including in the
alliance those elements of the agrarian, industrial and commercial
bourgeoisie who had remained in the country, and who opposed many
of the revolutionary policies aimed at achieving socio-economic
transformations. One has to recognise the relative success of this
strategy in terms of the ability of the Sandinista regime to sustain a
wide network of international relations which enabled them to resist
the assaults of the United States. Not only did it prove impossible to
isolate Nicaragua from the Western hemisphere, as it once had been
possible with Cuba; on the contrary, Sandinista diplomacy succeeded
in isolating the United States over its aggression against Nicaragua.

Nevertheless, the specific policies that financed the broad internal
alliances diluted the popular content of the revolutionary project and
led many people to reduce their level of participation in the
revolutionary process and in national defence. National unity with the
bourgeoisie was encouraged by slow progress in agrarian reform, by
an unequal distribution of incentives and bonuses, and by a
pronounced bias of sacrifice towards the peasants and workers. In the
context of a growing contraction of the economy, new incentives were
offered to the middle sectors and the employers, and carried through
at the cost of a decline in the wages and working and living conditions
of the masses, a greater administrative centralization and increasing
bureaucratic control over the popular organizations.[16] At the same
time, the maintenance of a network of broad international alliances
flowing from the principle of non-alignment, but based too on a
redrawn internal alliance, forced the Sandinista regime, especially
after 1987, to make a series of political concessions to the right wing
internally — for example the wide-ranging amnesty for members of
Somoza's army and of the counterrevolutionary forces who had been
sentenced for acts of terrorism and violations of human rights. This
contributed to a perceptible reduction in the level of military conflict,
but also flew in the face of the projected socio-economic transformations and broad popular participation.

The restrictions arising from the crisis, and the policies developed
by the government in response to it, together with the concessions to
the right, created in their turn a difficult situation for the Sandinista
mass organizations and above all for the workers and peasants

movement. The revolutionary transformations were slowed down or frozen, the possibilities for winning economic demands were dramatically reduced, centralization and the limitations placed on popular participation were increased. The space available to the opposition organizations consequently grew, not only because they had at their disposal financial resources coming from outside the country, but also because the Sandinista organizations proved incapable of asserting their relative autonomy from the political leadership of the state, while their demands and criticisms found little resonance in the Sandinista political leadership.

The new perspectives and policies of the Sandinistas were facilitated by the multiclass character of the FSLN. The Sandinista Revolution was a revolution of workers, peasants, semiproletarians, petty bourgeois youth, the poor of country and city; but it was also a revolution which, for reasons which I have dealt with elsewhere,[17] was joined shortly before 1979 by important sectors of the old conservative agrarian and commercial bourgeoisie who were opposed to Somoza. The relationship between the FSLN and the bourgeoisie, therefore, was not exclusively an external one, for sectors of the Nicaraguan bourgeoisie formed part of the FSLN even before the fall of Somoza. The weight of these sectors was consolidated by their role in the apparatus of the revolutionary state; they were particularly significant in the design and execution of agricultural and financial policies and in the mode of articulation of the mass organizations with government agencies. From 1987-88 onwards their influence grew in almost all areas of state administration and government political discourse.

At the same time, it was increasingly obvious that a kind of Sandinista new bourgeoisie was emerging, embracing bureaucrats and leaders who, as a result of their long exercise of public office and in the absence of any institutional controls, were able to accumulate and rapidly enrich themselves. The issue was addressed from a moral point of view and under the heading of corruption. But independently of the ethical issues, what was happening was the formation of sectors of the bourgeoisie who are found everywhere in Latin America and indeed throughout the capitalist world at certain stages of its development — a patrimonial exercise of political power whose explanation gains more from Max Weber than from Karl Marx. The Sandinistas were not responsible for the restrictions on access to information and resources, nor for the persistence of clientilistic styles of exercising power — they were deeply rooted in Nicaraguan political traditions and culture — but they did contribute to reproducing them, opening the way to the formation of capitals and enterprises and to a rapid social mobility which was in stark contrast to the austerity and probity of many other activists, leaders and functionaries, and above all to the hard life of the masses.

After the elections of November 1984 and as soon as the Presidency of Daniel Ortega was under way, the Sandinista government decided to confront the increasing economic decline by recourse to a conventional programme of monetary adjustment (9th February 1985). The attempt was frustrated by a recognition of the negative impact that a programme of this type would have on the mass base of the revolution at a time when the war was intensifying and it was the masses who had to bear the direct and indirect costs of defence. Nevertheless the strategy of broad alliances blocked any possibility of carrying through any economic adjustment which might impose burdens on the most backward sectors of the bourgeoisie. The result of these reciprocal tensions and blockages, in the context of a dramatic increase in the intensity of military conflict, was a sudden collapse of the economy, and the beginning of a traumatic phase in which it moved beyond all control.

At the same time the need to develop a political strategy that coincided with the military effort, produced in mid-1985 a new direction in government policies, adapting them to the actual contours of the Nicaraguan social map and to the demands of the rural masses. The insistence of the FSLN cadres on these changes, in defiance of the rigid technocrats of the state, made possible this shift in government policy. The agrarian reform was redrafted to correspond more closely to the demands of the peasantry; land distribution was speeded up. On the Atlantic Coast, populated by ethnic minorities who had confronted the revolutionary regime at an early stage, a plan for regional autonomy was set in motion, creating an atmosphere conducive to peace and encouraging the armed groups to lay down their weapons.[18] The redirection and acceleration of agrarian reform emphasised the popular character of the political project which the counter-revolution had set out to destroy, and in whose defence the peasants and rural workers had been the first to be mobilized. This introduced tensions into the alliance with the big landowners and middle farmers, but it was a risk that the government took in order to consolidate the internal front in the war against the counterrevolution.

This change of direction in the conceptions and strategies for development and defence bore fruit. The defeat of the counter-revolution on the battlefronts was the result both of the military effort and of these redrawn government policies. Nonetheless, it was a tactical turn and it was abandoned as soon as the war ended with the ceasefire agreements of March 1988. A few months later the Sandinista government decided to confront the crisis with a crude programme of monetary adjustment which produced its usual effects

— unemployment, reduction of basic consumption, recession, deterioration of living standards etc. — effects which were borne by the very people who had sacrificed themselves for the war effort throughout the decade.[19]

Real wages, which were already falling, now plummeted; peasant debts to the financial system grew exponentially; basic supplies fell and the redistribution of land was suspended. Simultaneously with these developments, the government redoubled its efforts to reach agreement with the employers within the framework of regional negotiations to resolve the Central American crisis. The Sandinistas put their hopes in agreements with private enterprise to reactivate private investment and win favour with the international economic community. Through generous concessions over incentives, prices, credits, supplies and subsidies, the Sandinistas hoped to win the good-will of the capitalist groups and, with an eye to the Presidential elections, to compete with the opposition parties for the votes of these groups. The alliance of the FSLN with the peasants and the rural workers, as well as with the urban masses, which they had attempted to reconstitute through the measures adopted from mid-1985 onwards, now underwent dramatic erosion.

To an extent the Sandinistas were trying to rebuild the broad alliance that had fought the Somoza dictatorship ten years earlier. But the conditions were completely different and the resources available dramatically limited. The original version of the alliance had been built on a widespread hegemony and a high level of popular mobiliza-tion, on open support from the international community and economic regeneration fuelled by broad external cooperation. Now there was a general demobilization of the people, the international community was exercising pressure from the right, the absence of external finance served to aggravate the prolonged economic recession and the masses were on the defensive.

The bourgeoisie understood that the attempt was proof of the weakness of a regime desperately in need of investments and convertible currency, and seeking international encouragement. As a consequence, it accepted the incentives of economic policy, but it kept a low profile and did not change its political inclinations towards the opposition — if not directly to the counterrevolution. The popular masses, for their part, heavily affected by the policies of economic readjustment, reduced even further their level of participation and mobilization; they were disorientated by a Sandinista rhetoric which was trying to revive the climate of mobilization of the war years when it was clear to everyone that the war was now a thing of the past; the government itself was freeing ex-members of Somoza's National Guard and offering an amnesty to the counterrevolutionaries.

Determined to improve their image abroad, the Sandinistas made a series of significant turns in international policy, the most far-reaching of which took place at the Central American Presidential Summit at San Isidro Coronado, Costa Rica, on December 12th 1989. There Daniel Ortega supported his colleagues in backing the Salvadorean President Alfredo Cristiani and condemning the FMLN and its recent military offensive. The *quid pro quo* was that the other presidents joined in the demand that the "contras" complete their demobilization by the 5th of February 1990 at the latest. It is well known that the demand met no response either from the contras or from the US government, but the repudiation of the FMLN linked Nicaragua with the most conservative positions on the Salvadorean question. Broad sectors of the Nicaraguan population were left disconcerted by Ortega's signature on the San Isidro document. Solidarity with the Salvadorean revolution had been one of the best known positions of Sandinista diplomacy and one of the points of conflict with the United States government. The FMLN rejected the document "with indignation", while the Guatemalan URNG evinced its "dissatisfaction, concern and surprise"; the USSR, by contrast, expressed its satisfaction.[20]

The failure to reconstitute the alliances that had emerged at other stages of the revolutionary process added to the tensions and contradictions arising from the timetable of the shift to the right in the economy and the timetable of the rightward move in the political arena. In June 1988 the Sandinista government launched its first programme of economic adjustment since its failed attempt of February 1985. The absolute lack of short term external financial assistance ensured that its impact on the masses was savage. But the Sandinistas were confident that the initial blow would be followed by beneficial effects, and that from the beginning of 1989 there would be a stage of reactivation of the economy which would consolidate their prospects for the Presidential elections of 1990.

Hurricane Joan, in October 1988, whose effects were disastrous in many areas of the country, obliged the government to alter its financial objectives and to relax its controls over the economy. At the end of January 1989 the government insisted once again on its programme of adjustment; there were still two years left before the elections in which to cure the country's ills, put the economy back on its feet and assuage the negative effects on the masses of the economic programme. But in February of that year, Sandinista diplomacy gave way to international pressure and decided to bring forward the election date to February 1990, cutting the room for manoeuvre for the economists. The FSLN thus came to the elections in the middle of the worst economic situation the country had ever known, whose ultimate effect was to reverse many of the gains of the early years which had brought with them real improvements in the living standards of the masses: the education system was on the edge of collapse, there was a major crisis in the public health service, unemployment and underemployment were reaching levels of nearly 30%, real wages were worth almost nothing, and there was a major contraction in production. The adjustment programme was very successful in a technical sense; hyperinflation was reduced, the fiscal deficit was drastically cut, exports grew slightly. But the social cost for the masses was enormous.

From this point of view, the fundamental error made by the Sandinistas was to have embarked on a policy of economic adjustment in the latter part of a presidential term. It is not by chance that this type of policy is always carried through in Latin America at the beginning of a period of government, in the hope that after the initial negative impact the situation will improve and the party in government may then aspire to reelection. The Sandinistas on the other hand turned to policies of economic adjustment virtually on the eve of the elections; yet they still hoped for an electoral victory, not just for the FSLN, but for the very Presidential team — Daniel Ortega and Sergio Ramirez — which had introduced the antipopular measures of the previous two years.

These miscalculations had their origin in the wider problem of a revolution bogged down in its own tensions and contradictions, and operating in an international context of increasing conflict. The project of national liberation and anti-imperialist struggle was reduced in the end to a military confrontation and a defensive struggle with no class basis or correlation. The strategy of national unity and broad alliances was financed by the sacrifices of the masses, yet did not succeed in winning the active support of the bourgeoisie or the better part of the middle classes. In these conditions, the regime's limitations and the extravagance of many of its functionaries became all the more disgraceful in the eyes of the masses, who were themselves increasingly impoverished and disorientated.

The insistence on a type of alliance for which the space no longer existed not only stopped the revolution from advancing in its project for socio-economic and political transformation — it also violated those which had already been achieved. Towards the beginning of 1990, for a significant proportion of those Nicaraguans who had supported or sympathised with the Sandinistas in previous years, there was little left of the revolution.

The incapacity of the Sandinistas to advance beyond the limits of the initial broad alliance of groups and social classes, despite the obvious defection of elements of the bourgeoisie and a major part of the middle classes, made all the more visible its later compromises with the right and with the international community, the reinforcement of traditional clientilistic and bureaucratic styles of politics, and the increasing influence over government and FSLN decisions of people closely linked to middle and employers sectors. All these factors served to demobilize the masses, without winning the loyalty of the elites or the benevolence of the government of the United States. In fact the weaknesses of the revolutionary regime underlined the effectiveness of the White House's policy of aggression and destabilization.

For those who once dreamed of a Red October in Masaya or Esteli, this was Thermidor; for others, it was one more example of Sandinista pragmatism. Some said that the Sandinistas were dismantling the gains of the early part of the revolution; others argued that they were rebuilding at this late stage what they had previously destroyed. These comings and goings, all of which took place out of sight of the masses or above their heads, fuelled the opposition vote of the 25th February. It is not the first time in the history of the Sandinista Revolution that the people have expressed their rejection of what they regard as the retreats or errors of the government, turning to their enemies or even collaborating with the contras. The peasants of Jinotega and Matagalpa did it in the mid-eighties, and before them it was the Indians and Creoles of the Atlantic Coast. In both these instances, the Sandinistas understood the message and changed their policies in response to popular demands.

In 1990 the contras were militarily defeated and their political leaders had entered the electoral contest; everyone was sick of war and violence and the great mass mobilizations were now a thing of the past. In the 1984 elections, Nicarguans had a choice between the revolution and the counterrevolution. In 1990 the choice was between the continuation of a regime entangled in its own indecision and whose revolutionary credentials belonged almost entirely to the past, and the promise of peace and prosperity coming from the allies of the White House.

The combination of internal contradictions and external pressures, and their reciprocal articulation provided fertile ground for the electoral defeat of the Sandinistas. It underlines the specific difficulties faced in the current world situation by anti-imperialist and national liberation revolutions in small, underdeveloped societies located in zones under the direct military or political influence of the United States. For reasons I have discussed elsewhere, and which have to do with the mode of constitution of peripheral capitalism and its class structure, rather than with ideological interpretations,[21] anti-imperialism and national liberation are essential ingredients of social revolutions in this type of society.

The experience of 20th century revolutions, with the exceptions of the Russian and the Chinese, are that they were consolidated thanks to the cooperation they received from the socialist bloc. Now that bloc no longer exists, and that cooperation can no longer be called upon. The events in Eastern Europe and the growing understanding between the USA and the USSR on how to manage the Central American crisis hit the Sandinistas at a moment when the revolution was undergoing serious deterioration. It is obvious that the reduction of economic assistance from the beginning of 1989, and the new direction of Soviet diplomacy reduced the FSLN's margin for manoeuvre or at the very least strengthened the arguments of those within the FSLN who were advocating a strategy of less revolution and more negotiation.

The strategy of international negotiation to survive the war and its effects by calling for a low intensity revolution, together with the reconstitution of internal alliances and the projection of an image more acceptable to external interlocutors, had a price — the winding down of the revolution, the inversion of its economic policies and the reversal of many of its social and political advances. The situation was all the more serious because the way that the Sandinistas had chosen to deal with the crisis was already having serious effects on the living standards of the masses. The weakening of the social base of the Sandinistas also restricted the room for movement at their disposal in the face of external pressures, and thus affected the viability of the project for national sovereignty.

The national liberation component of the Sandinista revolution was now more than ever reduced to a rhetoric with no actual correlation in internal or external policies. The discourse of war, which continued beyond the ceasefire agreements and was sustained at the same intensity despite the visible reduction in the level of armed conflict, lost credibility among the masses.

During the final phase of the electoral campaign, the competition for the votes of the middle sectors and the properties classes, gave rise among the masses to an image of the Sandinistas as promising all sorts of concessions to the right and to the outside world in order to hold on to power, yet unable to guarantee, in exchange for these concessions, that the contras would lay down their arms or that the economy would improve. Having defeated the contras militarily, yet unable to dismantle their organization, the Sandinistas opted to confront the US government through a strategy of less revolution; this brought them the raucous applause and the democratic blessing of their enemies, but also ensured their loss of power, as a significant section of the people rejected them at the ballot box.

4. *Transition to counterrevolution, or to popular autonomy?*

The elections of February 25th 1990 placed the government of Nicaragua in the hands of a heterogenous coalition united by a common denominator — their opposition to the Sandinistas. The new government is determined to overturn the institutions and gains of the revolution that were able to survive the doubts and ambiguities of the Sandinistas and the policies they adopted to confront the crisis. The object is to put Nicaragua in the sociopolitical position which it would have occupied in 1978 if Anastasio Somoza had accepted United States pressure and abandoned power in time: a "Somocismo without Somoza" in its most restricted sense. Although there has not been an invasion as there was in Guatemala in 1954 or Grenada in 1983, nor a *coup d'état* as in Chile in 1973, the new government is a counter-revolutionary one, in the literal sense that it is opposed to what the revolution had built. They will dismantle everything that was a product or a consequence of the revolutionary overthrow of the Somoza dictatorship. The substantial difference between the counter-revolutionary project in Nicaragua, and the other cases to which I have referred, does not have to do with the civilian method that was employed, but rather as Fred Halliday so perceptively pointed out, with the fact that unlike Chile, Guatemala or Grenada, in Nicaragua the counterrevolution carried out its masacres before rather than after the fall of the popular government.[22]

In these conditions, what then remains of the Sandinista revolution? If we think of it as a socialist revolution, or at least one that had embarked on a transition to socialism, then the reply can only be devastating. If, as I do, we think of the Sandinista revolution as a popular, democratic, anti-imperialist revolution, the response is much more hopeful.

There was an almost universal consensus after the 25th of February in emphasising the democratization of the political process as a great contribution of the Sandinistas in a country where for the first time in its history the opposition came to power by institutional means. The FSLN also shares in this consensus view; indeed it is curious to note the contrast between the insistence of the international sympathisers of the revolution on the extent to which the elections were conditioned by the war, the crisis, the "votes with arms in the air", the "blackmail from Washington" etc., with the often self-satisfied discourse of many Sandinista leaders.[23] If we are to speak sensibly of democratization, we should look at what is actually happening in Nicaragua, where the revenge of the bosses and the (ex?)supporters of Somoza is the first item on the agenda, and where the peasants, the workers, the rural and urban poor (and their numbers are constantly increasing) are being beaten by right wing gangs, expelled from their land, dismissed from their jobs, left hungry by the economic policies, and subjected to a climate of daily violence which degrades their lives and revives old hatreds. What has this to do with democracy?

Before we can speak of democracy, we shall have to wait until 1996 and see whether, if the FSLN win the elections, the present government does agree democratically to yield power and acknowledge that victory. Doubts persist, however, in a region where the forces of the Right have always violated the rules of the game of institutional politics whenever the popular masses, accepting those institutions, have threatened to increase their social and political influence.

Clearly, many of the socio-economic achievements of the revolution, which hd been considered irreversible, are now being turned back by the new government: job security, basic levels of consumption, which had been considered irreversible, are now being turned back by the new government: job security, basic levels of consump- were already in reverse for reasons that I have discussed earlier.

What remains intact, however, is what in my view is the most important contribution of the Sandinista revolution — the popular organizations. The great achievements of the revolution rested on those organizations: the awareness of the political effectiveness of direct popular participation, the reconstruction of the economy, the social development of the early years, the defence of the peasantry against the counterrevolution, overcoming the difficulties created by the lack of spare parts and the embargo on supplies, the militant anti-imperialism without which there can be neither revolution nor democracy nor development nor homeland. These popular organizations, reborn out of the fall of the Sandinista government, in the midst of the vengeance and the wild desire to restore everything to the way it was before on the part of the bosses and the landlords, the bankers and the oligharchs, is the richest inheritance of a traumatic decade of revolution, crisis and war. Those popular organizations are the guarantee that the hope for a life of dignity will remain alive at the en-during heart of Nicaragua, and that that hope will flower again with the same strength and certainty with which the barricades and trenches reappeared during the strikes of July 1990. Those organizations above all are the guarantee of the authentic autonomy of the popular forces in the struggle for national dignity and social transformation.

Notwithstanding their predominantly defensive character, the combativity of the popular organizations and in particular of the workers today contrasts with their passivity of previous years and con-tradicts the strategy of negotiation and compromise with the new government to which the highest level of political leadership of the Sandinistas remains devoted. At a time of deep tensions and internal confrontations within the FSLN, the mass organizations and above all the trade union movement have assumed the leadership of the popular opposition and the defence of what remains of the revolution. If the policies of agrarian counter-reform and the dismantling of the social area of the economy have not been allowed to progress at the pace envisaged by the new government, that is above all due to the combativity of those organizations.

The popular demonstrations and the contending strategies for relating to the new government point to the unfolding of a process of progressive differentiation between the popular and trade union organizations and the FSLN as a political party. It is as if the fall of the government of Daniel Ortega had detonated an explosion of energies and initiatives of social struggle hitherto suffocated by its strategic shift to the right and by its bureaucratization. The same situation is occurring in intellectual circles and within the mass media, with a profusion of newspapers, ratio stations, weekly magazines, information bulletins, debates and circulation of news and ideas that contrasts with the general experience of previous years. The reactivation of the popular movement can also be seen reflected within the party structures of the FSLN itself, in a process of renewal of leaders from below in which few of yesterday's leaders have escaped the sanction of the people's criticisms and the people's vote.

The contrast between the negotiating posture of the highest leaders of the FSLN and the combativity of the masses and the trade union leaders points ahead to a developing differentiation between the FSLN as a political party and the popular and working class movement. This does not mean, for the moment or in the near future, that the movement will lose its Sandinista character; but it does mean a growing autonomy from the party's political leadership and thus a change in the relationship that has existed in the past between the party and the movement. The top-down character of many aspects of the relationship FSLN/mass organizations up to February 1990 is now being rejected and replaced by a politics of negotiation between the Sandinista political leadership and the popular movement in the context of conflicts in which the terms of agreement are defined above all by the struggles of the masses.

It is difficult to imagine that this combativity will be able to substantially modify the dominant tendencies within the highest levels of leadership of the FSLN until that leadership also feels the winds of change upon it; the shift to the right of the Sandinistas has been going on for a long time and it has an inertia which makes it unlikely that it will change in any significant way in the immediate future. The lack of an alternative strategy with which to face the crisis, in particular, encourages caution among the political leadership of the FSLN and further underlines their ambivalence towards the popular protests. The Sandinistas need to preserve the political leadership of the popular movements if they are to keep their base and their role as chief interlocutor with the government; but they also need to control the intensity and spread of the mass protests in order to guarantee a minimum stability for the government. For if it fell, the threat of direct US intervention would again arise; at the very least it would force the leadership of the FSLN to take the risk of offering some concrete propoals in response to a chaotic socio-economic situation.

It is still unclear how the current conflicts and tensions will unfold. What is clear is that Nicaragua after the elections of February 25th 1990 is quite unlike Nicaragua prior to the Sandinista assumption of power on July 19th 1979. The difference is above all the consequence of popular struggles and the demands they have pursued. It is this which constitutes the sharp difference from the events of Eastern Europe.

One could say of revolutions what young Adso, the protagonist of Umberto Eco's *The Name of the Rose* said of his ephemeral and anonymous lover, who was "as beautiful and terrible as an army prepared for battle". Revolutions are beautiful and seductive, because they express what is best and most noble in human beings; the limitless capacity for solidarity and sacrifice to build a life more worth living. But they are also terrible because together with these heights of altruism and generosity, there are moments of incredible meanness and small-mindedness, and the great achievements mingle with the most monstrous errors.

But when they are real, revolutions are not ephemeral. Even if they fail, or experience reverses, nothing returns to the way it was. And they are not anonymous; they have the face of the people and they bear the name of their aspirations.

NOTES

1. See for example James Petras, "La derrota electoral de los sandinistas: reflexiones críticas" in *El Gallo Ilustrado*, Mexico, April 8th 1990.
2. See for example Jorge Castaneda, "Latin America and the end of cold war" in *World Policy Journal*, Summer, 1990.
3. Carlos M. Vilas: *The Sandinista revolution*: Monthly Review Press, New York, 1986; (hereafter Vilas 1986).
4. See *Resoluciones de la Asamblea Nacional de Militantes del FSLN en El Crucero, Departamento de Managua*, Managua, 17th June 1990.
5. See C. M. Vilas, "La contribución de la política económica a la caída del sandinismo" in *Crítica*, Managua, no. 2, July 1990, pp. 34-42; and "Nicaragua, what went wrong?" in *NACLA Report on the Amedricas*, XXIV (1), July 1990, pp.   10-18.
6. For example in "Unidad nacional y contradicciones sociales en una economia mixta: Nicaragua 1979-84" in R. Harris and Carlos M. Vilas (eds.): *La*

revolución en Nicaragua: ERA, Medico, 1985, pp. 17-50. "Nicaragua: the fifth year. Contradictions and tensions in the economy" in *Capital and Class*, 28, Spring 1986, pp. 105-138; *Transición desde el subdesarrollo*; Nueva Sociedad, Caracas, 1989; (hereafter Vilas 1989), chapters III, IV and VI.

7.   See for example the speech by President Daniel Ortega published in *Barricada*, February 1st 1989.

8.   On the increasing rundown of mass participation and their progressive subordination to the state apparatus see Marvin Ortega: "Workers' participation in the management of the agro-enterprises of the APP", in *Latin American Perspectives*, 45, Spring 1985, pp. 69-81; C. M. Vilas: "The mass organizations in Nicaragua: the current problematic and perspectives for the future" in *Monthly Review*, 38 (6), November 1986, pp. 20-31; Luis Serra, "Limitada por la guerra, pendiente al futuro: La participación y organización popular en Nicaragua" in *Nueva Sociedad*, 104, Nov.-Dec. 1989.

9.   See for example the speeches by Daniel Ortega published in *Barricada* on June 15th and 20th July 1988 and 1st February 1989.

10.   C. M. Vilas, "Revolution and Democracy in Latin America" in R. Miliband et al (eds.), *Socialist Register 1989*, Merlin Press, London, 1989, pp. 30-36.

11.   The rapid pace of the transition in Cuba reflected the specificities of capitalism on the island; among them, the high level of centralization and concentration of capital, the level of organization of the rural and urban working class, the comparatively advanced level of development of the productive forces.

12.   The worst part is that these tendencies often develop spontaneously and at all levels. Consider the following case: In mid-1982, when the tensions in the economy began to bring pressure to bear on the supplies of basic goods, the FSLN called meetings of the CDS (Sandinista Defence Committees, organizations in urban areas) so that popular debate might produce criteria for rationing and distribution. In the section of my own district (Monsenor Lezcano in Managua) where there were 450 CDS activists for 5-6,000 people, barely 200 of us attended the meeting. We decided that, since it was important to have the broadest possible discussion and take our decisions in the most democratic way possible, we should call a second meeting and guarantee the real participation of as many people as possible. There were less than 100 of us at this second meeting, and since we could not go on postponing the drawing up of a plan of supply, less than 100 of us present at the meeting made decisions in the name of 500 which affected the diet of 6,000.

13.   *Barricada*, 5th October 1989, p. 4; also Michael Kramer, "Anger, bluff and cooperation" in *Time*, June 4th 1990, pp. 38-45.

14.   See Vilas 1986, Ch. IV.

15.   See Vilas 1989, pp. 93 ff.

16.   See for example Peter Utting, *The peasant question and development policy in Nicaragua*, UNRISD, Geneva, 1988. On the progressive transformation of the trade union organizations into organs of the state, see Vilas, "The mass organisations in Nicaragua. . ." in *Monthly Review*, 38 (6), November 1986, pp. 20-31 and Vilas 1986, Ch. V.

17.   See Vilas 1986, Chs. II and IV; Vilas 1989, Ch. I.

18.   See C. M. Vilas, "War and revolution in Nicaragua" in R. Miliband et al (eds.), *Socialist Register 1988*, Merlin Press, London, 1988, pp. 182-219; and *Class, state and ethnicity in Nicaragua*, Lynne Riener Publishers, Boulder and London, 1989, Ch. V.

19.   See Asociación de Profesionales de la Economia (APEN), *Breve evaluación de las políticas de 1988 y propuesta para 1989*, Managua, December 1988; Rene Pilarte et al, "Reforma económica: hacia nuevas contradicciones" in *Boletín socioeconómico de INIES*, Managua, 9, Sept.-Oct. 1988, pp. 3-12.

20. See respectively *Crónica*, Managua, no. 57, 14th-20th December 1989, *El nuevo Diario*, 30th December 1989, and *Barricada*, 14th December 1989.
21. Vilas 1986, Ch. I.
22. Fred Halliday, "The Ends of Cold War", in *New Left Review*, 180, March-April 1990, pp. 5-23.
23. See for example Sergio Ramírez, "Nicaragua, la democracia a prueba" in *La Jornada*, Mexico, 14th and 15th August 1990, and "Nicaragua, confesión de amor" in *Nexos*, Mexico, 152, August 1990, pp. 29-48; Comandante Victor Tirado López, "Hacia nuevas estrategias revolucionarias" in *El Día Latinoamericano*, 18, 24th September 1990.

SOVIET REHEARSAL IN YUGOSLAVIA? CONTRADICTIONS OF THE SOCIALIST LIBERAL STRATEGY

Susan L. Woodward

For a generation of East Europeans, party stalwarts, and Balkanologists raised to view the Yugoslav path as heresy, the current changes in the Soviet Union must present one of those great ironies of history. A liberal communist programme once labelled Revisionist is now viewed as the guiding hope of a post-Cold War world and Soviet prosperity. A conflict that went public in June 1948 within days of the currency reform in Germany that finalized its division is now forgotten in the congratulations over Soviet acceptance of German reunion. In places where anti-Titoist purges paved the way to Stalinist rearmament in eastern Europe, there now comes criticism of Yugoslavs for their slow pace of anti-communist purge. And 41 years after Yugoslavia's path to reform — its "sell-out to Wall Street" — was assured in the fall of 1949 with US commitment of military aid and then food, the Soviet Foreign Minister, Edward Shevardnadze, presented Washington with a request for food to protect Soviet reforms.

Despite their substantial difference in international significance, power, and wealth, the similarity between the Yugoslav path since the late 1940s and the one chosen by the Soviets in the 1980s is unavoidable. So, too, is the relation between their introduction and international conditions. The parallels are neither chance events nor limited to their common multinational federalism. The Yugoslav experience provides direct lessons for analysis of the roots, possibilities, and contradictions of the Soviet reforms. These parallels originate in two fundamental characteristics of communist party governance: first, the crucial importance of the strategy of accumulation that its leaders choose for the whole pattern of institutional development and domestic conflict; and second, the importance that international conditions play in that choice of strategy.

In the Yugoslav case, the outcome of this strategy for growth and its implementing institutions has been long-term foreign indebtedness, economic cycles closely tied to international economic cycles, and by the 1970s stagflation, moving into hyperinflation and mass unemployment in the 1980s. Ever more divisive nationalist conflict accompanied economic problems and, by 1991, seriously threatened the break-up of the Yugoslav state itself.

These economic troubles have largely been blamed on worker self-management, on the erroneous assumption that workers have power over wages and employment in Yugoslavia. Avoiding the "Yugoslav path" thus has become a code word for preventing "worker control" in firms. Conflicts between the republics and the recent political movement toward independence by Slovenia and Croatia are laid to a history of "primordial" ethnic antagonisms exacerbated by the communist party's ostensible denial of the democratic right of national self-determination. And like analyses of reform programmes in other communist states, discussion tends to focus on political opposition, especially in the phases of implementation.

By focusing instead, however, on their common strategy of accumulation one can see these outcomes as the result of internal contradictions in the strategy itself (including assumptions about integration into a non-socialist and global economy) and the political conflicts they generate that would need to be addressed even if a purge of conservative opposition were final and complete. Problems seen as external obstacles to the success of reform*— ethnic conflict, a disintegrating central authority and its reaction, urban middle class disenchantment, and economic difficulties of rising inflation and unemployment — are instead its products. And the story in Yugoslavia and Eastern Europe is that the strain of these internal contradictions is felt most intensely by the socialist elements of their programme — the absence of capital markets and independent banks, the failure of a labour market to discipline wages and work effort, and the role of the party.

Analyzing Communist Regimes

Most analyses of communist party-governed states focus on characteristics that seem blatantly to *distinguish* them from non-communist party systems. Leninism as an organizational form necessary to the concept of a political vanguard, one party rule, democratic centralism, the bureaucratic hierarchy required by a *command* economy, relations between state and society based on the political dominance of the former, even "totalitarianism" seem to form a syndrome worth contrasting to the political forms of competitive party parliamentary polities. But in both communist and non-communist systems the organizational characteristics and distribution of political power and authority they institutionalize are instrumental. Behind these instruments and the different agents of change lies a common inheritance of the principal European discourse of the modern era — rational approaches to the material world and its development.

Although Marxists may place material development more consciously and openly at the core of their visions of the world than some social movements, they are far from unusual in their developmentalism and emphasis on economic growth as the basis for human possibilities, or in their internal disagreement over optimal strategies for development. The regimes they created also share the central dilemma of all modern states — how to respond and adapt to the consequences of the internationalization of markets and the subsequent global system of industrial capitalism.

This common dilemma presented the communist regimes with particularly painful constraints, however. First, it was in the market for labour and the livelihoods of small producers that local societies did (and still do) their adjusting. Since they represented the material interests of these groups, communist governments were less free in their choices of adjustment. Second, their revolutions succeeded in societies where delayed industrialization and imperial political systems compounded the local effects of international markets; their programme for societal transformation based on the most developed aspects of capitalism confronted societies that were underdeveloped, backward in self-perception, agrarian in culture, and heterogeneous in their level and extent of incorporation into the world market. The effect on peasants and farmers of highly variable commodity markets, on workers of global depressions, on national minorities of centralizing and rationalizing empires, and on the literate or travelled of a sense of relative material and cultural poverty (translated as "backwardness") enlarged their potential political constituency and allies. But it also brought populist, liberal, and nationalist concerns and tendencies into the proletarian movement.

Their agenda altered to a programme of rapid industrialization. Communist parties in power responded to this dilemma and its constraints with wracking debates on the best strategy of accumulation. For reasons worthy of serious scrutiny, these gelled early into two, and there emerged quite regularized political factions around their respective conceptions of economic development and the related political assumptions about how to put those beliefs into practice. Although the labels "Stalinist" (or conservative) and "reform communist" are now common, their kinship with analogous non-Marxian debates and traditions can be better understood if one contrasts these as "developmentalist" and "liberal". It was only in the institutions for implementing each strategy that communist parties made their particular contribution to the common dilemma. And even these institutions borrowed extensively from their allies in revolution and the preoccupation in Central and Eastern Europe between the global depressions of the 1880s and 1930s with social control over finance and nationalization (although parties differed in their notion of the "nation", or "people"[1]) to protect against the global crises of capitalist accumulation and dependence on foreign capital.

It is commonplace to argue that economic policy in socialist states pursues for some time an "extensive" strategy for development and that its exhaustion as a strategy of accumulation leads to an agonizing political struggle before it is replaced by its natural successor, an "intensive" strategy. In fact, in socialist states no less than capitalist ones, both the advocates of different strategies and their interests and institutions coexist, and the influence of each ebbs and flows with some frequency. Although this is not the place to elaborate the two strategies, some sense of their differences — between what Lenin called the "Prussian" and the "American" roads[2] — is necessary to understand this ongoing conflict.

The primary economic problem for the developmentalists is structural change from agrarian backwardness to advanced industrial economies. Productivity is measured in societal, economy-wide terms and achieved through sectorally-calculated investment in goods necessary for long term stable growth (capital goods, raw materials, infrastructure), though organizational economies of the productive process, concentration of scarce resources, and central allocation when shortages prevail so that social priorities take precedence over market power. Investment decisions for developmental projects are necessarily taken at the centre and implemented by functional ministries while microrationality is the world of the engineer more than the economist. Although there is nothing inherently militaristic about this programme, the economic needs of defence and self-sufficiency in strategic raw materials, food grains, textiles, and capital goods, independently of comparative price advantages in a world market, tend to ally developmentalists with security interests and to ensure their greater influence over economic policy when leaders perceive a national security threat.

For liberals, the purpose of an economy is to provide final consumption goods to the population, and the best strategy of economic policy and institutions is to favour the most modern and successful of the commodity producers. In words associated forever with Bukharin, the more developed industries, regions, and people lead the way, gradually absorbing at the most economically rational pace, the backward regions.[3] Efficiency in the use of labour in production is the primary source of productivity, and the global market is the best standard. This demands substantial autonomy to producers, local initiative, and decentralized operations and even investment in response to consumer demand in goods markets. Societal productivity is a sum of microefficiencies and is enhanced through trade, especially the import of wage goods and advanced technology produced more cheaply elsewhere, and through minimizing expenditures that do not yield a consumable output, hence rents, bureaucracies, the coercive apparatus of the state, welfare transfers, and so forth. At its core are producers of light manufactures and processed goods that can also be exported and of foods that are best suited to intensive household production such as vegetables, fruits, and meats.

The differences of communist-designed systems from capitalist ones in how these strategies were to be implemented had political and economic components. Politically, of course, the tactics of revolution were to unify the working class behind one movement and leadership so as to break capital's ability to use the labour market (competition between workers over wages and jobs) to divide and conquer; to create a popular front of all working people — medium and small farmers, landless labourers, free professionals (called in the east the "liberal or progressive, intelligentsia") and even lower white collar groups and civil servants — that would make revolution possible on both home and foreign front; and to seize the state. This was a prelude to the economic component: handing control over surplus value (that part of society's product that was not consumed in the course of producing it) to those who produced it — through social ownership of capital assets and a system that kept money the servant of production and prevented the economic crises that were only resolved under capitalism by the devaluation of labour.

The organization of the system of money and credit was no less critical than that of production to those who actually made the revolution: because of their understanding of the role of independent finance and the circulation of money in capitalist crises; because a programme of rapid industrialization and structural change required the ability to direct new investment, and therefore credit; and because the basis of solidarity in the revolutionary coalition of industrial workers, peasants and farmers, small producers, and other wage- and salaried-employees was stable purchasing power, and therefore the capacity to maintain a stable value for the currency and prevent inflation, debt, and financial crisis. Its characteristics were the elimination of markets for production supplies (labour, capital, and land); wages calculated to serve as incentives to increased output at the same time that they kept in line with real productivity; unified and uniform accounts for the entire economy; a cash plan based on the plan of production; and strictly balanced budgets of both firms and governments. [4]

The unity principle in both state and economy — one party rule and social ownership — and the strategic mentality of revolutionary parties contributed a systemic character to economic policy. Like developmentalist states everywhere, the approach to development chosen in the offices of state becomes a society-wide programme for change. Assessments of that programme seek systemic explanations. When the ruling party decides to change economic strategy, it sets in motion an entire series of alterations in the organization of the economy at both the macro and micro levels so that the instruments of incentive, implementation, and supervision are appropriate to the new strategy. Adjustment is a society-wide project.

If the instrumental and institutional elements of these states were based on the principle of unity, but the politically active divided over the optimal approach to development, how do choices between competing strategies of accumulation and shifts between dominant factions occur? The internationalism of Marxian interpretation and the nationalism of the states they created continues to dominate perceptions after the revolution, focusing the attention of party leaders and other influentials on international standards. They could not separate their goal of improving the living conditions of working people from "catching up" with the West and competing successfully in the international arena. Only when the domestic economic strategy appears to fail internationally is there sufficient pressure at home to resolve the many specific disagreements with the prevailing policy and build momentum for a reform of the system itself. Declining growth rates *relative* to other countries, chronic trade deficits, declining foreign reserves that interfere with critical imports, perceived threats to national security or of falling behind technologically, whether measured by armaments or trade and production of leading firms, rising costs of defence or strategic commodities, or new opportunities in trade: these are the generators of internal reform. And because the primary international characteristic of socialist states has always been their relative disadvantage — it was the birthmark of their revolutions and after World War II became the primary organizing factor of pax Americana — the dilemmas of adjustment to international changes (their reading of opportunities as well as threats and costs) remains the dominant force for domestic strategy. Similarly, the current turmoil in the communist world is inseparable from changed international conditions after 1978-79 in both trade and security. The response was a shift back to the liberal, reformist strategy, with the consequence in Eastern Europe of the end of communist party rule altogether and in the Soviet Union of the contradictions and conflicts all too familiar from Yugoslavia.

The Yugoslav Model

The Yugoslav party stands apart, not because of its early break with Moscow, but in the early dominance in party policy and state institutions of the approach to economic development and to socialism of the "reform", or liberal faction. This dominance did not emerge without a struggle and without confronting international conditions that favoured the opposing strategy and faction, so that the reformed state of 1952 was in fact a composite of both. Nonetheless, each stage of institutional change in the economy and the state, sealed each decade by a new constitution, was written by these liberal reformers. Moreover, the leadership pursued this reform strategy with an economy open to world trade and finance and for the most part in cooperation with western countries and institutions. This makes its forty-odd years of experience virtually unique and more directly relevant to the post-Cold War international environment than any other.

This early victory led to a system with significant differences from the Soviet Union. Above all the institutional ground of the developmental faction was thin. Central planning and its control over supplies and production decisions also never took institutional hold, although the institutions of the first step toward a socialist market strategy — the institutions of monetary planning and the cartellization of product markets by branch organization of producers' associations — have been extremely resilient. There was less need for the massive de-legitimation of "Stalinists" as occurred under Khrushchev and even more so under Gorbachev. Arguments against them in the first decade of power played on the popular association of defence and centralism with the Serb-dominated pre-war Kingdom and the substantial economic interest of many Serbs (but by no means all) in a strong military, investment in agriculture, and central fiscal capacity. From then on the debate over economic policy and institutional design could not be disentangled from a quarrel between nations and between central authority and "democratic" impulse, forcing the developmentalists and their very real concerns into defensive retreat. The smaller size of Yugoslavia and its greater vulnerability to external shocks on the economy also exposed the reformists' programme far more to dependence on international conditions than a country the size and international weight of the Soviet Union. This is particularly the case with the significance that balance of payments deficits and assessment of their cause must necessarily play in economic policy.

Nonetheless, the logic of the liberal programme in Yugoslavia that guided the Yugoslav leadership for four decades is the same as the strategy guiding the current Soviet leadership. To understand its internal contradictions and problematic practice, one must first have in mind its dominant model of intention. How that model plays out in practice also depends on the alliance of social forces behind it in each country, and the particular international conditions at the time of its introduction and resurgence.

The liberal "reform" programme in Yugoslavia originated before the war and revolution among leaders from the more developed regions of Slovenia and Croatia: an industrial working class employed in processing and light manufacturing; external trade, communications, and cultural links with Europe; and neopopulist agrarian parties which had organized large sections of the peasantry as well as local cooperatives — all this gave salience to the Bukharinist (or as they saw it, Leninist) strategy that would make the more modern manufacturers and commercialized farmers the engine of the economy's growth. Material self-interest and cultural preference have reinforced this coalition over time with a shared orientation to the west and resentment at large expenditures on developing capital goods and primary commodities at home.

At the same time, like Lenin's programme of 1921, the immediate cause of its selection after the war lay in international conditions: the need to stabilize the economy under pressure of a serious balance of payments deficit and unfilled trade agreements — both of which had to be met if the conditions for national security set by the leaders' policy of peaceful coexistence and a strong national defence were to prevail. Military assistance from the west allowed them to end the mass mobilizations and investment in military industries and stockpiles of 1948-1949, and western financial assistance (the IMF especially) and food aid came with conditions that reinforced the weight of the northerners' liberal approach in responding to the greater demand for exports and the inflationary conditions in domestic goods markets. As in Russia in 1921-1923, the choice of a Bukharinist strategy in Yugoslavia could be justified as, and indeed felt sincerely to be, the only choice where circumstances required radically increasing additional output from existing resources.

But this was more than a tactical choice, or one based solely on reconstructing a political alliance and base of support.[5] Its approach is based on an entire conception of the best way to develop an economy, independently of conditions calling for austerity.[6] Implementing this conception involved more than a change in the central party line and the defeat or concurrence of those who held opposing views. To put in place the institutions it required, legislation and constitutional revision created a "new economic system" and its accompanying political reform.

In Marxian terms, the core objective of the liberal strategy for economic growth is to reduce the socially necessary labour time of the economy. The source of accumulation at the level of the firm and of society is higher marginal productivity of labour and lowered costs of labour in production. Relative labour cost can be reduced within production by increasing mechanization and technological moderniza- tion, labour's skills ("human capital"), the efficiency of the productive process, and work effort. At the aggregate level, labour costs can be cut by finding cheaper sources of wage goods so that workers' consumption standards rise without consuming a greater proportion of output. The "aggregate wage fund" can also decline if the non-productive use of economic resources, and above all that of labour, is minimized. The more human effort contributes to the sum of goods that will be consumed, and the less people are engaged in activities that do not yield a consumable product, the higher will be society's overall growth and the possibility of rising standards of consumption for all.

As this economic strategy unfolded institutionally in Yugoslavia, one could see a social vision emerging of the early Marxian model of an association of free producers. The state would diminish as a force extracting surplus value, and become a small administration to ensure the basic condition of their mutual exchange — monetary stability — and a set of deliberative councils of elected representatives of producers who agree on policies of mutual interest.[7]

Although the blueprint of constitutional reform actually looked very much like this ideal, the structure of society it imagined could also have been designed to satisfy the members of a coalition of the political forces put together for revolution in Yugoslavia. The core was to be a socialized public sector of firms producing final goods for domestic consumption and export with the most advanced machinery available, managed by a staff of engineers and economists, kept in check by representatives of skilled industrial workers. The core is surrounded by efficient private farmers and craftsmen organized into local cooperatives, producing for the market and for socialized sector firms on long term contract. Movement of people and goods across borders is free with few regulations. At the same time the definition of community for this worker-peasant, or Marxist-populist, alliance shows in its mix of internationalist and nationalist principles the hard reality of revolution in the east where the history of state- building and capitalist expansion, the persistence of war, the political and economic importance of land, and the cultural and political influence of the liberal intelligentsia forced the national question near the top of the agenda.

The fundamental question facing leaders who held this ideal was, of course, how to achieve its objectives. Like all liberals elsewhere, socialist market reformers believe that the solution lies in individual economic interest. A system that structures its incentives to produce — and produce efficiently — around material self-interest will be most effective. Decisions on the use of economic resources should be made by those who have a direct economic stake in how they are used. Those who actually produce value, therefore, should be given the autonomy to make economic decisions. Workers will produce more per unit of labour if they expect a proportionately higher wage, and they will contribute to reducing costs if they are given a voice in production decisions. Managers will organize production more efficiently and respond to market demand if they see the consequences in profits and the revenues they can retain for themselves and their firm. Farmers will produce and market higher yields if they can increase their market income thereby. Although largely unspoken, this belief in the rational behaviour and potential initiative of "direct producers" left more or less alone to respond to material incentives has the character of a political faith.

The more directly related is this material return to the behaviour that enhanced value, moreover, the more effective it is seen to be. Variable wages and bonuses should replace political campaigns and status rewards. Wage differentials should directly reflect the embodied capital of skill and expertise as an incentive to skilling. While producers should orient their economic calculation to demand and realization in goods markets, the allocation of labour or capital by a free market would only distort the direct relation between effort and reward, cost and use. Exchanges between producers should be on the principle of mutual interest, and thus cooperation and bilateral contracts should replace both market and state allocation. Socialist liberals propose a system of "socialist commodity production", not a market economy.

This calls for a very different system of macrocoordination than the administered instructions and centralized accounts of developmental planning. Financial instruments take over the function of transmitting information, coordinating relations between enterprises, and enforcing state preferences over investment and society-wide rules and regulations. Autonomy over supplies and labour deprives the ministerial hierarchy of its instruments of influence and supervision. The strategy of accumulation thus has direct consequences for the organization of the economy as a whole and the role of the state in it. Although political authorities do not abandon their right to formulate economic policy or their interest in the health and direction of the economy, they must give priority to the value of the currency and monetary stabilization because their economic power is only as great as the monetary stability that their financial system demands: that the money in circulation never be greater than that supported by real value produced and that the total wage fund be kept in balance with the fund of commodities available for purchase.

There is a potential conflict in this strategy between the macro-economic concern with stability and a shrinking wage fund, on the one hand, and the role of direct and positive economic incentives to workers, managers, and independent producers and operational autonomy over labour and supplies in increasing productivity, on the other. The resolution, as Economics Minister Boris Kidric was fond of repeating in 1949-1950, is "economic coercion".[8] Balancing the initiative that comes from greater latitude of choice with responsibility for the economic consequences of those choices, whether good or bad, economic units are made financially accountable for their budgets. In the language of economic reformers in Eastern Europe in the 1970s and 1980s, both increased production to relieve shortages and limits on the aggregate wage fund to prevent spiralling inflation require "hard budget constraints". *Khozrascët* should apply to all using economic assets — not only firms and households but also governments, independent social services, and other non-profit organizations. Some supervision of financial responsibility is possible through banks that issue cash and send their accountants periodically to check the books of public sector depositors, but to retain the initiative and incentive to use resources wisely, authority over decisions on that use has to lie with the budgetary unit itself. Socialist liberals expect economic actors to make the same rationalizing and budget balancing calculations as capitalists — deciding how to make cuts when profits decline sufficient to threaten investment and trading off wages and employment — but they want to hand this authority to all those who "add value" with socially owned assets. *Labour is expected to think like capital.*

In Yugoslavia, the liberals secured control over institutional design as well as economic strategy in a time of severe shortages of both goods and skilled labour. Unions were still active in ways developed under capitalist ownership, and managers were acceding to wage demands from skilled workers in short supply. In order to limit the wage fund and stabilize the economy at the same time that they increased rapidly the productivity of domestic firms, leaders sought the assistance of workers themselves. The propaganda advantage of the slogan, "handing control of factories to the workers" (and farms to the farmers), obscures their real purpose in introducing workers' self-management: extending the "economic coercion" of market profit and loss to the employees (and above all production workers) of firms.[9] Restraints on consumption until justified by real increases in production and marginal output; cuts in labour costs by firing less productive workers, lowering wage rates, or reducing non-wage benefits; and intensified work norms remained managerial decisions, but they had to be reviewed and approved by workers' elected representatives. Unions would then organize the election of workers' councils and could advise and mobilize on ways to increase productivity. Democratic participation was a way to buy labour's support for the sacrifices needed to bring accounts into line with what was being produced and sold and to increase surplus value; and it was a way to check managerial power without the time lost and potential inflationary pressure of union-led bargaining and strikes. Self-restraint on wages might be voluntary if it promised greater return later on, and appealing to workers' economic interest yielded a more effective guide to specific decisions on layoff and dismissal.

This principle of financial self-management, and its necessary component of democratic participation in internal decisions, was first applied in Yugoslavia in critical export firms but was gradually extended to all workplaces that could be organized according to autonomous budgets. Not only does democracy enter the workplace; public functionaries were also expected to think in financially accountable and profitability terms. Non-profit services, such as schools and hospitals, might not add real value, but they can improve the use of the resources granted them from tax revenues if motivated by the right to retain a portion of their savings. Governments still spend monies obtained by taxing producers, but limits on those revenues and the legal obligation to balance the budget — with the participation of tax and fee payers — can encourage less potential waste. Parliaments elected from those who add value, because their direct economic interest in the use of their surplus should make policy and its financing economically rational, become ever more important in reviewing and debating policy. Executives composed of councils seating representatives of societal groups with economic interests (governments, unions, branch and commercial associations of firms) replace the ministerial hierarchy of decision and surveillance of a planned economy. Units of the economic ministries, in turn, are transformed from executive organs into properly "economic" units operating on commercial terms.

The attitude toward labour productivity at the core of this strategy for economic growth includes a notion of what is productive that requires additional organizational restructuring (in Russian, *perestroika*). To cut labour costs, firms are urged to reduce administrative and transfer costs by consolidating staffs and integrating vertically. Enterprises should employ internally the services they need, such as marketing and professionals (doctors, lawyers). Clerical and lower managerial staff should be transferred into production or dismissed. Less productive workers — almost as if by definition, unskilled and semi-skilled workers, the aged, handicapped, peasant-workers who migrate between land and jobs, and women — should be sent to more appropriate jobs or fired.

This concept of productive labour is an old one, but its prejudice is a core of the classical thought that informs so much of the liberal strategy. Above all, the idea that bureaucrats and rents are a waste of productive resources encourages a deep antipathy to the state; political campaigns to reduce government expenditures and enterprises' taxation by cutting state functions become "anti-bureaucratic" crusades. Most vulnerable is the military, which becomes the symbol of misuse and waste. But transfers of all kinds, including ones necessary to production such as monies for infrastructure and social services, as well as income supplements and welfare benefits, come under the axe of the orthodox budget balancers, are assigned to subordinate governments or to firms, or become independent funds and their offices in order to remove them from the central state budget and make them economically accountable. Even the party apparatus is "sent down" into the factories and local governments which will pay their salaries to tie their personal interest in the economic success of their employer to their tasks of supervision and persuasion in the economy. Democratic participation, political activism, and freer speech and criticism (in Russian, *glasnost*) are not only intended to gain popular support for the austerity of increased accumulation. The voice of the people was seen as a powerful tool of enforcement "from below" that involved no state office or budgetary penny for salaries and as a way to transmit information about citizens' preferences directly, without fluctuating prices.

Another way to cut wage costs so that wage incentives to workers retain their force is through lower prices (or higher productivity) of wage goods. Foreign trade and household agriculture hold a special place in the liberal strategy for this reason. If imported wage goods are cheaper than those produced at home, they should be substituted. Price competition with efficient foreign firms — only possible with liberalized trade — is an additional way to coerce firms economically to increase their efficiency without abandoning socialist methods of accumulation at home, such as the strict limits on price competition in production supplies between domestic firms, economic concentration for purposes of rationalization, and redistribution of rents from natural monopolies. Private plots for garden vegetables and livestock and financial autonomy and accountability for agricultural and marketing cooperatives can encourage farmers to increase their marketed yields, if necessary by working longer hours or other forms of peasant self-exploitation. The farms are also the logical place for labour dismissed from the industrial sector so that budgetary reductions from welfare and layoffs of the "less productive" do not create unemployment (in the sense of people without some source of subsistence). Those without land can turn to petty services and trades that the freed consumer goods market encourage. Indeed, the liberals place substantial stock in the growth and "initiative" of independent (private) petty bourgeois activities — the sphere of "small firms" and "second economy" — that improve the range and lower the cost of consumer goods without any drain at all on the state budget or public sector firms.

Finally, in defining the political borders of this economy, liberals attempt to recognize simultaneously the global operation of economic competition and technological progress and the national definition of community. One need not enter the tortuous history of the Yugoslav Communist Party's approach to the national question to note that this approach settled by 1940 on the Croat and Slovene version against objections. Nations, in line with their view of Marx's analysis, are not classes but economic spaces that, as historical-territorial units with a culturally-defined collective consciousness and sense of unity as a "people", have the right to administration. As the product of bourgeois competition this form of the nation was more advanced on the road to global community than the feudal form (tied to land-holding) still dominant in the southern regions such as Macedonia and Bosnia; their union into a multinational federation for mutual benefit was only the next stage on the road to this global community. National minorities ("nationalities" as opposed to "nations") resident within a nation's historical territory have a right to separate cultural expression but not economic governance.

This logic necessitates a federal constitution. Its premises are the same as the party's stance toward the rest of the world: a strong "national" defence based on local territorial forces, and the presumption of peaceful coexistence and economic redistribution from rich to poor as the basis for peace and prosperity. Liberals and developmentalists differ on the content of this federal arrangement, however, and in the early days the goal of developing Yugoslavia as one economic space led them beyond simple redistribution between nations to Lenin's formulation of a federal division of labour according to Marxian schemes of reproduction. By this, the federal government owns (with its attendant right to revenues and obligation to invest) projects for defence and country-wide development. Republican governments own the manufacturing, agriculture, transportation, and other activities of Department II located in their territory. Local governments receive jurisdiction over local consumption — local roads, elementary schools, trades and services, and small consumer goods — as well as relations between the socialized and private sectors (basically, industry and agriculture).

For the liberals, however, the same logic for producers' operational and financial autonomy should apply to republics. Governmental decentralization, fiscal federalism, and republican control over economic assets allegedly encourages economic rationality — on the grounds that the closer the responsibility for economic resources is to those who actually employ them, the greater the care in their rational use. Moreover, activities under republican jurisdiction are seen as the engine of growth while those of federal jurisdiction are a drain on that growth. Thus, the economic attack on the state does not apply to republican governments; drawing on the arguments of political and cultural nationalists, they see the federal government — Yugoslavia — as an artificial creation against the natural and legitimate communities of nations ("peoples") in the republics. The liberal strategy even gave new life to the territorial governments of the republics and localities in several ways: the attack on the ministerial hierarchy as a non-productive method of economic coordination; the shift in policy-making to parliaments and deliberative councils of delegates chosen by republic; and the expansion of foreign and private markets and a private sector to discipline the public sector and receive its rationalizing expulsion of less productive workers and welfare claims requires economic coordination on territorial grounds, not the branch ministries of the public sector alone.

Contradictions: From Model to Reality

Much is known about the problem of a pure liberal strategy for economic growth, from the Polanyian critique that markets need social supports and a political counterforce of state policy to keep them functioning properly,[10] through the Keynesian critique of the many aggregate paradoxes of a system of autonomous actors, such as the paradox of thrift to explain the failure of investment in business downturns, to the theorists of unequal exchange in the international economy. These receive little attention in states of reform communism, and one suspects this is because they believe in the socialist institutionalization of that strategy as safeguard against its problems.

The application of this model to Yugoslav reality over the past four decades has revealed a host of problems, however. As a strategy favouring the most developed, it did not take into account the range of underdevelopment in Yugoslavia, its internal heterogeneity, or the extent to which these differences were geographically defined. The liberal economic approach together with republican autonomy produced inequalities between firms, in relation to their initial fixed assets, and also between the republics.

Above all, the idea that the international economy could serve as a source of developmental finance, cheaper wage goods, advanced technology, and competitive stimulus to domestic economic efficiency in a world where socialist states remained outside major trading blocs and were subject to both regularized and quixotic trade discrimination after 1947, and where the government's protection of living standards and employment at home depended on monetary control and preventing domestic price competition between firms and labour, turned out to be wishful thinking. Adjustment to trade deficits and foreign debt preoccupied the country for the entire postwar period, and the choices alternated between delay, short-term administrative and political control over demand and social unrest, and orthodox stabilization that hit the poorest and least developed the hardest. While some had no option but economic restraint, those with greater influence created their own financial instruments and contributed to the inflationary spiral induced by their form of foreign integration. The loss of control over money, above all to foreign creditors, undermined the economic basis of stability in both the economy and the state — the economic security and predictability necessary to rational calculation, of stable growth in consumption across groups that was the basis of solidarity in their political coalition, and of manageable conflicts over distribution.

These two problems eventually exposed the highly problematic concept of the state embedded in the strategy's mix of socialist and liberal assumptions about economic behaviour. From unstable compromises and unending dissensus, to growing inflexibility of economic adjustment, and ever declining authority of state and party, the instabilities and vicious circles of its political-economic system found few counteracting influences from creative political action.

Critical to the early success of the liberal strategy (as recorded in growth rates) was the investment in mining, agriculture, and producers' goods in the brief attempt to build military self-sufficiency in 1947-49, and the international conditions of the 1950s. This was an era of development aid to poorer countries and American military and economic aid to support its strategic interests and anti-communist policies. The foreign financing necessary to get this opening strategy off the ground was there. By the late 1950s, the terms of foreign financing changed dramatically — loans of shorter maturities and higher rates, and increasingly bilateral, suppliers' credits between firms. Expectations that the expansion of the European community after 1958 and Yugoslav membership in GATT, achieved by 1965, would give them greater access to western markets were disappointed; continuing trade discrimination and protectionist barriers made it extremely difficult to reduce trade deficits and repay credits, while import dependence rose and the frequent trade recession in European and world markets during the 1960s were transmitted ever more readily into the domestic market.

This did not change the Yugoslav orientation to the international economy as a source of goods to increase productivity at home, but it began to require the adjustments in labour that the socialist movement was pledged to prevent. Reformers emphasized the necessity of cutting labour costs in production further to be internationally competitive. The remittances of Yugoslavs migrating temporarily to work in northern Europe came to foot nearly half the bill of the growing import dependence for intermediate goods of firms, and their exodus had the side effect of diluting conditions that might have led to political organization against the steeply rising unemployment. Macroeconomic stabilization policies to reduce rising domestic inflation followed the orthodox demand-restricting and budget-cutting approach of their domestic monetary system while they increased supply-side incentives to production. With the rescheduling of loans after 1969 and the hyperlending of recycled petrodollars to developing countries, the influence of international finance (especially the International Monetary Fund) grew, strengthening this orthodox approach, giving the liberals substantial foreign allies, and removing, it appears, any pressure for political reassessment of policy. Stabilization policies and their stop-go cycles of recession and un-intended expansion became the order of the day after 1970 without reducing the deficit or need to finance it further.

If one read the rhetoric of domestic politics and economic debate in the 1970s, one would be convinced that the reformists' "market" strategy had been defeated by popular reaction and replaced by a system of politicized negotiations and excessive political centralization and economic decentralization that interferred with any rational calculation of the kind reformers had sought. What really changed, however, were the supply shocks and their accompanying price rises in the world economy, and thus the interests of the most influential producers in finding cheaper, more reliable sources of raw materials (and even some producers' goods) at home and in producing for export goods whose prices were rising and, unlike more highly processed manufactures, were less vulnerable to unpredictable trade barriers. State preoccupation with the balance of payments doubled the interest in changing investment policy, and its sectoral shift gave greater importance to lowering costs of production and quantity increases than to revenues on consumer goods markets. Popular anger at rising inequalities, unemployment, and private wealth helped to ease the politics of this transition with an attack on commercially-oriented managers and liberal politicians.

What did not change was the concept of growth through micro-productivity, direct incentives, and budgetary discipline that had always defined the liberal reformists' strategy. The mergers and concentration of the 1960s to save on administrative costs, shift redundant labour, and gain market advantage were now attacked for diluting incentives to greater productivity. Firms were subdivided into units that "produced market value", and could therefore have an autonomous budget, so as to make incentives and accountability more direct and to find in this anti-trust drive toward smaller units a domestic rather than foreign source of competition. That this period also saw a rise in employment figures (with no compensating fall in unemployment), alongside stagflation, placed Yugoslavia squarely in the camp of most of the world's economies as they struggled to respond to the same global conditions. By the early 1980s manu-facturing firms oriented to western markets (especially in Slovenia), chafing at productivity comparisons that showed their relative decline, and harsher conditions from foreign commercial banks and the IMF over the foreign debt and terms of rescheduling, succeeded in shifting the policy agenda to technological modernization through imports, expanded exports to pay this bill and reduce the deficit, and more onerous austerity to stabilize the currency.

The full extent to which international conditions defined shifts in economic policy and prevented any change in the ruling strategy cannot be explained without its domestic political counterpart: the ambivalence toward the central state and quarrels over redistribution. The international functions of sovereignty remained in the scaled-down state — its responsibility for the country's balance of foreign payments, its legal guarantee of foreign inscribed debt, both public and commercial, and its protection of territorial integrity and national security. Yet neither the authority nor the revenues to perform these functions went unchallenged. Disagreements over defence policy had been "resolved" in the 1950s by combining a standing army with local territorial defence forces, but once the nuclear goal was abandoned for conventional warfare (assisted by the 1968 invasion of Czechoslovakia), the supremacy of the army was increasingly challenged. Only as long as Tito was alive was there an arbiter for Slovene and Croat demands for sovereignty of the territorial militias, cuts in the military budget, and republican precedence in cases of disagreement.

Even more frequent shifts occurred in the foreign exchange regime defining internal allocation. The importance of foreign exchange for production supplies and technology, the constant shortfall of export earnings against imports, and the insistence on nonconvertibility to retain some domestic control over living standards, employment, and economic stability turned disputes over access to and the right to use foreign exchange into the bitterest of quarrels. Yet each successive regime reduced the government's control further: ever greater liberalization of foreign capital flows to entice foreign investment; allowing firms to enter foreign capital markets freely, only to have European banking circles in the mid-1970s insist that the government regulate requests for loans that had become excessive; the decision after 1978 to divide the balance of payments into separate republican accounts to break the deadlock over responsibility for the deficit; and periodic efforts to recentralize control or create a foreign exchange market during the 1980s.

These quarrels reflect a larger unresolved problem of the state's authority to tax enterprise profits (surplus value) and the intentional limits on the revenue base of the federal government. Although it remains responsible for national defence, major developmental projects subject to republican free-riding, and currency stability, the state must bargain for income with representatives of producers; is obliged by the constitution to balance its budget; and cannot borrow from nonexistent capital markets. If it prints money to cover deficits, it only delays, and harshens, the obligatory budget-cutting of a stabilization programme. By the 1970s, there were few line items of the federal budget that had not been divested into financial self-governance. Thus, the federal government has always sought foreign funds to "supplement domestic accumulation" and to replace the domestic monies it cannot obtain. World Bank loans for major infrastructural projects such as roads; military assistance; public credits; bilateral trade agreements (not always fulfilled by other countries); and IMF balance of payments financing all have contributed their share to the foreign debt from the trade deficit, enterprise borrowing, and suppliers' credits.

Where the original objective of the socialist monetary system was to prevent the devaluation of labour power through producers' control and to protect the domestic economy from international trade cycles and foreign financial control, the opposite occurred. Frequent devaluation of the exchange rate, policy-induced recessions and with it declining real wages, rising unemployment, and by the mid-1980s, triple digit inflation, not only became a normal part of the economic scene, but disagreements about how to address these problems were only resolved (and that temporarily) by the pressures of international finance. The domestic economy came to reproduce cycles in the global economy rather than to protect its producers against it.

It is often said that these problems of macroeconomic instability and debt are the result of an insufficiently independent and disciplined Central Bank. Apart from the opposite assumption of the Yugoslav liberal system, that only if producers controlled finance could stability result, this commentary raises the difficulty of the system's assumption that producers and governments will be able to agree on mutually beneficial outcomes if they pursue their economic interest and have the right to self-determination. In the first case, the liberal strategy favours producers with greater initial assets, with links to the west, and with goods that can be sold abroad; developmentalists persist despite their institutional disadvantage because they represent another view and other interests. Since most distributive issues involve real conflicts of interest and disagreement, pareto optimal decisions are in fact quite rare and discussions can deteriorate rapidly into questions of fairness and accusations of injustice.[11] In federal offices, which are councils representing the republic governments (equally, rather than proportional to population), or in negotiations between producers, the discussion and bargaining takes time. Contracts are often out of date by the time they are signed, and the frequent resort to compromise encourages parties to cheat or seek alternative outlets. The governing board of the Central Bank, as a council of republican representatives, finds it very difficult to formulate a monetary policy on which all will agree.

Some of this difficulty of a system that eschews both central planning and market allocation for cooperative links between those who produce value — "the free exchange of labour" in an "association of free producers and free republics" — could be resolved by clear procedures and habits of mutuality developed over time. Yet government firefighting in response to the immediate pressures of deadlocked negotiations over economic policy and budgets, spiralling conflicts, inflation, and above all balance of payments deficits continuously interrupted the expectations of regular economic activity, and quarrels over principles of distribution have led to such frequent changes in the rules of allocation (of foreign exchange, of develoment funds, of taxes, of enterprise income) that stable procedures have little time to develop.

One of the reasons that these quarrels are difficult to resolve and rules can change so frequently is the virtual definition of ownership as the right to control realized surplus value (the net income after material costs and obligatory depreciation of the firm). Each person employed in the public sector has a right to a personal income commensurate with his or her contribution to that realized value; governments have a right to a portion of income earned on their territory; and so forth. But what is the source of value added? How ought income to be valued? Within firms, dispute has long raged between those who view income to be the result of lowered costs of production, and therefore due to the engineering staff or to production workers who in different ways increased output per unit of labour, and those who insist that income is realized sales from meeting market demand, and therefore the commercially-minded manager, the economists, and the marketing and sales staff. The basis for wage differentials according to skill levels, and whether the difficulty of a task (production workers) or its complexity (managers) is a better measure of added value, also led to disputes on wage determination.

Between firms there are disputes about relative contribution to the more prized final commodity. The pressure from more successful firms producing final goods for consumption and more developed republics with higher foreign currency receipts to retain an ever larger portion of their domestic and foreign market earnings against fiscal redistribution during the 1960s, for example, caused an uproar among producers of raw materials and intermediate goods and republics with less access because of production specializations and historical legacies to hard currency earnings. Had they not also contributed to the final product? The unsatisfactory solution in the 1970s and 1980s was to require that contracts between firms, whether for supplies or joint ventures and investment, include terms over the division of ultimate profits according to relative contribution.

Quarrels between republics over economic policy or redistributive transfers (for development aid, budgetary supplements, natural disasters and emergencies, or federal projects), in particular, tend to deteriorate into disputes over rightful ownership and efforts to realize their claims: by a progressive reduction in such transfers, by frequent charges that other republics are "laggards", and by a host of protectionist measures (especially by the wealthier republics) to keep revenues and investment at home. The division of product markets into non-competing territorial zones with ministerial decentralization and republican autonomy after 1950 has been reinforced ever since by local and republican government reaction against firms from outside their territory; by campaigns to get locals to "buy national" (Croatian, Slovenian, NovoSadian, Serbian); and by producers' enforcement of rules against "disloyal competition" (price wars). Trade wars erupted periodically between republics, particularly in the 1980s. By the mid-1980s, wealthier Slovenia and Croatia were refusing to pay their share into the federal budget and by 1990 they chose to pursue complete independence if they could not get a confederal constitution that gave them full sovereignty.

A consequence of decentralization, divestment of federal economic authority, and enterprise control has been, ironically, to increase the tax burden of firms and the redistribution they criticize. The burden of public goods and externalities fell heavily and unevenly on local governments, exacerbating the inequalities that already exist in development levels and local resources. Obliged to balance their budgets, and with the authority to tax as the country's tax collectors, local governments devised ever more taxes on firms (based on the wage bill, or net income of the firm), local bond issues for schools and hospitals, and fees and taxes on the private sector. This significantly dampened the development of the private sector, despite policy-makers' wish. Enterprises were frequently short of working capital to pay workers and had to beg banks to extend credit or shift the burden onto other firms with involuntary trade credits of unpaid obligations. The poorer the locality, the more local politicians and enterprise managers needed each other and the greater were the inducements to corruption and personal networks of mutual back-scratching and power. At the same time, because banks are governed by enterprises with voting power in direct proportion to deposits, credit decisions have tended to favour the largest firms — all within the republic borders of their jurisdiction — and the investment choices of the republican governments, whereas the risks of bank failure or the debt of large firms are socialized among all enterprises, large and small, within the republic. Because local governments are responsible for unemployment, they do everything possible to forestall bankruptcy of firms with temporary direct rule, restructuring, or loans, so as not to find their budgets and social service agencies over-whelmed. Ultimately, these practices move through the banking system, and the National Bank must choose between monetizing the accumulating debts of its member banks or risk a tidal wave of bankruptcies throughout the economy and renewed recession.

The microeconomic assumptions of macroeconomic stability, that enterprises and local governments would and even could be conservative, responsible financial managers, who balance budgets and make appropriate economic calculations regardless of the politics of distribution in recession and external economic shocks and demands, clearly failed in Yugoslavia. Over and over, the central government had to assert its responsibility for the balance of payments, the foreign debt, and the value of the domestic currency with demand-repressing policies — both monetary and physical restrictions — while supply-side policies aimed to revive domestic production and restore monetary equilibrium. Still assuming that production would respond best to material incentives to producers, this meant cutting governmental budgets and resources for investment first. Monies for transportation, basic human services, and collective goods were progressively cut, handed over to lower governments or independent funds (restricted in use and transfer to their original purpose), or abandoned to private sector mobilization ("the market" where those who could pay would restore the incentive to producers), with the eventual effect of progressive neglect. In place of the equilibrating objective, ever more frequent stabilization programmes addressed to external deficits and internal inflation created a downward cycle of recession, relieved only occasionally by monetary expansion accommodating debt of the previous period (rather than of Keynesian inspiration).

Its economic power contingent on monetary stability, the federal government tried to supplement its declining authority with the remaining political instruments under its control — the standing army and federal police powers that remain after substantial budgetary cuts, and the discipline of party members insofar as they remain unified and loyal. But monies for the military, authoritative positions and jobs for party cadre, and international diplomacy all require control over some economic resources. The idea that the party could remain a united force was in conflict with the republicanization of cadre policy, their assignment to firm or locality where common interest with their employer was meant to ensure rational decisions, and their loss (in 1951) of special privileges in goods markets. And because the army became increasingly entangled with domestic events, through civil disorder over growing inequalities (from those resisting redistribution and those in need of more), there were heavy political costs as well. The more the state is equated with coercive force, even when this is used to protect minorities, the more the legitimacy of its existence and expenditures are subject to question.

In the end, even the Yugoslav concept of democracy fell victim to its definition by the socialist liberal programme as a tactic to increase productivity with non-economic rewards: that people would find in the rights to democratic participation in decisions on production and distribution a substitute for immediate pay and a carrot for "waiting", for accepting the longer time horizon of capital. Where they sought to invigorate the "spiritual life" of the people (as Gorbachev also said frequently in 1988-1989), more intense consumerism resulted. And under prolonged recession and austerity policies, worsening shortages, and rising inflation, democracy became a burden, not a privilege. People used their democratic rights to claim fully the economic assets they are said to "own". In place of greater participation in public policy or social problems, they sought greater autonomy for their firm or national community from the state so as to be able to hold onto "their earnings" against their redistribution elsewhere. Yugoslavs mourn the loss by the early 1960s of a time when public service and individual work alike were motivated by devotion to the collective enterprise they shared, regardless of the immediate pecuniary reward, but few propose to slow the momentum away from autonomy. Instead the system of microrationality and decentralized

budgets places the locus of political activity within wage determination (usually, firms) for workers and within republics for
citizens. Free enterprise (and managerial power) and nationalist
independence became the choice of radicals, while the social base of
any society-wide movement disappeared.

The particular choices of an orthodox stabilization policy also
explain the most problematic social conflict of the liberal strategy.
Although it is often said that reform's greatest opposition comes from
workers threatened by unemployment and bureaucrats losing power,
it is the professionally-educated middle class — the original support
troops of liberalization — who chafe the most. Highly schooled and
urban, with expectations of status in employment commensurate with
their educational credentials, holding onto precious housing in ever
tighter housing markets and with few opportunities to return to the
countryside, they complain when their salaries diminish in comparison
with private sector incomes, when their relative advantage over
industrial workers is undercut by inflation, and their children
increasingly join the ranks of the unemployed as the attack on
"bureaucracy" and "non-productive" budgets reduces expansion in
white collar jobs. Although they have benefited from the wage gains
of industrial workers on which their salary rates are based, they are
also dependent on workers' collective bargaining for those gains.

Unlike the unskilled worker sent into private employ or the
bureaucrat reassigned to local jurisdictions, the flexibility of
adjustment to intensification and orthodox stabilization in this case
affects the most articulate social groups. Where budgetary restraints
reduce the number of local administrative and professional jobs, they
are quick to use cultural and ethnic criteria — nationalism — for
allocating jobs or mobilizing a collective grievance. And at the same
time that the staff of enterprises is expanding with the transfer of ever
more functions to the budgets and halls of firms, they succeed in
directing public attention to the "excessive" wages and wage increases
of industrial workers and their cause of price inflation. As we have
seen elsewhere in central and eastern Europe as well as the more
developed republics — Slovenia and Croatia — of Yugoslavia, it is a
very short step in political logic to claim the failure of the reform
strategy and the necessity of a "truly" liberal (i.e., fully
capitalist) system.

Even on the eve of the final showdown on the Yugoslav state, the
prime minister was fighting for one more version of economic reform,
introduced, he said, to get renewed financing from western creditors.
A constitutional debate of fateful proportions, between the two
republics that would accept only a confederation of sovereign states
and the four that wanted to retain a federal state, focused on

financing for the federal government, about whether monies for national defence, development aid to poorer regions, and agricultural investment could and should be found or whether the republics should be fully sovereign over their territorial defence forces, legislation, and budgets.

Conclusion

Despite the many differences between Yugoslavia and the Soviet Union, the expectations and contradictions of the reformists' strategy are the same. In an especially revealing statement in 1989, Gorbachev explained the reason for reform by reference to changes in the world situation: "this was not 1968" when the Vietnam war and escalating rearmament created a hostile security threat. Even if the USSR can bear rising balance of payments deficits more lightly than Yugoslavia, the infusion of foreign capital and a growing private sector undermine the monetary control of a planned economy and turn the passive role of money into a monetarist orthodoxy that western creditors are only too eager to reinforce. Monetary "overhang" has similar origins, and the resort to political compromises and administered rationing of goods evidence of the weakness of the state, not its power. Already the conflict over national sovereignty between republics, and nationalities within republics, has grown at least as violent, and the stage of conflict over budgets and trade in goods has moved rapidly to legislative sovereignty and military authority — local defence and paramilitary forces versus the standing army and all-union police.

The loss of central authority cannot, if the Yugoslav example is a lesson, be recaptured. Observers of Yugoslavia long believed that Tito's charismatic authority held the system together, not recognizing the importance he placed on international diplomacy and the tensions he had to balance between his preference for the reformers' strategy and his role as head of state. And those who attacked his centralizing reactions found the tension reproduced by the international community that will insist on both — the continuation of economic reform and the reassertion of a stable currency and political order — as conditions for the yearned-for foreign investment, technological imports, and membership in the West and as someone to hold financially responsible.

NOTES

1.   The word is inconveniently the same in much of the region, permitting not only confusion but also political obfuscation.
2.   A particularly useful introduction to the intertwining of developmental debates in this region, to Lenin's shared discourse of German developmentalism in

competition with Britain, and to neopopulist ideas can be found in Gavin Kitching, *Development and Underdevelopment in Historical Perspective* (London and New York: Methuen, 1982).

3. Cited and thoroughly discussed in Alexander Erlich, *The Soviet Industrialization Debate, 1924-1928* (Cambridge, Mass.: Harvard University Press, 1960), Chs. 1 and 2, pp. 3-59.

4. A useful introduction to this monetary system in practice is Marie Lavigne, "The Creation of Money by the State Bank of the USSR", *Economy and Society* (February 1978).

5. This is the usual interpretation: that the New Economic Policy aimed at regaining the peasantry, and that the Yugoslav reforms were an attempt to "return to the Yugoslav people" from domestically-grounded legitimacy after a period of anti-national "Stalinism" where relations with Moscow had defined policy choice and strategy.

6. This is one of the great achievements of Alexander Erlich's lucid study, *The Soviet Industrialization Debate* (see fn. 3), even if the absence of discussion about the political issues involved makes this less than obvious.

7. This was especially true of the writings and speeches of Edvard Kardelj, the main architect of the Yugoslav state until his death in 1979.

8. Boris Kidric, speaking on economic problems to the Third Plenum of the Central Committee of the Yugoslav Communist Party, the 29th and 30th of December, 1949, recorded in Branko Petranović, Ranko Koncar, Radovan Radonjić, eds., *Sednice Centralnog Komiteta KPJ (1948-1952)*, Izvori za Istoriju SKJ, Series A:II:2 (Belgrade: Komunist, 1985), p. 391.

9. This interpretation of the introduction of worker self-management in Yugoslavia is based on archival research, the primary piece of which is the record of central committee plenums in 1949 (see endnote 6), and discussed at length in chapters 5 and 6 of my manuscript, *Socialist Unemployment: Divisions of Labor in a Republic of Producers, Yugoslavia, 1945-1985*.

10. Karl Polanyi, *The Great Transformation* (Boston: Beacon Press, 1944).

11. Or its ultimate criticism, that redistribution undermines the incentives necessary to rising productivity, as Milan Vodopivec argues with substantial econometric evidence in his Ph.D. dissertation, *Productivity Effects of Redistribution in a Socialist Economy: The Case of Yugoslavia* (Department of Economics, University of Maryland, Ph.D. dissertation, 1989).

THE SOCIALIST FETTER: A CAUTIONARY TALE

Michael A. Lebowitz

> *Bishop, I can fly,*
> *The tailor said to the Bishop.*
> *Just watch how it works.*
> *And he climbed with things*
> *That looked like wings*
> *To the broad, broad roof of the church.*
> *The Bishop passed by.*
> *It's all a lie.*
> *Man is no bird,*
> *No one will ever fly,*
> *The Bishop said of the tailor.*
>
> *The tailor is done for,*
> *The people said to the Bishop.*
> *It was the talk of the fair.*
> *His wings were smashed*
> *And he was dashed*
> *On the hard, hard stones of the square.*
> *Toll the bells in the steeple,*
> *It was all a lie,*
> *Man is no bird,*
> *No one will ever fly,*
> *The Bishop said to the people.*

Bertolt Brecht[1]

The dreams of many have been dashed by the failures of actually existing socialism. For those who consider themselves Marxists, however, there are special complications. Few others are so congenitally disposed to accept historical experience as the Verdict of History.

The real as rational is the particular petard which has deprived Marxists of their footing. Prepared to accept every apparent crisis of capitalism as the reward for patient perseverance, as the revelation that the old is indeed dying, we look in shock at a machine gone mad. In the light of the economic and political crises of actually existing socialism (hereafter AES), the Marxian conception of history appears as the intellectual weapon not of the proletariat but, rather, of capital.

Consider what G. A. Cohen has aptly designated as the thesis of "the primacy of productive forces" — the dictum that the existence of a set of productive relations is explained by the level of development of the productive forces and that a new set of relations of production emerges when the old set "fetters" the productive forces.[2] For generations of Marxists, this was the promise of victories to come and come.

Yet, today there can be little doubt that this systemization of the spare propositions of Marx's Preface of 1859 carries with it distinctly uncomfortable implications. It is bad enough that it follows from this thesis, as Cohen indicates, that capitalism "persists because and as long as it is optimal for further development of productive power and. . . *is* optimal for further development of productive power".[3] There is also the inference that the present era of social revolution in the countries of AES is proof that socialism fetters the development of productive forces. Schumpeter's proposal in 1942 that Marxism permits a conservative interpretation thus has moved from insight to challenge.[4] It is important to understand, however, that a quite different lesson may be drawn from the fall of AES.

I. *The Austrian Challenge*

Credit for the most consistent and systematic argument that socialism inherently stifles the development of productive forces must go to the Austrian School in economics. Beginning with Ludwig von Mises in 1920 and followed by Frederick Hayek and more recent adherents to this school, they have argued that, as a system for progressively developing productivity and satisfying human needs, socialism is unworkable.

At the core of their argument is the absence of the entrepreneur in socialism. Austrians stress the alertness of individual entrepreneurs to opportunities for new ways of doing things (eg., new markets, new combinations of factors of production, new forms of organisation, etc.) as the driving force behind the development of productivity.[5] That alertness has as its basis the search for profits: "Human beings tend to notice that which is in their interest to notice."[6]

In this argument, too, the market plays a special role. By providing the information that permits decentralised decision-makers to discover the productive potential of their resources and by penalizing (via competitive rivalry) those who are not alert to the potential opportunities for gain, the market process is an essential part of the dynamism of capitalism. From this perspective, socialism with its common ownership of the means of production (and, *a fortiori*, with central planning) must inevitably fail.

For many years, Oscar Lange's theoretical demonstration that a market socialist economy could satisfy the efficiency criteria of neoclassical economics was widely accepted as an adequate refutation of the early Austrian argument. [7] Yet, in recent years, buoyed perhaps by the failures of AES, modern Austrians have gone back to re-interpret the Lange debate. In the course of this, they have drawn a much clearer line between mainstream neoclassical arguments which emphasize static efficiency market considerations and the Austrian focus on the entrepreneur as the driving force in the market process. [8] As Don Lavoie, the most influential of these revisionists, has argued, only a mainstream neoclassical (Walrasian) argument against the possibility of socialist efficiency was refuted by Lange; indeed, the Lange argument itself is shown to be completely within the bounds of the static, competitive equilibrium argument of neoclassical economics. [9] Thus, the Austrian focus on entrepreneurs in a dynamic disequilibrium market process emerges unscathed in the recent readings of the famous debate.

To be sure, since the main focus of von Mises' original argument stressed the impossibility of forming prices for means of production (and thus permitting rational economic calculation) under common ownership of the means of production, it is somewhat high-handed to declare that Lange's demonstration that prices do not require markets scored no points. [10] Our concern here, however, is not with the retrospective determination of winners and losers in an old debate. (Indeed, Lavoie is sensitive to the charge that he may be reading "modern Austrian positions into the earlier Austrian contributions." [11]) Rather, it is the product of the conjunction of the resurrected Austrian position and the failures of AES which bears attention.

For market reformers despairing of effective reform of the economies of AES, the new reading of the Lange debate has facilitated the explicit incorporation of Austrian arguments. Thus, the Polish economists Brus and Laski (in their new book, *From Marx to the Market*) explicitly accept Lavoie's updated version of the old exchanges. [12] Lange, they note, responded to the Austrian challenge "by presenting an essentially Walrasian system without the capitalists". Yet, that model "overlooks the true central figure of the capitalist system, namely the entrepreneur *sensu stricto*." [13]

Rather than the "robots" (Lavoie called them automatons) who populate mainstream neoclassical economics (and Lange's model) and mechanically optimize on the basis of given data, Brus and Laski indicate that the real entrepreneur must be "an acute observer of the emergence of new alternatives, as well as a creator of them". And, the entrepreneurial "intuition" itself is "generated by actually finding oneself in a competitive situation" (as in capitalism's competitive struggle for profits). [14] Since none of this is present in Lange's model of market socialism, one cannot conclude that Lange refuted the "Mises/Hayek challenge". That challenge is whether the entrepreneurial behaviour necessary for static and dynamic efficiency is "at all imaginable for economic actors who are not principals operating on their own risk and responsibility, but only agents employed by a public body which in itself is rather unfit for entrepreneurial behaviour".[15]

Although Brus has long stood out among market reformers for his unequivocal advocacy of a democratic socialism, the acceptance of the Austrian *desiderata* has made an undeniable mark on the Brus and Laski arguments.[16] While granting AES's successes in expanding the industrial base of backward economies through the use of central planning, Brus and Laski stress both the very high costs and the inherent limits of the particular growth strategies followed.[17] At the core of the problem is the discouragement of innovation and the inbred conservatism of the command system. Accordingly, having indicted the Marxian theory of socialism and the command system of AES for failing to acknowledge the importance of prices in conveying accurate information (in order to compare economic alternatives) and for providing weak incentives for innovation, Brus and Laski turn their attention to the market-oriented reforms in countries of AES.[18]

And, here again, the Austrian influence is telling. It surfaces in their criticism of early market reform models which, in accordance with Marxist theory, reserved decisions over the extent and direction of accumulation to the state.[19] Without a capital market (providing autonomy for individual state enterprises in following market signals), the functioning of competition in product markets is weakened: the "kind of competition generated by the entrepreneurial spirit of 'creative destruction' " is unlikely "without access to venture capital and new spheres of activity".[20]

Similarly, the absence of a proper labour market has also reduced the possibility of effective market coordination. "The absence of market-type opposition between 'buyers' and 'sellers' as far as labour is concerned presents a formidable obstacle to the achievement of a market ('rational') price of labour, and by itself throws the door open to bureaucratic coordination."[21] Thus, the problem is not enough reform, not enough of a movement to market coordination of the economy.

Yet, the Austrian spectre does not simply haunt their criticisms of the early reform efforts. For, it is striking that, having constructed a model of the "consistently reformed system" of "market socialism proper" (MS) which includes capital and labour markets, Brus and Laski proceed to question that system itself on the grounds of the appropriateness of state ownership at all.[22] At issue is whether state enterprises "will behave exactly as their capitalist counterparts, displaying the same level of microeconomic efficiency and the same alertness to opportunities offered by technical progress and by changes in the parameters of the system". In short, "is MS — requiring full independence of firms and true entrepreneurship — compatible with the dominant position of public (state) ownership of the means of production?" [23]

Their answer is — probably not. Even if the state were to adopt the position of mere rentier, remaining an interested observer of recreated wage struggles within enterprises, the real problem of entrepreneurship at the level of the firm would remain. What the socialist manager would still lack is "the material foundation of responsibility for risks when the venture fails. He does not risk his own capital, and this, as emphasized by Hayek long ago, makes it highly probable that he will err either on the side of recklessness or on the side of over-cautiousness." [24] In short, "fully fledged market conditions resemble. . . the game of poker, which can hardly be played without risking one's own stake". [25]

Yet, Brus and Laski do not give up on their idea of a "consistently reformed system" of market socialism. Despite its inherent problems, state ownership remains important to them as a source of revenue, as an instrument of Keynesian-type policy and as a means of ameliorating income and wealth inequality. [26] Thus, although admitting that the "pure logic of the fully fledged market mechanism" suggests private enterprise as "the more natural constituent of the enterprise sector of MS", they claim "the case for state enterprise should not be regarded as inevitably lost". Brus and Laski remain supporters of socialism — although the "open-ended" system they describe is one which Marxists (as well as von Mises) would deny the designation of socialism. [27]

Brus and Laski are not alone, however, in their absorption of the Austrian theory. Janos Kornai, the Hungarian economist, has similarly valorized that theory in his studies of the failures of the economies of AES. In the case of Kornai, on the other hand, the adherence to socialism ends with a bang.

In his 1986 review of the Hungarian reform process, Kornai also accepted Lavoie's ("outstanding") reconstruction of the Lange debate and dismissed Lange's "sterile world of Walrasian pure theory":

> What got lost was the crucial Mises-Hayek-Schumpeter idea regarding "rivalry". In a genuine market process actors participate who want to make use, and can make use, of their specific knowledge and opportunities. They are rivals. In that sense the market is always in a state of dynamic disequilibrium. The total potential of all rivals normally exceeds actual demand. Some win and some lose. Victory brings rewards: survival, growth, more profit, more income. Defeat means penalties: losses, less income, and in the ultimate case, exit. [28]

Whereas Kornai at this point endorsed the proposals of "radical reformers" in Hungary for a market socialist model similar to that of Brus and Laski, he expressed muted concerns about the adequacy of their treatment of the substantial question of ownership and property rights.[29] With the revolution in Hungary, however, Kornai has emerged as a full-blown adherent to the Austrian School; the title of his recent book, *The Road to a Free Economy*, indeed, is a conscious echo of Hayek's earlier *The Road to Serfdom*, and the book itself is an application of Austrian-type arguments for capitalism.[30]

There should be no surprise, then, that Kornai's paean for the "free economy" extols private property, the "flexibility, initiative, ability to quickly recognize and exploit opportunities, and freedom of entry and competition" within a market economy — and, of course, the entrepreneur (who includes "only those who are willing to risk personal financial loss").[31] Nor is he out of character here when he dismisses market socialism as a "fiasco" and scoffs at the futility of hoping that "the state unit will behave as if it were privately owned and will spontaneously act as if it were a market-oriented agent".[32]

Everywhere, the Austrian ethos prevails — whether it concerns a progressive income tax ("It gives me no moral satisfaction to see above-the-crowd people being pulled down to the lowest common denominator") or the difficulties facing the Hungarian people in the course of their transition to a "free economy":

"Respect should not go to those who moan the loudest, but to those who stop whining. . . The old adage 'God helps those who help themselves' has never been more appropriate."[33]

What is especially important, however, about Kornai's newly declared faith is his insistence that the ideas in his new book are not the result of a sudden epiphany but, rather, "follow closely" from his many years of concrete study of the economies of AES.[34] And, that bears some consideration. Kornai's analysis has achieved a significant degree of hegemony (and underlies much of the discussion of Brus and Laski and many others). Accordingly, it is important to examine that analysis to understand the extent to which it, indeed, provides support to the Austrian argument that socialism inherently fetters the development of productive forces.

II. *The Analysis of Kornai*

Perhaps the most intriguing aspect of Kornai's work has been his conscious effort to understand AES as an organic system and to uncover the laws of motion of that system.[35] In his early study of central planning in Hungary, for example, he emphasized the extent to which centralisation generated shortages which, in turn, generated the need for centralisation. Excessive centralisation, he proposed at the time, is a "coherent, unified mechanism, which has its own inner logic and several tendencies and regularities peculiar to itself".[36] Consistently, it has been "the immanent regularities of a socialist economy" which have interested Kornai, and much of his work has been the attempt to identify the "state permanently reproduced by the general economic laws and by the system-specific intrinsic regularities".[37]

Although Kornai's most recent book is more of a pamphlet (hastily written to influence Hungarian political decisions) than a systematic study, the same theoretical orientation shows itself in his concern for policy proposals that "add up to an organic whole". In this case, Kornai's efforts are directed to setting out the measures necessary for the development of capitalism as an organic system in Hungary and for the "organic historical development of private property".[38]

Kornai's fame (and his claim to a future "Nobel Prize in Economics") is based largely upon his analysis of the system-specific intrinsic regularities of AES as those producing a shortage economy as a normal state. As he indicated in his earlier works, the chronic shortage characteristic of AES brings with it many specific attributes — a dominating position for the seller (seller's markets), the burden of adjustment and forced substitution for buyers, the full utilisation of resources (including labour), hoarding (on the part of consumers and firms), a lack of discipline and diligence on the part of workers and a disinclination on the part of producers to innovate.[39]

Initially, Kornai attributed this pattern to the command system and to the centre's "impatient chasing of economic growth, the forcing of the acceleration of the growth rate", which reproduced both shortages and centralisation.[40] As long as this approach continued to achieve much (especially in drawing labour reserves into the production process), many of the dysfunctions associated with the shortage economy went ignored. Nevertheless, sooner or later, the system was bound to face inherent barriers with the emergence of chronic labour shortages. ("The exhaustion of labour reserves is sufficient in itself to force the economic system to leave its old growth path for a newer and much slower one.")[41] Accordingly, the apparent solution was an end to directive planning and its replacement by the introduction of a socialist market economy.

This is what Kornai subsequently described as characteristic of the position of the "naive reformer".[42] For, after all, it soon became clear that the pattern of chronic shortage continued *despite* the emergence of market reforms in Hungary. Kornai's subsequent explanation, then, focussed in particular upon the behaviour of the managers of state firms. Identifying with their positions and with the success of their enterprises, the managers had an insatiable demand for resources. ("He is convinced that the activity of the unit under his charge is important. Therefore it has to grow.")[43] Thus, in behaviour typical of bureaucrats, the enterprise managers were determined to maximize their own budgets. And, since it was not their own money they were spending, the result was an unquenchable expansion drive which became a more important explanation for the reproduction of shortages than the growth policy of the centre.[44]

Nevertheless, despite Kornai's emphasis upon the behaviour of the managers, the ultimate explanation of the production of shortages rested elsewhere. In particular, the problem was that the state adopted the paternalistic practice of bailing out firms when they were in difficulty. As a result, the firms functioned with "soft budget constraints"; and, not only were they able to expand without risk, but the absence of the potential penalties (eg., failure and bankruptcy) associated with a hard budget constraint meant that the firms were relatively unresponsive to the market. Rather, then, than truly functioning as market-oriented agents, the firms remained dependent upon the state in what Kornai described as a situation of "dual dependence" (a combination of bureaucratic and market co-ordination).[45] Thus, the hopes of the market reformers were disappointed; the experiment was a "fiasco".

What was needed, Kornai accordingly argued, was that the central authorities recognise the negative effects of their paternalism, harden the budget constraints of firms so that they were fully dependent on their own revenue, and introduce slack into the economy to permit it to operate more efficiently. But, this didn't happen. And, Kornai now argues it will *never* happen "as long as the state sector remains the dominant sector in the national economy".[46]

Unlike those who argue that it was the system of administrative planning and management (obsolete productive relations) that developed into a fetter or those who attribute continuing inadequacies to the failure as yet to adopt a "consistently reformed system", what makes Kornai's argument distinctive among the reformers is that he identifies the problem as one inherent in socialism.[47] In the "ethical principles of a socialist economy" (especially those of solidarity and security), Kornai finds an essential contradiction with the necessary conditions for economic efficiency.[48]

Thus, he argues that the budget constraint in socialism will not be hardened because of the concern of a socialist state for the maintenance of employment. ("It is practically incapable of deciding to eliminate jobs en masse.")[49] The elimination of unemployment (which "debases human dignity, forcing workers to humble themselves before the employers") is for Kornai an element of the security and solidarity which are essential principles of socialist ethics. But, that very commitment to full employment *also* is in contradiction to the universal requirements for efficiency. [50]

For Kornai, guaranteed full employment is a policy that protects the careless and the lazy. The chronic labour shortage (and the seller's market for labour it produces) "loosens workshop discipline, deteriorates work quality, lessens workers' diligence". In short, "the worker's *absolute* security, the unconditional guarantee of employment, encourages irresponsibility in anyone susceptible to it". [51] Yet it is not simply the lack of efficiency and discipline on the part of workers which makes market socialism inherently inferior to capitalism. [52] In this shortage economy, fostered by state paternalism, the wages paid by state firms are as well too *high*. [53]

State managers cannot enforce "wage discipline", and this "Achilles' heel" of socialist market reforms occurs because "the state-owned firm operates in a no-man's land that is neither a command economy, where wage discipline is enforced through bureaucratic means, nor a genuine market economy, where private ownership simulates this discipline". In contrast to capitalist relations, where "the natural interests of the *private* owners run counter to excessive wage increases" (and where increases will only occur "if the marginal productivity of the worker is not less than the wage"), the manager of a state firm faced with wage demands or tensions in the workforce "merely transfers the money of an impersonal state to his workers". [54] Only the "replacement of state ownership with private ownership" can alter this situation. "Only private ownership can pit a natural 'antagonist' against the employee who demands a wage raise; this antagonist is the owner, who pays wages out of his own pocket." [55]

Thus, for Kornai, market socialism is inherently flawed because it is unable to enforce either workplace or wage discipline — i.e., to stimulate the dependence of the wage-labourer regularly reproduced within capitalism. And, at the core of the problem is the adherence to the principles of socialist ethics, which prevents the hardening of the budget constraint. Ultimately, this is the bottom line. The "effective constraint" in socialism is neither the non-ownership of means of production by managers of state enterprises nor their desire to maximize their budgets. It is not that the managers, could they be relieved of state paternalism and be firmly subjected to hard budget constraints, would fail to display entrepreneurship in the market. *Rather, the effective constraint is the inability of the socialist state to discipline the managers of its various divisions and to act like a good capitalist owner.*

Accordingly, socialism is fated to reproduce conditions of chronic shortage, with all the inefficiencies that this entails. It inevitably must hold back the development of productive forces — because it lacks capitalists (either in the managers of state enterprises or in the state as owner of a multi-divisional firm).[56] It lacks entrepreneurs — because an entrepreneur by definition must be the antagonist of workers and must pay workers out of his own pocket. And, finally, it lacks a genuine market — because the characteristic of a market which will propel entrepreneurs into rivalrous competition with other sellers is one in which there is excess supply ("the total potential of all rivals normally exceeds actual demand"); neither the incentive nor the proper economic calculation thus can exist in the shortage economy characteristic of socialism.

Nothing is easier, of course, than to dismiss Kornai's findings as relevant to socialism as such. One need only state that AES was and is not socialism. There are certainly many bases upon which to do this. According to one's particular preferences, it can be argued that true (actually non-existing) socialism utilises neither money nor markets, requires democratic self-management by producers, is inconsistent with a one-party state, is free of bureaucratic rule or distortion and/or cannot exist in one country (or any subset of the world).[57]

Since it is rather difficult to reconcile Marx's concept of socialism as the association of free and equal producers with the domination over workers characteristic of AES, the point is certainly well taken. Accordingly, from this perspective, it may be confidently observed that between ill-starred AES (the object of Kornai's study) and socialism as such, there is a large and un-bridgeable gap.

Naturally, this stand would appear to be upon rather firmer ground if it could be demonstrated that the fetters on the development of productive forces identified by Kornai as characteristic of AES are not of the essence of socialism. Can we truly say this, however, about the principles of socialist ethics which, for Kornai, are in contradiction with the requirements for economic efficiency? Do we envision a socialism where, for example, the principles of solidarity and security for individuals and communities or the priority of the general interest over partial interest do *not* prevail?

On the contrary. These are not contingent characteristics of socialism. As Kornai notes, these principles can be traced back to the dawn of the labour movement in capitalism.[58] Not only do the very characteristics which for Kornai are antagonistic to efficiency — policies ensuring security of employment and insulation of workers' incomes from the effects of market forces — have workers in AES as the immediate beneficiaries, but they also correspond to the historic goals of workers as wage-labourers within capitalism. Michael Bleaney, indeed, has recently argued in his survey of the problems of AES that trade union attitudes within capitalism "are in large degree reactions against the everyday behaviour of market forces, and, in effect, against hard budget constraints".[59]

Rather than phenomena alien to socialism, the principles of socialist ethics identified by Kornai are inherent in one of its defining elements — the common ownership of the means of production. Not only does this element underlie guaranteed access to the means of production and security in the claim to the fruits of production for workers, but it also provides the impetus toward conscious co-ordination of the elements of production.[60] Given a socialist state's commitment to these goals and to common ownership, the persistent interference in the life of firms that Kornai identifies in the Hungrian experience thus also emerges as more than a chance phenomenon: "bureaucratic coordination is as much the *spontaneous* effect and natural mode of state property's existence as market coordination is of private property."[61]

In short, state property (which "belongs to everyone and to no one") is the socialist fetter; it is contrary to the requirement of adequate incentives, the disposition for innovation and risk-taking and the necessity for personal responsibility on the part of decision-makers.[62] The problem, it thus appears, is that whatever one may think about the legitimacy of the claim of AES to the designation of socialism, the specific features of AES identified as fetters *do* seem to be of the essence of socialism. In this respect, the analysis of Kornai *cannot* be so easily dismissed.

III. *The Dilemma of Socialism*

The tailor has fallen, and the Bishop has proclaimed that no one will ever fly. What is there left for a Marxist to say?

When the relations of production fetter the development of productive forces, an era of social revolution begins and a new set of productive relations emerges. Thus, a classic Marxist textbook case: the fettering of productive forces by the common ownership of means of production, social revolution and. . . capitalism. Twist and turn as they may, those Marxists who accept the thesis of the primacy of productive forces cannot escape the unambiguous logic of their own lessons.

But that thesis has always been a distortion of the essence of Marx's position. Consider the inference (noted earlier) drawn by G. A. Cohen that capitalism "persists because and as long as it is optimal for further development of productive power". Missing from this ready-made formula is any hint that capitalism may persist even if it is *not* optimal. Missing is the recognition that capitalism may persist because the very process of capitalist production reproduces workers who view the necessity of capital as self-evident:

The advance of capitalist production develops a working class which by education, tradition and habit looks upon the requirements of that mode as self-evident natural laws. The organization of the capitalist process of production, once it is fully developed, breaks down all resistance. [63]

The critical silence in the thesis of the primacy of productive forces revolves about the nature of human beings produced within an economic system. Those who fall prey to its determinist message can never explain why Marx believed that the political economy of the working class he elaborated in *Capital* was so important that it was worth sacrificing his "health, happiness and family" or why he never ceased to stress that workers make themselves fit to found society anew only through the process of struggle. Rather than reflecting Marx's position, the thesis in question is characteristic of a one-sided Marxism that has lost sight of the subjects of history. [64]

Yet, there is another side to this question. If productive relations can be suboptimal and nevertheless persist in the absence of people able and prepared to replace them, can we not also propose that productive relations may be optimal and yet be replaced in the absence of people prepared to support their continuation? Rather than the displacement of science by some variety of voluntarism, this is a rather fundamental aspect of Marx's discussion of capitalism. It is the very point of his distinction between the "natural laws" of capitalism "once it is fully developed" and the requirements "during the historical genesis of capitalist production" — when it was *not* possible to rely upon the worker's "dependence on capital, which springs from the conditions of production themselves and is guaranteed in perpetuity by them". [65]

Fully developed, capitalism produces a relative surplus population through its inherent tendency to alter the labour process and to increase the technical composition of capital; it thereby regularly reproduces the dependence of wage-labourers which is a condition of its existence. Until this point, however, Marx argued that "the rising bourgeoisie needs the power of the state" to enforce that dependence on capital. The mere existence of capitalist property relations in themselves was not sufficient. "It is not enough," Marx observed. [66]

It is not enough because, in the absence of the buyer's market for labour, neither the relation of dependence nor the feeling of dependence of the worker on capital were reproduced in the ordinary course of events. [67] Thus, in order to prevent the restoration of the private property of workers in their means of production (and the reproduction of forms of production resting upon the personal labour of the independent producer), "artificial means" were required:

In the old civilized countries the worker, although free, is by a law of nature dependent on the capitalist; in colonies this dependence must be created by artificial means.

The secret discovered in the New World by the political economy of the old world was simple: *the conditions necessary for the reproduction of a set of productive relations differ according to whether there is in existence an organic system or whether that system is in the state of becoming.*[68]

Characteristic of a fully developed organic system is that all its necessary presuppositions are reproduced as the result of its own existence:

> While in the completed bourgeois system every economic relation presupposes every other in its bourgeois economic form, and everything posited is thus also a presupposition, this is the case with every organic system.

An organic system, nevertheless, does not drop from the sky; its historical process of development "consists precisely in subordinating all elements of society to itself, or in creating out of it the organs which it still lacks". Only by reshaping its historical presuppositions, "the conditions of its becoming", into results of its own "being", can an economic system stand on its own foundations.[69] This was the mark of capitalism's completion — its material conditions and productive relations "are on the one hand the presuppositions of the capitalist production process, on the other its results and creations; they are both produced and reproduced by it".[70]

Kornai's arguments appear in a rather different light in the context of this distinction between a developed organic system and one in the process of becoming. All the aforementioned deficiencies of common ownership of the means of production and the principles of socialist ethics cannot be said to be deficiencies *in themselves*. Within what Marx envisioned as the higher phase of communist society (communism as it has "*developed* on its own foundations"), there is no such theoretical inconsistency between socialist ethics and the development of wealth: initiative, innovation, entrepreneurship are logically part of a society in which individuals produce ("as human beings") within a relationship marked by the conscious recognition of their interdependence and their unity and where their activity is its own reward ("life's prime want").[71]

If the inconsistency is not present in the utopia of the higher phase of communist society, it is however pervasive in Marx's lower phase (communism "as it *emerges* from capitalist society"). For, despite common ownership of the "material conditions of production" and co-operative production (present in both phases), what distinguishes the lower phase is the private ownership of "the personal condition of production, of labour-power".[72] It is precisely this particular productive relation which yields the well-known distribution relation of the lower phase of "to each according to his contribution". For, insofar as producers look upon their labour-power as their property, like all private owners they demand a *quid pro quo* for their property; they will not expend their productive energy (which includes not only their physical strength but also their initiative and innovative potential) unless they are assured of receiving its equivalent in return.

Let us admit frankly that where there is a combination of common ownership of the means of production and private ownership of labour-power, many of the characteristics of AES (as described by Kornai and others) will be produced. Regardless, indeed, of whether the principal means of coordination of economic activity is plan or market, each of these defining elements of socialism acts upon and deforms the natural tendencies of the other. Thus, whether it is, for example, the distortion of the information required for planning (due to the self-interest of the information-providers) or the reduction of personal incentive resulting from the focus on common property, characteristic of the combination of these two types of ownership is inconsistency. [73]

Yet, rather than an incidental conflict between the principles of efficiency and socialist ethics, *the underlying problem is that socialism is not itself an organic system.* Its defining characteristics belong to two different organic systems. [74] With respect to communism, the private ownership of labour-power and the associated characteristic of self-orientation are elements of an alien organic system. [75] Despite the existence of "the co-operative society based on common ownership of the means of production", socialism for Marx necessarily contained a historical premise yet to be reshaped — a "defect" as seen from the perspective of communism as a developed organic system.

Let us consider, then, communism as an organic system. What are the conditions which would lead producers to look upon the requirements of co-operative production based upon the common ownership of the means of production as self-evident natural laws? Among these is the condition that the productivity advantages arising from associated producers "expending their many different forms of labour-power in full self-awareness as one single social labour force" are manifest. [76] That is, given the superior productivity which emerges from the conscious combination of labour under conditions of common ownership of the means of production, the likelihood that individuals or groups could produce as efficiently by turning their back on common property and co-operative production would be slim.

Further, the fruits of this direct social labour would have to be sufficient both in general and particular to provide producers with the assurance that their individual needs could be satisfied (if not immediately, then in the future) simply by virtue of membership in the community. Implied here is a conscious means of identifying the particular needs of producers and ensuring the allocation of labour in such a way as to secure "the correct proportion between the different functions of labour and the various needs of the associations".[77] Under such conditions, the incentive for individual producers to seek alternative ways to satisfy their needs would be minimal.

We are, of course, describing a situation in which communism is clearly the optimal form for the development of productive forces and the satisfaction of needs. Given its superiority as a form of production, the dependence of individuals upon the community is regularly reinforced, and its requirements appear as self-evident natural laws.

Thus, the recognition of the benefits of production in common produces a particular attitude among producers such that any tendency on the part of individuals to shirk or free ride is minimised. (There is no need for surveillance other than that inherent in the disapproval of co-workers). Similarly, given the assurance that needs can be satisfied as the result of membership in the community ("to each according to his needs"), individuals work well because of the satisfaction they receive from their activity; they innovate and are alert to better ways of doing things for the very same reason — their contribution (and the approval of the community) is its own reward.[78] They "notice that which is in their interest to notice" as members of a community. Communist "entrepreneurship", in short, is inherent in the very nature of the relations among people within this society of associated producers.

In such a situation, common ownership of the means of production is reproduced in the ordinary run of things. Communism here is an organic system. All its premises are the result of its own functioning; it "proceeds from itself to create the conditions for its maintenance and growth".[79]

Thus, elements which appeared inconsistent in their combinations within earlier forms of production now are part of the logic of the system itself and are here able to develop fully. Clearly, the principles of socialist ethics noted earlier, which emerged historically in the opposition of workers to the logic of capital, find their full realisation in communism as an organic system. Rather than contrary to the principles of efficiency, they are here their condition.

Similarly, the desire of all to do the best possible job and therefore to have all the resources at one's disposal to achieve this goal does not appear here as a deficiency attributable to the "bureaucrat". Nor does this desire bring with it under these conditions an inherent check to efficiency; the democratic association of free producers would presumably recognise that at any given point there were limits to production and thus, necessarily, would place a hard "budget" constraint upon the satisfaction of particular needs. But, within this structure, such limits would be a spur to initiative by associated producers.

Within Communism as it has developed upon its own foundations, there is clearly no need for "artificial means" to ensure its reproduction. The dependence of producers on the community "springs from the conditions of production themselves and is guaranteed in perpetuity by them". But, what about the case where all communism's premises are *not* yet the product of its own functioning?

Assume that there is co-operative production based upon common ownership of the means of production and that communism is at this point the optimal form for the development of productive forces and the satisfaction of needs *but that the producers continue to treat their labour-power as their private property*. Under these circumstances, there will be recurring instances in which individual producers withhold their energy, initiative, etc. in the hope of securing higher private returns. Yet, under the assumed condition of the superiority of communist production, such self-oriented behaviour will increasingly be recognised as irrational and will become the exception.

Alternatively, assume that producers have accepted as common sense the logic of working in common *but where communism as a form of production is not yet the optimal means for satisfying needs and developing productive forces*. In this case, the very behaviour of producers will be the basis for the development of productive forces and the establishment of communism as the optimal system. In both these cases, we are describing the *development* of communism as an organic system, which "consists precisely in subordinating all elements of society to itself, or in creating out of it the organs which it still lacks".

Yet, the same conclusion would not follow if *several* elements were lacking at the same time. If communism is *both* not as yet a superior economic system and there is also a continuing orientation to the private ownership of labour-power, then the regular reproduction of common property and the free association of producers "comes up against the most mischievous obstacles, which are in part insuperable".[80] The combination of required material incentives *and* the advantages present for engaging in other than communist production means either that individual producers will have to be rewarded with a stake in the results of their past labour (thereby tending to the disintegration of common ownership of the means of production) or that the absence of sufficient personal incentive will produce the reduced activity which is manifested in stagnation.

Let us grant, then, the Austrian school its arguments. Selfishness is necessary for progress — insofar as no alternative motivation for human behaviour is present. The capitalist entrepreneur is essential — in the absence of the development of communist entrepreneurship. Communism, in short, requires more than the negation of capital. For the proletariat to truly abolish and transcend (aufheben) capital, it must also abolish the proletariat; it must absorb and preserve characteristics which formerly could only appear as attributes of capital and which were necessarily separated from wage-labour. In the completed communist system these economic relations presuppose every other — not in its capitalist but in its communist economic form.

We have here the dilemma of communism as it emerges from capitalism. Socialism, the lower phase of communist society, necessarily reproduces in the normal course of things neither the common ownership of the means of production nor the dependence of producers upon the community. The reproduction of the elements of communist production thus requires under these conditions the use of "artificial means".

IV. The "Artificial Means" of Socialism

Before capitalism produced its own presuppositions, there was a point when, even though capitalist property relations existed, capitalist production was neither manifestly superior nor did producers "by education, tradition and habit look upon the requirements of that mode as self-evident natural laws". There were cases of the restoration of older forms of production as the result of the struggles of those for whom security and solidarity was to be found in the community of peasant producers. And, there were alternatives to production under capitalist relations (such as co-operative production by artisans) — especially during that phase which historians designate as "proto-industrialisation".[81]

Under these circumstances, artificial means were required in order to secure the dependence of the wage-labourer upon capital. What artificial means are available to the communist society which still is dependent upon historical presuppositions?

The answer requires us, above all, to understand the socialist defect. And that is where Marx's discussion of the "inner dualism" of the village commune in Russia is useful. The commune, he noted, has "common land ownership" but, in practice, "each peasant cultivates and works. . . his plot, reaps the fruits of his field. . . on his own account".[82] This dualism, he proposed, "may eventually become a source of disintegration". The commune "bore within its own breast the elements which were poisoning its life"; and, "the key factor was fragmented labour as the source of private appropriation". It was this, Marx argued, which was the "dissolver of primitive economic and social inequality" and which "introduced heterogeneous elements into the commune, provoking conflicts of interest and passion liable to erode communal ownership first of the cultivable land, and then of the forests, pastures, waste ground, etc." [83]

The same inner dualism is present in the socialist combination of common ownership of the material conditions of production and private ownership of the personal condition of production. The very idea, however, that the path to communism as an organic system consists in relying upon the element which is both properly part of another organic system and which is a source of disintegration of common property seems rather perverse. *In the absence of the already-existing superiority of the communist form of production, the development of a new common sense which accepts the logic of production in common to satisfy human needs appears to be the only route to the creation of conditions in which communism produces its own presuppositions.*

The alternative (and historical) argument is well-known. It proposes that, rather, what is required is the development of the productive forces which can make communism a superior economic system and that this entails continuing dependence upon the distribution relations dictated by the private ownership of labour-power. [84] *Yet, this is what precisely the arguments of Kornai (and Brus and Laski) deny.*

Rather than demonstrating the potential for developing an advanced economic system in which the emergence of abundance permits the withering-away of the self-orientation of the producers, the inner dualism of socialism in this view produces a situation in which the combination of the alien principles of efficiency and socialist ethics "manifests the disadvantages of both conspicuously, and suppresses their advantages". [85] The inconsistency requires resolution. For those concerned about the development of productive forces and the growing satisfaction of needs, we have seen that the real choice appears to be one between the rejection of socialism in favour of capitalism and the rejection of socialism (in all but name) in favour of an "open-ended" simulation of capitalism. [86]

Perhaps this, then, is the major lesson to be drawn from the accounts of the disaffected reformers. They show that every concession to the old world is in itself inadequate and calls for ever further concessions until the common ownership of the means of production itself is seen as an aberration. In the process, as Brus and Laski show (by tracing out the "full implications" of the market-oriented resolution), the very conception of communism as a rational system is acknowledged as "utterly fallacious".[87] The point, to be sure, is not new. It was made clearly in 1965 by Che Guevara:

> The pipe dream that socialism can be achieved with the help of the dull instruments left to us by capitalism (the commodity as the economic cell, individual material interest as the lever, etc.) can lead into a blind alley. And you wind up there after having travelled a long distance with many crossroads, and it is hard to figure out just where you took the wrong turn. Meanwhile, the economic foundation that has been laid has done its work of undermining the development of consciousness. To build communism it is necessary, simultaneous with the new material foundations, to build the new man.[88]

Consider, then, some of the elements critical to the building of the new human beings for whom the requirements of communist production are self-evident. Self-management in the process of production (co-operation) is clearly an essential element. Not only did Marx consider the co-operative factories within capitalism to be "the first examples of the emergence of a new form", but co-operative production (the conscious recognition of the interdependence of producers within a productive unit) was identified as characteristic of both lower and higher phases of communist society.[89]

There is nothing very profound about this point. Insofar as people produce themselves in the course of all their activities, the very process of engaging in democratic forms of production is an essential part of producing people for whom the need for co-operation is second nature. In this respect, Marx's proposal that the Russian peasants' familiarity with occasional co-operative production in the artel "could greatly facilitate their transition from small-plot to collective farming" was a recognition of the importance of human experience.[90] "When the worker co-operates in a planned way with others," Marx noted, "he strips off the fetters of his individuality, and develops the capabilities of his species."[91]

Yet, self-management of particular productive units in itself cannot be sufficient. The attitudes of co-operation, community, solidarity and the spirit of volunteerism — which neither the market nor an overweening state can generate — are elements of a communist society which must be nurtured before it can develop on its own foundations. We need not say more about these values because they are a familiar part of every movement for social justice. It suffices to say that, in their conscious emphasis upon human needs, these values are the diametric opposite of the selfishness and self-orientation stressed by the Austrian school and its latter day adherents such as Kornai.

More than simply a focus on the centrality of human needs, however, what is critical is that the necessity to engage in collective solutions to their satisfaction become recognised as a responsibility of all individuals. Where a sense of community and a confidence in the benefits of acting "in full self-awareness as a single social labour force" are called for, a state over and above civil society cannot produce the people who have these characteristics. Rather, only through their own activities through autonomous organisations — at the neighbourhood, community and national levels — can people transform both circumstances and themselves. [92] What is called for, in short, is the conscious development of a socialist civil society.

Of course, it must be stressed that insofar as socialism does not proceed from human beings produced in a self-less way in a society founded upon common ownership, we necessarily are talking about a society in which personal material interest continues to play a central role. We cannot ignore this, and the attempt to do so can produce disaster. But, this does not mean inscribing a "defect" upon society's banner. The exclusive focus upon self-interest produces the wrong types of people, people who not only cannot build a new society but who also will tend to reproduce capitalist institutions. Thus, the project must be one of causing these attitudes to "wither away" — not through the apocryphal advance to "abundance" but through the conscious fostering of the development of a socialist civil society.

What, then, are the "artificial means" required to establish the conditions in which communism can become an organic system? Just as capitalism needed artificial means to ensure the dependence of the wage-labourer upon capital, socialism also requires them — to ensure the dependence of producers upon the community. Two measures appear especially important. As long, for example, as the self-orientation associated with the private ownership of labour-power continues, it is essential to prevent the disintegration of the common ownership of the means of production — as a holding action. [93] Secondly, until the requirements of communist production appear as self-evident, special efforts are needed to develop such attitudes — and this requires not merely exhortation but the *actual creation of* democratic and decentralised forms in which people change themselves in the course of changing circumstances. Both these measures are an essential part of the process of producing dependence of producers upon the community. *They are artificial in that neither is necessary in fully developed communism.*

There should be no illusion that this is a simple or short process. The general direction, however, is quite different to that suggested by the propositions associated with the thesis of the primacy of productive forces. Rather than a focus upon productive forces as the condition for the development of communism, there is a stress here upon human beings and the development of the institutions which will permit their emergence as people for whom the requirements of production in common appear as self-evident natural laws. The emphasis, in short, is upon the development of a process designed to remove the *real* socialist fetter.

V. *Where Do We Go From Here?*

De te fabula narratur. The story of the fall of AES is intended as a cautionary tale for us all. Its purpose is to explain that socialism cannot succeed. All attempts to build a just society will fail. Forget about social ownership; forget about all the accomplishments and inroads resulting from past struggles to satisfy needs. Privatise. Unleash the entrepreneur. Free capital from restraints. It was all a lie. No one will ever fly.

But, the struggles will continue — and, they will continue to advance an alternative logic to the logic of capital. Implicit in those struggles to satisfy human needs are the values of a communist society, the principles of socialist ethics. That process of struggle can displace capital from its position as mediator among producers, which it holds by virtue of its ownership of the products of labour; and, it also has the potential to create a socialist civil society within capitalism in which we produce ourselves as people capable of creating the just society we seek. [94]

Although different on the surface, the struggles are similar in AES. With its lack of democratic and co-operative production, its absence of a socialist civil society, and its actually existing bureaucratic rule, AES has certainly not produced the human beings for whom the requirements of communist production are self-evident. When we consider the cynicism, the retreat into private lives, the everyday accommodation to anti-social and illegal acts, the ripping off of social property, etc. described by so many observers, we are quite justified in wondering whether AES offers any prospects for the passage to a communist society. Indeed, the question which emerges is whether it is possible to get there from here? Is it, rather, necessary for people to retrace their steps back to capitalism and then to attempt, through the inevitable struggles which emerge from the contradiction between human beings and an inhuman existence, to try again?

We should not be so quick, however, to reach this conclusion. Even though bureaucratic rule has been in the name of the common ownership of means of production, it has always been constrained by the ideology associated with common ownership (which was a condition of its existence). That residue of common ownership remains. And, although it should not be assumed that such attitudes are in anyway permanent (especially given their coexistence with quite contradictory perspectives), neither should it be assumed that these principles of socialist ethics count for nothing.

Certainly, this is not a mistake that those advocating the re-institution of capitalism make. The campaign for the introduction of capitalism in AES has been overwhelmingly an ideological campaign — an attack on the attitudes towards solidarity, security, equality and egalitarianism associated with the common ownership of the means of production.[95] Small wonder that Kornai's *Road to a Free Economy* emphasises the need not only for "a revolutionary change in institutions, but also one in *thinking*"; small wonder that his not-entirely optimistic pamphlet identifies as paramount the dangers of the existing ideology.[96]

These values, insofar as they still remain, are clearly the basis within AES upon which to build. Will the people of AES be able to do so? Only they can determine that. For our part, we should support every struggle to prevent the privatisation of common property, to insert real content into that common ownership and to build a socialist civil society. It is their struggle, and it is ours.

Modern bishops will do their best to preach their lesson from the experience of AES. However, it is critical to remember that it is only from the perspective of capitalism that common ownership of the means of production and the associated principles of socialist ethics are the elements in socialism which appear as defects. The lesson to be drawn from the cautionary tale by socialists is different. No one should ever again try to fly with those things that only look like wings.

NOTES

1. Bertolt Brecht, "Songs for Children, Ulm 1592" in Bertolt Brecht, *Selected Poems*. Translation by H. R. Hays (New York: Grove Press, 1959).

2. G. A. Cohen, *Karl Marx's Theory of History: A Defence*. (Princeton; Princeton University Press, 1978), Ch. 6, *passim*.

3. *Ibid.*, p. 175. The implication is, of course, present in Marx's comment that "no social formation is ever destroyed before all the productive forces for which it is sufficient have been developed". Karl Marx, *"Preface"* to *A Contribution to the Critique of Political Economy* in Marx and Engels, *Collected Works*, Vol. 29. (New York: International Publishers, 1987), p. 263.

4. Joseph A. Schumpeter, *Capitalism, Socialism and Democracy*. (New York: Harper Torchbook, 1950 [1942]), p. 58.

5. The emphasis upon the "alertness" of the entrepreneur is most closely associated with the modern Austrian theorist, Israel Kirzner. In many respects, this focus parallels the central role that Schumpeter (considered not quite orthodox by other Austrians) earlier assigned to the entrepreneur. Cf. Israel M. Kirzner, *Discovery, Capitalism and Distributive Justice* (Oxford: Basil Blackwell, 1989), pp. 60-2. Joseph A. Schumpeter, *The Theory of Economic Development* (New York: Oxford Books, 1961 [1911]).

6. Israel M. Kirzner, "The Primacy of Entrepreneurial Discovery", in Institute of Economic Affairs, *The Prime Mover of Progress: The Entrepreneur in Capitalism and Socialism* (London: IEA, 1980), p. 16.

7. Oskar Lange, *On the Economic Theory of Socialism* (New York: McGraw Hill, 1964 [1938]).

8.   See, in particular, Don Lavoie, *Rivalry and Central Planning: The Socialist Calculation Debate Reconsidered* (Cambridge: Cambridge University Press, 1985), pp. 100-113.
9.   Quite early, Maurice Dobb noted in his review of the Lange book that the real economic problem of socialism was ignored and that increased productive power took "precedence over the question of securing a theoretically perfect adjustment between the output of various types of consumption goods". *The Modern Quarterly* (April 1939) reprinted in Maurice Dobb, *On Economic Theory and Socialism* (New York: International Publishers, 1955), pp. 244-5.
10.   Ludwig von Mises, "Economic Calculation in the Socialist Commonwealth [1920]", reprinted in Alec Nove and D. M. Nuti, eds., *Socialist Economics* (Middlesex: Penguin Books, 1972).
11.   Lavoie, *op. cit.*, p. 26. He argues, however, that the distinctions between neoclassical and Austrian arguments were always present but were clouded by the eagerness of the Austrians to "embrace neoclassical economists as marginalist allies against the threat of resurgent classical value theory in the form of Marxism". *Ibid.*, p. 3.
12.   Wlodzimierz Brus and Kazimierz Laski, *From Marx to the Market: Socialism in Search of an Economic System* (Oxford: Clarendon Press, 1989), pp. 57, 159.
13.   *Ibid.*, p. 57.
14.   *Ibid.*, p. 58. Lavoie, *op. cit.*, p. 107. In the Austrian argument, the data is not given but is discovered and created in the course of rivalrous competition.
15.   Brus and Laski, *op. cit.*, pp. 58-9.
16.   See, for example, W. Brus, *Socialist Ownership and Political Systems* (London: Routledge and Kegan Paul, 1975).
17.   Brus and Laski, *op. cit.*, Ch. 3, "The Objective of Catching Up", *passim*.
18.   *Ibid.*, pp. 43-6.
19.   They comment that the attitude of orthodox Marxist theory towards the capital market "must be that of outright and uncompromising rejection". *Ibid.*, pp. 73-6.
20.   *Ibid.*, pp. 80-1.
21.   *Ibid.*, pp. 84-5.
22.   *Ibid.*, p. 105.
23.   *Ibid.*, pp. 131-2.
24.   *Ibid.*, pp. 140-1, 145-6.
25.   *Ibid.*, p. 142.
26.   *Ibid.*, pp. 147-9. Since, however, "MS seems hardly feasible in practice without a sizeable non-state sector competing with state enterprises on equal terms, state ownership cannot be the only factor determining distribution", p. 149.
27.   *Ibid.*, p. 149. For von Mises' exclusion of such an economy as "socialist", see Ludwig von Mises, *Human Action: A Treatise on Economics* (Chicago: Henry Regnery Company, 1966 [1949]), pp. 258-9.
28.   Janos Kornai, *The Road to a Free Economy. Shifting from a Socialist Economy: The Case of Hungary* (New York: W. W. Norton & Company, 1990), p. 57n. Janos Kornai, "The Hungarian Reform Process: Visions, Hopes and Reality", *Journal of Economic Literature*, Vol. XXIV (December 1986), p. 1727.
29.   *Ibid.*, pp. 1733-4.
30.   He indicates that he was "greatly inspired" for his chapter on "Ownership" by works on property rights in socialism, and he singles out von Mises' 1920 essay and Lavoie's book, *The Road to a Free Economy*, p. 34n.
31.   *Ibid.*, pp. 22-3, 49, 175. In addition, he argues that "in some of the developed capitalist countries the intervention in the life of the individual and in the economic activity of private property is unnecessarily frequent", p. 45n.
32.   *Ibid.*, p. 58. In this respect, Kornai echoes von Mises' rejection of attempts to

have people "play market" and his assertion that "a socialist system with a market and market prices is as self-contradictory as is the notion of a triangular square", von Mises, *op. cit.*, pp. 707, 710.

33.   Among the suggestions that he makes is that people grow fruit and vegetables in their gardens. Kornai, *op. cit.*, pp. 123, 182.

34.   *Ibid.*, pp. 31, 211-2.

35.   The discussion here draws upon a more extensive consideration of Kornai's argument in Michael A. Lebowitz, "Kornai and Socialist Laws of Motion", *Studies in Political Economy*, No. 18 (Autumn, 1985).

36.   Janos Kornai, *Overcentralization in Economic Administration: A Critical Analysis Based on Experience in Hungarian Light Industry* (Oxford, 1959), p. 215.

37.   Janos Kornai, *Growth, Shortage and Efficiency: A Macrodynamic Model of the Socialist Economy* (Berkeley: University of California Press, 1982), p. 125; Janos Kornai, *Economics of Shortage* (Amsterdam: North-Holland, 1980), pp. 144-5.

38.   Kornai, *The Road to a Free Economy*, pp. 18, 52, 80, 93.

39.   See, in particular, Kornai, *Economics of Shortage*, Brus and Laski credit Kornai's "clear and comprehensive" demonstration that the reasons for the lack of success of AES are "systemic", *op. cit.*, p. 35.

40.   Janos Kornai, *Anti-Equilibrium: On Economic Systems Theory and the Tasks of Research* (Amsterdam: North-Holland, 1971), pp. 321, 168, 186.

41.   Kornai, *Growth, Shortage and Efficiency*, pp. 108, 114-7; *Economics of Shortage*, p. 235.

42.   Kornai, "The Hungarian Reform Process", p. 1728; Kornai, *The Road to a Free Economy*, p. 58.

43.   Kornai, *Economics of Shortage*, pp. 62-3, 191-4, 547.

44.   Kornai's argument here, as he notes, is consistent with that of the conservative economist, W. Niskanen. See, eg., W. Niskanen, "The Peculiar Economics of Bureaucracy", *American Economic Review* 58 (May 1968) reprinted in Eirik G. Furubotn and Svetozar Pejovich, eds., *The Economics of Property Rights* (Cambridge: Ballinger Publishing, 1974); Kornai, *The Road to a Free Economy*, p. 60n. Kornai, *Economics of Shortage*, pp. 63, 556.

45.   Kornai, "The Hungarian Reform Process", pp. 1693-7.

46.   Kornai, *The Road to a Free Economy*, pp. 62, 111.

47.   Abel Aganbegyan, *The Challenge: Economics of Perestroika* (London: Century Hutchinson, 1988), pp. 15-6, 22; Anders Aslund, *Gorbachev's Struggle for Economic Reform: The Soviet Reform Process, 1985-88* (London: Pinter Publishers), p. 26. Nikolai Shmelev and Vladimir Popov, *The Turning Point: Revitalizing the Soviet Economy* (New York: Doubleday, 1989), Ch. 3, "The Administered Economic System", *passim*. Brus and Laski, *op. cit.*, pp. 66-71, 75, 81-3, 105-6.

48.   The principles of solidarity and security imply the elimination of the fear of unemployment and of the "cruelty of capitalist competition, which casts out the weak". An associated principle, the priority of the general interest over the partial interest implies a focus on the long-term interests of society. Janos Kornai, "Efficiency and the Principles of Socialist Ethics", in *Contradictions and Dilemmas: Studies on the Socialist Economy and Society* (Budapest: Corvina, 1983), pp. 125-6. 132-5.

49.   Kornai, *The Road to a Free Economy*, pp. 111, 141.

50.   Janos Kornai, "Efficiency and the Principles of Socialist Ethics", *op. cit.*, pp. 124-6, 131-2.

51.   *Ibid.*, pp. 131-2; *Economics of Shortage*, p. 255.

52.   Note that von Mises argued that, in the capitalist market economy, workers

know that "laziness and inefficiency are heavily penalized on the labor market", *op. cit.*, p. 677.

53. Kornai's description is strikingly reminiscent of Marx's comment on the colonies where "not only does the degree of exploitation of the wage-labourer remain indecently low. . . (but) the wage labourer also loses, along with the relation of dependence, the feeling of dependence on the abstemious capitalist". Karl Marx, *Capital*, Vol. I (New York: Vintage Books, 1977), p. 936. See also Michal Kalecki, "Political Aspects of Full Employment [1943]", in E. K. Hunt and Jesse G. Schwartz, eds., *A Critique of Economic Theory* (Middlesex: Penguin Books, 1972).

54. *The Road to a Free Economy*, pp. 98-9.

55. *Ibid.*, p. 144. Recall the concern of Brus and Laski about the "absence of market-type opposition between 'buyers and sellers' as far as labour is concerned".

56. Kornai's analysis clearly offers little support to those who persist in describing the economies of AES as "capitalist".

57. Brus and Laski quite nicely set out the distinction between the conditions of backwardness under which AES emerged and the presumed requirement that socialism would issue forth from a mature capitalist system ("The Historical Regularity in Reverse"). Recognition of this gap, however, does not deter them from making inferences from AES about the "utopian" aspects of Marx's original conception. *Op. cit.*, Chs. 1 and 2, p. 36.

58. Kornai, "Efficiency and the Principles of Socialist Ethics", *op. cit.*, p. 125.

59. Lebowitz, "Kornai and Socialist Laws of Motion", *op. cit.*, pp. 59-60. Bleaney's comment should be understood as a criticism, one informed by his concern over the negative effect of soft budget constraints in AES. Michael Bleaney, *Do Socialist Economics Work? The Soviet and East European Experience* (Oxford: Basil Blackwell, 1988), pp. 157-8.

60. Insofar as all producers are common and equal owners of the means of production, there is as well the basis here for egalitarianism. Cf. Michael A. Lebowitz, "Contradictions in the 'Lower Phase' of Communist Society", *Socialism in the World*, No. 59 (Belgrade, 1987), pp. 123-4.

61. Kornai, *The Road to a Free Economy*, p. 59.

62. Kornai, *The Road to a Free Economy*, p. 51; Kornai, "Efficiency and the Principles of Socialist Ethics", *op. cit.*, p. 125.

63. Karl Marx, *Capital*, Vol. I (New York: Vintage, 1977), p. 899.

64. Marx to Sigfred Meyer, 30 April 1867 in Marx and Engels, *Collected Works*, Vol. 42 (New York: International Publishers, 1987), p. 366. Michael A. Lebowitz, *Beyond Capital: Marx's Political Economy of the Working Class* (London: Macmillan, 1991), cf. especially Chs. 7 and 8.

65. Marx, *Capital*, Vol. I, p. 899.

66. *Ibid.*

67. See note 53.

68. *Ibid.*, p. 935-7. Cf. Ch. 33 in general.

69. Marx, *Grundrisse*, pp. 278, 459-60.

70. Marx, *Capital*, Vol. III, p. 957.

71. See Marx, "Comments on James Mill", in Karl Marx and Frederick Engels, *Collected Works*, Vol. 3 (New York: International Publishers, 1975), pp. 227-8. Marx, *Critique of the Gotha Programme* in Marx and Engels, *Selected Works*, Vol. II (Moscow: Foreign Languages Publishing, 1962), pp. 23-4.

72. Marx, *Critique of the Gotha Programme*, p. 25.

73. Lebowitz, "Contradictions of the 'Lower Phase' of Communist Society", *op. cit.*, pp. 128-31.

74. In this respect, Kornai's conclusion that state ownership and market regulation

are inherently inconsistent elements should not be surprising.

75. Brus and Laski make this very point: "resorting to economic incentives. . . introduces into the postulated system an alien element threatening to come into conflict with the basic assumptions of the model", *op. cit.*, p. 12.

76. Marx, *Capital*, Vol. I, p. 171.

77. *Ibid.*, p. 172.

78. Alec Nove assumes that the Marxian argument is one in which, with abundance ("an unrealisable degree of plenty"), "acquisitiveness would wither away. . . because acquisitiveness would have lost all purpose". There is no suggestion above, however, that "abundance" is a necessary condition — if this is taken to mean the absence of scarcity and the need for choices under conditions of scarcity. Alec Nove, *The Economics of Feasible Socialism* (London: George Allen & Unwin, 1983), pp. 16, 59.

79. Marx, *Grundrisse*, p. 460.

80. Marx, *Capital*, Vol. I, p. 936.

81. For the implications of the solidity of the pre-capitalist peasant community, see the essays in T. S. Aston and C. H. E. Philpin, *The Brenner Debate* (Cambridge: Cambridge University Press, 1985); a more recent discussion by Robert Brenner (which is explicitly critical of the primacy of productive forces thesis) appears in "The Social Basis of Economic Development", in John Roemer, ed., *Analytical Marxism* (Cambridge: Cambridge University Press, 1986). For a discussion of alternative paths to industrialisation in Britain, see Maxine Berg, "Will the Real Bosses Please Stand Up: Marglin and Landes on the Origins of Capitalist Hierarchy", Warwick Economic Research Papers, No. 305 (October 1988); Maxine Berg, *The Age of Manufactures: Industry, Innovation and Work in Britain, 1700-1820* (London: Fontana, 1985); and M. Berg, P. Hudson and M. Sonenscher, eds., *Manufacture in Town and Country before the Factory* (Cambridge: Cambridge University Press, 1983).

82. Karl Marx, "Drafts of a Reply (to Vera Zasulich)" in Theodor Shanin, ed., *Late Marx and the Russian Road* (New York: Monthly Review Press, 1983), p. 104.

83. Rather than yielding to determinism, however, Marx did not think that the disintegration of the common ownership of those means of production in the village commune was *inevitable*:

> Its innate dualism admits of an alternative: either its property element will gain the upper hand over its collective element; or the reverse will take place. Everything depends on the historical context in which it is located.

   Ibid., pp. 109, 120-1.

84. This position appears most consistent with Keynes' argument that continued reliance upon "avarice and usury" is required to "lead us out of the tunnel of economic necessity into daylight". John Maynard Keynes, "Economic Possibilities for our Grandchildren", in *Essays in Persuasion* (New York: W. W. Norton & Co., 1963), pp. 369-72.

85. Kornai, "The Hungarian Reform Process", *op. cit.*, p. 1729; Kornai, "Efficiencies and the Principles of Socialist Ethics", *op. cit.*, p. 136.

86. Brus and Laski recognise the possibility of an alternative resolution but do not explore it because the "mood" in AES points in the direction of a consistently reformed system of market socialism proper. *Op. cit.*, p. 105.

87. Brus and Laski, *op. cit.*, Ch. 1, pp. 150-1.

88. Che Guevara, *Socialism and Man in Cuba*, reprinted in Carlos Tablada, *Che Guevara: Economics and Politics in the Transition to Socialism* (Sydney: Pathfinder, 1989), p. 92.

89. Marx, *Capital*, Vol. III (New York: Vintage, 1981), pp. 512, 571.

90. Shanin, *op. cit.*, pp. 104, 113.

91. Marx, *Capital*, Vol. I, p. 447.
92. The centrality of "revolutionary practice" in Marx's conception is stressed in Lebowitz, *Beyond Capital*.
93. Note Marx's comment that one of the fundamental characteristics of the Russian village commune, common land ownership, formed "the natural basis of collective production and appropriation", Shanin, *op. cit.,* pp. 112-3. What he would have had to say about the current proposals to privatise land and other means of production is easy to imagine.
94. The arguments made here are developed further in Lebowitz, *Beyond Capital*, Ch. 8.
95. See the discussion in David Mandel, " 'A Market Without Thorns': The Ideological Struggle for the Soviet Working Class", *Studies in Political Economy*, No. 33 (Autumn 1990).
96. Kornai, *The Road to a Free Economy*, pp. 20, 21, 23-4. In this context, his emphasis upon the need for a strong state which can impose necessary real wage reductions with "an iron hand" is an acknowledgement of the necessity for "artificial means" on the road to the organic system of capitalism. *Ibid.,* pp. 195, 206.

WHAT COMES AFTER COMMUNIST REGIMES?*

Ralph Miliband

I

The overthrow of the Communist dictatorships in Eastern and Central Europe in the second half of 1989 was the product of upsurges which were among the most spontaneous and popular revolutions to have occurred this century; and one of their most remarkable features was their mainly peaceful character. Once Soviet protection had been withdrawn from these regimes, their own police and military apparatus was soon paralysed in the face of sustained mass demonstrations. The speed with which events moved, once the process had begun, shows well enough how extreme had become the failure of ruling parties and governments to maintain any significcant measure of popular support.

As in the case of any revolution, however, these upheavals raised the question of what was to replace the regimes that had been overthrown. In fact, two distinct questions needed to be answered: the first was what kind of *political regime* was to be set up; the second concerned the nature of the *social order* that was to come into being. The same two distinct questions have also been posed by the crises which have gripped all Communist regimes apart from those in Eastern and Central Europe, most notably the Soviet Union.

There are many revolutions in the world which bring about a change of political regime, but which do not seriously affect the social order, or which do not affect it at all: the democratic successes in recent years in Latin and Central America are cases in point. There too, dictatorships have been swept away by popular upheavals. But the economic, military and administrative power blocs which had sustained the dictatorships, and which had been sustained by them, remained in place, with only some changes in personnel in the government and the state. The new political regimes, for all their

* This is a somewhat revised version of an essay which has appeared in *El Socialismo del Futuro*, vol. 1, no. 2, 1990 (Fundacion Sistema, Madrid). I am very grateful to Marion Kozak, David Miliband, and Leo Panitch, for their critical comments on the earlier version.

extreme shortcomings, are a distinct advance on the ones they have replaced; but for the vast majority, the social order has remained as alien and oppressive as it had previously been.

In the case of Communist regimes, on the other hand, economic, political, military, and administrative power had been so merged in the party-state that the break-up of the political regime was bound to bring into immediate question the issue of the social order itself; and this meant in particular the question of what was to happen to economies that were based on the public ownership of the predominant part (at least) of the means of economic activity.

In one case at least, that of the German Democratic Republic, an answer to the questions posed by the demise of its Communist regime has already been finally settled by the country's complete absorption into the Federal Republic, its integration into the Federal Republic's capitalist economy, with the intended privatisation of most of the state-owned firms in the defunct GDR. It may take quite a while to dispose of the great bulk of these firms, but it will no doubt be done, and the process will be helped by the closing down of many of these firms.

In other Communist or ex-Communist countries, the position is rather more complicated, but the dominant tendency is clearly towards the creation of economies in which most of the means of industrial, financial and commercial activity would be privatised and come under indigenous or foreign (or joint) ownership and control. This tendency is strongly encouraged by Western governments, the International Monetary Fund, the World Bank, reactionary foundations, and also private capitalist institutions; and it is further strengthened by an array of pro-capitalist advisers, who have taken full advantage of the failures of Communist regimes to press on the successor regimes economic policies derived from the law of the jungle.

What is at issue here is nothing less than the complete undoing of the social revolutions which occurred in these countries after World War II. That such social revolutions did occur may be obscured by the fact that most of them, in Eastern and Central Europe, were imposed from above, indeed from outside, and that the regimes issued from them turned out as they did; but this does not negate the immense, revolutionary changes, good or bad, which they all experienced. The authoritarian or semi-authoritarian political structures which had been in place in most of these countries in the pre-war years were dissolved; and so too were the social hierarchies which, save in East Germany and Czechoslovakia, had kept the great majority of their (mainly peasant) populations in a state of dire subjection. In all of them, property relations were profoundly transformed; in place of the traditional ruling classes, members of hitherto excluded, marginalised or persecuted layers of society gained access to positions of power; state structures were thoroughly reorganised; modernisation in every area of life was the order of the day; a rhetoric of socialist commitment and proletarian democracy was given pride of place; and great changes were made (or were at least proposed) in the whole national culture.

For a short couple of years after 1945, and before the imposition of the Communist monopoly of power, there was hope, nurtured in the terrible years of war, that there might be built a democratic and egalitarian order on the ruins of the old and discredited pre-war regimes; and there was even a very broad measure of popular support for the changes that were occurring. Whether there really ever was a possibility that a reasonably democratic and egalitarian order might be built is a matter of controversy. But if it did exist, it was quickly snuffed out by the onset of the Cold War and the imposition in all the countries of the Soviet sphere of influence of the Stalinist model of political rule and economic organisation, with the Communist monopoly of power and the stifling of all dissent, and the imposition of the command economy over all aspects of economic life.

Even so, there were two sides to these regimes, particularly in their earlier years: on the one hand, they were viciously repressive and cruel; on the other, their record, in terms of economic growth, modernisation, education, welfare, and new opportunities for a majority of hitherto greatly disadvantaged people, was far from negative, especially if account is taken of the lamentable conditions which most of them had inherited. Nor is it accurate to think of all the leaders of the Communist regimes in Eastern and Central Europe as mere scoundrels and stooges. Many of them had in fact spent many years in the anti-fascist struggle in their country, and had suffered grievous persecution for it. Their tragedy and that of their successors was that the system they built or accepted was based on unchecked power, and demonstrated to perfection how deeply corrupting such power is, and how wasteful and ultimately inefficient is economic management under its auspices.

Communist regimes did try a variety of economic reforms over the years, with the purpose of reducing the rigidities of the command economy. But the system of power, and the bureaucratic apparatus that went with it, remained in being and defeated all attempts at remedying an increasingly severe crisis. The reform programme in Czechoslovakia in 1968, the Prague Spring, might have provided the basis for a more successful renewal; its abrupt ending by Soviet military intervention meant that the crisis in all Communist regimes under Soviet control would not be seriously tackled. One of the merits of Mikhail Gorbachev was to have perceived early after his accession to power that a radical change in the political system in democratic directions was an essential though not a sufficient condition for economic renewal. Unfortunately, as he himself admitted in a speech to the Congress of Soviet Deputies in December 1990, the reforms he did engineer lacked coherence and consistency.

The upheavals of recent years have destroyed the power structure spawned by Stalinism. Conservative forces in the Soviet Union remain strongly entrenched in various parts of the administrative, military, economic and political system. An authoritarian outcome of present difficulties in one or other of the republics which make up the Soviet Union cannot be excluded; but a restoration of the iron dictatorship from the centre which once had the whole country in its grip now seems rather unlikely. In Eastern Europe, some people who occupied leading positions in the old regime have remained in positions of power in the new ones. But they have only been able to do so by repudiating the past, and remain highly vulnerable. In short, the revolutions of 1989 (and *perestroika* in the Soviet Union) have created a space for new political, economic, and social structures. The question is how that space is going to be filled.

II

In Eastern and Central Europe, the regimes which have replaced the Communist ones have declared their intention to adopt one variant or another of Western-style democracy. In formal constitutional and political terms, this may be taken to mean a regime based on stipulated civic and political rights, political competition, mandatory elections for parliamentary assemblies and local authorities, account-able executives, judiciaries free from executive dictation, and redress against arbitrary state action. Such a regime, in societies with a strong tradition of rights, and with well-entrenched and independent civil institutions (Gramsci's "earthworks" and "trenches") undoubtedly makes possible the voicing of opinions, grievances and demands, and the fostering of a public opinion to which governments and repre-sentatives, removable by way of general elections, must pay some heed.

These features of Western-type regimes stand in sharp contrast to the modes of rule which have been characteristic of Communist regimes; and the contrast has obviously been greatly in favour of the former. The installation in ex-Communist countries of such political regimes, however great their shortcomings may be, marks a real advance. On the other hand, the term "democracy", which is always used to describe Western-type regimes, carries a strong ideological and propagandistic charge, and begs many crucial questions about their nature and functioning. For it leaves out of account the fact that Western-style political democracy operates in the context of a capitalist social order, and that this imposes severe, even crippling limitations upon the meaning of democracy.

An essential requirement of democracy is that there should exist a general equality of condition between citizens, so that no group of people in society should have a built-in, permanent and vastly preponderant measure of power and influence in decision-making. But such inequality is precisely what obtains in capitalist-democratic regimes. The degree of inequality of income, wealth, influence and power between citizens varies from one country to another, but it is nowhere negligible, and it is certainly very pronounced in such countries as the United States, Britain and France, which never cease to congratulate themselves on their democratic character, and in most other capitalist-democratic countries as well.

The capitalist context in which the state functions means that the control of immense resources is concentrated in the hands of a relatively small number of people, who are thereby possessed of great power. Defenders of "free enterprise" tend to speak of it as if it consisted of a vast scatter of small and medium firms, all fiercely competing with each other, and none of them with much influence and power beyond the confines of their own narrow domain. In reality, contemporary capitalism is on the contrary dominated by great conglomerates and transnational firms, and the people who control them are able to make decisions which are of the greatest importance not only to the firms themselves, but also to their city, region, country, and, in many cases, to people and economies far beyond their own borders. A crucial feature of these decisions is that the people most affected by them have little or no control over them. Western-style democracy does not generally cross the threshold of the corporate boardroom. Nor does it have much access anywhere in the corporate economy.

Apologists for capitalism also argue that the decisions taken in the boardroom are inherently congruent with the public good and the general interest, because of the operation of that famous invisible hand guided by the market. But the claim is belied by the whole experience of capitalism. For wherever it has been allowed to proceed unchecked, capitalist enterprise has always proved to be a menace to those who work for it, and to society at large. This is to be expected, since its dynamic is the pursuit of private profit, with any other consideration a mere distraction from that pursuit, and therefore quite naturally ranking far behind it. This is why powerholders in the state, however dedicated they might be to "free enterprise" and the market, have always found it imperative, for the sake of the system itself, to curb the anti-social propensities which form an intrinsic part of its nature. The trouble, however, is that the state, save in a few exceptional countries, notably Sweden, where counter-capitalist forces have been strong, has been greatly (and willingly) constrained in its curbing endeavours, and only seeks to attenuate, at best, the depredations and derelictions of "free enterprise".

All this forms the necessary background to the arrangements which are now being proposed for the countries that once formed part of the "Soviet bloc", and which are already quite advanced in such countries as Poland and Hungary. The magic word everywhere is privatisation. But privatisation has implications which are seldom made clear by its devotees. One of them is that the transfer of public property to private agents means the creation of a new capitalist class, whose purposes would be no different from those of their counterparts in capitalist countries. The provenance of the members of this new class is still somewhat uncertain, since its formation is still in its early stages. But a good many of them, as is already happening in Poland and Hungary, would come, ironically enough, from the discredited *nomenklatura*, for these are the people who know their way around, have the right connections, and have money or can obtain credits and loans. Others would be people who had acquired wealth in the second or black economy; and there would no doubt emerge a host of budding entrepreneurs eager to take advantage of the opportunities offered by the sale at bargain prices of plants, equipment, land and other resources hitherto in the public domain. Any comparison with the New Economic Policy inaugurated by Lenin in the Soviet Union in 1921 is misleading: for NEP never brought into question the public ownership and control of the main means of economic activity. What is envisaged now is precisely the privatisation of these (and other) such means; and the process would of course involve the acquisition by foreign firms of many enterprises, particularly the most efficient and profitable ones. Local managers, as in Latin America, would then become the representatives and employees of faraway owners and controllers even more remote from national needs and concerns. The prospect of such a foreign takeover is openly — indeed eagerly — contemplated by many of the people who were in the forefront of the movements which brought down the Communist regimes in Eastern and Central Europe.

However it would be composed, it is quite certain that it would be a new capitalist class. It would be different in kind from the "new class" that was constituted by the "state bourgeoisie" of Communist regimes, for it would be based on ownership and control of private enterprises rather than on the control of public ones. Such control, operating in the context of dictatorial regimes, itself had many oppressive and arbitrary features; but it is pure prejudice to suggest that this is the only context in which it can conceivably operate, and that it is therefore bound to be oppressive and arbitrary.

The new capitalist class, like capitalist classes everywhere, will seek the greatest possible freedom from the tiresome constraints which the state in capitalist societies has been driven to impose upon private enterprise. In respect of labour relations, wages, hours and conditions of work, health and safety, consumer protection, environmental concerns, not to speak of such issues as the establishment of democratic procedures at the workplace, the new capitalists could be expected to be strongly opposed to any interference with managerial prerogatives, and to denounce such interference as an intolerable harking back to the bad old days, and as a sign that "communist" influences had not been finally rooted out.

No doubt, these entrepreneurs would not have it all their own way. There would be resistance from many quarters, particularly from workers. Workers in Communist regimes have always been told by their leaders of their worth, rights and power. The reality was for the most part very different from the rhetoric. But the message that workers do have rights and should have power will not have been forgotten. Having been freed from the managerial power of their Communist managers, and from retribution at the hands of the state for speaking out, they are not likely to accept without resistance the imposition of arbitrary power upon them by their new indigenous and foreign bosses.

Most of the new regimes are already members of the International Monetary Fund and the World Bank, or have applied to join; and most of their leaders are, to all appearances, perfectly willing to accept the philosophy which membership implies. In essence, what is involved is the acceptance of drastic cuts in public expenditure, privatisation and deregulation, tax concessions to national and international business, and whatever else capitalist rationality, as interpreted by bankers, entrepreneurs and conservative economists, is deemed to require. That rationality, on the other hand, does not include the notion of full employment and the right to work. Nor does it include the notion that the state has a prime responsibility for the provision of a high level of social and collective services in health, education, transport, the environment, amenities, etc. What is wanted instead is the greatest possible "recommodification" of life and the enthronment of the cash nexus as the essential mechanism of social relations. There are now many voices everywhere in Eastern and Central Europe, and in the Soviet Union, to proclaim that high un-employment, rising prices, reduced social services, and all other ills that accompany the rule of the market are part of the price that must be paid — mainly by those least able to afford it — to achieve a "healthy economy", a term which is itself laden with ideological and question-begging assumptions. Poland is one country which has already experienced the full effects of the "shock therapy" advocated by market fanatics and implemented since the beginning of 1990. The results have been catastrophic for the vast majority of the population, with a fall of some 30% in industrial production, a massive rise of unemployment, a drastic fall in purchasing power, and a considerable spread of dire poverty. Such "shock therapy" has had other consequences of which its advocates seldom take account — a vast increase in crime and prostitution, quick fortunes on the one side and multiplication of beggars on the other, and general demoralisation and cynicism. On the strength of what has already happened in countries in Latin America where a similar "shock therapy" has also been administered, there is no reason to believe that this "primitive capitalism" is capable of curing the ills which it has produced.

III

A capitalist restoration in ex-Communist countries will be based on a partnership between the new capitalist class and the controllers of the state. As in the case of all capitalist countries, the partnership will not be free of divergent purposes, tensions and conflicts. Capitalists have interests which may conflict with those of powerholders in the state; but there is sufficient congruity of purpose between them, including a dedication to the market economy, to ensure an adequate degree of accord.

This new power bloc will be concerned to do what all such power blocs seek to achieve, namely maintain, defend and strengthen the system which gives them their property, position, privileges and power. Such a purpose, in class societies, has large implications for the workings of the political system.

As already noted, the new capitalists and the new powerholders in the state will encounter a good deal of popular resistance to their endeavours. Such resistance has already occurred in many ex-Communist countries in the form of sporadic strikes and other manifestations of popular discontent; and this must be expected to grow as the negative consequences of the rule of the market come to be increasingly felt. Also, elections which have been held in these countries since the revolutions of 1989 clearly indicate that while their populations repudiate the former regimes, they do not repudiate the social benefits which these regimes proclaimed to be the due of all citizens, and which, however inadequately and imperfectly, they sought to provide in such realms as health, education, housing, transport, the right to work, etc. The enthusiasm which the new rulers display for the market economy is not shared by masses of people who rightly fear what it will mean for them. This indeed is one of the main problems which these new rulers face; and they speak with great feeling, at least in private, of how difficult it is to instil in the working class a new psychology, which would make it accept the notion that a "healthy economy" imperatively requires a great increase in inequality and the unfettered rule of the market.

Governments faced with popular resistance to their policies, and strongly pressed at the same time by powerful internal and external forces to pursue these policies, tend to find that the democratic forms which define capitalist democracy are exceedingly inconvenient; and they are therefore driven by a compelling political logic to reduce the effectiveness of these democratic forms. One common way of doing this is greatly to increase the power of the executive to the detriment of legislative and other sources of protest and resistance. Another is to curb trade union rights, for instance by limiting the right to strike, and to curb civic and political rights in general. Yet another is to increase the power of the police and the military to control and curb pressure from below against unpopular policies; and even though it is no longer possible to describe protest and opposition as Soviet-inspired, there is still much life in the denunciation and the repression of protesters as "communists", agitators and agents of dark forces bent on sabotaging national renewal. All capitalist-democratic regimes, for all their proclaimed dedication to pluralism, political competition, and freedom of expression, constantly seek to contain, deflect, subdue, and ultimately suppress inconvenient forms of dissent; and they all have a vast arsenal of emergency powers, which is readily drawn upon in times of crisis. In other words, the authoritarian side of these regimes, which is usually circumscribed (though not absent) in "normal" times, comes to the fore in conditions of stress, strife and turmoil, when the regular functioning of the political system can no longer ensure stability.

Given all the ills which a capitalist restoration in ex-Communist regimes is certain to produce, circumstances would undoubtedly favour a creeping authoritarianism *within* the framework of constitutionalism, with a steady erosion and perversion of democratic forms, in the name of the national interest, national salvation, and indeed democracy. The state in these regimes would be very weak in relation to international capitalism, and would preside over dependent economies; but this need not prevent it from being quite strong vis-à-vis its own citizens. Latin America offers many examples of such a combination of weakness and dependency abroad and oppressive power at home.

The tendency towards creeping authoritarianism is bound to be strengthened by the ethnic and national tensions which the demise of Communist regimes has again brought to the surface, often in virulent forms. Communist regimes obviously failed to resolve these tensions, and only managed to suppress their overt expression. The extent of their failure in this respect is clearly shown by the eruption of murderous ethnic strife in different parts of the Soviet Union, where generation after generation of Soviet citizens was drilled into giving a superior allegiance to the Soviet Union as a whole, but where conditions on the ground were such as to keep alive, though hidden, ancient grievances and antagonisms, which immediately surfaced once the repressive apparatus was loosened. Much the same goes for Eastern and Central Europe, where the new regimes have come into a bitter inheritance of national, ethnic, religious and racial enmities and prejudices, among which antisemitism occupies a choice place.

Regimes in which the market is the organising principle of life, with competition and individual striving for material advantage acclaimed as the highest virtues, cannot tackle any of these problems effectively. Nor can they generate the social morality which Communist regimes, because of the contradiction between their socialist rhetoric and their actual practice, were themselves unable to foster. Even rich capitalist countries, ruled by the same organising principle, have been unable to tackle effectively the economic and social ills which the system produces: why should poor countries, faced with a plague of problems of every sort, be expected to do better under the rule of the market?

The more reasonable expectation is that they will not and that this will provide a very fertile terrain for the further growth of movements based on a nationalism that readily slides into an exclusive, aggressive, xenophobic chauvinism, with other (or the same) movements drawing on the most backward and reactionary inter-pretations of religion. The influence of the Vatican in this respect should not be overlooked; for the present Pope does have a project — to "re-Christianise" ex-Communist countries, and for that matter the rest of Europe, and beyond, in directions which point very firmly towards an obscurantist past in which Rome was the unquestioned legislator of the true faith.

Times of crisis, with the political system under great strain, also offer a favourable terrain for the emergence of self-proclaimed saviours, spouting a populist rhetoric of national redemption, and fierce in their denunciations of a variety of suitable scapegoats. They would no doubt declare themselves to be ardent democrats; but they would nevertheless be bent on reproducing the kind of "strong" regimes which were characteristic of most of the countries of Eastern and Central Europe in the inter-war years.

The revolutions of 1989 were largely fought in the name of freedom and democracy; and enormous efforts have been made by a multitude of official and unofficial sources in the West to persuade ex-Communist countries that the essential, indispensable condition of freedom and democracy is free enterprise and the market, in other words capitalism. In fact, a capitalist restoration is much more likely to produce conditions where free enterprise does indeed flourish, but where freedom and democracy would be severely curtailed or even abrogated altogether.

IV

One of the main arguments used by advocates of wholesale privatisation and the rule of the market is that there is no alternative; or rather, that the only alternative is totally regimented economies. But this either/or categorisation should be treated for what it really is, namely prejudice and propaganda masquerading as objective judgment. For the issue is not whether a market should exist: it is rather what place it should occupy in economic and social life, and what degree of regulation it requires. Even the most committed of free marketeers admit that some matters cannot be left to the market and the workings of free enterprise, and that the state *has* to intervene in some areas if civilised life is to be maintained. Indeed, the same people turn heavily "statist" when it comes to such issues as "law and order", defence and the curbing of trade union and other rights, and are not in such respects in the least reluctant to see the state's power greatly increased.

The difference between them and their "interventionist" opponents is that the latter insist on the state's responsibility for the organisation of a wide range of collective services whose provision should not be governed by the rule of the market — health, education, public transport, the protection of the environment, the provision of amenities, the access to quick and cheap justice, and much else that defines the quality of life and the reality of citizenship for the vast majority of people. The point is not that the state itself run all such services; but it should ensure that provision, by whatever agencies, should be made for them.

As for productive activity, the point has already been made that a degree of regulation and control has always been imperatively required, given the a-social and anti-social dynamic of capitalist enterprise; and capitalist entrepreneurs, for all their proclaimed dislike of the state, have always been the most voracious consumers of state help by way of protection and subsidy, against the dictates of the market. So too is it well to remember that countries which have in recent years been most admired as examples of free enterprise — for instance South Korea and Taiwan, not to speak of Japan — would be better cited as examples of state intervention in economic life. In short, state interventionism has always been an intrinsic and crucial part of the history of capitalism: the point is to create the conditions in which that interventionism is placed at the service of society.

It is by now generally agreed on the Left that the state cannot possibly plan every detail of economic activity, or at least that it cannot do so in ways which are satisfactory. But this is very different from saying that a democratic state, mandated by popular will freely expressed after due debate and deliberation, should not determine economic and social priorities, and plan for their fulfillment. It is a perverse dogmatism which stipulates that all planning is by definition undesirable: controllers of the state, whatever their ideological dispositions may be, do plan for some years ahead in such areas as highway construction, the building of schools, hospitals, prisons, the procurement of weapons, etc., and they seek to ensure that the plans are fulfilled. The point is to extend this a great deal further, without any thought of controlling from the centre every aspect of economic activity.

Similarly in relation to private versus public enterprise, the issue is not at all whether there should exist a private sector or not, but what is to be the nature of the "mix" in "mixed economies". The term was invented as a euphemism for capitalism, and served to obscure the fact that in reality it denoted an overwhelmingly predominant private sector, with a subsidiary public sector largely confined to infrastructural concerns; and the drive to privatisation in the last decade in many capitalist countries has further reduced and weakened the public sector. The alternative to both the command economy and the "market economy" (another and more recent euphemism for capitalism) is a "mixed economy" *in which the position of the public sector vis-à-vis the private sector is reversed*, and where the commanding heights of the economy, including its strategic industrial, financial and commercial enterprises, and some of the lesser heights as well, come under one form or another of public or social ownership, under the scrutiny and regulation of a democratic state, itself strictly accountable.

State ownership is only one form of social ownership, suitable for some major industries and services, but to be complemented wherever possible by local and regional enterprises and partnerships, owned and run by municipal or regional authorities, and by various organisations and collectivities in society. All such bodies would enjoy a very considerable autonomy; and they would, in many instances, be competing with a private sector, located at the lower heights of the economy or at its grassroots, and providing a wide range of goods, services and amenities. This is the kind of economic pluralism which is truly congruent with political pluralism, all the more so because state ownership need not be thought of in terms of single, monopolistic corporations, but rather as areas of economic activity ruled wherever possible on the principle that more-than-one is better than one.

A fundamental tenet of the apostles of the free market economy is that a different economy, in which the public sector was predominant, is bound to be inefficient. The notion of "efficiency", like so much else in the vocabulary of such people, is heavy with ideological overtones; but even if taken on its own terms, the assertion must be treated as mere dogma. Even in Communist regimes, public ownership was not always inefficient; and Communist experience of public ownership cannot in any case be taken as proving anything, given the exceedingly unfavourable conditions under which it operated. Also, the experience of public ownership in capitalist countries shows that it can, to put it no higher, be at as efficient, innovative and "entrepreneurial" as capitalist-run concerns.

There are, however, reasons other than "efficiency" for wanting a mixed economy with a predominant public sector. One crucial such reason is that public ownership removes from private hands the control of assets and resources which, as was noted earlier, are of essential importance to society. Private armies in control of stocks of weapons are now thought to be an abomination, which no properly-run society could ever tolerate. However much it may offend conventional wisdom, and even much current thinking on the Left, it needs to be said that the private control of what are *social* assets and resources is scarcely less abominable. They too need to be subject to a degree of control, regulation and direction which private ownership and control makes difficult, ineffective, or impossible. The power concentrated in the hands of the owners and controllers of large corporations — the great oligarchs of industry, finance, commerce and communications — can only be effectively "socialised" by the transfer of the sources of their power into the public domain.

Among the objections which are raised against any such transfer is that it entails the danger of an inflation of state power. Against this, it is worth recalling that the free market economy has itself not only been perfectly compatible with a dictatorial state, but also that it profoundly corrupts and degrades the democratic forms of capitalist-democratic regimes. But the answer, more positively, is that an economy in which the public sector is dominant need not be tightly run from the centre; that it is intended, as noted earlier, to be marked by economic pluralism; that the state itself would be democratically constrained; and that it would function in a democratic context.

A predominant public sector is an essential condition for the creation of societies in which cooperation and fellowship are the dominant values; but nobody would now argue that it is a sufficient condition. The experience of Communist regimes is proof enough of that. A predominant public sector is no more than the indispensable "base" on which new social relations may be built, in a process that is certain to be long and difficult. But it is a process that opens up possibilities of human emancipation which are precluded by the spirit and the practice of capitalism.

It is that "base" which devotees of the free market economy, inside and outside Communist and ex-Communist regimes,, seek to destroy by their frantic pressure for privatisation. They are finding that the wholesale disposal of national assets to private buyers is likely to be a difficult and protracted business. Nevertheless, the privatisation campaign will no doubt succeed in some countries, say Czechoslovakia, Poland and Hungary, not to speak of the former German Democratic Republic, and will in due course produce an economy in which the private sector will be heavily predominant. Other ex-Communist countries, notably the Soviet Union, are still at a point where crucial choices in this respect have not yet been finally made. In the Soviet Union (and elsewhere) a struggle is still proceeding in a situation of great ideological confusion, but whose protagonists may be ranged, no doubt with many qualifications, into three sets of positions. First, there are the free marketeers, bent on wholesale privatisation and the free market economy, i.e. capitalist restoration, who enjoy the support of the West, and who are freely dubbed reformers, radicals, democrats, even though there are many such people in their ranks whose democratic credentials are exceedingly dubious. At the other end of the spectrum, secondly, there are those people who hanker for the good old days, when the *nomenklatura* ruled, the command economy was in place, and there was no nonsense about democracy, *perestroika* and *glasnost*. These ˙ are the "conservatives", whose numbers and strength are not easy to evaluate, since they are for the most part careful not to parade their opinions too openly. Somewhere in between these two positions, there are the protagonists of a "third way", who do want political pluralism but who are not willing to see the larger part of the economy, particularly its strategic heights, fall into the private domain and form the basis of a capitalist restoration. Such people are often assimilated to the "conservatives", and reproved or denounced, because of their opposition to such a restoration. In fact, they are the best hope — in all probability the slender hope — that what will follow Communist regimes may be something approximating to the beginnings of socialist democracy.

So far, socialists in the West have done very little to give encouragement to such people in their search for a "third way": the field has been virtually left to the Right, with its glowing prospectus of the virtues of the free market economy. An urgent task for people on the Left is to explain why the prospectus is fraudulent, and to help in the advancement of socialist alternatives to it.